Peter J. Angelos

AOA 1970

SUCCEEDING IN THE World
of Work

McKNIGHT & McKNIGHT PUBLISHING COMPANY · BLOOMINGTON, ILLINOIS

SUCCEEDING IN THE World of Work

GRADY KIMBRELL
Coordinator
Work-Experience Education
Santa Barbara High School District
Santa Barbara, California

BEN S. VINEYARD, Ed. D
Professor and Chairman
Trade and Technical Education
Kansas State College
Pittsburg, Kansas

FIRST EDITION

Copyright 1970

by McKnight & McKnight Publishing Company

Lithographed in U.S.A.

Library of Congress
Card Catalog Number: 77-134824

SBN: 87345-496-0

Foreword

Throughout the years, education has undergone many changes in emphasis. During the last decade emphasis has been placed at varying times on a purely academic education, consumer education, occupational guidance, and vocational training. It is good that education is able to change to meet the needs of our ever-changing society. The local community is playing a more significant role in education now than ever before. Students are demanding a realistic, relevant education. The business community, the consumer of the product of the educational system, is increasing its willingness to cooperate with the local school system in providing meaningful experiences in their places of business for interested students.

John Dewey stated "Man learns to do by doing." Now, many years later, we find a partnership being formed between the local school system and the local business community in which students are provided opportunities to "learn to do by doing" under the coordinated guidance of persons from business and education. This partnership is not limited to distributive occupations, but is being developed in virtually every occupational field represented in the community served by the school system. This coalition between the schools and business is taking the form of work experience education in which the skilled guidance of the professional educator is combined with the experience of the concerned, trained worker.

Learning the actual technical skills required for employment is not enough to make an individual successful on a job. The worker, whether he is in a job requiring professional training, or in a skilled or semi-skilled occupation, must have an understanding of certain principles which are fundamental to success on any job. This book brings together under one cover the essentials every worker needs to understand in order to be successful on his job. Most workers eventually learn what is contained in this book. Unfortunately, it is usually learned by trial and error over a period of many years—after many disappointments.

It is important that "education" be added to the student's work experience to give it maximum value. One factor which is important in adding the "education" to any work experience is related classroom instruction. This book should prove to be extremely valuable to all coordinators of work experience education programs in bringing together in a logical, easy to comprehend manner those items important to "job success" which are best learned in the classroom.

The authors of this book bring together unique backgrounds of experience and success in the business community combined with many years' experience as professional educators. Their vast experience as classroom teachers and work experience educators has made it possible for them to develop a complete text which can help the young worker succeed in the world of work.

Vern C. Gillmore
President, California Association
of Work Experience Educators

Acknowledgments

The authors are grateful to all who assisted and cooperated in the preparation of this book. Special acknowledgment is made to the following:

American Express Travelers Cheques

American Telephone and Telegraph

Ball State University

Bank America Service Corporation

Caterpillar Tractor Company

Chicago Tribune

Ford Motor Company

General Electric

General Research Corporation, Systems Research Division

Homelite, Division of Textron, Inc.

Internal Revenue Service

International Business Machines Corporation

Johns Manville Corporation

Kansas Employment Security Division

The Lincoln Electric Company

Mutual of Omaha Insurance Company

National Aeronautics Space Administration

The National Bank of Pittsburg, Kansas

The National Cash Register Company

New York Life

Oklahoma State University Extension

Pacific Gas and Electric Company

Sears, Roebuck and Company

Shell Oil Company

State Farm Insurance Company

State of Kansas Labor Department

Tennessee Valley Authority

United Benefit Life Insurance Company

United States Bureau of Census

United States Department of Health, Education, and Welfare

United States Forest Service

Table of Contents

FOREWORD   v   ACKNOWLEDGMENTS   vii

Part I   Entering the World of Work   1

Chapter 1   You and Work   3

What's Ahead in Part I   9
Study Helps   10

Chapter 2   JOBS: Choices and Opportunities . . .   11

Your Part-Time Job   13
Qualifications and Interests   15
Growing Occupational Fields   17
Where to Look   26
Career Planning   34
Study Helps   36

Chapter 3   Applying for a Job   38

Application Forms   39
Letters of Application   43
Personal Data Sheets   47
Interviews   52
Questions Often Asked During the Interview . . .   60
Why People Aren't Hired   61
Why the Other Boy Was Hired   63
Study Helps   64
Cases   65

Chapter 4   You, Your Employees, and Your Co-Workers   .   67

The Importance of Attitude   67
What Your Employer May Expect   69
What You, the Employee, May Expect   75
Getting Along with Co-Workers   79
Unions and Professional Groups   83
Study Helps   85

Chapter 5   Your Progress on the Job   87

Your Success and Achievement   87
Performance Review and Evaluation   102
Terminating the Job   108
Study Helps   110

**Chapter 6   SELF INVENTORY: Knowing and Understanding
Yourself 111**

Values   111
Interests   113
Aptitudes and Abilities   119
Personality   122
Study Helps   137

Chapter 7   Personal Effectiveness   138

How Others Know You   138
How to Improve   143
Understanding and Influencing Others   145
Study Helps   149

Part II   Meeting Your Adult Responsibilities   151

Chapter 8   Managing Money   153

Wise Use of Money   153
Levels of Responsibility   156
Planning Your Program of Spending   165
Planning a Budget   166
Putting a Budget into Use   173
Where to Get Additional Help   175
Study Helps   177

Chapter 9   Buying Goods and Services **178**

Consumer Problems **178**
Consumer Fraud **182**
Buying Women's Clothes **190**
Buying a Car **192**
Contracts **197**
Influences on Choice **198**
Study Helps **202**

Chapter 10 Credit and Installment Buying **204**

Establishing and Maintaining Credit **204**
Estimating the Cost of Credit **212**
Types of Credit **221**
Study Helps **228**

Chapter 11 Contracting for Goods and Services . . . **229**

The Use of Legal Advice **230**
Contracts **230**
Preparing Contracts **237**
Defective Contracts **237**
When to See a Lawyer **238**
Study Helps **242**

Chapter 12 Using Bank Services **244**

Banking Institutions **244**
Bank Classifications **246**
The Federal Reserve System **247**
Federal Deposit Insurance Corporation **247**
Use of a Checking Account **248**
Substitutes for Cash **256**
The Savings Account **261**
Study Helps **263**

Chapter 13 Buying and Using Government Services . . **265**

Understanding Taxation **265**
Types of Taxes **266**
Preparing Income Tax Returns **277**
Characteristics of a Good Tax System **285**
Study Helps **287**

Chapter 14   Social Security and Retirement 290

    Social Security Act of 1935 292
    Basic Ideas of Social Security 294
    Benefits 294
    Health Insurance and Medical Care Under Social Security 299
    Your Social Security Card 299
    Unemployment Insurance 303
    Workmen's Compensation 308
    Study Helps 310

Chapter 15   Insurance 313

    Sharing Economic Losses 313
    Insurance Needs of Young Workers 314
    Planning for Personal Insurance 315
    Types of Insurance 318
    What Life Insurance Should You Buy? 331
    Health Insurance 332
    Suggestions for Buying Insurance 334
    Study Helps 335

Part III   Meeting Future Responsibilities 338

Chapter 16   Vocation Development, Changing Responsibility 340

    Average Person's Vocational and Responsibility Growth 340
    Case Studies 345
    Study Helps 354

Chapter 17   Post High School Education and Training . . 355

    The Nature of Work Today 355
    Preparation for Work 358
    Study Helps 385

Appendix 1   Understanding Mathematics 387

    Answers to Math Problems 403

Appendix 2   Parliamentary Procedure 409

Appendix 3 **Oppressive Child Labor Is Defined
As Employment of Children Under
the Legal Minimum Ages** **417**

Appendix 4 **Bibliography of Vocational Guidance Materials** . **455**

Index **478**

PART I

Entering the World of Work

Introduction

In America, the work we do to earn a living determines our *way of life*. It is the chief factor in our identity as a person. It affects our choice of friends and the way we spend our leisure time. It also provides our cultural boundaries. Work is the *central activity* around which we plan our lives. Successful work activity is necessary to a mentally healthy person.

During the first 100 years of our nation, the variety of work activity available to a young person was limited. Few women worked outside the home at all. Most boys followed in the same line of work as their fathers. Most boys became farmers, having learned how to work at an early age by helping their fathers who were farmers. Others learned a trade by helping their fathers or a friend of the family. There wasn't much choice about the kind of work a person would do.

During the past 50 years, our society has become much more complex. There are now more than 20,000 different jobs. Most women work for at least 25 years of their lives. Men no longer perform their work activities in the home — *they travel to work*. Thus, many young people never see their fathers engaged in the work activity which earns the family livelihood. While there are several thousand *kinds* of work which are available to young people, there is less opportunity to closely observe work activity today than there was 50 years ago.

Psychologists tell us that the one thing which most disturbs young people is the lack of an occupational identity. That is, too many young people have no picture of themselves some five or ten years in the future. They have no goals. They don't know where they are going. These are the young people, lacking an occupational identity, who are most often involved in burglary, drug abuse, and other illegal acts. They are the ones most often involved in campus violence. Young people who know where they are going, occupationally, go about their business without causing a lot of problems for their fellow man. They have a goal to pursue. They have a purpose.

How can you, somewhere between the ages of 15 and 25, make career decisions which will determine the central activity of your daily life for the next 40 or 50 years? Some say, "Sit at your desk, and you will be told about the world." Others say, "School won't help too much, you've got to *experience* the world." Most psychologists who have studied this problem agree that the two most important factors in gaining identity as a worker between the ages of 15 and 25 are (1) getting work experience to guide in choosing a career and (2) choosing and preparing for an occupation. Thus, the best approach seems to be through cooperative work-experience education.

Part I of this text deals with the meaning of work and appraising your interests, abilities and aptitudes, values, and personality — and then considering many occupational fields to determine which is most appropriate for you. We shall discuss setting short-range and long-range goals which are realistic for you. You will learn how to locate, apply for, and progress on a job which will lead toward your long-range goal. You will learn how you can become a more effective person in your relationships with others both on and off the job.

Chapter 1

You and Work

After completion of high school, you can expect to live for about another fifty years.[1] If you are a boy, you will probably work for about forty of these years. Boys usually understand this as they know that men are the primary "bread winners" in our society. The average girl in high school today will work for about 25 years. Many high school girls find this difficult to believe. However, here is a typical example:

Sally graduated from high school when she was eighteen and began working as a typist in an insurance office in her home town. Soon after she began working she met Dave. They began dating regularly and were married shortly after Sally's twentieth birthday. Dave was twenty-two and had a good job, but his income was barely enough to meet the expenses of a newly married couple. They decided that it would be best if Sally continued working for a while so that they could rent a nicer apartment, trade in Dave's six-year-old Chevrolet, and maybe even save a little money for a down payment on a house in a couple of years.

---

[1]The life expectancy for an 18-year-old boy is 70.19 years; for an 18-year-old girl it is 72.95 years.

3

A month before their first child, Carol, was born, Sally quit her job. She did not begin working again until after their second child, Tracy, was in the first grade. The family had moved to another city, and Sally began working part time as a typist at the local high school. She was soon offered a better-paying job as a secretary in a real estate office, and Sally was again a full-time member of the working world. Although she changed jobs twice more, Sally continued working until Tracy had completed two years of college, got his own apartment, and began his first full-time job.

Sally has spent the last two years at home as a full-time housewife. But she is bored with inactivity after being a working girl for seventeen years. Sally will go back to work as soon as she finds a job she likes and feels she can do well.

You, too, will spend many years of your life working. Why will you work? Why do people work? They work for three reasons:

(1) Economic,

(2) Social, and

(3) Psychological

If you were asked the question, "Why do you *want* to work?" your first answer would probably be "for money!" This is one good reason to work. During your lifetime, you will need at least $250,000 to pay for the goods and services which you will purchase. Some of these goods and services are necessary to your life and well-being. These necessities include such goods as food, clothing, and shelter (housing). Some services are also necessary. These include medical attention and education. An automobile is also a necessity if you must have one to get to work or to the places where necessary goods and services are purchased.

None of us is satisfied with only being able to purchase the goods and services which are necessary. Our *wants* are greater than our *needs*. Whatever you desire in addition to the necessities of life are called *luxuries*. Of course, what is a *necessity* to one person may be a *luxury* to another. If you live on a bus line that can take you to work and shopping, then a car would not be a *necessity* — it would be a *luxury*.

Ways of handling your money so that you can get more goods and services for the amount of money you earn will be discussed in a later chapter. Money is *only one* reason for working. There are other important ones.

As an Adult, You Will Be Identified by the Work You Do

As a young person of school age, it is assumed that your major activity is that of a student. After you are introduced to another person, perhaps, you are often asked, "Where do you go to school?" or "What grade are you in?" Your "identity" is that of a *student*. As an adult, you will be identified by the work you do. After being introduced to another person, you may be asked, "What do you do?", "What kind of work do you do?" or simply "Where do you work?" Of course, other things go into making up your identity, but the work you will do is probably the chief ingredient. Even the work you *plan* to do affects your identity. For example, college students are sometimes identified as *pre-law* or *pre-med* students. If you are concerned about your own identity, keep in mind that the work you do will largely identify you to others. By knowing the work a person does, you can estimate:

1. His income
2. His educational background
3. Where he lives
4. Where he works
5. What his political views are
6. Who his friends are
7. How he spends his spare time
8. What clubs he belongs to

Do you believe that your work can affect your life in so many ways? Consider these situations:

Leonard is a bookkeeper in a Ford agency. He moved to the community two years ago after being released from the Navy. While in the Navy, Leonard's favorite form of recreation was bowling. When he heard that Tom, the agency's service manager, was on a bowling team, it was natural that Leonard and Tom should become good friends. They had two common interests: their place of work and bowling as a form of recreation.

George is a typewriter repairman. His boss is very much interested in politics and is on the city council. During the last election, George came to share his boss's political views and even became his campaign manager.

As you can see, your work does affect your life in many ways. Your outlook on life or your satisfaction with life depends to a large extent on how you feel about your work. The importance of work differs from person to person. Some think it is important only because it earns them a living. To others, it is a *way of life!*

How successful a person is in *life* is measured largely by his success in his work. Being successful on a job which interests you develops a sense of pride. It gives you self respect. *Those without job success cannot have the same respect for themselves as those with job success.* This is the chief way we measure our *own* usefulness, our worth. It also greatly affects our personality. Without *respect for self,* it is impossible to accept yourself as being a *person of worth;* and if you cannot accept yourself as a worthy person, you cannot accept others and truly be concerned about them.

Well, as you can see, you receive many things from work! As with anything else, however, you will not receive all this unless you give something. What you receive from working depends directly upon what you give to the work and to your employer. *If you expect a full-day's pay, you must give a full-day's work.*

When you attend a movie, you must purchase a ticket and pay the full fare. If the theater only showed you three-fourths of the film and turned off the projector, you would feel that you hadn't received your money's worth. Your attitude toward the theater manager would be distrust and, perhaps, even anger.

Likewise, if your employer pays you for four hours' work and you have worked only three hours because you arrived late and took too much time for a coffee break or otherwise wasted time, you are being unfair. Your employer will learn to distrust you. Those who cheat their employers this way are not likely to be promoted to a better-paying job. Many times they are fired! *Remember that you must make money for your employer's business* in order for him to be able to pay your salary. When you begin work, or if you are working now, put in a day's work for a day's pay!

In addition to giving your employer a fair day's work for your salary, you owe him your loyalty. You should be *for him.* If you have minor complaints about your work or your company, do not discuss them with those outside the company. It is important to the welfare of the company that it have a good name, a good *image*. This good name, or *good will,* is partly what makes it possible for the company to make a profit so that it can meet its expenses — and this includes your salary!

You know that you will probably be working for a big part, perhaps most of your adult life. You will work:

(1) For money to purchase goods and services (necessities and luxuries),

(2) For a social identity, and

(3) Because you will have greater respect for yourself and be a happier person if you are interested in and successful in your work.

It is thus possible to gain a great deal from the many hours, days, and years you will spend working. You must give something too. You must *give* a full day's work for a full day's pay; and you must be *honest* with and loyal to your employer.

If You Expect a Full Day's Pay, You Must Give a Full Day's Work

What's Ahead in Part I

Many young people today are searching for identity. They will find it only after setting (and making progress toward) some realistic goals. Occupational success in their chosen field is one of the most significant goals which people can set for themselves, but there is a difference between *goals* and *realistic goals*. You can decide upon a realistic goal for *you* only after a very careful study of your own special (1) abilities and talents, (2) interests, and (3) personality. In addition, you must give consideration to the occupational outlook. In the next chapter you will learn how to set a realistic vocational or career goal for yourself and also how to choose an occupation and a job rather than being *chosen by it*. You will learn how to look for and apply for a job. There are certain techniques which improve your chances of getting the job you want. These techniques, along with how to make the best impression in an interview, are discussed.

Although successful in obtaining a job, many young workers are not successful *on* the first job. Some are fired, others are *laid off*. Some employers tell these young workers the real reason for their failure, while others just say they "must cut back the number of employees," or make some other excuse. The *real* reason for 90 percent of these failures is discussed in Chapter 4. You will also have a chance to learn what the employer (boss) usually expects of a young worker and what you can reasonably expect of him. You will receive some helpful ideas on how to get along with those who work with you — which makes your job much easier.

After you have worked for a while, if you do a good job, you may be given additional responsibility. This is discussed in Chapter 5 along with salary increases, promotions, and what to do if you are fired!

In the remaining chapters of Part I, you will have an opportunity to learn how to better understand *yourself*. You will also learn how to find out what others think about you and how to become more effective in your personal relationships with others. You may even learn ways of getting others to do and see things *your way!*

Study Helps

Study Questions

1. How many years can the average boy graduating from high school expect to work?
2. How long does the average girl work? Why so long?
3. Why is work important?
4. What must you give your employer in return for a day's pay?

Chapter 2

JOBS:

Choices and

Opportunities

If the work you do has such a great influence upon your life, then finding appropriate work is one of the most important considerations in your life as a young adult. You ought to involve yourself in experiences which will prepare you for work in which you can succeed, and which will be properly challenging to you according to your aptitudes, interests, and personality.

It is estimated that the majority of today's workers simply "fell into" the kind of work they do. If the work you do is such an important part of your life, your *way of life,* shouldn't you *choose* your work instead of being *chosen by it?* The first step in choosing your work is to set some goals. You may select one goal or several, and you may change your mind many times before reaching your goal. However, if you have some goals in mind, you have something to work toward. You will be on your way to *choosing* your work. One more thing about career goals — they must be realistic! *Let's look at this sentence again:* Your primary concern should be to involve yourself in experiences which will prepare you for work in which you can succeed, and which will be properly challenging to you according to your aptitudes, interests, and personality. A realistic career goal, then, would be a kind of work in which it is likely that you would be successful. It would be one in which you could do well because you have an aptitude, a *knack,* for it. It would be one in which you are interested. It would be one which fits your personality.

Finally, it should be challenging to you — but not so great a challenge that you would be unable to meet it. More will be said later about general ability and aptitude tests, but in setting a career goal, you should be realistic. If your general ability is slightly below average, it would *not* be realistic to select a career goal which requires many years of college. It would probably result in disappointment to you, and it would delay your reaching a more realistic goal. If your general ability is above average, you would probably not be challenged by many routine jobs which would seem quite easy for you. Of course, to prepare for many of the more complex jobs, some college study may be necessary — and the first step toward college is a good high school record. Selecting a realistic goal for yourself also depends upon your personality. If you are the kind of person who likes to talk and you make friends easily, you are an *outgoing* person. You may have the kind of personality it takes to be a salesman.

Many People Simply Fall into the Kind of Work They Do

If you are usually quiet and find it difficult to make friends, you would probably be very unhappy as a salesman. You would, perhaps, be a happier, more successful worker in a job where you work alone or with only a few other people.

Your Part-Time Job

If you have a part-time job, or if you are looking for one, this is your main job interest. You may find it difficult to look ahead to a full-time job which may be several years away. We have mentioned the importance of realistic career goals because of their relationship to your part-time job. They are related in these ways:

1. The attitudes you develop toward your part-time job, and toward your fellow workers, will carry over to your permanent work.
2. If you can get a part-time job which is similar to your career goal, you can "test out" that field of work to see how interesting it is to you and find out if you have the aptitudes and personality which make for success. In this way you will be able to make the right choice when you become a full-time worker.
3. If you are successful on your part-time job, you will have a valuable recommendation from your employer when you are ready for a full-time job.

Work-Experience Programs

If your school has a work-experience education program, that office can be of great help to you in selecting realistic career goals and finding part-time employment which is related to your career goals. The program in your school may be known by another name, such as Cooperative Work-Experience, Cooperative Education, Work-Study, or Diversified Occupations. Some schools offer an "exploratory" work-experience program on a non-paid basis. The advantages of this program are (1) many more kinds of job opportunities are available, and you can choose the one which is related to your career goal; and (2) because employers are not paying you for your services, they can take more time to let you observe and "try out" many work activities instead of assigning you just the duties that you would perform as a paid worker.

Relationship to Career Goals

If your school does not have a work-experience education program, you can still profit from a part-time job after school or a summer job. In addition to the money, you will benefit from the experience in these ways:

1. You can still explore occupations which interest you and determine your suitability for them.
2. You can broaden your understanding of the working world and of working conditions — even if the job is not closely related to your long-range career goal.

Look into Many Fields of Work Before Choosing Your Career

3. You can develop the kind of work habits which will make for success.
4. Your transition from school to work will be easier.

Qualifications and Interests

With one or perhaps several possible career goals in mind, it is time to consider your qualifications and take a look at what jobs are available to you. In the Dictionary of Occupational Titles, Third Edition[1], more than 20,000 separate occupations are listed and defined. Of course, it would not be practical to read through the more than 800 pages of fine print describing all of these occupations; and many of the jobs are very much alike. However, it does make sense to look at a few job descriptions so that you will be able to consider which types of work seem to fit your interests. In this way, you can begin to set some career goals. On the following eight pages, 12 major fields of work are listed. Several examples of specific jobs are shown for each field, with a brief job description of one or two jobs in each field. These are all jobs for which there is a growing need for more workers. Some of the jobs require, or prefer, college training. For others, high school graduation is all the formal education required. Study these jobs, and ask yourself as you read each description:

(1) "What qualifications do I have for this work?"
(2) "Would I be interested in this work?" and
(3) "Would my personality allow me to succeed in this kind of work?"

To answer the first question, "What qualifications do I have for this work?", consider all related experiences. If you have not worked before, this means the classes you have taken or are now taking which help prepare you for work. For example, if you have taken courses in automobile mechanics, you might be considered for a job as a beginning or trainee auto mechanic. If you have learned typewriting, bookkeeping, print-

---

[1]*Dictionary of Occupational Titles*, Vol. I, Definitions of Titles, Third Edition (Washington: U.S. Government Printing Office, 1965).

ing, or radio and TV repair in school, you will feel at least partly qualified to apply for work in these fields. Of course, you will be expected to begin at the beginning — at the bottom and work up. For some of the fields of work mentioned, there are courses in your school which can help you prepare for work. To qualify for some of the jobs mentioned, it will be necessary to attend a special school.

Visit with Someone Who Does the Kind of Work That Interests You

If you have difficulty in deciding whether a certain kind of work would be interesting to you and fit your personality, ask your school counselor or work-experience coordinator to set up an appointment for you to visit someone who does that kind of work. In this way you may discuss *with the professional* the job qualifications, working conditions, salaries, and need for workers in that field.

These descriptions will give you some idea of the kinds of beginning jobs that may be available. Some of these jobs would be suitable as permanent employment. Others will appeal to you only as part-time or temporary work.

Growing Occupational Fields

College Usually Required

Accountant
Personnel
   Manager
Public Relations
   Worker

Business Administration

Maintains accounts and records or supervises others in such bookkeeping activities as recording expenses, income, and payments. Audits contracts, orders, and vouchers. Prepares financial reports and income tax returns.

Building Trades

Bricklayer
Carpenter
Cement Mason
Plasterer

Constructs, installs, and repairs structures of wood, plywood, and wallboard, using carpenter's handtools and power tools. Studies blueprints and selects type of lumber. Shapes material to prescribed measurements using saws, chisels, and planes.

Clerical

Bookkeeper
Clerk Typist
Secretary
Stenographer

Schedules appointments and gives information to callers; takes dictation, uses stenotype machine or transcribing machine. Reads and routes mail, locates and attaches appropriate file to correspondence. Keeps records. May arrange travel schedules and reservations.

College
Usually
Preferred

Forester
Range Manager

Conservation Occupations

Manages forest lands, plans reforestation, and maps forest areas. Plans cutting programs, gives fire prevention programs, and puts out fires. Works to prevent floods, erosion, and insect pest problems. Conducts research in cutting methods.

**HS Grad.
Preferred**

Routeman
Taxi Driver
Truck Driver

Driving Occupations

Drives a truck to transport materials in liquid or package form to and from such destinations as railroad stations, plants, residences, or within industrial yards. Prepares receipts, collects payment. May load and unload truck.

**College
Required**

Dentist
Pharmacist
Physician

Health Occupations

Compounds and dispenses medicines, following prescriptions issued by physicians, dentists, or other authorized medical practitioner. Weighs, measures, and mixes drugs. Fills bottles or capsules with correct amount and composition of preparation.

Some College Preferred

Dental Assistant
Medical Technologist
Laboratory Assistant

Obtains and records patient's personal information and medical history. Seats patient and prepares him for treatment. Arranges dental instruments and materials, handing them to dentist as needed.

HS Grad. Preferred

Assembler
Furniture
  Upholsterer
Jeweler
Photo Lab Worker
Service Station
  Attendant
Shoe Repairman
Welder

Manual Occupations

Puts together mechanical parts, such as switches, terminal boards, and devices. May fit together electrical parts, test operation, and adjust. May use handtools such as pliers, screwdriver, tweezers, wire cutter, and soldering iron.

Welds metal parts together according to diagram or instructions, using electrical arc or gas welding equipment. Positions material to be welded, adjusts equipment, and feeds welding rod into weld. Uses hood or goggles for eye protection.

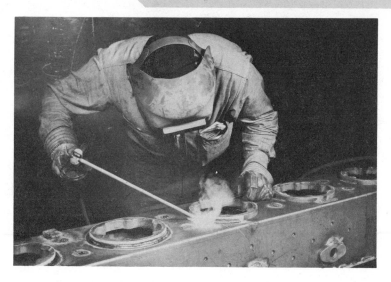

College Required

Actuary
Mathematician
Statistician
Biochemist
Chemist
Geologist
Oceanographer
Physicist

Math & Science

Determines mortality, accident, sickness, disability, and retirement rates for insurance purposes. Designs insurance and pension plans and determines premiums. Applies knowledge of mathematics, probability, statistics, and principles of finance.

Examines rocks, minerals, and fossil remains. Prepares maps and interprets research data. May explore earth to locate gas and oil deposits (petroleum industry). May analyze and classify minerals, gems, and precious stones (mineralogist).

Mechanics & Repairmen

Appliance
 Serviceman
Auto Body
 Repairman
Auto Mechanic
Diesel Mechanic

Repairs household appliances, such as fans, heaters, vacuum cleaners, toasters, mixers, and irons. Disassembles appliance to remove defective parts, using handtools. Installs new parts and reassembles appliance. Records type of repair.

Sales Occupations

Auto Parts
 Counterman
Salesman (Retail)
Salesman
 (Manufacturer)

Sells merchandise to individuals, using knowledge of merchandise. Displays merchandise, refers to catalog, demonstrates use of merchandise. Quotes prices, prepares sales slips or contracts. Prepares reports of sales transactions.

College Required

Anthropologist
Economist
Sociologist

Social Sciences

Studies groups of human beings in society, collecting and analyzing scientific data on their culture. May specialize in relationship between law and crime, special problems of large cities, crime prevention, or juvenile delinquency.

College Required

Architect
Lawyer
Librarian
Teacher
Psychologist
Systems Analyst
Urban Planner

Other Professional Occupations

Plans and designs residences, office buildings, theaters, public buildings, factories, and other structures. Consults with client to determine size and space requirements, provides information on costs, prepares sketches of proposed project.

Diagnoses mental and emotional disorders and administers treatment. Interviews patients in clinics, hospitals, prisons, and other institutions. Observes patients in play or other situations. Selects, gives, and interprets tests of intelligence, achievement, and personality.

A summer job or a part-time job after school can lead in many directions, depending on your interests. The same job may be good training for several young people whose interests are quite different. Consider the case of Alan and Mark:

Between their junior and senior years in high school, Alan and Mark got jobs at Charter Motor Company — a local repair garage and service station. They were hired as service station attendants, and they worked full time until school began in the fall. They pumped gas, cleaned windshields, checked oil and water levels, checked tire pressure, and wrote out credit slips and made change for cash customers. When there were no gasoline customers, they helped the shop mechanics with servicing and minor repairs, such as lubrication, installing fan belts and batteries, and occasionally assisted with brake overhauls.

When summer was over and school began, a full-time worker replaced them during school hours, but Alan and Mark continued working part time after school. By that time, however, Alan knew he didn't care much for the direct contact with the customers which was part of being a service station attendant. He preferred helping the mechanics. He mentioned this to his boss, and because there was an increase in their repair business, he became an assistant to one of the shop mechanics. Mark enjoyed the contact with the customers more than any other part of his job. He liked talking with the customers, and was soon selling them tires, batteries, and other accessories.

After graduation from high school, Alan stayed with Charter Motor Company as a full-time mechanic. Mark began a training program for salesmen with the oil company whose products were sold by Charter Motor Company.

Where to Look

If you have decided upon one or several possible career goals, and have considered your interests, aptitudes, skills, experience — if any, and your personality, *you are ready to choose a job*. You will not let it choose you! By studying the job descriptions on the preceding pages, you now have some idea of the kinds of work that are available to beginning workers. You may be looking for a part-time job to support a car, buy some clothes, or save some money for a trip or college. You may already be looking for the full-time job you will begin after you are out of school. In either case, there are some proven sources and ways of locating vacancies.

In order that you will be able to choose the job that is right for you, it is necessary to organize a plan for locating vacancies. Of course you may have heard a friend tell you about how lucky he was because he was offered a job as soon as he was out of school and that he didn't have to look for a job. If it turns out to be the right job for him, then he was lucky indeed! More often, those who take the first job that is available are among those who are *chosen by their jobs*. They may spend months or even years on a job which is *not* really suited to them before they break loose and begin an organized search for the job they might have had from the beginning — one that is right for them. This is a job in which they can be successful, are interested in and can take some pride in, yet is challenging to them. It just makes sense that the more job opportunities you have to choose from, the better your chances of finding this kind of job. Some of the sources of good job leads are discussed here.

School Work-Experience and Placement Offices

Most schools have someone assigned the responsibility of assisting students in locating job vacancies. The larger high schools often have a well-organized program of work-experience education which provides both vocational counseling and job placement. Smaller schools may have a counselor or teacher who works with the community in locating jobs for students and graduates. The schools can be quite effective in placement because they know you well. They know your ability, aptitudes, grades, attendance record, and have information on your attitudes and personality. No one will be more interested in your

Most Schools Assist Students in Locating Job Vacancies,
But Don't Just Sit Back and Expect the School to Take Care of Everything

getting the right job than the school from which you are graduating. However, don't just sit back thinking that the school will take care of everything. It is usually necessary to refer several of the best applicants for each job, so you will have competition from others in your school. It is possible that the school could refer you to a number of jobs and yet you would not be hired. Your chances of getting a job that is right for you are good if you

There Is Nothing Wrong with Obtaining a Job through a Member of Your Family or a Friend—As Long As You Are Qualified to Do the Work

are willing to work hard at both locating and obtaining it. You should make a list of all job leads so that you will be able to follow up every possibility. When you are job hunting, your chances are better if you know exactly which places you will go to make application when you walk out of your front door. While the school work-experience or placement office is an important source for job leads, there are other good sources.

Family and Friends

One of the best sources of job leads may be members of your own family and friends. They may not have jobs to offer you, but if they are working, then they are involved in the business world daily and may learn of job opportunities for which you are qualified. If you have a friend who has recently begun working, then he or she may have some job leads which are right for *you* even though they may not be right for your friend. Then too, leads often lead to other leads. Because of this, it is wise to follow up on every job lead even though it does not seem to be just what you are looking for.

Make a list of those who might help you with job leads beginning with the members of your own family and add to it the names of friends of your family. This should include those who are in business and might be able to hire you or know others who are looking for workers to fill job vacancies. You should also include those friends who work for companies where you think you might like to work. Add the names of your own school friends and your neighbors who are in any way related to business. A schoolmate's father may work for a company that is looking for someone with your qualifications. Some young people hesitate to ask their "influential friends" about job possibilities, saying that they do not want to get a job by using *pull*. However, there is nothing wrong with obtaining a job through a member of your family or a friend as long as you are qualified to do the work. Pressuring someone to hire you for a job for which you are not qualified is the kind of "pull" to be avoided as both you and the company suffer. Many jobs, however, for which you are qualified are never listed with any placement agency or otherwise advertised — because they are filled by friends of present company employees.

Employment Agencies

Most larger cities have both public and private employment agencies. The public employment agencies are set up under federal and state laws and are known according to the name of the state in which the particular office is located, as *Minnesota State Employment Service* or *Texas State Employment Service*. In California, the state employment service is now a part of the new *Department of Human Resources Development*. By whatever name, their service is free; and in some cities, this is the only employment service offered. Many businessmen list jobs with these state departments of employment, and you should fill out an application form in your local office. You will be interviewed to determine what your interests and qualifications are; and when a job is listed which seems right for you, you will be called into the office and given a referral card to go for a personal interview.

Private employment agencies provide placement for a fee. They usually will not accept an application from someone they think is not qualified for work in the field of his choice. When you make application with a private agency, you must sign an agreement to pay a certain amount or, more often, a percentage of your first few months' salary. Private agencies often know about jobs which are not listed with the state employment service. They should not be overlooked.

City, County, State, and Federal Government

City, county, state, and federal government agencies hire many kinds of workers. Such jobs have a number of advantages, as most are under a civil service or merit system which protects workers from unfair dismissal. The pay and working conditions are usually quite good. As the U.S. Government is the largest employer in the country, thousands of new employees are hired each year for many kinds of jobs.

Schools

In most cities, another important source of jobs is the local school district. In addition to teachers, schools must hire many other kinds of workers. Among them are accountants, secretaries, stenographers, file clerks, PBX (switchboard) operators, library clerks, gardeners, custodians, cooks, nurses, and maintenance workers. Working conditions are usually very good. If you are interested in working in your local schools, check with the school district's personnel office or the superintendent's office.

Colleges and Universities

Colleges, too, must hire many workers besides teachers and professors. Many people enjoy working on a college campus where they can be associated with those who are interested in learning and improving themselves. If there is a college in your city and this sounds interesting to you, apply at the personnel office of the college.

Newspaper Advertisements

If you get into the habit of reading the *Help Wanted* advertisements in your local newspaper (or those in a city where you would like to work), you will learn quite a bit about the job market. You will have a good idea about what salaries are being offered for what kinds of work. It will also give you an idea about what the qualifications are for the kind of work which interests you. You should follow up every newspaper ad which looks like it might lead to the job you are seeking. However, you must be careful. Do not apply for a job which requires you to make a deposit of money. These are often not jobs at all but attempts to sell goods. Other ads may require that you take a course for which you must pay a fee before you are hired. These are usually attempts to get you to enroll in a special school rather than an employer trying to hire someone to fill a job.

The More Possible Employers on Your List,
the Better Your Chance of Getting the Job That Is Right for You

Direct Calling

In addition to the sources of job leads which have been mentioned, you may find it necessary or desirable to do some direct contacting without the benefit of leads. If you do this, you will find it helpful to go through the yellow pages of the telephone directory for ideas of companies which you may call. Looking for a job in this way is difficult because you do not know whether there are any openings, and you do not know anyone connected with the company. However, if you contact enough businesses, you will probably find some who are looking for workers with your skills.

We have said that it is important to have as many job leads as you can so that you can *choose* the job that is right for you. Remember, too, that *there are lots of others looking for work.* You may not get the job you want most, and you may decide not to take some jobs offered to you. In such cases, you will simply follow up another lead. For this reason it is a very good idea to have a list of possible employers written down. Remember that:

1. The more possible employers you have written on your list, the better your chance of getting the job that is right for you.

2. A list of a number of possible employers will lessen the chance that you will jump at the first job offered even if it is not right for you.

3. If you are turned down several times, it is encouraging to have additional employers to whom you may apply.

In deciding which job to accept, you should consider one which:

1. Interests you
2. You can do well
3. Fits your personality
4. Pays reasonably well
5. Provides opportunity for advancement
6. Provides good working conditions

Career Planning[2]

1. Most young people daydream about the kind of work or career they will do when they are adults. What career would you *most like* to follow if you had the opportunity and ability? Describe it.

2. Of course, there can be a big difference between a person's daydreams and what, seriously, he or she really expects to do. A few students your age have made their minds up *definitely* on a choice of career or occupation, but not very many. Most students are thinking of possibilities rather than definite choices. What careers have you given serious thought to as your possible life work? (List three choices in order of preference.)

3. What is your father's occupation?

4. Why do you think you would like the work you listed as your first choice?

5. Why do you think you would like the work you listed as your second choice?

6. Why do you think you would like the work you listed as your third choice?

7. What *facts* should you know about yourself *before* choosing a career?

8. How much education is required for the work you listed as your first choice? (High school, apprenticeship, trade school, business school, college or university, or or special school?)

9. In your first choice for a career, what would your duties be?

10. How do your parents feel about your career choice?

---

[2]Adapted from material prepared by Covina-Valley Unified School District, Covina, California.

11. Suppose your parents didn't agree with your plans — what would you do? (Consider that they are unwilling to support you in your plans.)

12. Who do you feel should be responsible for your career choice?

13. List some of your interests, hobbies, and activities both in school and outside of school.

14. Which of your interests would your career (first choice) satisfy and why?

15. Discuss your scholastic abilities. What are your strong points and weak points in school? How do you know this?

16. Which abilities do you have that will help you in the work you are planning?

17. Which scholastic ability do you *not have* that would help you in the work you are planning? Note: If you honestly feel you have no lack of ability for this work, say so.

18. List the grades you received at your last grading period.

19. Things that are important to us personally are called our values. List some of your values.

20. Which of your values would be satisfied by the work you are planning?

21. What do you plan to do after graduating from high school? (Such as working full time; enlisting in the military service; attending trade or business school; attending junior college, 4-year college; no plans, etc.)

22. After considering your interests, abilities, and values, is your career choice right for you? Why?

23. Are the courses that you are planning to take the right ones to help you in your career choice? If not, how do you know they are not?

Most Young People Daydream about the Kind of Work They Will Do As Adults

Study Helps

Discussion Problems

1. Why are most workers doing the *kind of work* they are doing?
2. What is a better way to become involved in work?
3. What is meant by a *realistic goal*?
4. Does the person who finds it difficult to make friends usually make a good salesman? Why?
5. There are several ways in which part-time jobs are related to career goals. What are they? How does this apply to you?

6. Some schools have exploratory work-experience programs which allow students to try out different kinds of work on a non-paid basis. What are some of the advantages of doing this?
7. In considering different kinds of occupations, what questions should you ask yourself about them?
8. With whom should you talk to get first-hand information about job fields in which you are interested?
9. Where can you get information about conditions of work, salaries, and job requirements on many hundreds of jobs?
10. When you are looking for a job, there are a number of good sources for leads. What are they?
11. Is it a good idea to take the first job you hear about? Why?
12. Why is it a good idea to have a written list of possible employers?
13. In deciding which job to accept when more than one is offered, what should you consider?

Suggested Activities for Chapter 2

1. **Vocational Speakers**—Arrange for several vocational speakers to talk with the class, each on a separate day. They may be workers in whatever kinds of work interest the class. Those who earn their living by doing a particular kind of work can provide a lot of information about how much education is required, what the salaries are, what the working conditions are like, and whether there is a need for more workers in a particular field of work.
2. **Field Trips**—Arrange for two field trips to businesses chosen according to the interests of the class. Actually seeing the conditions under which the employees work and watching them in their work activities can provide accurate, up-to-date information on many occupations.

Chapter 3

Applying for a Job

After you have decided what kind of job you are looking for and have made out a list of job leads, you are ready to apply for some of these jobs. You will be applying to employers who are shopping for the best person to fill the job. Their selections will be based upon about the same things that cause you to decide upon which car to buy. Before buying a car, you will want to know some facts about its condition, how it looks, and how it performs. The employer interviewing you will want to know:

1. Some facts about you, such as how much and what kind of education and experience you have.
2. How you look and behave.
3. How you perform.

This usually means filling out an *application form*. It may mean that you must write a *letter of application* and prepare a *personal data sheet*. Almost always it means that you must be interviewed before you will be hired. Sometimes you may be asked to take some kind of performance test. If you are applying for a job as a secretary, you will probably be given shorthand and typing tests. If you are applying for a job as a welder, you will be asked to do some welding to show how well you perform. Experience shows that employers look for certain things in each of these. If you present the employer with the information he wants, the way he wants it, you have a much better chance of being hired!

Application Forms

As most employers will ask you to fill out an application form, following these suggestions will help *sell* you to the employer:

1. Fill out the application form in ink — or use a typewriter.
2. Answer every question that applies to you (if a question does not apply, you may write "NA", meaning *not applicable,* or draw a line through the space to show that you did not overlook the question).

An Employer Will Want to See How You Look, Behave, and Perform

3. Give your *complete address,* including your zip code.

4. The question on marital status simply means whether you are single, married, separated, divorced, or widowed.

5. Spell correctly (if you aren't sure about how to spell a word, try to use another word with the same meaning).

6. The question on place of birth means the city and state in which you were born — not the name of the hospital.

7. A question on job preference or "job for which you are applying" should be answered with a specific job title or type of work. Do not write "anything" — employers expect you to state clearly what kind of work you can do.

8. Try to have in mind all of the schools you have attended and the dates of your attendance (if there are several, it is a good idea to write them down before you apply for a job).

9. Be prepared to list several good references. It is much better to ask permission of those you plan to list. Those considered good references include (a) the pastor of your church, (b) a former employer, (c) a teacher who knows you well, (d) friends who are established in business.

10. When you write or sign your name on the application, use your correct name — not a "nickname." Your first name, middle initial, and last name is usually preferred.

11. Be as neat as possible (the employer expects that your application will be an example of your *best* work.)

An example of an application form appears on the following two pages. To prepare you to do your best on the application you will fill out for a real job, practice filling out one or two such forms. Your teacher can probably obtain a supply of these from local firms.

FF-75 (5-68) rev. (TEMPO)

GENERAL ⊛ ELECTRIC

APPLICATION FOR EMPLOYMENT

PRINT NAME_____					SOC. SEC. NO.			
	LAST	FIRST	MIDDLE	(MAIDEN)				

TEMPORARY ADDRESS_____

PERMANENT ADDRESS_____

NO. & STREET   CITY   STATE   ZIP CODE   TELEPHONE

CHECK ALL THAT APPLY
- ☐ SINGLE   CITIZEN ⎫   ☐ YES
- ☐ MARRIED   OF   ⎬   ☐ NO
- ☐ DIVORCED   U.S.A.?⎭
- ☐ SEPARATED
- ☐ WIDOWED   ☐ MAN
- ☐ REMARRIED   ☐ WOMAN

	NAME	RELATION & AGE	NAME	RELATION & AGE
NAME, RELATIONSHIP & AGE OF HUSBAND OR WIFE, AND DEPENDENT CHILDREN				
IF SINGLE, GIVE PARENTS' NAMES				

HEIGHT_____ WEIGHT_____

BIRTH DATE_____
MONTH   DAY   YEAR

NOTIFY IN EMERGENCY_____
NAME   ADDRESS   TELEPHONE

HAVE YOU ANY DEFECTS OR LIMITATIONS?
(Physical, Mental, other.)
☐ YES   ☐ NO
IF YES, EXPLAIN FULLY

HAVE YOU EVER BEEN CONVICTED OF A MISDEMEANOR OR A FELONY?
☐ YES   ☐ NO
IF YES, EXPLAIN FULLY

POSITION DESIRED

WAGES OR SALARY EXPECTED $_____ PER ⎰ HR.
⎱ WK.
⎱ MO.

OTHER POSITIONS FOR WHICH YOU ARE QUALIFIED

DATE AVAILABLE

WHAT INTERESTED YOU IN G.E.?

LIST NAMES AND COMPANY LOCATIONS OF RELATIVES EMPLOYED BY G.E.

WERE YOU EVER EMPLOYED BY G.E.? IF YES, WHERE & WHEN?

HAVE YOU EVER APPLIED FOR WORK AT G.E.? IF YES, WHERE & WHEN?

CIRCLE HIGHEST GRADE COMPLETED IN EACH SCHOOL CATEGORY	GRADE SCHOOL	HIGH SCHOOL	COLLEGE	GRAD. SCHOOL
	1 2 3 4 5 6 7 8	9 10 11 12	1 2 3 4	1 2 3 4

	NAME	LOCATION	COURSE–DEGREE	YEAR GRADUATED	CLASS STANDING
GRADE SCHOOL					
HIGH SCHOOL					
COLLEGE					
GRADUATE SCHOOL					
ADDITIONAL GRADUATE SCHOOL; BUSINESS OR VOCATIONAL SCHOOL					
OTHER TRAINING OR SKILLS (Special Courses, Office Machines Operated, Typing and/or Shorthand Speed, etc.)					

HOBBIES

BRANCH OF U.S. SERVICE	DATE ENTERED	DATE DISCHARGED	FINAL RANK	SERVICE NO.

SERVICE SCHOOLS OR SPECIAL EXPERIENCE	TYPE DISCHARGE
SELECTIVE SERVICE NO. CLASSIFICATION & DATE	LOCAL BOARD NO. AND ADDRESS
RESERVE OR NATIONAL GUARD STATUS	NAME & ADDRESS OF COMMANDING OFFICER

PLEASE COMPLETE OTHER SIDE

(MAIDEN) MIDDLE FIRST LAST

EMPLOYMENT HISTORY

PLEASE LIST ALL EMPLOYMENT STARTING WITH PRESENT OR MOST RECENT EMPLOYER.

ACCOUNT FOR ALL PERIODS, INCLUDING UNEMPLOYMENT & SERVICE WITH U.S. ARMED FORCES. USE ADDITIONAL SHEET IF NECESSARY.

DATES	NAME & ADDRESS—EMPLOYER	1 JOB TITLE / 2 DEPARTMENT / 3 NAME OF SUPERVISOR	DESCRIBE MAJOR DUTIES	WAGES	REASON FOR LEAVING
FROM _MONTH_ _YEAR_ / TO _MONTH_ _YEAR_		1 / 2 / 3		STARTING $ ____ per / FINAL $ ____ per	
FROM _MONTH_ _YEAR_ / TO _MONTH_ _YEAR_		1 / 2 / 3		STARTING $ ____ per / FINAL $ ____ per	
FROM _MONTH_ _YEAR_ / TO _MONTH_ _YEAR_		1 / 2 / 3		STARTING $ ____ per / FINAL $ ____ per	
FROM _MONTH_ _YEAR_ / TO _MONTH_ _YEAR_		1 / 2 / 3		STARTING $ ____ per / FINAL $ ____ per	
FROM _MONTH_ _YEAR_ / TO _MONTH_ _YEAR_		1 / 2 / 3		STARTING $ ____ per / FINAL $ ____ per	
FROM _MONTH_ _YEAR_ / TO _MONTH_ _YEAR_		1 / 2 / 3		STARTING $ ____ per / FINAL $ ____ per	

PRE-EMPLOYMENT STATEMENT

I voluntarily give the General Electric Company the right to make a thorough investigation of my past employment and activities, agree to cooperate in such investigation, and release from all liability or responsibility all persons, companies or corporations supplying such information.

I consent to taking the pre-employment physical examination and such future physical examinations as may be required by the Company. I agree to wear or use protective clothing or devices as required by the Company and to comply with the safety rules.

I agree that the entire contents of this application form, as well as the report of any such examination, may be used by the Company in whatever manner it may wish.

If employed by the Company, I understand that such employment is subject to the security policies of the Company. I further understand that if the position for which I am hired requires access to classified information and I am not able to obtain a security clearance, I will not be allowed to work in this position. My employment with the Company in a position not requiring security clearance depends upon the existence of such a position for which I am qualified.

I further understand that any false answers or statements made by me on this application or any supplement thereto, or in connection with the above mentioned investigation, will be sufficient grounds for immediate discharge.

APPLICANT'S SIGNATURE _____ DATE _____

INTERVIEWER'S COMMENTS

INTERVIEWER BY _____ DATE _____

Letters of Application

We have discussed the importance of filling out the application form completely and neatly. This alone, of course, will not get you a job. Most often it is in the personal interview that the employer decides who will be hired. Both the application form and the letter of application (if well done) can get you into the employer's office for the interview. There are times when writing a letter of application is the only way of getting a personal interview. You should write a letter of application in these situations:

1. When you wish to apply for an out-of-town job (especially if it is a business or professional position).
2. When you answer a newspaper advertisement which asks that you apply by mail.
3. When you wish to be interviewed by business friends of your family.

Telling the Employer How Badly You Need a Job Will Not Get Him to Hire You

4. When an employer asks that you write a letter of application. (Sometimes this is done to see how well you can use correctly written English and also to see how well you type or how neatly you write.)

When you apply for a job it is necessary to sell yourself to the employer. Telling the employer how badly you need a job will not get him to hire you — in fact, you shouldn't even mention this. You must convince him that hiring you would benefit the company, but you must not pressure him in any way. A letter of application, then, is a sales letter. As with any kind of sales letter, you must make a good first impression. This means that you will type your letter unless you are answering an advertisement that asks you to apply in your own handwriting. (If you do not type, handwritten letters are acceptable.) If you are applying for a job as a typist, stenographer, or other clerical office worker, this is an excellent chance to show the employer how neatly you can set up and type a letter. No matter what job you applying for, a neatly typed letter with all words spelled correctly is impressive.

Here are some suggestions which will help you write a letter of application that will get atention:

1. Write a *first copy* so that you can develop what you should say the way you should say it. This will be re-written or typed after you have polished it up. (You might ask a teacher or a friend in business to help you with this.)

2. In your first sentence establish a point of contact. This should tell where or from whom you learned about the job. You might say, "At the suggestion of Mr. Benson (a mutual friend), I am writing regarding the job as messenger in your office." If you are writing in answer to a newspaper advertisement, you might begin, "Your advertisement in today's *Times* for a typist clerk describes the work which I think I do best."

3. In the second sentence, state that you are applying for the job. You might say, "Please consider me an applicant for this position." or "I should like to be considered an applicant for this job."

4. If you have little to say about how your education and experience qualifies you for the job, this can all go in the

second paragraph. If you have no experience, don't mention it at all — just tell how your education (classes in typing, bookkeeping, auto shop, etc.) will help you in this job. If you have more to say about both your education and experience, separate paragraphs should be used for each.

5. If you include references in your letter, these should appear in the next paragraph. Be sure you get permission from those you wish to name as references.

6. In your last paragraph, ask for a personal interview at the employer's convenience; and tell him how he may reach you by phone.

Some businesses receive dozens of application letters for each job. If they have advertised in the newspaper, they may

A Carefully Written Letter of Application Can Help Land the Job You Want

receive hundreds of letters. Interviews are usually given only to those whose letters show that the applicant is qualified for the job and whose letters themselves are neat and well-written, with all words spelled correctly. This means that if you are very careful about how you write your letter, you will have a big advantage. After you have written one really good letter, you can make it the basis for letters of application for other jobs. Of course, you would have to change the first paragraph about what job you are applying for and where you learned about it. However, the paragraphs on your education and experience, references, and the last paragraph in which you ask for an interview would change very little.

Before you rewrite or type your letter for mailing, carefully read the sample letters on pages 48 and 50. They may give you some additional ideas for polishing up your letter. These suggestions will help you in preparing your copy for mailing:

1. If you are typing your letter, clean your type before you begin. A letter typed on a dirty machine will show a's, e's, and p's with blackened areas which should be white. Set your margins about 1½" on the left and right sides of your paper.

2. Type your street address 2" from the top of the sheet. This can begin at the left margin or end even with the right margin. On the next line, type your city, state, and zip code. On the third line, type the date.

3. Begin the inside address (person or company to whom you are writing) about 1½" down from the date line. If your letter is very short, you will need to leave several more spaces between the date and inside address so that your letter will be centered on the sheet when completed. Check to be certain you have spelled correctly the name of the person and company and that the address is correct. People are particular about how their names are spelled.

4. If you are addressing your letter to an individual, your salutation should be *Dear Mr. Fox:*, *Dear Miss Doe:*, or *Dear Mrs. Winn:*. If you are writing to a company or to a personnel office and do not know the name of the person who will read and act upon your letter, you

should use the salutation, *Gentlemen*:. The salutation should be followed by a *colon*.

5. Type the main part of your letter very carefully. It will make the best impression if there are no mistakes, but one or two careful erasures are acceptable.

6. Your closing should be *Yours truly, Yours very truly,* or *Very truly yours.* Only the first word of closing should begin with a capital, and the closing should be followed by a *comma.*

7. After the closing, space down four (4) spaces and type your name.

8. Before you remove the letter from your typewriter, read it carefully to see if there are any mistakes which could be more easily corrected while still in the machine.

9. Sign your name in ink above the typewritten signature.

Personal Data Sheets

We have said that the letter of application, if done well, can get you into the employer's office for an interview. However, it is to your advantage to give the employer some additional information about you which is not usually put into the letter of application. The accepted way of presenting this information is in the form of a personal data sheet. This information includes details about the courses you have taken in school; experience — if any; your age, height, weight, and general health; and hobbies which might be related to the job for which you are applying. It is generally better to list these details on a data sheet as they can be more easily referred to than if they were a part of your letter of application. Another name for a personal data sheet is *resume.*

Remember, if you have no experience, don't mention it! You should tell about the qualities you *do have* — not what you don't have! References, too, are often made a part of the resume instead of the letter of application. You should make a number of copies of your resume and include one with each letter of application to employers.

In order to help you in making up your own personal data sheet, or resume, study the samples on pages 49 and 51.

714 Channel Drive
Santa Barbara, California 93105
May 10, 19

Mr. Kenneth Smith, Personnel Director
Electrophysics Incorporated
8462 Main Street
Santa Barbara, California 93105

Dear Mr. Smith:

Mr. Charles Winfield, the Work-Experience Counselor at Santa Barbara High School suggested that I contact you about the typist clerk job in your firm. Please consider me an applicant for this position.

On June 12, I shall graduate from Santa Barbara High School where I have majored in business education. My courses have included two years of typewriting, two years of shorthand and transcription, business machines, and office practice. My typing speed is 65 words per minute, and I take shorthand at 100 words per minute.

During my senior year in high school I participated in work-experience education. My job assignment was in the accounting office of Radford Oil Company where I made use of and improved the skills I learned in school.

I plan to continue my education in night school and hope someday to be a top secretary. May I have an interview? I shall be glad to call at your convenience. My home telephone is 769-1401.

Yours truly,

Ann Fisher

Ann Fisher

PERSONAL DATA

Personal

Name--Ann Fisher
Address--714 Channel Drive, Santa Barbara, California 93105, Phone--769-1401
Age--18
Height--5 feet, 6 inches
Weight--120 pounds
Health--excellent

Skills

Typing--65 words a minute
Shorthand--100 words a minute
Filing
Adding machine--10-key and full-key
Key-driven calculator

Education

Graduate of Santa Barbara High School, June 12, 19__

Subjects studies--

Typewriting, 2 years
Shorthand, $1\frac{1}{2}$ years
Transcription, $\frac{1}{2}$ year
Business machines, $\frac{1}{2}$ year
Office practice, $\frac{1}{2}$ year
English, 4 years
Math, 3 years
Science, 2 years
History, 3 years

Experience

One year as part-time stenographer-clerk in the accounting office of
Radford Oil Company.

Outside Interests and Hobbies

Dramatic Arts, Tennis

References

Mr. Louis Johnston, Personnel Manager, Radford Oil Company, 1726 Main
Street, Santa Barbara, California 93101
Mr. Charles Winfield, Work-Experience Counselor, Santa Barbara High
School, 700 East Anapamu, Santa Barbara, California 93103
Miss MaryEllen Boxberger, Business Education Teacher, Santa Barbara
High School, 700 East Anapamu, Santa Barbara, California 93103

516 Elm Street
Peabody, Kansas 51683
May 5, 19

Mr. James Duncan
Manager
First State Bank
715 Pine Street
Peabody, Kansas 51683

Dear Mr. Duncan:

My counselor at Peabody High School, Mr. Walter Smith, told me that you plan to hire a young man as a bank trainee. I would like to apply for this position.

On May 17, I shall graduate from Peabody High School. As you will see on the attached personal data sheet, I have taken some subjects in business education which should prove helpful in this job. I would also be willing to continue my education either in night school or part time if it would be helpful in my work.

Several months ago I was with a group which toured your bank, and I feel that it would be a very interesting place to work. Some day I would like to work up to the management level in banking.

May I have a personal interview? You may reach me any day after 3 p.m. at 846-6489.

Very truly yours,

John Grant

John Grant

PERSONAL DATA of
JOHN GRANT
516 Elm Street
Peabody, Kansas 51683
PHONE 846-6489

Skills

Typing--40 words a minute
Adding machine

Education

Graduate of Peabody High School, May 17, 19__

Subjects studied--

Typewriting, 1 year
Bookkeeping, 1 year
English, 3 years
Business math, 1 year
General science, 1 year
Band, 3 years
History, 2 years
Physical education, 4 years

Outside Interests and Hobbies

Play piano and trumpet
Photography
Tennis
Swimming

References

Mr. Walter Smith, Counselor, Peabody High School, 100 Walnut Street
Peabody, Kansas 61583

Mrs. George Lewis, Bookkeeping Teacher, Peabody High School, 100 Walnut
Street, Peabody, Kansas 61583

Mr. Robert Carson, Photographer, 614 Sycamore Street, Newton, Kansas 61543

Mr. Larry Williams, Assistant Manager, First National Bank, 1864 Main
Street, Newton, Kansas 61543

Interviews

We have studied the use of application forms, letters of application, and personal data sheets, but you will be hired only after you have been interviewed by the employer or his representative. The employment interview can be one of your most important life experiences. What happens in this twenty or thirty minute period may direct your whole future career. Yet, some applicants for jobs give the impression that they might as well get interviewed for a job since they have nothing better to do at the moment. A personnel manager of a large corporation on the West Coast recently told about a young woman who came into his office seeking a job wearing a bathing suit. She was on her way home from the beach!

Some Applicants Give the Impression They Might As Well Get Interviewed for a Job Since They Have Nothing Better to Do at The Moment

Preparing for the Interview

Before your first interview, you should look over your personal data so that you will be able to answer whatever questions may be asked of you. You will either be called by the employer's secretary and agree on a time for an interview or you will call to make an appointment. If you call for an appointment, you must clearly state your name and how you learned of the job opening. Be sure that you know the exact place and time of the interview — and write it down. Check the correct spelling of the interviewer's name and how to pronounce it.

Usually, you will be interviewed by the employer or the personnel manager. It is normal to be a little nervous, but there is really nothing to be afraid of. It may help you to know that the purpose of the interview is to allow the employer to learn about: (1) your attitude toward people and work, (2) your education and work experience, and (3) your future career plans. It also gives you a chance to see whether you would like to work in a particular job or for a particular company. As you want to make a good impression, find out something about the company before the interview. Try to learn what its products or services are, how large the company is, and whether it is a growing company. This will give you something besides yourself to talk about during the interview.

The Interview

There are several things which you should take with you when you are going for an interview for a job. They are:
1. A pen and pencil.
2. Your social security card.
3. A work permit if required (your school counselor or work-experience coordinator can advise you).
4. If you have prepared a personal data sheet, take a copy with you to the interview.

Go alone! Do not take a parent or friend with you. One high school senior girl was referred to a job and decided that she would take her friend along. As her friend was also looking for work and the employer liked her qualifications better, he hired her friend for the job. Employers seldom hire anyone who cannot sell himself in an interview without the help of another person.

Check your appearance. The employer's first impression of you when you arrive will be based on how you look. You must, therefore, be careful about your grooming and the clothes you choose for the interview. You should, of course, take a bath before dressing for the interview. You would think that it would not be necessary to mention this; but, unfortunately for them, some young people do show up for a job interview wearing a body odor that loses the job as soon as they walk into

The Employer's First Impression of You Will Be Based on How You Look

the interviewer's office. The strong smell of cigarettes, too, has lost jobs. This odor is very annoying to those who do not smoke.

Boys should be very careful about their hair, fingernails, and a fresh shave. Their hair should be clean, trimmed, and well groomed. More boys have probably lost jobs because they were in need of a haircut than for any other reason. The fingernails, too, must be cleaned and trimmed if one is to make a good impression. Some boys in their upper teens do not shave as often as they should to make a good appearance. Girls should use only a small amount of makeup and should have a neat hair style.

When You Chose the Clothes You Will Wear,
Remember That You Are Looking for a Job—Not Going to a Party

When you choose the clothes that you wear, remember that you are looking for a job, not going to a party. The type of clothes you wear for the interview depends upon the kind of job you are applying for. If it is a factory or construction job, clean, unwrinkled work clothes are appropriate. If you are a boy looking for a sales or office job, wear a shirt and tie with a suit or sports coat. Girls should wear a dress or blouse and skirt. Your clothes should be conservative, not faddish. They need not be expensive, but they should be clean and unwrinkled. Boys with well-shined shoes make a better impression than those who don't think enough of the interview to take time for this important part of proper dress. Leather shoes are much preferred to tennis or canvas shoes for an interview. Matching dress socks are correct for the interview — white athletic socks are not. Hose and dress shoes are appropriate for girls. The employer will look at you as one who will represent his company if you are hired. If your working qualifications and another applicant's are about the same, he will hire the one that makes the best appearance.

Arrive five minutes early. If you are driving, allow some extra time in case traffic slows you up. If you are even *one minute* late or rush in at the last minute, it will look like you are a careless person. However, don't be too early. If you arrive about five minutes before the time set up for the interview, that is about right. When you arrive, the first person you speak with is usually the receptionist or the interviewer's secretary. You must be very cooperative with her. She may be asked her opinion about you by the employer after you are gone.

You may have to introduce yourself. When you walk into the interviewer's office, you may be introduced by his receptionist or secretary — or he may introduce himself and call you by name. If not, then you should introduce yourself by saying something like, "I'm John Grant, and I'm interested in the job as trainee in your bank." You should speak clearly and loudly enough to be heard — and you should smile. You should stand up straight, but do not offer to shake hands unless the interviewer offers his hand first. Wait for his lead. If he offers his hand, then grasp it *firmly*. A "limp fish" handshake will cause him to think you have a "weak personality." Of course you should not prove how strong you are by grabbing his hand and crushing it!

Stand until the interviewer asks you to sit. If he does not ask you to sit down, then you must stand during the interview. When you sit, sit alertly. Don't slouch. Although you will feel nervous at the beginning, you will become more relaxed after the interview has begun. Your eyes should meet the interviewer's eyes regularly. Some people do not trust a person who can't look them in the eye. Perhaps the biggest mistake you could make at the beginning of an interview would be to place your purse or some other article on the edge of the interviewer's desk. If you are carrying a purse or a book with you, keep it beside you. Try to keep your hands quiet. Usually it is best to keep them in your lap. Do not lean on the interviewer's desk or try to read papers on his desk. You know, of course, that you should not chew gum or smoke.

Don't Prove Your Strength by Grabbing the Interviewer's Hand and Crushing It

There are two basic ways of interviewing. You may simply be asked to "tell about yourself." In this case you must do most of the talking, and include all of your qualifications for the job. The interviewer will be pleased if you also say why you would like to work for his company. This is why it is important to do some checking on the company before the interview. The other way in which the interviewer finds out about your qualifications is by asking questions. This is probably the way most interviewers learn about you. Some of the questions most often asked are (1) "Why do you want to work for this company?", (2) "What do you plan to be doing five years from now?", (3) "Are you looking for permanent or temporary work?", and (4) "Which courses in school did you like best?".

Apply for a Specific Job, Not "Anything"

A more complete list of questions which may be asked of you appears on page 60. Be prepared to answer these questions completely. If you do not know the answer to a question, say that you don't know. If you try to "fake it," the interviewer can usually tell. If so, he won't hire you even if your other qualifications are good. There are two questions that we should give special attention to: (1) "What kind of work would you like to do?" and (2) "What salary do you expect?". Too many young people answer the first question by saying "anything." This is irritating to many interviewers because they want to put you in a job for which you are applying. *There is no such job title as "anything."* If you are asked about the salary you expect, it is best *not* to mention a specific amount. It may be too low. If you are hired, you could be paid less than others are getting for the same work. If you mention an amount too high, you may not be hired at all because the interviewer may feel that you would not be satisfied. You might say, "I'm sure you know more about what a fair salary would be than I do — what do you pay for this kind of work?" If you are pressed for an answer, you could mention the amount that you know others are getting for this kind of work. If the interviewer does not mention salary and you can tell that the interview is about over, it is all right to ask what you will be paid if your are hired. If you bring it up too early in the interview, it will look like you are only interested in what you get out of the job. If you are applying for a permanent, full-time job, it is all right to ask whether you get a vacation — but only toward the end of the interview if it hasn't been mentioned by the interviewer. Part-time or temporary workers usually do not get vacations.

Show that you are interested in the company. This is easy if you have thought about two or three questions to ask about the company. These could be about a product or service, the number of employees, etc.

You may be asked to talk with someone in the company besides the interviewer. This might be a department head or someone with whom you would be working if you are hired. If so, it usually means that the interviewer thinks that you would be a good worker. Your chances of being hired are good.

When the interview is over — go! If you have given the interviewer your qualifications, and he seems to have run out of questions, the interview is over. If you do not leave at this time, you may lose your chance of being hired. If you have not been offered the job, it is all right to ask whether you will be called or if you may call back in a few days to learn the interviewer's decision. Say "thank you," and leave. If you pass the receptionist or the secretary, thank her too.

Questions Often Asked During the Interview

1. Why would you like to work for this company?
2. Are you looking for permanent or temporary work?
3. What job would you most like?
4. What do you want to be doing in five years? In 10 years?
5. What qualifications do you have for this job?
6. What subjects in school did you like best? Least?
7. Do you prefer working alone or with others?
8. How do you spend your spare time?
9. What magazines do you read?
10. What is your main strength? Your main weakness?

When the Interview Is Over, GO

11. What jobs have you had? Why did you leave?
12. What salary do you expect?
13. Do you have any debts?
14. Have you had any serious illnesses?
15. Do you smoke?
16. How do you feel about working overtime?
17. Did you attend school regularly? How many days were you out last year?
18. What grades have you gotten in your school work?
19. When can you begin work?
20. How did you become interested in this company?

Why People Aren't Hired

Negative Factors Evaluated During the Employment Interview and which Frequently Lead to Rejection of the Applicant, in Order of Frequency (As Reported by 153 Companies Surveyed by Frank S. Endicott, Director of Placement, Northwestern University).

1. Poor personal appearance
2. Overbearing — overaggressive — conceited "superiority complex" — "know-it-all"
3. Inability to express himself clearly — poor voice, diction, grammar
4. Lack of planning for career — no purpose and goals
5. Lack of interest and enthusiasm — passive, indifferent
6. Lack of confidence and poise—nervousness—ill-at-ease
7. Failure to participate in activities
8. Overemphasis on money — interest only in best dollar offer
9. Poor scholastic record — just got by
10. Unwilling to start at the bottom — expects too much too soon
11. Makes excuses — evasiveness — hedges on unfavorable factors in record
12. Lack of tact
13. Lack of maturity
14. Lack of courtesy — ill mannered
15. Condemnation of past employers

16. Lack of social understanding
17. Marked dislike for school work
18. Lack of vitality
19. Fails to look interviewer in the eye
20. Limp, fishy handshake
21. Indecision
22. Loafs during vacations — lakeside pleasures
23. Unhappy married life
24. Friction with parents
25. Sloppy application blank
26. Merely shopping around
27. Wants job only for short time
28. Little sense of humor
29. Lack of knowledge of field of specialization
30. Parents make decisions for him
31. No interest in company or in industry
32. Emphasis on whom he knows
33. Unwillingness to go where sent
34. Cynical
35. Low moral standards
36. Lazy
37. Intolerant — strong prejudices
38. Narrow interests
39. Spends much time in movies
40. Poor handling of personal finances
41. No interest in community activities
42. Inability to take criticism
43. Lack of appreciation of the value of experience
44. Radical ideas
45. Late to interview without good reason
46. Never heard of company
47. Failure to express appreciation for interviewer's time
48. Asks no questions about the job
49. High pressure type
50. Indefinite response to questions

Why the Other Boy Was Hired

There's a good deal of talk these days about teenage unemployment. Some of it makes sense and some of it does not.

Donald E. Wood wrote a letter to a teenage boy who had applied to him for a job. It represents a point of view shared by many employers. It is reprinted here to help you see how employers look at applicants.

Dear Kid:

Today you asked me for a job. From the look of your shoulders as you walked out, I suspect you've been turned down before, and maybe you believe by now that kids out of high school can't find work.

But, I hired a teenager today. You saw him. He was the one with the polished shoes and a necktie. What was so special about him? Not experience. Neither of you had any. It was his attitude that put him on the payroll instead of you. Attitude, son. A-T-T-I-T-U-D-E. He wanted that job badly enough to shuck the leather jacket, get a haircut, and look in the phone book to find out what this company makes. He did his best to impress me. That's where he edged you out.

You see, Kid, people who hire aren't "with" a lot of things. We know more about Bing than about Ringo, and we have some Stone-Age ideas about who owes whom a living. Maybe that makes us prehistoric, but there's nothing wrong with the checks we sign, and if you want one you'd better tune to our wave length.

Ever heard of "empathy?" It's the trick of seeing the other fellow's side of things. I couldn't have cared less that you're behind in your car payments. That's your problem and the President's. What I needed was someone who'd go out in the plant, keep his eyes open, and work for me like he'd work for himself. If you have even the vaguest idea of what I'm trying to say, let it show the next time you ask for a job. You'll be head and shoulders above the rest.

Look Kid: The only time jobs grew on trees was while most of the manpower was wearing G.I.'s and pulling K.P. For all the rest of history you've had to get a job like you get a girl: "Case the situation, wear a clean shirt, and try to appear reasonably willing."

Maybe jobs aren't as plentiful right now, but a lot of us can remember when master craftsmen walked the streets. By comparison, you don't know the meaning of "scarce."

You may not believe it, but all around you employers are looking for young men smart enough to go after a job in the old-fashioned way. When they find one, they can't wait to unload some of their worries on him. For both our sakes, get eager, will you?

Donald E. Wood

Study Helps

Study Questions

1. Should an application for a job be written in pencil, ink, or completed on a typewriter?
2. On most application forms some questions will not apply to you. What should you do to show that you have not overlooked these questions?
3. What is meant by marital status?
4. How should you answer the question on place of birth?
5. Why do you think employers ask for an applicant's job preference? Is it a good idea to answer this question with "anything?"
6. Who do you think you should list as references?
7. How should you sign your application?
8. In what situations should you write a letter of application?
9. Should a letter of application be typed or handwritten?
10. Should you rewrite your letter of application or send the first copy? Why?

11. What is the purpose of the first paragraph of a letter of application?
12. What is the purpose of the last paragraph of a letter of application?
13. What kind of information should be presented in the resume or personal data sheet?
14. What does the employer hope to learn from interviewing an applicant?

Suggested Activities for Chapter 3

1. **Write A Letter of Application**—From the job leads you found in doing the suggested activities in Chapter 2 or from the advertisements in your local newspaper, select one job and write a letter of application. Carefully follow the instructions on writing application letters which are given in Chapter 3.

2. **Role Playing the Interview**—Select someone to take the role of the interviewer and several other students to take the role of job applicant. The others in the class can listen and watch carefully to see which applicant would most likely be hired. After several have been interviewed, discuss the correct and incorrect behavior shown in the interviews.

Cases

The Wellington Company has an opening for a clerk typist. Suppose that you are the personnel manager and you have just interviewed three girls for the job:

Mary is an attractive girl and has a pleasing personality. She typed 50 words a minute on the typing test, and she has taken one year of shorthand in addition to two years of typing. Her grades in school were mostly B's and C's. She arrived five minutes late for the interview.

Just the idea of being interviewed was frightening to Karen so she brought her friend, Carol, along for support. They arrived five minutes early and, although nervous, Karen presented herself well. She was clean, neat, and well dressed. She typed 55 words a minute on the typing test, and took one year of bookkeeping in addition to two years of typing in high school. Her grades in school were mostly C's.

Vera arrived for the interview five minutes early. She answered each question accurately and pleasantly. On the typing test she scored 48 words per minute. Vera took one year of bookkeeping and two years of typing in high school. Her grades were mostly C's.

Who would you hire? Why?
If you can't decide, what additional information is needed?

Chapter 4

You, Your Employer, and Your Co-Workers

The Importance of Attitude

In the first three chapters we discussed the meaning of work and how to locate and apply for a job. After you have a job, there are certain things you must do to be successful on your job. *The most important factor in job success is attitude!* This is shown in the fact that the main reason young workers lose jobs is because of poor attitude. In fact, a recent study of beginning workers who had been fired showed that eighty percent lost their jobs because they couldn't get along well with other people. Getting along well with others does not just happen. It must be learned. Those who do learn to get along well with almost everyone are usually happier persons because people like them, they enjoy a greater feeling of job success, and they often receive higher salaries.

The study of physical anthropology has recently indicated that our behavior depends in part upon who our parents are. It is, to a degree, inherited. Much more important in the way we behave is what happens to us while we are growing up. The behavior we exhibit and the attitudes we develop up to graduation from high school usually carry over into adult life. They are with us both on the job and in social relationships. Basically, your attitude is your outlook on life. It is shown by the way you behave in the presence of other people. If you look at life as something exciting and worthwhile — if you really enjoy life most of the time, your attitude toward other people will show this. You will be the kind of person who looks at the good side of things. If, on the other hand, you tend to see others — and life in general — as being unfair to you, then you probably don't like people very much. If this is you, you will be happy to learn that you *can* change. By practice, you can do a lot to become the kind of person who likes other people and whom others like. The younger we are when we begin to exercise some control over our own personalities, the more we can do toward becoming the kind of person we would like to be.

Your attitude can show up in many ways on the job. Consider Sara's attitude:

Sara, 18, is a waitress. She works in a restaurant known for its fine food and excellent service. She dresses neatly and is always well groomed. She has a good memory and never makes mistakes on orders. She arithmetic is always correct on customer's checks. However, Sara does not smile easily. This, even though she is a good worker, makes her less popular with customers; and her tips usually amount to less than that received by the other girls. The busiest day of the year for the restaurant where Sara works is Mother's Day. Every girl is expected to work on that day. However, Sara wanted to visit her own mother in Chicago on Mother's Day — so she begged the restaurant manager to let her off on the busiest day of the year. Although the manager gave Sara the day off, he and the other waitresses felt that Sara had let them down. Everyone else had to work that much harder. Two months later Sara was fired from her job because she couldn't get along with the other employees and was irritable toward the customers.

Sara was an intelligent girl and a good worker, yet she was fired. Could she have done anything which would have saved her job?

Behavior characteristics of those who have healthy, desirable attitudes are compared in the following chart with those who have negative or poor attitudes. If your behavior is similar to that described on the negative side, you should know that such behavior causes others to react to you negatively. If you can work on just one or two areas so that your behavior shows a desirable, positive attitude instead of a negative attitude, the behavior of others toward you will change. People will like you better, and you will like them better. Study the chart to see where you fit in.

POSITIVE ATTITUDE	NEGATIVE ATTITUDE
1. Smiles easily	1. Rarely smiles
2. Willing to change his ideas, dress, behavior when appropriate	2. Unwilling to change
3. Able to see the other person's point of view	3. Unable to see the other person's point of view
4. Almost never complains	4. Complains about nearly everything
5. Accepts responsibility for mistakes	5. Blames others for own mistakes or shortcomings
6. Seldom criticizes others	6. Very critical of others
7. Considers what is good for or helpful to others	7. Thinks only of himself, "What's in it for me?"
8. When talking with another person, looks him in the eye—but does not try to stare him down	8. Unwilling or unable to look the other person in the eye
9. Respects the ideas and opinions of others	9. Tries to force his ideas and opinions on others
10. Never makes excuses	10. Often makes excuses
11. Has a variety of interests	11. Few interests, is often bored

What Your Employer May Expect

We have said that you must make money for your employer's business in order for him to be able to pay your salary. In addition to a day's work for a day's pay, your employer will expect certain things from you. Most employers expect these things from their employees:

1. Cooperation
2. Honesty
3. Initiative
4. Willingness to Learn
5. Willingness to Follow Directions
6. Dependability
7. Enthusiasm
8. Acceptance of Criticism
9. Loyalty

There Are Tasks Nobody Likes to Do,
But Those Who Do Them Make a Good Impression on the Boss

Cooperation

The employer who pays your salary has a right to expect your full cooperation. This means that you will be cooperative with everyone with whom you work — your boss and everyone else with whom you come in contact. One of the best ways to show your cooperation is to offer to help other employees if your duties are completed. In many companies there are certain tasks that nobody likes to do. The employee who is willing to do these tasks will make a good impression on the boss and also gain the cooperation of his fellow workers.

Honesty

Your employer will expect you to be honest with him and with the company. Being dishonest on the job can take many forms. One form of dishonesty is stealing time by coming to work a few minutes late every day. Some workers cheat their employers by stopping work before the end of the work day. If the hours of work are eight to five, you should be on the job a few minutes early so that you will be able to actually start at eight. Your employer will expect you to continue working, except for breaks and lunch, until five. Your time during working hours belongs to your employer. Stealing this time costs him money — money that might be used in part to increase salaries or otherwise benefit you. Stealing time is probably the most costly form of dishonesty in business.

Another form of dishonesty on the job is stealing company property. Several years ago I worked in an office with a young man who regularly used the office postage for his personal letters. Although he was not fired, when it came time to select a new office manager he was passed over mainly because of the dishonesty shown in his stealing postage stamps. Other employees have been fired for stealing supplies or tools.

Initiative

Employers have a right to expect you to complete whatever duties you are given and then, if you haven't been told what to do next, look around to see what needs to be done and do it. Of course, you must use good judgment. Don't attempt to do work that you are not qualified to do.

When I worked as an assistant to a personnel manager a few years ago, I hired a girl who had just graduated from high school for my secretary. She was a charming girl and a good typist. However, she had never learned about initiative. When she completed whatever tasks I had given her, she sat and read a magazine. There was other work that could be done, but she didn't do it. She did nothing except when told directly each task to be done. Such constant supervision required so much of my time that I couldn't get my own work done. I discussed the problem with her on two occasions but had to let her go because she was not able or willing to change. The next girl I hired always kept busy and required little supervision.

Exercising initiative is probably the best way to show your employer that you are capable of accepting greater responsibility — which often leads to a promotion and salary increase. If you never do any more than you get paid for, you will never get paid for any more than you do.

Willingness to Learn

Your employer will expect you to learn the way things are done in his company. This is usually not so much of a problem for a young worker as with the person who has worked for years and developed his own ways of doing things. However, it is worth a special effort to show an eagerness to learn everything you can about your job and the company for which you work. Those who are promoted to jobs with greater responsibility and higher salaries are usually the workers who have taken the trouble to learn about more than just their own daily tasks.

Willingness to Follow Directions

When you are given directions about how to do your work, you are expected to follow them *exactly*. That is why they are given. Sometimes you may not understand the reason for doing things a certain way, but your employer or supervisor has his own reason. Do the work as you are directed. After you have worked on the job for a while, you may suggest other ways of doing certain tasks if you think your ideas will be well received. Be careful about this, though. A new worker may be resented for making suggestions even if they are good ones.

Dependability

Your employer will count on you to be on the job every day and to arrive on time. Those who come to work late — even if they are not fired — are resented by the other workers who do come to work on time. Thus, the worker who is not dependable will also find it difficult to work cooperatively with his fellow workers. If you are ill, call your employer and let him know about your absence as early as possible. This is usually before the time you would normally start work. Many workers lose their jobs because they do not take time to call their employers when they must be absent due to illness.

Enthusiasm

The best employees are those who like their work and show enthusiasm for it. You are fortunate indeed if you find everything connected with your work interesting. Most likely, however, you will find certain things about the job which are interesting to you. When others ask you how you like your new job, tell them the things about it that you like. By concentrating on the positive — the things you like — you will find the total job more interesting to you. When you are interested in and enjoy your work, life itself is more interesting and enjoyable; and you will become a more interesting person because of it.

Acceptance of Criticism

Nancy was a bookkeeper in a bank managed by a friend of mine. She was a good worker, always arrived on time, and

almost never missed a day of work. Nancy's problem was that
she could not accept criticism and benefit from it. On several
occasions she made incorrect entries on her records. She was
told by her supervisor that she must give more careful attention
to certain details of her job. Each time this happened Nancy
would sulk — not speaking or smiling for the rest of the day.
This placed the supervisor under a severe strain because it was
difficult to criticize Nancy's work even though it was necessary.
Nancy was "let go" because it took so much of the supervisor's
time figuring out how to approach Nancy without hurting her
feelings.

Criticism is necessary. It is the way in which the employer
lets us know how he expects the job to be done. Your employer
will expect you to accept criticism — with a smile (not a smirk!)
— and to improve because of it. Regardless of how you may
feel when another person criticizes you, you will be better off
if you *appear* to take it good naturedly. When a friend's criticism
is off base, it may be all right to laugh it off. If it is connected
with your work, it is best to take your critic seriously and
thank him for his attempt to help you. Accepting criticism
means more then just listening politely. It means *making use*
of the criticism. Think about your critic's remarks after you
are alone and try to see how they can help you become a better
worker. Of course, there are employers and supervisors who are
unfairly critical; but there is nothing you can do about the
boss's bad temper — except quit if it is too difficult a work
situation. You must be able to take it, but you can't lose your own
temper. Regardless of how a criticism was meant, it will be
constructive or destructive depending upon how you use it. It
will give you an idea of what is expected of you.

Loyalty

You have probably heard it said that you should not bite
the hand that feeds you. This certainly applies to your relationship with your employer and the company for which you work.
You must be *for* them. Just as none of us is perfect as a person,
neither is any company perfect in every way. You may not
agree with everything your employer does or with some of the

policies of the company, but you must not complain to your
friends or try to "run down" the company which pays your
salary. Employers expect their workers to keep confidential
those things that pertain to the business.

If you cannot be loyal to your employer and your company,
look for another job. You will not be happy working for an
employer of whom you cannot speak well; and while you are
looking for a new job, resist the temptation to be critical of
your present employer.

What You, the Employee, May Expect

After reading what most employers expect of their employees, you may feel that you are expected to give a lot and not
get much consideration from your employer in return. This is
not so. You have a right to expect certain things from your
employer. Of course, some employers are more considerate than
others; but most will do these things for you as a worker:

1. Pay your salary
2. Provide safe working conditions
3. Provide training
4. Introduce you to co-workers
5. Explain policies, rules, and regulations
6. Change your duties
7. Evaluate your work
8. Discipline you if you break rules
9. Encourage an honest relationship

Pay Your Salary

Your employer will pay you for the work you do. The
amount you are paid will depend upon state and federal minimum wage laws, the "going" rate for the work you do, union
contracts, and your ability to perform your job. As a part-time
or beginning worker, your pay will be less than that paid other
employees who have had more experience.

Safe Working Conditions

Your employer should provide reasonably safe working conditions. If you are under eighteen years of age, federal law prohibits your working in certain occupations considered dangerous, such as coal mining, logging, and jobs requiring the use of certain power machinery.

Federal Law Prohibits Those Under 18
from Working in Certain Dangerous Occupations

Provide Training

Your employer should provide whatever on-the-job training is necessary in order for you to do your job. The way this is done will differ from job to job and between companies. You may be asked simply to observe another worker performing the job you will be doing — or another worker may be assigned to teach you how to do a particular job.

Introductions

Your employer should introduce you to all of the workers with whom you will be working. This is a courtesy which is not always observed. If your employer does not show you this consideration, you will have to make your own introductions — or perhaps the other workers will do it for you.

Explanations

Your employer should explain company policies, rules, and regulations so that you understand them. If you do not understand exactly how these affect you, ask for further explanation.

Changes

Your employer should tell you about changes in your duties, responsibilities, working relationships, rate of pay, vacation schedule, and anything else which affects you and your work.

Evaluations

Your employer should evaluate your work. This does not mean that he should tell you only the things he doesn't like about your work. He should let you know what is both bad and good, in his opinion, about how you do your job. If he is a considerate employer, he will do this in private.

Discipline

If you do not follow the rules and regulations — or if you do not live up to the things mentioned in what the employer expects of his employees, then you may be disciplined. Most employers are fair in penalizing their employees. If you have not fulfilled your responsibilities, you should not resent disciplinary action.

Honesty

Most employees are honest with their employers, and you have as much right to expect honesty from your boss as he has to expect it from you.

Other Responsibilities

Your employer is required by law to pay half the amount paid into your Social Security account — that is, he matches the amount you pay. In addition, he contributes to workman's compensation for your protection in case you are injured on the job.

Some employer's responsibilities are enforceable by law; others are not. If you become dissatisfied with your job because you feel that your employer is not being fair with you, you may wish to talk things over with him. This will depend upon your own personality, your employer's personality, and how well you get along together and understand each other. If you decide to talk about the problem with your employer, remember that you will have a much better chance of getting him to see things your way if you are cooperative rather than if you simply lay the blame on him. If things cannot be worked out, look for another job — but don't quit until you have found a job you like better. Some workers quit a job they are dissatisfied with only to find that they cannot find another one they like as well.

Getting Along with Co-Workers

We have discussed what the employer, your boss, is likely to expect from you and what you can reasonably expect from him. Because most everyone works with other people, it is necessary that we be able to get along well with these co-workers in addition to living up to the boss's expectations. There are many reasons why it is important that you get along well with your co-workers. If employees enjoy working with one another, they will get more work done — which will make the employer happy and may result in salary raises and promotions. In addition, if you are pleasant and fair with others with whom you work, they are more likely to be pleasant and fair with you. No one can become truly successful in his work completely by himself. An old saying in the business world is, "Make friends of those below you on your way up, for you'll meet the same people on the way down." Of course, as a beginning worker, you will be at the bottom of the ladder; but it is just as important to make friends of your co-workers from the beginning. When you are put in charge of other workers, you will probably have formed the habit of treating those around you with respect and courtesy.

Getting along well with co-workers is an art that is too often neglected. This is because it does not happen automatically. It takes work but it is worth it. If you and your co-workers do not cooperate with one another on the job, it will be damaging to everyone involved. The amount and quality of work will be down — and so will be your chances for pay raises and promotions.

Every individual reacts differently in any given situation. The main reason for this is that each of us sees things through the eyes of our own experiences. If you had a very unpleasant experience with dogs as a child — perhaps badly bitten, you will react toward all dogs quite differently from the person who grew up having dogs as pets which meant a great deal to him. I have known young women who were quite frightened by a close working relationship with any man because their fathers had been unreasonably demanding and unfair to them. The point is that each of us has had experiences which are different from those of every other person. Each of us, then, will see every situation a little differently from any other person. If you are to get along well in your working relationships with your co-workers, you must accept them as worthy individuals even though they are different in many ways from you. Nobody is perfect, but everyone has some good qualities. If you can accept those with whom you work as worthy persons and really try to understand them, you will be more apt to do your part in developing good working relationships.

If it seems to you that one of your co-workers is extremely difficult to get along with, don't judge him too harshly. There are reasons for such behavior. Experiences in his past — or perhaps difficulties he is having at home — are most often causes. It is your responsibility, as his co-worker and as a fellow human being, to do *more* than your share at such times to strive for a smoother working relationship. *You* may sometime need such understanding from those with whom you work.

As a Beginner

As a beginning worker you will be wise to keep your eyes and ears open and your mouth shut — except to ask questions about your work. After you have worked for a while, you will learn which employees are the better workers and which employees receive a paycheck but aren't going anywhere. You will probably find that those who have been working longer than you are happy to help you get started. The worker who tells you about a mistake you are making is doing you a favor. Accept it as a favor — and thank him. Some of your co-workers will offer suggestions for better ways of doing things. They have more experience than you. If their suggestions do not conflict with what your "boss" has told you, try them out. If they work well, adopt them. When help is offered by other workers, accept their suggestions pleasantly and with a smile. However, once you understand your job, do it yourself. Don't depend too much on others. They have their own jobs to do.

I have too often heard the phrase, "That's not my job; let someone else do it." This attitude is sure to create unhappy co-worker relationships. In every company there are tasks which must be performed that are not pleasant. But someone must do them. Don't say that you are "too busy" with other work to do the things you may not feel you were hired to do. Employers react most favorably toward those who are most willing to take on extra or unpleasant duties; and it is a fact that those who are most agreeable to performing these extra tasks are the first to be rewarded with salary increases.

Formality in Business Relationships

If you aren't sure about how friendly — or how formal you should be as a beginning worker, it is better to err in the direction of too much formality than to be *too* friendly. Of

It Is Better to Err in the Direction of Too Much Formality
Than to Be Too Friendly

course, you should smile and be pleasant to everyone, as we have discussed. But don't get too "chummy" too soon. You may find that, after you get to know all of your co-workers, you have become associated with those that you would not really like for your close friends — and it may be difficult to adjust your relationship with these persons and still retain working relationships.

You may work where everyone is called by his first name, and it will seem natural for you to call your co-workers by their first names. In many companies, however, beginning workers are expected to call their older co-workers and especially their boss by their last names, such as Mr. Smith or Mrs. Jones. If you are not sure about how to address your co-workers, again it is better to err in the direction of too much formality than to be *too* friendly.

Stay Neutral in Disputes

One of the best ways to keep up a good working relationship with *all* of your co-workers is to mind your own business. No matter where you work, there will likely be disputes between some workers. If you get involved in such disagreements, you will be the loser every time. You may feel that you have strengthened your friendship with one person for the moment, but you will likely cause a strain on your working relationship with others for a long time. The best thing to do is remain neutral.

Keep Your Sense of Humor

If you have, or can develop, a good sense of humor, it will do more to make you a happy, well-adjusted worker than anything else. A sense of humor is the ability to laugh when the joke is on you. Not too many people can do this. If you can, your co-workers will accept you much more readily than they will the person who laughs only at others.

Unions and Professional Groups

About 17 million workers in the United States belong to *labor unions*. About half of them are factory workers, such as those involved in the production of automobiles. Many others are carpenters, electricians, plumbers, or other skilled craftsmen. They pay dues to the union ranging from about $8 to more than $30 a month — in addition to an initiation fee that often runs more than $100 when they become members. Why do so many workers join unions? They join unions because it is beneficial for them to do so, as we shall see.

Today, Americans are paid higher salaries, work shorter hours, and work under safer and better conditions than any other people in the world. However, in the early days of manufacturing in the United States, workers labored long hours (often 12 hours a day, six days a week) under unsafe working conditions, and were paid only enough to buy the bare necessities of life. If a worker complained, he was often fired — for there were plenty of others who were willing to take his job. This situation caused workers to organize into *labor unions*. In this way, instead of each worker trying to bargain with his employer, all or many of the workers joined together to bargain collectively with their employer. Wherever there are large numbers of employees working for one employer, there are certain to be disagreements over such things as salaries, fringe benefits, and hours of work. When representatives of organized labor and the employer or his representatives (management) sit down together to try to settle such disagreements, each side knows that it must compromise. Negotiation between organized labor and management is known as *collective bargaining*. Under collective bargaining, labor and management discuss what they expect of each other concerning salaries (wages), hours of work, seniority rights, and other common concerns. When an agreement is reached, a *labor contract* is signed by representatives of labor and management. Such contracts usually are written for periods of one to five years, after which a new contract is negotiated.

The things most often covered in a labor contract include wages, fringe benefits, hours of work, seniority, and grievance procedures. The labor unions are, of course, mainly concerned with the welfare of the workers. Unions are constantly seeking higher wages, more fringe benefits, shorter hours of work, and greater benefits for its members. Fringe benefits are vacations, sick leave, retirement pensions, life and health insurance, coffee breaks, and other employee benefits other than wages. For every $100 paid in wages, most employers pay about $20 in fringe benefits for employees.

Management is also interested in the welfare of its employees, because happy workers produce more. However, the purpose of being in business is to make a profit. Profit is the money left from income after all expenses have been paid. In most businesses, wages paid to employees is the biggest expense of all. Management is therefore opposed to raising wages so high that a reasonable profit cannot be made. When this does happen, either the business fails (*goes broke*) or it raises the price of its product. If the prices are increased, then the higher wages of the workers do not buy any more than their old wages purchased before the price increase. This upward spiral of wages and prices, known as *inflation*, has been the pattern in recent years.

Collective bargaining requires that each side be willing to give a little. If one side refuses to compromise, agreement is impossible. In an effort to force management to agree to its demands, unions may strike. A strike is a refusal by employees to work, causing a loss in production and therefore a loss of profits to the company. Employees on strike receive no wages, but may receive some pay from the union called *strike benefits*. If employees strike without the approval of the union, they receive no strike benefits. This is known as a *wildcat strike*. Workers on strike usually picket the entrance of the business which has not met their demands. You have probably seen them carrying signs indicating that they consider the company "unfair" — or simply that the union is "on strike."

Unions must be given much of the credit for the high pay and good working conditions enjoyed by American workers. In addition, union-negotiated health and welfare funds provide medical care for employees and their families regardless of their income.

Much has been written about the constant increase in the cost of living since World War II. It is true that prices of food items, clothing, automobiles, and most other consumer goods have gone up in price each year. Workers' demands for higher wages have resulted in price increases and lowered the purchasing power of the dollar. Many people are asking whether unions and management should have the right to make agreements which bring about higher prices.

Certain occupational fields requiring four, five, six, or more years of college are known as *professions*. These include medicine, dentistry, law, teaching, and many others. Professional organizations, like unions, are mainly interested in the welfare of their members. Unlike unions, the professional organizations do not ordinarily strike to achieve their demands. The most widely known professional organizations are the American Medical Association, the American Bar Association, and the National Education Association.

Study Helps

Study Questions

1. What is the most important factor in job success?
2. Eighty percent of the beginning workers who lose their jobs are fired for the same reason. Why do you think this happens?
3. How can you tell if a person has a positive attitude?
4. In addition to a day's work for a day's pay, your employer has a right to expect certain things from you. What are they?
5. What can you reasonably expect from your employer?
6. Why is it important to get along with your co-workers?
7. Why is it a good idea to do some of the unpleasant tasks which you may not feel you were hired to do?
8. Is it best to become close friends with a co-worker during the first week or two on the job? Why?
9. Should you call your boss by his or her first name? Should you call your co-workers by their first names?
10. If two of your co-workers have a dispute, should you take sides? Should you try to settle it?

5-MINUTE TIMED TEST ON FOLLOWING DIRECTIONS

How well do you follow directions? You should be able to complete all the things required in five minutes by following the directions below. Your teacher may wish to time you to see who can finish first, second, etc., so close your book to show when you have completed all the work.

Do not begin until your teacher says "go," then follow directions *exactly* as given. You will need one sheet of notebook paper.

1. Read all directions before doing anything.
2. On a sheet of notebook paper, write your name in the upper right corner.
3. Number from 1 to 7, leaving three blank lines between each number.
4. Draw five small squares beside the number 1 on your paper.
5. Put an "X' in each square beside number 1.
6. Put a circle around the number 2 on your paper.
7. Count the number of pages in Chapter 4 of this book and write the answer beside number 3 on your paper.
8. Multiply the answer above by your age.
9. Say your name out loud.
10. Beside number 4, write today's date.
11. Beside number 5, write the city and state where you were born.
12. Count the number of persons in the room and write the answer beside number 6.
13. Say, "I have reached number 13, and I am following directions carefully."
14. Now that you have completed the reading, omit all directions except the first two.

Chapter 5

Your Progress

on the Job

Your Success and Achievement

If you are presently working and have (1) been doing what your employer expects of you and (2) learned to get along well with your co-workers, you are on your way to success. You can now begin thinking about plans for your future advancement. By carefully studying this chapter, you will know how to win that promotion or pay raise.

Promotions

The time to find out about opportunities for advancement in a company is when you are interviewed for the job. You may ask, "What are my chances for advancement if I do well?" or "What can this job lead to?" After you have begun work, do not bother your supervisor by continuously asking questions about promotions or pay raises.

When you think you should be given a promotion, ask yourself these questions: "Have I learned everything there is to know about my present job?" and "Have I done my work in the best possible way?" Promotions must be earned.

In working for a promotion, keep in mind the realistic, long-range career goal discussed in Chapter 2. That is, the kind of work you would like to be doing five or ten years from now. It is what you are working toward. It is important that long-range goals be kept flexible. Many young people set two or three possible long-range goals knowing that it may be some time before they decide which is the most appropriate. By keeping your long-range goal flexible, you will be able to take advantage of more opportunities when they come your way. Suppose, for example, that you have decided to become a secretary and you begin work as a typist in an advertising firm. After you have worked for a year, you are asked to do some of the layout and design work for the advertising — and you find that this work is actually more interesting to you than your typing duties. Because your design work is good, you are offered a different job which would be mostly layout and design of advertising at a higher salary. Should you turn it down because it does not fit your long range goal? Or do you change your long range goal? In this case you would probably change your long range goal. However, it was important to have a long range goal as it led to something you enjoy doing even more than secretarial work.

In addition to your long range career goal, you should have intermediate and immediate goals. Your intermediate goal in the example above might have been a stenographer because you would expect that it would lead to your long range goal of becoming a secretary. Your immediate goal was to perform your duties as a typist to the best of your ability.

Promotions may be of three kinds: (1) a better job in the department or plant where you are now working, (2) a job with greater responsibility in a different department or plant within the same company, and (3) a job with more responsibility with another company.

If you are thinking about quitting your present job to accept one with another company because you think chances for advancement are not good where you now work, make sure that this would bring you closer to your long range career goal. We said that long range goals should be flexible, but it is not wise to job-hop unless the new job is related to your long range goal or you have decided to change your long range goal. Would a new job with a new company really increase your chances for promotion? Does the new company usually give the more responsible jobs to its present employees or does it hire outsiders to fill the best jobs? Then too, how well do you think you would fit in with the new set of co-workers? Sometimes taking a new job with another company is the best thing to do, sometimes it is not. However, it is always best to have the new job before quitting the old one. Those who quit their jobs to look for something better seldom find it, and they are without a paycheck all the time they are looking.

Everyone likes to be offered a promotion. It makes us feel important and shows us that we are appreciated by our fellow man — in this case, our employer. Promotions increase our

It Is Not Wise to Job-Hop Unless
Your New Job Is a Step Toward Your Long Range Goal

personal feeling of worth; and often, give us a larger paycheck. In addition, promotions usually result in an increase in responsibility. Sometimes this means greater authority over other workers.

When the time comes for your employer to decide who will be promoted, he will give careful attention to each employee being considered, and to his work. The things most often considered by employers in deciding who shall be promoted are these:

(Not in order of importance)

1. Seniority
2. Knowledge of job
3. Quality of work
4. Quantity of work
5. Initiative
6. Perseverance
7. Cooperativeness
8. Ability to think
9. Adaptability
10. Adequacy of training

Seniority is a privileged status attained by continuous service with a company. Those who have worked for the company the longest have the greatest seniority. Most companies take seniority into consideration when making promotions, but they usually don't give employees promotions simply because they have been with the company a long time.

Your *knowledge of the job* you are presently doing is one of the things that employers notice about you when they are considering you for a promotion. If you know your present job well, they can expect that you will be able to learn to do a more responsible job.

The *quality of work* that you do is also carefully considered by your employer. If your work is done very well on the job you are now doing, you will probably perform well in another job with more responsibility.

Some employees do their work well but are slow. The *quantity of work* you turn out will be checked to see whether it is likely that you would turn out a greater than average amount of work on a more responsible job.

Your employer will learn how much *initiative* you have by observing how often you look around to see what tasks need to be done and then go ahead and do them without being told. If you are a person with initiative, you will require less supervision than the person who must be told about each task to be done. If you are able to perform your work without much supervision and then do whatever else needs to be done, your employer is likely to think that you would make a good supervisor yourself.

Once you begin a task, do you always carry it through to completion? Of course, you may have to leave it until something more urgent is done — but do you always come back to the unfinished task and complete it? If you are a person with *perseverance,* you will finish what you start. You probably have

Can You Stick to a Project Until It Is Completed?

known people who begin many projects either at home or as a part of their jobs, but never finish them. Can you stick to a task or project until it is completed, even if it is tiresome or boring? Being able to do this is important to your future job success.

Cooperation with others was discussed in a previous chapter. We said that most of the beginning workers who lose their jobs lose them because they are not able to get along with their employers, supervisors, or co-workers. While cooperation with others is necessary simply to keep your job, an even greater degree of *cooperativeness* must be shown if you are looking for a promotion. As promotions usually mean that the new job will place greater responsibility on you, *a special ability to get along well is required, even with those who are difficult to work with.*

Very often a promotion will mean a job which requires you to make decisions. This means that your employer will consider your *ability to think* for yourself. If you are able to consider new situations and come up with the right answer most of the time, or the right way of doing particular tasks, then you are better able to think for yourself than the employee who must always ask someone else.

How *adaptable* are you? Can you learn to do many kinds of tasks? Are you willing to do things other than those for which you were originally hired? When your salary is paid by an employer, he usually expects you to do whatever needs to be done — even if certain tasks were not mentioned when you were hired. Jobs and duties change. If you are adaptable, you are a more valuable employee than the person who feels he should only do those things for which he was hired.

In considering you for a promotion, your employer will ask himself whether you have *adequate training* for the new job. Long before you have a chance for a promotion, think about what training you should have to bring you closer to your long range career goal. You may find that there are several levels of training required for intermediate goals along the way. The *Occupational Outlook Handbook,* published by the U.S. Department of Labor, may help you decide what training is required by your intermediate and long range goals. Your school work-experience or counseling office probably has a copy. It is also in your public library. Suppose that your long range career goal is to become a store manager, and your present job is salesman in the automobile department. In planning your advancement toward this goal, you and your work must meet a high standard of excellence concerning items 2 through 9 on page 90 which we have just discussed.

In addition, you will need to find out how much and what kind of training is required for each of the intermediate goals which may someday bring you to your long range goal. You can learn this by asking your employer what training is required or suggested for various positions with the company. Most companies have an organizational chart which may help you to more clearly see some of your intermediate goals. You will find that the more education you have, the faster you will move along toward your long range goal. If there are two employees who are otherwise equally well qualified, the promotion will always go to the one with more education. But how do you get this training if you are working full time? Some companies provide their own courses for employees, because they know that money for education is money well spent. Both the company and the employee benefit. If you live in a city where there is a college or university, there will probably be night classes available to you. Also, many public schools conduct adult evening classes. If no formal training is available in your area, you can still take correspondence courses and read trade magazines and books.

If you are promoted, you will probably have greater responsibility. Many times this means responsibility over other employees. In this case, you must see that others perform their jobs well. This kind of promotion means that there will be a different kind of relationship between you and the employees you will be supervising. You are no longer their co-worker. You are the boss. If you can be the boss without being bossy, you will probably enjoy this new relationship. If not, you may be miserable. If you think that you will not be able to handle the responsibility or that you will be unhappy with it, perhaps you should turn down the promotion. This is not often done, but in rare cases it is better to wait until you are more ready to accept greater responsibility. For instance, if you are having problems at home which are very upsetting to you, it may not be wise to take on added responsibilities at work. Then too, there are some people who can be happy with a job in which they have great responsibility for the performance of special duties, but simply don't like supervising other workers.

Suppose that you have been offered a promotion which places you in charge of a number of other employees. What will your actions towards them be? What will their reactions be? Consider these ideas:

George worked as a gas station attendant at Walker's Auto Shop after school during his senior year in high school. When he graduated, Mr. Walker asked him if he would like to learn to be a mechanic. George was very interested in this work and quickly learned the many jobs that were required. He was a hard worker and willing to do something extra to help out a co-worker. After five years George was promoted to shop foreman. He was in charge of six mechanics. On the first day after his promotion, one of the other mechanics, Bob, arrived at work ten minutes late. George felt that he must let Bob know that this would not be permitted. "Hey you!" he yelled when Bob walked into the shop. "Where were you? You think we are paying you to sleep in all morning?"

To Jack, another mechanic, George said, "If there is one thing I can't stand it's somebody who leaves engine parts all over his bench. Where were you brought up? Learn to be neat and orderly if you want to keep working here!"

Perhaps George did need to say something to Bob and Jack. After all, he was responsible for their work. But the way in which he handled these situations might make Bob and Jack feel that they did not want to keep working under a supervisor like George.

Ellen began working for the Maddox Company as a typist after one year of college. After she had been with the company for a year, she was promoted to stenographer. Three years later she became secretary to one of the vice presidents of the company. She was an excellent worker and everyone liked her very much. When the office manager left the company to take another job,

Ellen was asked to be the new manager. Company officials thought that she would make a good office manager, though she had never been placed in charge of other workers before. Ellen was placed in charge of an office staff of 16 men and women. When several workers started coming into work late and leaving early, she knew that she should do something; but she was afraid that she might make them angry with her. When some of the workers took a half-hour coffee break, Ellen didn't know what to do, so she did nothing — except worry about it.

Ellen wanted to be popular with the others in the office but felt she couldn't if she talked to them about their shortcomings. Soon the others in the office became disrespectful toward Ellen. Some talked back to her when she gave them work to do. Finally, in tears, Ellen went to the vice president and asked to be relieved of her responsibilities as office manager. Ellen was an excellent worker when she worked for someone else or as a co-worker, but she was afraid to accept the responsibilities of manager.

Handling Responsibility

In the cases above, neither George nor Ellen made a good supervisor. George felt that he had to show those under his supervision who was boss, and he became "bossy." Ellen's need to be popular with all of the other employees kept her from being a good supervisor. She wanted everyone to like her but felt they wouldn't if she critized them in any way. The other employees took advantage of Ellen's fears.

We have said that promotions often mean that you are given an increase in pay and are expected to handle greater responsibility. These responsibilities may be either of two types: (1) you may be performing a different set of duties not requiring supervision over other workers, or (2) you may supervise the work of one or more employees. Sometimes a promotion means both a change in your non-supervisory tasks and also requires that you supervise the work of others. If you are promoted to a job which does not require that you supervise the work of other employees, you will probably be given work which makes use of the training and experience that you have gained while on the job. Earning such a promotion will give you a real feeling of accomplishment. It will increase your feeling of worth as a person, and — if you can accept the new responsibility — you will be a happier person because of it. Probably you will be paid more for your work, too.

If your promotion carries responsibilities for the work of others, then you must learn to be a good supervisor. This is easy for some people and difficult for others. Of course, if you have no supervisory experience you are seldom placed in charge of a large number of workers. Your first promotion to a supervisory position may place you in charge of only one or two workers. If so, you will have a better chance to learn how to be a good supervisor, but you must work at it. The following list will give you an idea of what you should work on if you are to become a really effective supervisor:

1. Give directions clearly
2. Plan training for new workers
3. Be consistent
4. Treat workers fairly
5. Be firm when necessary
6. Be mindful of workers' welfare
7. Set a good example

If you directly supervise and are responsible for the work of others, you will find that your job will be a much easier one if you can give directions so that they are always understood. Communication is often the biggest problem a supervisor has. If his workers cannot understand exactly what, and how the job is to be done, then even the best employee is useless. Too often, the supervisor is at fault because he gives too little direction about the work to be done. Give all the direction needed for each particular job. If you are not sure that it was completely understood, ask the worker some questions about it until you are certain that he understands clearly.

New workers coming under your supervision require special handling. Of course, they are usually given a tour of the office or plant and introduced to the other workers. But to have really good workers, a plan of training is necessary. Teach him how to be a good worker. This may be done by you as his supervisor, or you may assign him to someone else who knows the work and has a flair for teaching. New workers trained by good workers who are enthusiastic about their jobs are more apt to become good workers themselves.

Be consistent in handling your supervisory duties. For example, if you say that a certain duty must be performed a certain way, insist that it always be done that way and by every worker. Also, follow through on what you say. If you tell an employee that you will deduct part of his salary if he is late to work, do it. If you don't follow through, your workers will not respect you and will tend to do as they please.

If You Are the Supervisor, Don't Play Favorites

If you expect those under your supervision to do their best work for you, you must treat them fairly. Don't permit one worker to come to work late or get by with sloppy work while requiring others to arrive on time and perform well. A part of being fair with your workers is being reasonable. Don't set up requirements which cannot be met by the employees. If a worker feels that you are being unfair, listen to his complaint calmly and consider it. If he is right, you may wish to change your mind about the matter. If he is wrong, explain to him why a change cannot be made — that it would not be in the best interest of the workers, the company, etc.

As a person with supervisory responsibilities, you must sometimes be firm with your workers. Avoid yelling or losing your temper, but do not allow an employee to take unfair advantage of you, the company, or other workers. Just as every person differs, every situation dealing with workers will be different from every other. With some workers, a friendly suggestion is all that is required. To get others to perform as you require them to on the job, you may have to be a bit more firm: "Do it this way," and show them *how* the job is to be done. Sometimes a problem will come up because of the behavior of one or more employees toward other employees. Again, be firm when necessary. If it is too severe a problem to be corrected, it may be necessary to move an employee to another office or section of the plant. If he fails to adjust to other workers and to the work after being moved, it will probably be necessary to let him go.

Be mindful of the workers' welfare. Consider what is best for them. I do not mean that you should put their desires above the interests of the company, but often think about whether they are getting a fair deal. Do what you can to make their work easier while keeping the amount of work done at a high level, or even increasing it. Be willing to go to your boss when necessary to request that changes be made for the benefit of your workers.

Set a good example for your workers. I remember the supervisor on a job where I worked one summer while in college. He was a bright young man, but he always came to work 20 or 30 minutes late. He dressed well and made a good appearance, but his work was sloppy. I think his mind was on things other than his work. This example was followed by some of the other workers. Their work was also sloppy. When the supervisor was replaced by an ambitious young man whose work was a good example for other workers, the other employees' work also improved. One worker, who had regularly come to work 15 minutes late — just in time to beat the supervisor — also followed the example of our new boss and arrived at work at five minutes to eight.

Just as you are responsible for the work of those under your supervision, someone else (your boss) is responsible for your work, unless you own your own business. As the workers whom you supervise must account to you for their performance on the job, so must you account to your supervisor, or boss, for your own performance on the job. You must "answer to" the person who is responsible for your work. Your relationship with your supervisor or boss will be further discussed in the section on performance review and evaluation.

There are a number of advantages in holding a supervisory job. One advantage is that supervisors usually are paid more money than the workers they supervise. They should be, of course, since they have greater responsibilities. The job as a supervisor usually carries a certain amount of prestige, too. The supervisor is "looked up to" by other workers — if he is a good supervisor. Then too, the supervisor is often free from some of the more routine or even dull jobs. His work may thus be more interesting. He has a greater chance to be creative than other workers. He can try some things out that he feels will prove beneficial to the company. He has a greater "say" about how the company will be run. One of the most important advantages of being the supervisor is that he has a chance to show that he can be a leader of others. If he does well as a supervisor, he is probably on his way to further advancement with the company.

There are disadvantages in being a supervisor, too. As a supervisor, you do not have the same kind of relationship with your employees that you had with your co-workers. You are the boss. People say different things to the boss than to their co-workers, and say them in different ways. They usually aren't quite so free in what they say. Some think this is a disadvantage, others prefer this kind of relationship. As the boss, you are a target for criticism. Most of it you won't hear. You get a bigger paycheck than the other workers, and they must feel you earn it. Another disadvantage is that when you do make a mistake, it is usually more costly to the company than the mistakes made by other workers. This is because your mistakes are made on the bigger things. Sometimes a supervisor errs in giving directions on how a job is to be done, and other workers make the same mistake.

If You Are the Boss, Don't Try to Do Everything Yourself

Sometimes a person responsible for the entire output of work for a department or company tries to do too much. You may have known someone who was so "overworked" that he had to take work home every night in order to keep up with it. Some people, of course, do have such a heavy burden of work that this is necessary. Often, however, the person who is so busy that he just never catches up with all the work to be done is himself at fault. There may be others in his department, plant, or company who have a light schedule of work. The wise boss — whether he is a company executive, department manager, or job supervisor — will delegate some responsibilities to those who work under him. Why do some people try to keep all the responsibilities for themselves? One man does it because he is a poor organizer. Another because he thinks that he is the only one able to handle the job. Another will not delegate responsibility because he wants everyone else to depend upon him. This makes him feel important.

If you are the boss, don't try to do everything yourself. Organize the work responsibilities that go with it according to (1) who can handle these duties and responsibilities in the best manner, and (2) what is a fair work load for each worker. Of course, don't give away *all* of the work and responsibility. Doing this, you would lose the respect of your workers — and perhaps your job too. But by giving up some responsibilities to others who can handle them, you will be able to better handle the responsibilities left to you. In addition, those under your supervision will appreciate the opportunity to show that they, too, can be counted upon to handle important work.

Salary Increases

If you receive a *salary*, you are paid a fixed sum each week, month, or perhaps twice a month. You may not even know how much you are paid for one hour's work. The word *wage* usually refers to the amount paid a worker for one hour's work. If you receive a wage, you will know how much you get per hour, but your paychecks will probably differ from payday to payday because of the number of hours worked in one pay period differs from that worked in another. Those paid a wage, by the hour, usually are paid for overtime work. Those on salary usually are not. For the purpose of our discussion on salary increases, both wages and salaries will be considered as "salaries."

A millionaire was once asked if he thought he had enough money. "No, not until I get just a little more," was his answer. Everyone would like to have more than he has; but when he gets a raise, it's not enough. He wants more.

If you get a raise in pay, you will be able to have a higher standard of living. Perhaps just as important is the feeling of increased worth you have about yourself. In some companies, employees are given a raise in salary after working for a certain length of time — usually six months or a year. If you work for such a firm, you are almost sure of a raise if you are a good worker and do the things expected by your employer. Before you get a raise in such a company, however, you will probably be evaluated in writing by your supervisor or some official of the company. This will be discussed in the next section.

In other companies, pay raises are not so automatic. If there is not a specified length of time employees must work before they are considered for a salary raise, then it is left completely up to the employer to decide when a worker deserves a raise. In such companies, the best workers are given raises fairly often — others may work for years without a raise at all.

Performance Review and Evaluation

In addition to seeing you perform your duties on the job daily and noticing how you get along with the other workers, your employer may make a written report on your effectiveness. This, of course, will be used in deciding whether you will be promoted, given a raise, allowed to continue working at the same job and salary, or fired.

Employers gain much useful information about their workers from employee evaluations. Individual strengths and weaknesses of workers show up more clearly when the supervisor is taking a close look at each employee. It may be found that a particular employee would do better work if he were transferred to another plant or to another type of job within the company.

It gives the company, and the workers, a better chance to make use of individual strengths. Each employee is most valuable to the company when he is doing those things he can do really well. The evaluation may show a need for special training programs for workers with common weaknesses. In addition, the employee evaluation usually causes the worker to improve his own work.

Employees generally are allowed to see how their supervisors evaluated them. This is, of course, best; otherwise the evaluation could hardly cause the employee to improve his work. Evaluation reports which are not shown to the workers can still serve as a basis for promotion and dismissal. After the supervisor has rated the employee according to whatever form is used by his company, he will most often discuss the results with the employee rated. This is done in private to avoid unnecessary embarrassment.

During the evaluation interview, the supervisor—or boss— may discuss both strengths and weaknesses of the worker. Some supervisors try to save time by discussing *only the weaknesses*. This is not a good way to conduct evaluation interviews, but if your boss does it this way, you must still try to profit from the criticism. The only purpose of pointing out your weaknesses to you is so that you will be able to become a better worker by improving in certain things. It is to your advantage as well as to the company's that you improve in your job. If you follow the recommendations made by your supervisor for the continued improvement of your work, you will receive more pay raises. Even more important, you will take greater pride in your work — which helps make you a happier person. If you are truly pleased with your work efforts, it will affect every part of your life. You will become a better friend, a better father or mother to your children, and a more loving husband or wife.

If your supervisor points out your weaknesses but does not make any recommendations about how you can improve, ask him for some suggestions. Your boss will probably be able to help you, and it shows him that you are genuinely interested in improving your work.

Study each item in the employee evaluations on the next pages. By knowing in advance what you will be "tested on," you will be better prepared for advancement in the world of work.

GENERAL RESEARCH CORPORATION

SYSTEMS RESEARCH DIVISION

PERFORMANCE EVALUATION REVIEW

Support Staff

Name _____

Position _____

Employee No. _____

Date Hired _____

Date _____

Date of Last Review _____

To be filled out by immediate supervisor and department head as appropriate. On the basis of your personal contact with this employee, your opinion and analysis of the employee's performance on the job is requested. Please evaluate by checking the square which best describes the employee's performance. If you have not observed the factor well enough to evaluate it, please leave blank.

JOB KNOWLEDGE

Consider the employee's fundamental understanding of basic techniques and procedures relating to his position.

Unsatisfactory		GRC Norm		Excellent
☐	☐	☐	☐	☐
Does not have enough understanding to handle present work properly.		Well-informed on all aspects of job.		Expert in his job, and has good knowledge of related jobs.

Comments: _____

WORK OUTPUT

Consider the volume of work consistently done in relation to the volume required for fully proficient performance of the job.

Unsatisfactory		GRC Norm		Excellent
☐	☐	☐	☐	☐
Work output consistently falls below the daily requirements of the job.		Work output is consistently good.		Work output is always above the standard requirements of the job.

Comments: _____

QUALITY OF WORK

Disregard volume. Consider accuracy, thoroughness and related characteristics of work.

Unsatisfactory		GRC Norm		Excellent
☐	☐	☐	☐	☐
Careless. Time required for revisions noted to be excessive.		Does a good job. Seldom has errors. Checks quality frequently.		All work performed is exceptionally accurate, and thorough. Catches errors in the work of others.

Comments: _____

JUDGEMENT

Consider the ability to think through a problem, select pertinent factors and arrive at a sound course of action.

Unsatisfactory	GRC Norm	Excellent
☐	☐	☐
Jumps to conclusions. Judgment is not dependable.	Judgment is dependable	Sound judgment. Decisions always based on thorough analysis.

Comments: _____

RELIABILITY

Consider the responsibility assumed by employee for his own actions.

Unsatisfactory	GRC Norm	Excellent
☐	☐	☐
Can rarely be counted on to carry out work as directed.	Can be relied upon	Never any doubt about his carrying out duties with a minimum of supervision.

Comments: _____

COOPERATION

Consider employee's attitude toward his work, associates, company, and its effect on others. Also consider his willingness to work with and for others.

Unsatisfactory	GRC Norm	Excellent
☐	☐	☐
Shows reluctance to cooperate. Constant friction with others. Antagonistic.	Gets along well with associates. Meets others halfway.	Good team worker, always helpful. Goes out of way to cooperate.

Comments: _____

INITIATIVE

Consider ability to originate actions and take necessary steps in attacking new problems.

Unsatisfactory	GRC Norm	Excellent
☐	☐	☐
Relies on others. Must be told what to do and consistently needs help in getting started.	Solves problems pertaining to his own work and occasionally offers suggestions for improvement.	Outstandingly active in making new suggestions.

Comments: _____

COMMUNICATION (expression)

Consider the ability to transmit knowledge and ideas orally and in writing with effectiveness and clarity.

Unsatisfactory	GRC Norm	Excellent
☐	☐	☐
Inarticulate.	Transmits information well both verbally and in writing.	Speaks and writes exceptionally well.

Comments: _____

JOB PLANNING

Consider success in planning and organizing work.

Unsatisfactory	GRC Norm	Excellent
☐	☐	☐
Work shows serious lack of proper planning.	Plans effectively.	Effective under the most difficult circumstances.

Comments: _____

For Evaluation of Supervisors Only

DEVELOPMENT OF OTHERS

Consider the extent to which the supervisor recognizes and develops the aptitudes, abilities and capacities of others.

Unsatisfactory	GRC Norm	Excellent
☐	☐	☐
Contributes very little to the development of his subordinates.	Successful in recognizing and developing the potential of others.	Extremely capable and active in developing his subordinates.

Comments: _____

LEADERSHIP

	Unsatisfactory	GRC Norm	Excellent
Consider the supervisor's ability to inspire in others the willingness and desire to achieve.	☐ Ineffective as a leader.	☐ Obtains satisfactory results.	☐ Inspirational and effective leader.

Comments: _____

_____

OVERALL PERFORMANCE

	Unsatisfactory	GRC Norm	Excellent
	☐	☐	☐

1. Does this employee's present position place him in the line of endeavor best suited to his temperament and ability?   Please comment: _____

_____

_____

2. What are the employee's particular strong points? _____

_____

3. In what areas is improvement needed?   (If applicable) _____

_____

4. General Comments: _____

_____

_____

_____

Employee's Signature _____ Date _____ Evaluated by _____ Date _____

Employee's Comments _____

_____

_____

_____

Terminating the Job

Ann Winfield was a high school senior who worked part time as a typist in a law firm. She assisted a legal secretary by typing letters and memoranda from a transcribing machine. One day Ann had difficulty adjusting the machine properly and asked Mrs. Allen, her supervisor, for help. Mrs. Allen was upset over the illness of her mother and, although she quickly made the simple adjustment of the machine, she spoke sharply to Ann about her not being able to do anything herself. Ann was crushed. She soon developed a dislike for both Mrs. Allen and everything about her job. Three weeks before school was out, Ann called Mrs. Allen on the phone and "told her off." Ann quit her job without giving any advance notice of her intention to do so. In the weeks following graduation, Ann looked everywhere for a job. It seemed that word had gotten around town about her behavior in quitting her part-time job. Nobody wanted to take a chance on getting an employee like that. She did finally get a job in another city.

Hopefully, Ann learned from this experience that if you have a problem on the job it is best to at least try to see the good things about the work and the employer. You may get interested in your work and find that the boss isn't so bad after all. Sometimes workers forget that the boss has problems, too. Often, the boss spends many more hours on the job than the employees he supervises. Many business owners and company executives, for instance, work 50 to 60 hours a week. The extra time your boss is working may increase company profits — thus helping to pay your salary.

Giving Notice of Termination

There are, of course, good reasons to quit a job. If you have accepted a better job with another company or if you must quit your job because you are attending college in another city, you have good reason to terminate employment. In this case, there are certain courtesies which should be observed.

Notice of your intent to leave your job should be given to your immediate supervisor unless company policy states that it should be given to someone else. It is often necessary to notify the personnel office in larger firms. You may be asked to make written notification. If this is the policy, follow it.

You should give notice of termination soon enough for the company to find a replacement by the time you leave. Courtesy requires that you give at least two weeks' notice. If you are paid once a month, then it is customary to give at least a month's notice. Failure to do this may make it difficult to find suitable work in other firms.

If You're Fired . . .

If business is off and you are one of the last employees hired by the company, you may be one of the first to be "laid off." When this happens, you are not really "fired." That is, your loss of the job was not due to your being an unsatisfactory employee. If your boss feels that you are unsatisfactory either in your performance on your job or in your ability to work well with the other employees, then you may indeed be fired! Then what happens? If you are wise, you will think about what happened and how you could have prevented it. You will learn from your mistakes. If you place all the blame on your employer, you probably won't learn much. If you can see what *you* did wrong, then you will be more able to avoid being fired from another job. Then begin immediately to look for the job which you think will be "right for you." The places to go and the methods to use are the same as when looking for your first job. These were discussed in Chapter 3.

We said that if you are paid once a month, it is customary to give your employer at least a month's notice if you plan to quit your job. If you are paid once a week, you should give at least a week's notice. It is customary for the employer to give similar notice if he intends to lay you off. If you are not given any advance notice, you are entitled to *severance pay*. That is, because you are *severed* (cut off) from your job without notice, you are entitled to receive a check for one week's work if you are paid each week, two weeks' work if you are paid every two weeks, etc.

If you are laid off or fired from a job on which you have been working for some time, you may be eligible for some *unemployment compensation*. Unemployment compensation checks are provided for a limited time to those who are able to work, available to accept work, and actively seeking work. Students working part time do not usually qualify because their yearly earnings do not meet the minimum required.

Study Helps

Study Questions

1. When is the best time to find out about opportunities for advancement with a company?
2. What questions should you ask yourself about whether you deserve a promotion?
3. What are long range goals? What are your long range goals?
4. Three kinds of promotions were discussed. What were they?
5. What things will your employer consider in deciding who will be promoted?
6. If you are working full time, can you still continue your education? How?
7. Do you think you would like to have a job in which you would be responsible for the work of others?
8. In relationship to his workers, what qualities does the good supervisor have?
9. What disadvantages are there in being a supervisor?
10. Why do some people refuse to delegate work, keeping all responsibilities for themselves?
11. Why do most companies use a written evaluation of employee's work?
12. If you decide to quit a job, what do you tell your employer?
13. What should you do if you are fired?

Chapter 6

SELF INVENTORY:

Knowing and Understanding

Yourself

Those who study the employment scene predict that the average person will change the kind of work he does five times in his lifetime. This does not simply mean that you may change *jobs* several times. The *kind* or *type of work* may change a number of times. We have already discussed the importance of having one or several career goals, and we said that our long range goals must be kept flexible to take advantage of appropriate opportunities. But which opportunities will be the appropriate ones—the right ones—for you? You probably won't know unless you learn to know and understand yourself better than you do now. In discussing job choices and opportunities, we said that each career goal considered should be realistic. Each goal must be one that you *can reach*, and it must be one that will give you satisfaction after you reach it. If you are anything like the average person and will be changing the kind of work you do several times, then you must learn all you can about yourself—especially your values, interests, aptitudes and abilities, and your personality.

Values

Our values are those things that we think are important. Up to the age of about 15 or 16, our values are pretty much those of our parents. If our parents consider taking part in religious activities important, so do we. It is one of our values. If they feel that having a daily bath and being neatly dressed are important, so do we. When we are in about the tenth or eleventh grade in high school, we begin to set our own values. We keep some of the values of our parents and reject others. We take a look at life and try to decide how we want to fit into it. We

Set Goals That You Can Reach

think about such questions as those below, and our answers have a great deal to do with the kind of work we eventually go into. Answer each question for yourself. Which are most important to you?

1. Being helpful to other people
2. Earning a lot of money
3. Having high moral standards
4. Being active in a religion
5. Becoming famous
6. Having a successful marriage
7. Being well dressed
8. Having lots of friends
9. Good health
10. Having power over others

What other things are important to you? Can you see how your values can affect how satisfied you are with the work you do?

Interests

Part of getting to know and understand yourself is to take inventory of your interests. This can be done informally by thinking about and perhaps making some notes on the things you like best. Those activities in which you feel comfortable are exciting to you, or in which you perform well are often the most interesting to you. Think about your hobbies. How do you like to spend your spare time? Many successful photographers were once interested in taking pictures only as a hobby. What classes in school have been your favorites? If you have taken some vocational classes, you may have developed an interest in a particular career field. Have you been active in school clubs? Are you involved in any social activities outside of school, perhaps your church, YMCA, YWCA, or others? These and other questions can be asked and answered by you. Your answers will help you to a better understanding of yourself.

If you feel that you won't know enough about your likes and dislikes to profit from an informal inventory, perhaps the more formal approach is best for you. There are interest inventories which can be taken very much like you would take a test.

In fact, you may have already taken one at your school. If not, your school counselor can probably arrange for you to take one. In one of the widely used interest inventories, the Kuder, your scores show how interested you are in activities common to these 10 areas:

1. OUTDOOR interest means that you prefer work that keeps you outside most of the time and usually deals with animals and growing things. Forest rangers, naturalists, and farmers are among those high in outdoor interests.
2. MECHANICAL interest means you like to work with machines and tools. Jobs in this area include automobile repairmen, watchmakers, drill press operators, and engineers.
3. COMPUTATIONAL interest means you like to work with numbers. A high score in this area suggests that you might like such jobs as bookkeeper, accountant, or bank teller.
4. SCIENTIFIC interest means that you like to discover new facts and solve problems. Doctors, chemists, nurses, engineers, radio repairmen, aviators, and dietitians usually have high scientific interests.
5. PERSUASIVE interest means that you like to meet and deal with people and to promote projects or things to sell. Most actors, politicians, radio announcers, authors, salesmen, and store clerks have high persuasive interests.
6. ARTISTIC interest means you like to do creative work with your hands. It is usually work that has "eye appeal" involving attractive design, color, and materials. Painters, sculptors, architects, dress designers, hairdressers, and interior decorators all do "artistic" work.
7. LITERARY interest shows that you like to read and write. Literary jobs include novelist, historian, teacher, actor, news reporter, editor, drama critic, librarian, and book reviewer.
8. MUSICAL interest shows you like going to concerts, playing instruments, singing, or reading about music and musicians.

9. SOCIAL SERVICE interest indicates a preference for helping people. Nurses, Boy or Girl Scout leaders, vocational counselors, tutors, ministers, personnel workers, and hospital attendants spend much of their time helping other people.

10. CLERICAL interest means you like office work that requires precision and accuracy. Jobs such as bookkeeper, accountant, file clerk, salesclerk, secretary, statistician, and traffic manager fall in this area.

If You Prefer to Work with People, Some Jobs Will Not Appeal to You

People, Things, and Ideas

Besides the kind of work activity which seems interesting to you, think about whether you would prefer to work mainly with other people, things, or ideas. If you enjoy the company of others and tend to feel lonely and unhappy when left alone for more than an hour or two, you would probably prefer to work where you are in the company of other people. You probably would not enjoy being a forest ranger or a lighthouse keeper. If you would rather spend an evening alone building a model than go to a party with friends, you might like a job where you work alone. You might enjoy working with "things." If you like to spend your spare time solving difficult problems or writing, you might like a job in which you work with ideas.

In some kinds of work, you would deal with only one of these—people, things, or ideas. In many careers, you would deal with a combination of people and things, people and ideas, or things and ideas. Some careers involve all three—people, things, and ideas.

If you like to be in the company of or to come in contact with other people, and you also like working with things, you might enjoy such jobs as:

1. Salesman
2. Dental hygienist
3. Grocery checker

If you enjoy being with people but also like working with ideas, you might like such jobs as:

1. Advertising copywriter
2. Lawyer
3. Play director

If you like working with things and ideas, but prefer to work alone, these jobs might appeal to you:

1. Research biologist
2. Interior decorator
3. Engineer

If you like working with people, things, and ideas, these jobs might interest you:

1. Office manager
2. Teacher
3. Librarian

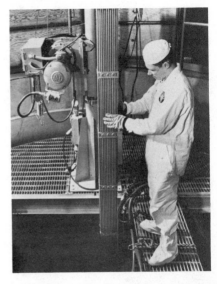

After you are out of school, you will spend more time working than in any other activity. The wise person chooses the kind of work which interests him. People tend to leave jobs which do not interest them and stay with and advance on those jobs which do interest them. Do you know what your interests are? Do you have many interests? If you have been involved in a lot of school and social activities, you may have many interests.

You Must Have an Aptitude As Well As an Interest in Your Work to Succeed

If your activities have been few, you may need to be exposed to new ones. You do not know whether you will have an interest in something until you have tried it. The more interests you can develop, the better your chances of finding a career which will be satisfying to you; and the satisfaction you get from your job is more important to you as a person than the money you earn. The interest you have in your career contributes greatly to the satisfaction you get from it.

Aptitudes and Abilities

Having an interest in a career is not all that is necessary to successfully pursue it. You must have the necessary aptitude or ability too. I once knew a girl who wanted more than anything in the world to become a singer. Her parents arranged for her to take singing lessons, which she did for several years, but her voice simply wouldn't cooperate. Becoming a singer was not a realistic goal for her. She didn't have the natural talent for it.

When we say that a person has *ability* to do something, we mean that he is *able* to do it. We usually mean that he is rather skillful at it too. He may have this ability because he has worked very hard to develop it or because he has a natural talent for it. When a person seems to be born with natural talent which makes it easy to learn certain things, we say that he has an *aptitude* for these things. It is much easier to learn those things for which we have an aptitude. For instance, you may have known someone who learned to play the piano with little or no instruction, while others develop little ability after years of study. In some careers, such as music, a fair share of natural talent (aptitude) is necessary in order to be successful.

If you are to set and work toward realistic career goals, you must know something about your abilities. Otherwise, you wouldn't know whether a particular goal was realistic for you or not. How do you learn about your abilities—and perhaps more important, your aptitudes, since these can be developed into abilities? It isn't too difficult if you know where to look. We will talk about two kinds of aptitudes and abilities: (1) those which are mainly mental and (2) those which are mainly physical.

Mental Aptitudes and Abilities

Your mental abilities are indicated by the grades you achieve in your classes in school. If you try to do all the work asked by your teachers, your grades can be a fairly accurate measurement of your aptitudes and abilities. If your efforts are not very great, you may have more aptitude than your grades indicate. However, to develop these aptitudes into useful abilities may be difficult for you until you decide to make greater effort.

Your teachers can provide information about your ability to do certain kinds of work. If you are taking shorthand, your shorthand teacher will be able to give you an idea about how useful your shorthand ability would be to a businessman. The same goes for other skill courses, such as auto mechanics, electronics, drafting, typing, bookkeeping, etc.

If you have a school counselor, he can help you learn what your strengths and weaknesses are. You have probably already taken one or perhaps several tests which give a good indication of your general ability. You may have taken an aptitude test. Your counselor can give you information about your aptitudes and abilities as shown by the results of these tests. If you have not taken any aptitude or ability tests, ask your counselor to arrange for some.

Your general intelligence is commonly reported as an intelligence quotient score, or IQ. Those whose IQ score is between 90 and 110 are considered to have "average" intelligence. IQ tests usually measure three different kinds of intelligence. They are (1) verbal ability, (2) arithmetic ability, and (3) reasoning.

Your verbal ability is measured by how well you understand the meaning of words—your reading vocabulary. This is considered a most important part of general intelligence because so much learning depends upon your ability to understand written material in instructions, articles, the newspaper, and books. Your verbal ability can be increased by working on your vocabulary. Develop the practice of using the dictionary to look up the meaning of words you do not understand.

Your arithmetic ability is measured by how fast and how accurately you can solve arithmetic problems. This part of most intelligence tests usually begins with simple arithmetic problems, then goes on to more difficult problems for those who can do them. Your arithmetic ability, too, can be increased by practice. If you do not know how to add, subtract, multiply, and divide accurately and with fair speed, it will show up in your IQ score. If you practice these kinds of problems, including the "multiplication tables," your IQ score will go up. Another factor measured in this part of most intelligence tests is your ability to figure percentages. Do you know what 10 percent of any number is? How about 1 percent? It will show up in your IQ. If you are not as good as you would like to be in arithmetic ability and you would like to raise your IQ (and your ability to learn), study the basic math skills section in the appendix of this book. If you need additional work on this, ask one of the math teachers in your school how you can further improve your arithmetic skills.

Reasoning is the ability to see how things do or do not fit together and then find the reasons why. Reasoning may also involve looking at past experiences and coming up with logical plans. It is difficult to improve your score on this part of an intelligence test.

There are other kinds of tests which can measure your aptitude for certain kinds of mental activities. Tests will show whether it would be easy or difficult to develop ability in special fields. These tests are used successfully to determine a person's ability to learn clerical skills, radio code, to play a musical instrument, etc.

Physical Aptitudes and Abilities

Some of the aptitudes measured by aptitude tests are more physical than mental. The general aptitude test battery (GATB), developed by the United States Employment Service, measures 12 kinds of aptitudes, some mainly physical. Two of these are finger dexterity and manual dexterity. Your finger dexterity is how well you can use your fingers to move small articles rapidly and accurately. Manual dexterity is the ability to move your hands easily and skillfully. Finger and manual dexterity are necessary in many kinds of work. Assemblers, sewing machine operators, and welders must have at least good finger and manual dexterity.

You may have other physical abilities which are not so easily measured. Or, you may lack some physical ability which is necessary to succeed in certain kinds of work. We mentioned the the girl who wanted to become a singer but whose voice wouldn't cooperate. Many boys would like to become professional baseball players, but they lack the natural talent to learn to play the game well—even if they practiced for a hundred years! If you are considering a career which requires special talent, try to be realistic. A goal is worthwhile only if there is a possibility of reaching it. Each of us has shortcomings, but each of us has some strengths too. As you look toward the future and plan your career, do so with a positive attitude. Do the best you can with what you have, and you will find that you are a happier worker and a more satisfied human being that the person who had more talent but did little with it.

Personality

Employers often look for job applicants with "pleasing personalities." For several years, I was in charge of the student employment office of a large high school on the West Coast. Employers regularly called me to discuss the kind of student workers they wished to hire. Their remarks often went like this:

"Send me a girl with a nice personality; she is the first person my clients will see when they come into the office and I want her to make a good impression."

"Send me a boy with a clean-cut personality."

"I want a girl who can type and has a good personality."

After referring several students for each job vacancy, I would call the employer to see which student was hired and why the others were rejected. Their comments often were similar to these:

"I hired Jan because she has such a nice smile and a pleasing personality. She'll make a great first impression on my clients."

"Nora was a whiz at typing, but she didn't have much personality."

"I hired Vance because he had more personality than the other boys you sent."

Personality is the one most important thing which causes people to like you. What is this thing called personality? Webster defines it as "the complex of characteristics that distinguishes an individual." It is the combination of personal traits that make you different from every other person. It is the set of habits which you develop in reacting to people and situations. Because your personality is shown to others through these habits, it is not something you can put on and take off. It is always with you. It is through your personality that you show others what kind of a person you are. Earlier in this chapter, we discussed values—those things which are important to you. Your values are shown to others through your *personality traits*. These personality traits are generally considered to be among those which make up your personality:

1. Attitude
2. Courtesy
3. Dependability
4. Desire to succeed
5. Enthusiasm

6. Foresight
7. Friendliness
8. Health
9. Honesty
10. Initiative

11. Loyalty
12. Morality
13. Neatness
14. Open-mindedness
15. Personal appearance

16. Punctuality
17. Self-control
18. Sense of humor
19. Tact
20. Use of voice

The *value* which has the greatest effect upon your personality is shown in your *attitude toward other people*. The person whose list of values is topped by a real concern for and desire to be of help to other people is the unselfish person. He accepts every person as a worthy human being. *He cares for people.* To him, people are the important things in the world. The selfish person does not really care about what happens to others. This is shown in his attitude toward them. We mentioned earlier that most of the beginning workers who lose their jobs are those whose attitudes show little concern for others. They are uncooperative. Those who are most satisfied with life are those who have a positive attitude. They look for the good in others. They are *optimists.* Those who are least satisfied with life are *pessimists.* A pessimist is a person who can see all of another person's faults but none of his virtues. He can only see the bad things in life. No wonder he is usually unhappy.

In the next chapter we shall discuss ways in which you can improve your personality and become a more effective person in all of your relationships. To do that, you must take a rather complete inventory of your personality. You probably have a pretty good idea about what is meant by attitude, and you may have learned of some areas in which you will need improvement. We haven't said much about other personality traits.

Courtesy

The attitude you have toward other people is shown in how you behave in every situation. One of the most obvious ways it shows up is in how courteous you are. The people I have known who were most lacking in courtesy showed it to everyone with whom they talked. They were only interested in what they had to say. They interrupted another person at any time because they didn't care what anybody else had to say. Have you known someone who wouldn't let you finish a sentence? If you have, you probably didn't tell him about it. Courtesy is like that. It's like having bad breath—even your best friend won't tell you. Because of this, it is up to you to watch your own courtesy.

Courtesy involves a true concern for the comfort of others and good manners. Do you say "please" and "thank you"? If you are late arriving at a friend's house, do you call so that he (or she) will not be expecting you momentarily? Thinking about and doing what you can to make others comfortable is worth more than gold in making others like you. Nothing so valuable costs so little as courtesy. It's free.

Dependability

A dependable person can be "counted on." The lineman on a football team who always blocks his man is dependable. He gets the job done every time. Nobody else has to worry about it. The person who always completes the work given him on the job is dependable. The person who sometimes does not complete his work as assigned can't be counted upon and isn't worth much to an employer. Someone else must be ready to take over. If this happens very often, of course, the employee doesn't have a job at all.

Desire to Succeed

Everyone wants to be happy and satisfied with life, and we have learned that satisfaction in life depends a great deal upon how satisfied you are in your work. If you are successful in an interesting job that is challenging to you, then you will gain a great amount of satisfaction from it. But becoming a success in your work doesn't just happen to you, like waking up one morning with measles. In a recent survey, the most successful young men and women were asked, "What is the one most important thing that led to your success?" Their answers were pretty much all alike. It was *desire*. They simply wanted it more than those who were not so successful. You know that the members of a football or basketball team have to have a strong desire to do their best, to win. If you have watched them practice, you know how hard they work to succeed. Those who are the most successful on the field or court are those who want it the most. It's like that in your career too.

Enthusiasm

The person who is enthusiastic about life is an optimist. He is happy and excited about the good things that are happening to him. If his job is "right for him," he is especially enthusiastic about his work. Enthusiasm is a personality trait that makes it a pleasure to work with or be around the person who has it.

Foresight

Foresight means to look ahead, to plan ahead. It means that you don't just let things happen to you. You plan things. When you apply for a job, you have thought about what questions may be asked of you—and you have the answers. During a job interview, you find out what the opportunities are for advancement. On a job, your employer may not remind you of the time when certain assignments must be completed. You must plan your work so that deadlines will be met. The person with foresight is *alive*. He doesn't just let things happen, he *makes them happen*. How well do you plan the use of your time and money? Are you "broke" before each payday? Do you plan the use of your time so that your school assignments are always completed on time?

Friendliness

If you find that most people are friendly toward you, you are probably friendly yourself. The person who is most liked has many friends because he is sincerely interested in others. He has a nice smile and smiles often. To have more friends, give your friendship to more people.

Health

Some people with poor health have been very successful because of their talent and desire to succeed. Many healthy people have not been successful because they lacked ability, desire, or certain personal qualities. However, other things being equal, good health is very important to success. When you feel good, your work is easier. It may even be fun. Healthy workers are more productive too, and employers often consider health when hiring new employees and giving promotions. Young people are often careless about their eating and sleeping habits. They punish their bodies by trying to get along on improper foods and too little sleep. They get by with it for a while, but they don't know what their limit is until they have gone past it. Good health habits help you to feel, act, and look your best.

Honesty

Whether you are an honest person or a dishonest person is your choice. You can be whichever you choose to be. Because of the peace of mind you will have and the trust others will have in you, it will be to your advantage to be an honest person. Wherever you work, there will be opportunities to be honest or to be dishonest. Your employer pays you for your time. Show him that you are honest by your willingness to give a day's work for a day's pay. Do not fake sickness and stay away from work. This is not fair to your employer or to the other workers who must do at least part of your work. When you give your word for something, make it good. If you are given credit for something someone else did, place the credit where it is due. Do not steal time, money, supplies, or ideas. To do so will cause others to distrust you.

Initiative

If you can see things that need to be done and do them, you have initiative. As a beginning worker, you will do your work exactly as your employer directs you. Your suggestions in the beginning would probably not be too well thought out and might make your employer think that you don't respect his experience. After you have been on the job for a while, you can begin to take a bit more initiative. After your assigned duties are completed, look around to see what else needs to be done. If you are *sure that you can do well* this "extra work," do it. Start with small things. In this way, you will learn just how much initiative your boss likes you to take. If you do a really outstanding job on the little jobs in which you show initiative, your employer will probably allow you to take more and more responsibility. If you are able to handle these additional responsibilities well, you will probably be promoted.

Loyalty

You are loyal to your company and to your employer if you think well and speak well of them. You will respect the men and women who run the company. You will be happy about company successes. To be loyal to your company also means that you will not tell those who do not work for the company about things which should be kept confidential. To do so might result in an advantage to another company and lower profits for your own company. If you are truly loyal to your work and the company for which you work, they become of great interest and importance in your life. If you find that you cannot be loyal to your employer and to the company for which you work, it is best to look for another job.

Morality

Man is a societal creature. That is, he sets up certain patterns of behavior which guide the lives of all men and women in his society. This is true wherever man lives, in all parts of the world; and it was true long before man learned to speak, read, and write. In our American society, the ideals of honesty, fair play and justice are important. Therefore, if we are to be happy in this society, if we are to make a good adjustment to it, we must accept these moral principles. We may add other standards to our own moral code. These may or may not involve belief in a certain religious faith. Regardless of your feelings toward religion, the rule of doing for others as you would like them to do for you is a good one.

Neatness

If you are a neat person, it shows up in many ways. You are probably a neat dresser, always personally clean and free of body odor. In addition, you will do the necessary house-cleaning to keep your work area tidied up. If you make out reports, they will be done neatly. If you are a typist, you will regularly clean the type on your machine; and when you erase, you will move the typewriter carriage all the way to one side so that the erasure crumbs will not fall into the machine. If you are not a neat person, this will show up in many ways too.

Open-Mindedness

Open-mindedness means being able to see both sides of a question or argument. It means considering, carefully, what the other person has to say even when you don't agree with him. It is very much to your advantage to keep an open mind in all things. The moment you close your mind to something, you can no longer learn anything which is not in agreement with your belief. Thus, to close your mind prevents you from becoming a more intelligent person. Such people are sometimes referred to as being dogmatic and opinionated. They think their beliefs and opinions are correct and they will never be changed. The open-minded person freely allows others to question his beliefs and opinions. The open-minded person tends to be a happy worker. He accepts criticism of his work without feeling that his worth as a person is being questioned. He takes the criticism seriously and tries to see how he can improve because of it. If he decides that criticism of his work is not accurate, he is not hostile toward the person making the criticism. The open-minded person always gives the other person the benefit of any doubt in a situation.

Personal Appearance

Your personal appearance was discussed in Chapter 3. Of course, it is just as important to keep your good appearance everyday on the job as it is during an interview for a job. Wear clothes which are appropriate for the kind of work you are doing and have them regularly cleaned or washed. Polish your shoes regularly. Boys and girls need to shave regularly—the boys their faces and girls their legs. Make it a habit to take a bath or shower every night or morning. Use a deodorant and change underwear every day. By doing this, the other workers won't avoid being around you.

Punctuality

Time is money. In an earlier chapter we said that if you went to a movie and paid the full price, you probably would be unhappy if the theater projectionist switched off the projector before the movie was over. You would expect to see the full movie for the full price. Your employer also expects a full day's work for a full day's pay. If you get into the habit of arriving late to work, you are cheating your employer. He will, of course, be unhappy with you about it. If you go to a movie and you get to see it all, but it starts twenty minutes late, you won't be quite so angry as if they switched off the projector. But you still wouldn't be very happy about their not starting on time. In some companies, if you are late to work, they will take the time out of your paycheck. Even so, your employer wouldn't be very happy about your being late. Just as it would be an inconvenience to you if the movie started late, it would be an inconvenience to your employer if you are late. Being punctual is more than simply arriving at work on time. It means *starting* work on time. If it takes you 15 minutes to get settled and begin work, you are still not being punctual. Punctuality is a habit. You are forming your habit of punctuality right now. Are you always on time to each class in school?

Self Control

Self control means how well you can control (1) your emotions and (2) your efforts. The person who often loses his temper has little control over his emotions. He would do well to try very hard to (A) see the other side of whatever makes him angry, giving the other person the benefit of the doubt, and (B) hold back his anger until he can let it off in a way that is not damaging to his relationship with another person. The person who takes out his anger by whacking a golf ball around the course will probably have more friends than the person who allows his anger to explode in the presence of others. Most everyone wishes to accomplish something, to reach some kind of goal. But it takes work to do it. If the boss is looking over your shoulder, you will probably get the job done. But what if you are not supervised? Getting the job done when working on your own requires self control. Self control, too, becomes a habit. If you have a great deal of self control, you will be able to answer "yes" to most of these questions:

1. Do I sit down and complete my school assignments when I would rather watch a television program?
2. Do I set up a schedule of work and stick to it?
3. Do I avoid "telling off" another person who makes me angry?
4. Do I work well when tired?
5. Do I take criticism without becoming upset?
6. Do I avoid pleasures that injure the body, mind, or emotions?
7. Am I patient with other people?

If you had several "no" answers, you had better spend some time thinking about the kind of person you would like to become.

Sense of Humor

If you can see the funny side of life, you have a sense of humor. Being able to enjoy the humorous makes life a lot easier and much more interesting. Having a good sense of humor is healthy both physically and mentally. The person whose thoughts are always serious ones will seldom laugh. Doctors tell us that these people are more apt to develop illnesses such as heart disease and ulcers than the person who can enjoy the lighter side of life. Those who do not balance the serious with the humorous are also more apt to need the services of a psychiatrist. Don't take life seriously *all the time*. Look for and enjoy the funny side of life, and learn to laugh even when the joke is on you.

Tact

Can you say the right thing at the right time? Can you handle situations so that no one becomes offended? If so, you are tactful. Being tactful does not require that you be dishonest. If a co-worker wears a dress which you do not like, you do not have to say that you like it. If you can see something *about it* that you like, mention that. You might like the color or texture of the material. Part of being tactful is knowing *how* and *when* to discuss things with your friends, your co-workers, and your boss. Try to sense the *feelings* of those around you. Once you discover what pleases and displeases them, what their moods are, and when they are happiest and most agreeable, you will find that they will be cooperative.

Use of Voice

Your voice and the way you speak is just as important as your personal appearance in attracting or repelling others. Your voice and speech habits are very revealing. A person trained to do so can tell what kind of an attitude you have toward your family and friends, about how much education you have, how much self control you have over your emotions, and how mentally and physically healthy you are. Even so, you can control the use of your voice considerably. By practicing, you can develop the habit of speaking in the tonal range that is most pleasant. However, it must not sound artificial. A speaking voice which is attractive involves these qualities:

1. A medium to low tonal range.
2. Relaxed rather than tense.
3. Loud enough to be heard, but not booming. (A booming voice—too loud—will cause others to resist you.)
4. Clearly and properly enunciated words.
5. Correct pronounciation.
6. Variation in talking speed but not too fast nor to slow.
7. Inflections properly used. (What you say will be more interesting if you raise and lower the inflection to accent meaning.)

An attractive voice will go a long way in developing a satisfying relationship with others. When you speak on the telephone, your voice becomes even more important than in a face-to-face conversation. The person with whom you are speaking on the telephone cannot see you, and his only impression of you is what he hears. When your phone rings, answer it promptly. In business, the full cooperation of the other person often depends upon this. Usually, the name of the company or department is given first and then the name of the person answering. "Maddox Company, Miss Jones." However, this varies; ask your employer how he wishes you to answer the phone. Speak clearly and directly into the mouthpiece. Speak loud enough that the other person does not have to strain to hear you, but don't yell! Develop the habit of being courteous, *never interrupting* the other person.

An Attractive Voice Will Go a Long Way
in Developing a Satisfying Relationship with Others

You now know what traits make up your personality. Rate your own personality according to the traits in the chart below. Do not write in this book, but list these traits and your rating on a separate sheet of paper.

PERSONALITY RATING					
Trait	Excellent	Good	Fair	Poor	Very Poor
ATTITUDE					
COURTESY					
DEPENDABILITY					
DESIRE TO SUCCEED					
ENTHUSIASM					
FORESIGHT					
FRIENDLINESS					
HEALTH					
HONESTY					
INITIATIVE					
LOYALTY					
MORALITY					
NEATNESS					
OPEN-MINDEDNESS					
PERSONAL APPEARANCE					
PUNCTUALITY					
SELF CONTROL					
SENSE OF HUMOR					
TACT					
USE OF VOICE					

The kind of work you choose to go into as your career will depend, in part, upon your personality; and the degree to which you are satisfied with life in general will depend a great deal upon your adjustment to your work. Recent surveys show that many people, as many as 90 percent in some occupations, are *not* satisfied with their work situation. Often it is because their work does not fit their personalities. While you *can* change your personality—and even improve it—you should also choose your work to suit your basic personality insofar as possible.

ATTITUDINAL INVENTORY

Because the matter of *attitude* is the *most important* of all personal traits, it is important that you take inventory of your own attitudes toward people and situations. Read each of the following questions and answer honestly. A careful study of your answers can help you to see those areas that need improvement. On a separate sheet of paper, write the number that represents your answer in this manner: 5 = positively yes; 4 = mostly yes; 3 = undecided; 2 = mostly no; 1 = positively no. Answer with your *first reaction*.

1. Do you make new friends easily?
2. Do you refrain from being a "complainer"?
3. Are you careful never to interrupt when another person is speaking?
4. Can you be optimistic when others around you are depressed?
5. Do you refrain from boasting or bragging?
6. Do you control your temper?
7. Are you genuinely interested in the other person's point of view?
8. Do you speak well of your employer?
9. Do you keep the same friends for years?
10. Do you feel well most of the time?
11. Do you use proper English?
12. Do you keep promises?
13. Are you at ease with the opposite sex?
14. Do you have good table manners?
15. Do you organize your work and keep up with it?

16. Do you get along well with your parents?
17. Do you readily admit your mistakes?
18. Can you be a leader without being "bossy?"
19. Is it easy for you to like nearly everyone?
20. Can you stick to a tiresome task without being "prodded?"
21. Do you finish each task you begin?
22. Do you realize your weaknesses and attempt to correct them?
23. Can you take being teased?
24. Do you avoid feeling sorry for yourself?
25. Are you courteous to your fellow workers?
26. Are you usually well groomed and neatly dressed?
27. Are you a good loser?
28. Do you enjoy a joke even when it is on you?
29. Do you like children?
30. Do you keep your own room in good order?
31. Are you aware of the rules of etiquette?
32. Do you refrain from giving alibis?
33. Are you tolerant of other people's beliefs?
34. Do you respect the opinions of your parents?
35. Do you introduce people easily and correctly?
36. Do you refrain from pouting when things go differently than you like?
37. Are you a good listener?
38. Can you speak before a group without feeling self-conscious?
39. Do you like to attend parties?
40. Are you the kind of friend you expect others to be?
41. Do you accept compliments or gifts graciously?
42. Can you disagree without being disagreeable?
43. Do you like to give parties?
44. Are you "on time" for engagements?
45. Do you generally speak well of other people?
46. Can you take criticism without being resentful or feeling hurt?
47. Are you careful to pay back all loans, however small?
48. Are you always on time for your appointments?
49. Does your voice usually sound cheerful?
50. Can you work well with those you dislike?

51. Do you contribute to the conversation at the family dinner table?
52. Do you try as hard to get along well with your family as with friends?
53. Do you like people who are much older than you?
54. Are you pleasant to others even when you feel "out of sorts?"
55. Are you free from prejudices?

There are 55 questions; a perfect score would be 275. If you rate from —

250 - 275 You're too good to be true.
200 - 249 Your attitude toward others is commendable.
150 - 199 Your attitude needs improvement in certain areas.
Below 150 You need a general overhauling.

Study Helps

Discussion Problems

1. It is estimated that the average person will change the *kind of work* he does five times during his lifetime. What effect does this have on planning your career?
2. What do we mean by the word *values*? What are some of your *values*?
3. Why are your interests important in choosing a career? What are some of your interests?
4. Do you prefer working with people, things, or ideas? Why is this important to your career choice?
5. What are your best abilities? What kind of work is related to your abilities?
6. What classes have you done best work in? What kind of work is related to what you did in these classes?
7. Do you have greater ability in math or reading? What can you do to improve the area in which you are the weakest?
8. What is meant by the word *personality*? What are some of the things that make up your *personality*?

Chapter 7

Personal Effectiveness

There are two kinds of people in this world: (1) those that let things happen and (2) those that *make things happen*. We mentioned earlier that most people simply drift into an occupation pretty much by accident. We said that those who plan ahead and *choose their work* are often more satisfied with their work and happier with life then those who do not plan this important part of their lives. The ability to make things happen is important in many situations. We call this ability *personal effectiveness*. How effective you are in making things happen depends largely upon the degree to which you can get others to see things your way, to influence them. And this, in turn, depends upon (1) your personality—how others know you, and (2) how well you are able to understand others.

How Others Know You

In the last chapter, we discussed twenty personality traits. You probably know pretty much where you are strong and where you are weak. So that you can get an even better picture of what kinds of behavior are displayed by those with certain personality traits, we will be more specific. We shall look at the specific actions of behavior, appearance, etc. which are most liked and most disliked by others. These were the things found most important according to high school seniors and recent graduates, and they have considerable effect upon those with whom you work and those in whom you have romantic interests.

Qualities in Men

First, the things women most admired in men:

1. **Cleanliness and good grooming.** "I like a man that looks and smells clean and has clean, well-cared-for hair. Too many fellows today have hair that makes them look like they just crawled out of a cave."

2. **Courtesy.** "A fellow who is courteous makes others feel like he cares for them. He usually isn't selfish. Saying 'please,' 'thank you,' and just being thoughtful go a long way in influencing me."

3. **Cheerfulness.** "Nobody likes the guy who is always gloomy. He tends to make those around him gloomy too."

4. **Honesty.** "I like a man who is honest in what he says and what he does. You must be able to trust him. If you can't, a close relationship just isn't worth the pain."

5. **Respect for others.** "The man who has respect for others is usually the man who has respect for himself. I think this is a good tip-off to his overall character."

6. **Clean, appropriate clothing.** "I feel uncomfortable around the fellow who is not clean. The man who wears clothes that are somewhat stylish is more interesting."

7. **Interest in and concern for others.** "Selfish men I can do without. The person who is really interested in and concerned for others is a real human being."

8. **Good morals.** "While standards of morality have undergone a change in recent years, it is still important to a girl that a fellow have good morals."

9. **Desire to succeed.** "Anybody I'd be interested in would have to want to be a success. Too many guys just don't seem to care what happens to them; they don't *do* anything to bring success."

10. **Dependability.** "I admire a man who can be counted on. I once had a date with a boy who was, for no reason at all, a half hour late. I went with him once, but never again."

11. **Ability to hold a job and enjoy it.** "A girl needs the security of knowing that her fellow can hold a job and be a good provider. If he really likes his work, he is a much happier person and more fun."

12. **Gallantry.** "A girl likes to be treated like a lady. A gentleman does this."

13. **Respect for self.** "The man who doesn't respect himself won't have much respect for others."

A Woman Needs the Security of Knowing That
Her Husband Can Hold a Job and Be a Good Provider

14. **Self control.** "A girl feels very uncomfortable with a fellow who 'blows his stack' in public. I was with a boy once who got mad at the waiter during dinner, and I just wanted to hide."

15. **Sense of humor.** "Being serious *all the time* is a bore. I prefer to be with people who can see the funny side of life."

16. **Good health.** "I like people who are healthy and full of pep."

17. **Intelligence.** "I prefer being with fellows who can hold an intelligent conversation."

18. **Well-cared-for teeth.** "I always look at a fellow's teeth. Clean teeth and a clean breath are musts. Can you imagine kissing a boy who has dirty teeth?"

Do you agree with these comments? Probably you could add some additional qualities which you admire in a man. Now let's see what the men had to say about what they look for in a woman.

Qualities in Women

1. **Cleanliness and good grooming.** "I was all ready to ask this girl for a date, then I saw she had dirty ears!"

2. **Friendliness.** "Men like women who are cheerful most of the time, gals who are friendly toward people in general."

3. **Intelligence.** "The popularity of the 'dumb blonde' is no more. I prefer to know and be with girls who are real people, people who can think."

4. **Honesty.** "A girl who is dishonest, one who can't be trusted, is to be avoided like the plague."

5. **Courtesy.** "I think, in general, girls are more courteous than the fellows—but now and then you run across one that doesn't know the meaning of the word. Lack of courtesy shows up worse in girls than it does in boys."

6. **A good figure.** "Men look at women with a good figure. It's probably the first thing that catches my attention about a woman. It's too bad how some gals let themselves go until they aren't even noticed."

7. **Clean, appropriate clothing.** Most of the girls I know wear clothes that are clean and appropriate for the occasion. I have seen some who don't seem to have any 'clothes sense,' but I wouldn't consider them my friends."

8. **Dependability.** "All my friends are people who can be counted on. I guess I just don't cultivate a friendship with the kind of person who isn't dependable."

9. **Good morals.** "I am simply not interested in a girl who doesn't know right from wrong. Fellows talk about promiscuous girls, but they aren't interested in them as people—and they seldom marry one."

10. **Respect for others.** "I like women who can value other people for whatever good qualities they have and not worry about their faults too much."

11. **Respect for self.** "If a girl doesn't think much of herself, I don't think much of her either."

12. **Unselfishness.** "Can you imagine having to cater to the wishes of a selfish dame? I like a girl who considers the interests of others at least half the time."

13. **Sense of humor.** "A girl who can take a joke when it is on her is loved by everyone."

14. **Beauty.** "I know beauty is only skin deep, but it is what attracts men. Once attracted, other things are more important.

15. **Socially at ease.** "It makes a fellow proud to be with a girl who is at ease—not tense—in any situation."

16. **Good health.** "I used to go with a girl who didn't take care of her health—seldom got enough sleep, wouldn't eat properly, things like that. She never had any energy and consequently wasn't much fun."

17. **An even temper.** "How would you like to go with a girl who exploded in anger at the least little thing? I like a girl with a dependable disposition."

18. **Attractive, clean teeth.** "When a girl smiles, I like to see some pretty teeth. The main thing, of course, is that they be clean and well-cared for. There's a bit of truth in these toothpaste ads."

These are the things people like in their friends. What do they dislike about people? These comments are representative of the things that are most irritating to others:

"I can't stand people who smoke just to impress others."

"Body odor and bad breath make me want to vomit."

"People with dirty fingernails remind me of animals."

"I can't stand people who are always putting others down. I guess they do it to try to make themselves look better, but it doesn't work."

"People who are rude I'd like to kick in the shin, but of course I can't."

"People who are cynical, hateful toward others, are sick."

"Some people think they are always right. They contradict and argue every point. They are a bore."

"My pet peeve is the person who is only interested in himself. He usually starts every sentence with 'I.' "

"Some off-color jokes are all right. But I get disgusted with the person who tells jokes that have more dirt than humor."

"People who have formed the habit of filling their conversations with swear words just aren't too smart. They can't think of really descriptive words."

Perhaps these comments will give you some ideas about how you might improve your own personality. It might be interesting, too, to talk with your friends about *their* pet peeves.

How to Improve

None of us is perfect, and none can expect to develop a perfect personality. Yet, each of us *can improve.* Many schools are now teaching classes in personal improvement and personality development. Correcting those things that irritate others and improving your personality is possible, but it is not easy. Your personality has been developing since you were born. The

reason you act the way you do in a given situation may be partly
due to your relationship with other people before you entered
school. Habits which were formed years ago are difficult to
break, but it is easier to change them this year than it will be
next year or five years from now. If you feel that improving
your personality is really important to you, it can be done. The
procedure outlined here can help you:

(1) **Find out what your shortcomings are and admit them.**
At the close of the last chapter, you were asked to rate yourself
on 20 personality traits. If you were honest, you probably found
some traits which can stand some improvement. If you are not
satisfied that you really know enough about your personality to
begin a meaningful plan of improvement, ask your school counselor to give you a personality inventory.

(2) **Decide on one habit or trait for improvement.** If you
try to improve on many traits at once, you will not be able to
follow through on any of them. By concentrating all your effort
on just one trait, you will develop new—and more satisfying—
ways of thinking and behaving.

(3) **Develop a plan for improvement.** Make a plan and
stick to it, without exception! If you wish to correct an undesirable habit, such as biting your fingernails, try to develop a
habit which is opposite. Begin taking pride in how your fingernails look—or how they are going to look. Clean them, file them,
and—if you are a girl, use some nail polish. Then, to use up the
nervous energy formerly expended in biting your nails, try
some new activity which is more acceptable—perhaps doodling.
Chewing gum or eating mints may also be helpful in ridding
yourself of the habit of nail biting.

(4) **Check your progress.** Check yourself regularly and
often at first. If the trait you wish to improve is something that
gives you opportunity for improvement every day, check yourself every day. After you have followed a plan for improvement
for several weeks, you may find that you have indeed made progress; but keep checking yourself for weeks or even months so that
you will not slip back into the old ways! If you feel that a
friend will be honest in his judgment, it a good idea to ask him
how *he* (or she) thinks you are progressing.

(5) **When you feel that improvement is permanent, begin
working on another trait or habit.**

Yes, you *can* improve your personality, but you must want very much to do so. If it is not really important to you, if you don't have a *good reason* to improve, then you will probably go right on being your *old* self. Some good reasons to improve your personality might be to become more popular, to be happier and have more satisfying relationships with others, or to become a better salesman. It can be done *if you want it*. One final word about personality improvement. Psychologists tell us that, in general, doing things *with* and *for others* tends to improve our personalities.

Understanding and Influencing Others

There are times when our personal effectiveness takes the form of convincing others to see things our way, to do what we want. This is especially important to company executives and to salesmen in any field. Can you usually get others to do things your way, when yours is a good way? If you wish to influence someone to accept your way of thinking, it is first necessary to understand how that person thinks and, in addition, make use of certain psychological advantages. In this way you will be able to approach that person in the manner which will most likely cause him to go along with your wishes. Since every person is different from every other person, the right approach with one person may be the worst approach with someone else. Learn all you can about the person you wish to influence. Consider each of the personality traits discussed in the last chapter. They are important to your understanding of others. Be careful, though, not to condemn a person because you see many personality faults. The idea is simply to *understand* him.

Another thing to be considered in understanding another person is his range of interests. His hobbies, how he spends his leisure time will give you a clue to his values.

Additional ways of "sizing up" a person include observations about his:
(1) Voice
(2) Eyes
(3) Eating habits
(4) Driving habits

Voice

A pleasant sounding voice most often accompanies a pleasing, well-balanced personality. Personal conflicts and negative attitudes often show up in an unpleasant voice due to tension of the throat muscles. Psychological tests have shown that those with a pleasant voice have greater self control and self satisfaction than those with unpleasant voices. If the person you wish to influence has a very unpleasant voice, perhaps you should look into his personality further before you try to exert your influence.

Eyes

The eyes have been described as the "windows of the soul," and they are indeed very revealing. Do you know someone who cannot, or will not, look you in the eye while you are talking with him? The person whose eyes flit from place to place likely does things on impulse and may be difficult to reason with. The person who looks you in the eye and whose eye movements are rather slow tends to be open-minded and realistic.

A person's eyes can also tell you whether he is usually nervous, deceitful, and whether he likes or dislikes what you have

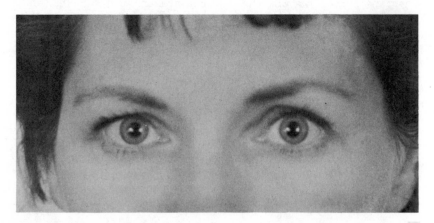

The Pupils of a Person's Eyes Reveal Likes and Dislikes

to say! The person who blinks his eyes rapidly is likely quite nervous. If you are talking with a person whose blinking suddenly becomes more rapid, you have probably caused him concern about something. He is worried. Blinking is the outward sign of nervousness which is most difficult to control. Psychiatrists have recently found that the unusually nervous person is more likely to be deceitful than any other type of personality. Calm, easy-going persons are least likely to be deceitful. Recent experiments show that the eyes are quite reliable in giving away the liar. When telling a lie, the pupils of the eyes usually grow slowly larger and then suddenly become smaller. This is easily observed in some people, difficult in others. Based upon this discovery, improved lie detectors may make use of high speed motion picture photography to record suspects' eye movements during questioning. The pupils of a person's eyes also react to what the person sees and what he hears. If he likes what he sees and hears, his pupils become larger. If he dislikes what he sees and hears, they become smaller. Of course, this is true only if there are no sudden changes in lighting—since light also makes the pupils enlarge. Although a person may be able to hide his true feelings in every other way, the pupils of his eyes reveal his likes and dislikes.

Eating Habits

You may wonder how eating habits can help you size up a person. The fact is that there is a relationship between a person's eating habits and certain personality traits. Why there is this connection is not known, but we do know that it exists. For instance, those who are heavy meat eaters tend to get along well with others and usually have a good deal of initiative. Those who especially enjoy salads tend to be outgoing persons who like the company of others. They may be restless and hurried in their speech and actions. Those who consider dessert as the best part of any meal tend to be impulsive and do things without giving much thought to the consequenses. Those who like all kinds of foods usually have well-balanced personalities.

Driving Habits

The driving habits of a man can tell you a great deal about his personality. This may not hold true for women. But for a man, the number of dents in the fender often shows the degree to which he is antisocial. Men who repress their emotions, that is keep them under control in most every other situation, may reveal their hostilities behind the wheel of a car. The fellow who crowds out other drivers, speeds through traffic taking chances, starts and stops unusually fast, and follows other cars dangerously close is often a basically weak person. The only time he feels confident is when he is in control of a ton of steel. This kind of driver will likely feel that cheating the other fellow is all right if it brings him his own selfish wants. He often thinks that life is unfair to him. He probably has few close friends and may have trouble holding a job.

Another important factor in influencing others is catching the person in the right mood. A person is much more likely to agree to whatever ideas you present if he is in a good mood. How can you tell when a person is in a good mood? You can tell by his answers to a greeting. Listen to his voice. When you say, "Good morning. How are you?" his reply will likely be something like, "Fine, thank you." If the "Fine, thank you" is said

The Driving Habits of a Man Tell a Great Deal About His Personality

with a rising inflection, the person is probably in a good mood. If it is said with a lowering of pitch, he is probably *not* in a good mood—and it may be wise to wait until later to discuss an important item.

Executives and top salesmen know that the best time to talk anybody into anything is while he (or she) is enjoying a good meal. We are more susceptible to influence from others while eating something we especially like. But this period lasts only a short time; it starts with the first bite and ends shortly after it has all been eaten. If you wish to persuade someone to see things your way, it may be worth the price of a steak!

Study Helps

Discussion Problems

1. What is *personal effectiveness?*
2. What do you most admire in men?
3. What do you most admire in women?
4. What are your "pet peeves?"
5. What are the steps in improving an undesirable personality trait?
6. What can you learn about a person by listening to his voice?
7. What can you learn about a person by watching his eyes?
8. What can you learn about a person by observing his driving habits?
9. How can you tell whether a person is in a good mood?
10. When is a person most likely to be in a receptive mood?

PREDICTING YOUR SUCCESS

You have now completed Part I, which has dealt with selecting, locating, applying for, and being successful on the job. You have a pretty good idea of what is required of you to become successful. Will you succeed? The more "yes" answers you have to the following questions, the better your chances—*but be honest!*

1. Will you dress neatly, wearing clothes appropriate for the job?

2. Have you worn appropriate school clothes while attending high school?
3. Will you plan to be a few minutes early for work so that small emergencies will not make you late?
4. Do you always arrive at school in time for your first class?
5. Will you, on the job, take criticism without resentment—and learn from it?
6. Have you taken well and learned from the constructive criticism given by your teachers and parents?
7. Will you do the best job you can wherever you work?
8. Are you putting forth your best efforts while in school?
9. Will you be on the job every day—unless you are really too ill to go to work?
10. Have you attended school regularly—being absent only when you were too ill to attend?
11. Will you do your work on the job in a neat and orderly manner?
12. Have you done your work in this class completely and neatly?
13. Will you do any task asked of you, even though you were hired to do something else?
14. While in school, or on a part-time job, have you been willing to do whatever tasks were asked of you?
15. If you finish your own work early, will you help a co-worker?
16. Around your own household, or on a part-time job, have you been willing to help others with their tasks?
17. On the job, will you be considerate of others' feelings?
18. Are you considerate of the feelings of your friends, parents, and even those whom you do not consider your friends?
19. Will you stick to a difficult task until it is completed?
20. In your school work, have you usually completed whatever work has been assigned to you?
21. Will you do what you can to keep your good health so that you will be able to give your work your best effort and not be absent frequently?
22. Do you regularly eat those foods which contribute to good health; get regular, vigorous exercise; and sleep at least eight hours every night?
23. Do you believe that if you never do any more than you get paid for, you will never get paid for any more than you do?

PART II

Meeting Your
Adult Responsibilities

Introduction

One of the most thrilling and exciting experiences in your lifetime is to secure and start work on your first full-time job. The transition from school to work is more than finding a job. It is obtaining a freedom from dependence on your parents. It is becoming independent. It is the beginning of full adulthood when you accept adult responsibility and citizenship.

Becoming a good citizen requires more than holding a job and making a contribution with your skill and energy at work. You must join other consumers and use your earnings to achieve the most happiness for yourself and those you care about.

Learning to become a wise consumer is not easy. The well-being of a family depends to a great extent on learning and using good buying habits. In the last few years, much has been done to assist Americans to become better consumers. Programs on radio and television have been designed to assist consumers in getting the most for their money. The federal government and state governments have recently passed laws to assist and protect the consumer. Many agencies of the government now perform services which assist the public in becoming wise consumers. However, you must be alert to good buying procedures—and make them a habit!

In Part I of this book, you learned about selecting a career and preparing for employment, succeeding on the job, and advancing in your career. The purpose of Part II is to assist you in becoming a better consumer and a well-informed citizen. As an independent consumer in a complex and competitive industrial society, you need to learn how to receive the most benefits from your money by studying and observing different products.

Learning good habits in the management of money and the art of spending will greatly help you become a happy and productive citizen. In Part II you will learn how to budget your money for successful spending. You will learn ways of getting the best buy for your money. Everyone needs to learn about available services and how and when to use credit to an advantage. The information in Part II will be both useful and interesting. As a worker on your first job, you can apply much of the consumer information provided in Part II.

Chapter 8

Managing Money

Wise Use of Money

Most of us have problems in managing our money. One problem is that few of us have enough money to buy all the things we would like to buy and do all the things we would like to do. Another problem is that we do not plan the use of our money well enough to receive the full value of each dollar. Often, it is wasted. Some people waste money without even knowing it.

Learning to use money wisely isn't easy. It takes some knowledge on how to use your money and a lot of *careful planning*. Since few people have a lot of money to spend, it is good business to learn how to use what we have wisely.

You can learn to manage your money just like learning to drive a car. It gets easier as you become more experienced. Managing your money, like driving your car, requires that you develop good habits. The good driver or good manager need not work any harder than the poor driver or poor manager. He knows what to do and does it consistently, with the confidence that comes from developing competency in driving—or in managing money. Good driving will save you costly repairs—and court fines as well. Good money management will help you get the most out of the money you have.

Have you ever noticed two people who earn about the same amount of money each month, but one seems to have more to show for his earnings? Is this because one does a better job in managing his money?

You may know a family who seems to have more of a money problem that the average family. This family is always behind in paying bills. Even though the father makes a good salary, this family is never quite able to catch up in paying bills. Such a family is not living within its means. You have heard this term before. What is meant by "Living within your means?" It means the wise use of the money you earn. Also, it means spending no more than you earn, or not buying things for which you cannot pay.

Manage Your Money for Things You Want
(Courtesy of Oklahoma State University Extension)

Learning to live within your means is very important when you start on your first job, just as it is to the head of a family. Many economic and family problems can be avoided by careful attention in this area.

Every worker has a certain financial responsibility to himself, to his family, and to his community. Just as the poor driver wrecks his car and injures others, the poor manager of his money wastes his money, lessens his chances of economic success, and creates problems for his family.

It Is Important to Live Within One's Means

Levels of Responsibility

The level of responsibilty for the use of money may vary from individual to individual. The use of money is probably more important to young people today than it was 100 years ago. In 1870 about 53% of the population was engaged in farming. Today less than 7% of our population is engaged directly in agriculture. The family income in 1870 was low, and consumer goods were not available in the quality and quantity they are in the 1970's. The median family income had increased to $8,400 in 1967, and many more consumer items are available today. Life has become more complex for everyone.

To better understand some of the problems of the young consumer and his level of financial responsibility, let us look at a few case studies involving young people.

CONNIE MARTIN

Connie Martin is 16 years old and a junior at Washington High School. She lives within a few blocks of the school with her father and mother, Fred and Marjorie Martin; her brother, Larry; and her sister, Linda. Larry is 14 years old and a freshman at Washington. Both Connie and Larry walk to school each day. Linda attends Lincoln School which is eight blocks from their home on West Sycamore Street.

Fred Martin is a carpenter. Bad weather and strikes have caused Fred to lose considerable work time the last three years, and the family has found it necessary to adjust the budget several times.

Connie has been given a small allowance for school supplies and clothing. Any extra money Connie has for luxuries and entertainment must come from her own earnings. She has been earning and saving some of her money for the last two years. Connie understands that the family financial picture is not too bright at the present time and that she will need to be responsible for herself after she graduates from high school.

Connie has studied the occupations that are available to young women, and cosmetology appears to be very interesting. Connie's friend, Jane, has an older sister who is a licensed cosmetologist; and Connie enjoys visiting her shop and watching the work.

After discussing future goals with her school counselor, her mother and father, and with friends, Connie has decided to take a cosmetology course after graduating from high school.

The cost of a cosmetology course is about $500. Connie has started saving one-half of the money she earns working at the public library three hours after school each day. With the additional money Connie makes baby-sitting, she expects to have the $500 saved before graduation. Is this a realistic goal?

JOSEPH THOMPSON

Joe Thompson is 6' tall, 190 pounds, 18 years old, and a senior at East High School. He is interested in sports and has made the varsity football team the last three years. Joe is a good worker and a jolly fellow, but has not been too successful in his business ventures.

Joe's father, Jim, and his older brother, Bill, are salesmen for the Johnson Wholesale Plumbing Supply Company. Both have rather high gross earnings from their salaries and commissions. However, they have a lot of expenses since they must furnish a car for travel and entertain customers out of expense accounts which are not adequate.

Joe has two brothers and three sisters younger than he, and all in school. Even though Joe's mother shops wisely, it is quite a task to meet the expenses of a large family living in an expensive section of Waynesville, a city of 125,000 people.

Last summer, Joe decided he would help the family by going to work as a hardware salesman. He purchased a three-year-old automobile for $1200 and spent $500 for clothing needed to meet his customers. Joe worked very hard during June, July, and August selling a special aluminum kitchenware. His earnings were high, but he was not able to make enough money to pay for his car and clothes.

Joe has a different level of financial responsibility than most of his friends; but rather than admit defeat, he is determined to pay for his car and go to work full time as a hardware salesman upon graduating from high school.

MILDRED AND STANLEY WOODWARD

Mildred Sharp had known Stanley Woodward since they started to Lincoln School in Mount Vernon eight years ago. They seemed to be fond of each other since their first year in school together.

Mildred lived with her father and mother, Dennis and Marie Sharp, in a large house on Elm Street. Dennis owned and operated the Main Street Garage where he had developed a good business during the last 15 years. Mildred's mother helped keep the accounts in the garage for her husband.

Stanley Woodward lived 10 blocks north of the Sharp's. His father, John Woodword, was a plumber and worked for the Mount Vernon Plumbing Company, where he had been employed for the last 10 years. Stanley was the oldest of four children in the Woodward family. His sister, Mary, was 15 years old, and brothers, Keith and Bruce, were 12 and 10 years old. Stanley's mother, Gladys, was always busy keeping their clothes clean and repaired and doing all the jobs needed for a busy family of six.

Mildred and Stanley had dated since the ninth grade in high school, and it was taken for granted that they would be married later. Last fall Mildred and Stanley were both seniors at Jackson High School and both enrolled in the distributive class. Mildred applied for a job at Bradley's, a children's clothing store, and was employed in the dress department. She was very happy with her work and was making a good salary while learning to be skilled in selling.

Stanley had worked in the Kroger store for the last three summers and liked the grocery business. Thus, the first place he made application was at the Tenth Street Kroger store. He was employed as a trainee to work in all areas of the store.

In October, Mildred and Stanley decided to get married. Both had saved some money and had enough clothing to last them the rest of the year. If they both worked, they thought they could manage to get married and still finish their senior year in high school. Neither was interested in going to college. Stanley was hopeful that some day he could become a store manager and Mr. Kyser, the store manager, had promised him full time work when he graduated from high school. Mildred was happy working in retailing, and she agreed with Stanley that retailing would be a good life's work.

Mildred and Stanley were married during the Christmas holidays with the blessings of both the Sharp and Woodward families. Knowing that Mildred and Stanley would have to budget carefully the money they earned, the Sharps asked Stanley and Mildred to live with them until both were through high school. A financial agreement was reached between the Sharps and the newlywed Woodwards. Stanley and Mildred agreed to take over specific responsibilities around the home and to contribute a percentage of the cost of maintaining the home.

In this case, the arrangement worked very well. Mildred and Stanley were, for the most part, independent. Both were employed and taking their places in the adult world, as well as completing the last year of high school. Their level of responsibility had been well defined and they were able to handle their financial, employment, and school responsibilities. The study of consumer education in the distributive education class also provided them with additional knowledge and skill to manage their affairs.

HELEN LANE

Helen Lane had always wanted to become a secretary. Even as a high school freshman, she had informed her typing teacher of plans to become a legal secretary. Helen lived with her parents on a large ranch in Kansas. Helen's mother encouraged her to prepare for secretarial work by attending the Northern Area Vocational School.

The idea of leaving the ranch where she had lived all her life to live in a small apartment was frightening to Helen, who had graduated from the small Madison County Rural High School last June. Only Helen's strong determination could force her into this new level of responsibility where she would have to be completely independent.

Helen found a small apartment about five blocks from the school. She selected the apartment on Maple Street because it was about equal distance to the shopping center and to the school. It was very important to live near the shopping center since Helen didn't want to be bothered with a car. A shopping center with a bank, a number of stores, and a restaurant would serve her needs quite well. The apartment was furnished with just about everything a student would need in furniture and appliances. Helen enjoyed entertaining the students in her class by cooking special dishes.

After four months of managing her affairs, Helen found she was quite capable at managing a budget, buying food and clothing, and maintaining the apartment. Her mother and father were proud of the ability she displayed.

Managing for herself was easy for Helen because she had practice. Her mother and father had encouraged self reliance. Helen had also received instruction which built her confidence. The study of consumer education in homemaking classes had been very useful, as was the study of budgeting in high school business courses. Helen's success was partly because she knew how to plan. Helen not only knew how to keep accounts, she knew how to be a good consumer. The allowance Helen's father sent her each month was more than adequate.

PHIL AND MARY KIRBY

Phil and Mary Kirby had wanted to buy their own home for several years. Only recently had they been able to save enough money for a down payment on a new home in the North Hill addition. Phil and Mary had been married for six years. Phil, who is 29, liked to live in the three room apartment on Tenth Street because it was close to the plant where he worked.

Mary, who is a nurse, had worked at the Memorial Hospital for the first three years after marriage. Now that Bruce, their two-year-old son, needed more room to play, they were anxious to find a small home. Six months ago they found a small, three bedroom home on Kennedy Street in North Hills. The planning for selecting, financing, and contracting for the house was done over a number of months. With Phil's latest raise in salary, they were sure that they could pay off the mortgage in twenty years.

After Phil and Mary had reviewed their budget plan several times, they visited Mr. Jones at the First National Bank. He reviewed their financial situation and recommended that they pay no more than $175 per month on house payments. He also recommended that they be given a loan and promised to help in appraising the property selected.

The little house on Kennedy Street was the best they could find to fit their particular needs and still be within their financial range. A check list to be used in buying a house was furnished by their bank. According to the check list, it appeared the house had a good location for their needs. A school was within five blocks, and the neighborhood appeared to be quiet—with few busy streets. Most of the houses in the addition were less than three years old and were occupied by young families. The exterior of the house was in good condition, newly painted and well landscaped.

The interior of the house also was in good condition, but a little painting was needed before occupancy. The room arrangement was satisfactory; all the equipment and appliances were a good brand and were nearly new.

Phil and Mary liked the house even more after moving in four months ago. The payments of $160 per month were not easy to make; so a number of cuts in spending had to be made. The family budget for recreation was reduced by dropping their membership in the country club. It would not be possible to pay dues each month as they had before. After three monthly payments were paid, it seemed that by using savings for a 20% down payment and using 25% of their earnings based on an average of the last three years, Phil and Mary would not be overburdened with their payments. They had shown considerable responsibility in the planning and buying of their first home.

Phil and Mary acted wisely in managing their money. First, they saved enough money to make a good

down payment. Second, they planned their spending
and selected a house within their financial ability.
Responsibility in financial matters is extremely important to the young family.

Planning Your Program of Spending

A spending plan, or budget, is most important for managing your money. At the end of the week have you ever
thought, "Just look at the money I have spent this week. How
did I spend so much with so little to show for it?" The secret
of knowing where your money is spent is to develop a good
budget. If you are paid at the end of each week, perhaps a
weekly plan could be used; but such planning offers no con-
tinuation from week to week. Therefore, long range plans with
some flexibility appear to be the best.

A family budget should be planned on a yearly basis. Your
spending plan should be based on what you wish to do with the
money you earn. Planning a budget has certain advantages to
you whether you are a student in a work-experience program
or the head of a family.

(1) It will force you to establish goals in using your
money.

(2) It will help you live on the money you earn.

(3) It will help you eliminate wasteful habits of spending
your money.

(4) It can help you achieve long range goals.

(5) It can give you valuable experience and develop
competency in money management.

Budgets can be simple or complex. The budget of the
federal government is a document that requires the work of thousands of people and is a major document when printed. The budget of a student working part time can be written on a single
sheet.

Your budget may not look like a major auto manufacturer's
budget, yet the two are basically the same. Two steps are
involved in planning your budget.

1. First you must estimate how much money you will
earn for the week, month, or year. In estimating your

income, all sources should be included in your budget.

2. Then you must estimate expenses for the year.

In preparing an estimate of income for the year, it is helpful to review income for the last year. A city manager will use figures from the last year's budget and the present year's spending to estimate the amount of money needed for the next year.

The second step in planning your budget is to determine how to use the money you earn. This may be difficult because you will be deciding what things you must buy, how much you will save, how much you will spend on recreation, etc. This part of the planning can be fun as well as difficult. At this point you must set goals and make some compromises in spending money. You will need to make cuts in different items to balance your expenses with income.

The experiences of John Smith, a recent high school graduate, will help you understand the principles of making a simple budget.

Planning a Budget

John Smith enjoyed working in his first full time job as a lathe operator. He had worked part time last year for the Acme Tool Company as a student learner. The part time work was a part of his high school work in the cooperative work-experience program. Wages paid for the part time work were not high, but he learned to operate the lathe. Mr. Jones, his foreman, promoted him to a lathe operator.

John had learned about consumer education in his high school program and was anxious to make plans and set goals for the year. He decided to use the budget plan developed by the Household Finance Corporation as his guide in making a budget for the year. The booklet titled, "Money Management— Your Budget," had been very helpful to him in completing one of his school assignments in consumer education.[1]

---

[1]Household Finance Corporation, "Money Management-Your Budget," (Leone Ann Heuer), Chicago, 1950.

John remembered from his studies that a successful money manager uses goals as a guide for planning the use of money. This part of the planning was not difficult for him. He had always wanted a more stylish wardrobe, and since it would soon be football weather, sport clothing was listed first. The old car his uncle had given him last year was needing repair, but would probably last for another year without too much trouble. A good car was a definite need and something to budget money for next year.

There was no steady girl friend, but John wanted to start saving money for a home when the right girl came along. Thus, he listed money for getting married and starting a home as number one for "Buy things you want in the future."

Estimating Income

Estimating income for the year is quite a challenge for most people. No one knows what the coming year will hold for him. It is wise to begin by listing the minimum income you expect to receive for the coming year.

John was hopeful that he would receive a raise before the end of the year. However, since he could not be sure, he decided to use the amount of his weekly check as a basis for estimating income. Only "take home" pay was listed as income. Federal

How to Make a Spending Plan
(Courtesy of Oklahoma State University Extension)

and state income taxes were deducted by the company along with his social security tax.

The "take home" amount of his check was $125 per week which totals approximately $500 per month and $6,000 per year. The monthly and total amounts were listed on page 1 of his budget form.

Future Fixed Expenses

Everyone has bills which fall due at certain times during the year. Some of the bills may be paid out of the weekly pay check. The larger bills which fall due monthly, quarterly, semi-annually, or annually are special problems to those who do not have a spending plan. A good way to pay such bills is to plan a chart with names and the dates they are due. John reviewed a list of possible future expenses and planned his fixed expenses in the categories that applied to him. He listed all fixed expenses on page two of his budget form. The total was $1,540.

INCOME

List budget periods	List sources of income				Total for each budget period
	Wages	Rents	Other Income	Dividends	
Jan. 1 - Jan. 31	$500	—	—	—	$500
Feb. 1 - Feb. 28	$500	—	—	—	$500
March 1 - March 31	$500	—	—	—	$500
April 1 - April 30	$500	—	—	—	$500
May 1 - May 31	$500	—	—	—	$500
June 1 - June 30	$500	—	—	—	$500
July 1 - July 31	$500	—	—	—	$500
Aug. 1 - Aug. 31	$500	—	—	—	$500
Sept. 1 - Sept. 30	$500	—	—	—	$500
Oct. 1 - Oct. 31	$500	—	—	—	$500
Nov. 1 - Nov. 30	$500	—	—	—	$500
Dec. 1 - Dec. 31	$500	—	—	—	$500
Total for Year	$6,000	—	—	—	$6,000

FIXED EXPENSES?
(Omit items already deducted from paycheck)

TAXES
    Federal income tax
    State income tax
    Property taxes

MONTHLY RENT OF MORTGAGE PAYMENTS

UTILITIES
    Telephone
    Gas
    Electricity
    Water

INSURANCE
    Life
    Health and accident
    Hospitalization
    Fire and theft
    Automobile
    Personal property
    Social security
    Others

ANNUITIES and other investments
    toward retirement

FUEL for home heating

UNION DUES

PROFESSIONAL ASSOCIATION DUES

INTEREST on loans where principal
    is not being repaid along with
    interest

REGULAR PAYMENTS—may include
    interest on loans
    on furniture or equipment
    on car
    Christmas Club

SAFETY DEPOSIT BOX

CAR LICENSES—state and city

SCHOOL TUITION, TEXTBOOKS AND FEES

FUTURE FIXED EXPENSES

ITEM	Amount Due	Date Due	Jan.	Feb.	March	April	May	June	July	Aug.	Sept.	Oct.	Nov.	Dec.
			In Top of Columns List Budget Periods											
Taxes														
Property	$50.00													$50.00
Rent														
Apartment	$900.00		$75.00	$75.00	$75.00	$75.00	$75.00	$75.00	$75.00	$75.00	$75.00	$75.00	$75.00	$75.00
Safety Dep. Box	$10.00													$10.00
Telephone	$80.00		$6.66	$6.66	$6.66	$6.66	$6.66	$6.66	$6.66	$6.66	$6.66	$6.66	$6.66	$6.66
Union Dues	$150.00		$12.50	$12.50	$12.50	$12.50	$12.50	$12.50	$12.50	$12.50	$12.50	$12.50	$12.50	$12.50
Insurance														
Hospital	$150.00		$50.00				$50.00				$50.00			
Car	$100							$50.00						$50.00
Life	$150.00							$75.00						$75.00
	$1,540.00		$144.16	$94.16	$94.16	$94.16	$144.16	$219.16	$94.16	$94.16	$94.16	$144.16	$94.16	$279.16

Future Flexible Expenses

The flexible expenses which are certain to appear offer an opportunity for making budget adjustments in order to meet unexpected changes in spending. Many items listed in this group will vary in cost and will occur at different times during the year.

John examined the list of suggested items which appear as possible expenses in the budget. He budgeted for clothing, charities, subscriptions, recreation, and gifts. He also budgeted a part of his income for emergencies. His budget items are listed on page three of his budget form in the flexible expense section. The total amount in this section of the budget was $1,830.

FUTURE FLEXIBLE BUDGET ITEMS

CLOTHING

HOME FURNISHINGS AND
HOUSEHOLD EQUIPMENT
   including repairs

HOME IMPROVEMENT
   including equipment and repairs

CONTRIBUTIONS
   Church
   Charities
   Civic Groups
   Professional Groups
   Fraternal Groups
   Social Clubs

ANNUAL SUBSCRIPTIONS
   Papers
   Magazines

MEDICAL AND DENTAL CARE
   not covered by insurance,
   including medicines

RECREATION
   including hobbies unless
   included under personal allowances or day-to-day expenses

GIFTS AND ENTERTAINMENT
   Birthdays
   Wedding and Anniversaries
   Christmas
   Babies
   Graduation

A CUSHION for the unexpected
   and emergencies

FUTURE FLEXIBLE EXPENSES

In Top of Columns List Budget Periods

ITEM	Amount Needed	Jan.	Feb.	March	April	May	June	July	Aug.	Sept.	Oct.	Nov.	Dec.
Clothing	$ 500.00												
Contributions													
Church	$ 20.00												
Charities	$ 20.00												
Civic Group	$ 20.00												
Annual Subs.													
Local Paper	$ 15.00												
Magazines	$ 15.00												
Medical Care	$ 100.00												
Recreation	$ 640.00												
Emergencies	$ 500.00												
TOTALS	$1,830.00												

Day-to-Day Living Costs

The amount of money used for day-to-day living costs makes up a sizeable percentage of your expenses. These expenses are flexible. Budgeting for expenses in this area helps to control spending and provide information on how money is used.

John examined the possible expense items below and made estimates of expenses in the categories which applied to his budget. The total expense for day-to-day cost of living was $1,592. John purchased a special record book to record daily expenses to compare with the amount budgeted.

CAR UPKEEP AND TRANSPORTATION

ENTERTAINMENT—extra food;
    candies; flowers

FAMILY PERSONALS—toothpaste; first
    aid; shaving supplies; cosmetics

FOOD—meals eaten at home;
    meals eaten out.

HOUSEHOLD HELP—care of
    house; yard; baby

HOUSEHOLD SUPPLIES—soaps
    and cleansers; small items
    for the home

LAUNDRY; DRY CLEANING; CLOTHING
    REPAIRS

STATIONERY; POSTAGE; NEWSPAPERS

DAY-TO-DAY COSTS

ITEM	Four Week Period				Total for Four Weeks	Total for Year	Monthly Costs
	1	2	3	4			
Food	$20.00	$20.00	$20.00	$20.00	$ 80.00	$1,040.00	$ 80.00
Laundry, Dry Cleaning,							
Clothing Repair	$ 4.00	$ 4.00	$ 4.00	$ 4.00	$ 16.00	$ 192.00	$ 16.00
Personal Supplies	$ 3.00	$ 3.00	$ 3.00	$ 3.00	$ 12.00	$ 144.00	$ 12.00
Household Supplies,							
Soap & Cleaners	$ 2.00	$ 2.00	$ 2.00	$ 2.00	$ 8.00	$ 96.00	$ 8.00
Car Expense	$10.00	$10.00	$10.00	$10.00	$ 40.00	$ 120.00	$ 40.00
TOTAL	$39.00	$39.00	$39.00	$39.00	$156.00	$1,592.00	$156.00

The Trial Plan

After John had completed estimates of all the expenses which were likely to occur, he made a total of all the expenses in each category. The totals were brought forward and listed in the trial plan which appears on page four of his budget form. If John can live on the $4,962 budgeted for the year, he will have made considerable progress toward his long-range goals. Saving $1,038 or 15% of the take-home-pay may be very difficult for most young people.

A TRIAL PLAN

	For One Budget Period	For One Year
INCOME Subtract FUTURE FIXED EXPENSES	$500.00 $120.83	$6,000.00 $1,540.00
Balance: Subtract FUTURE FLEXIBLE EXPENSES	$379.17 $152.50	$4,460.00 $1,830.00
Balance: Subtract PAST-DUE BILLS	$226.67 None	$2,630.00 None
Balance: Subtract DAY-TO-DAY LIVING COSTS	$226.67 $156.00	$2,630.00 $1,592.00
SAVINGS FOR GOALS	$ 70.67	$1,038.00

Putting a Budget into Use

Do you remember the first time you tried to drive a car? It took patience and practice before driving was easy and a joy to you. Making and using a budget is difficult at first, but with the same patience and practice you will be able to use a budget as a tool for managing your money. Once you have developed good habits in money matters, you have built a good foundation for success. It may take several budget periods before your actual expenses match the budgeted amounts. However, this does not mean that your budget was a failure. Most budgets need to be adjusted at the end of the period.

A budget cannot provide an immediate cure for serious financial problems. It may take a long time to recover from some unexpected expense. A good budget plan should alert those not living within their means and help them adjust their expenses to their income.

Here are some suggestions to keep your plan running smoothly:

1. Keep your plan for managing money simple. The more convenient the system is to use, the easier it will be to get it going and to stick to it.

2. Be realistic in setting up your plan. If your income or that of the entire family is balanced against a complete and accurate list of expenses, any problems that come up may be faced squarely.

3. Make your spending plan adjustable to changing circumstances. If fixed expenses are grouped together, the family has a clear picture of what must be paid and when. Flexible expenses may offer opportunities for adjustment if there is need for rearranging or refiguring.

4. Develop a system for handling the details of budgeting— keeping necessary records . . . paying bills . . . setting aside money for future expenses . . .

5. Decide on a place to keep materials and information: YOUR BUDGET booklet . . . incoming bills . . . receipts . . . cancelled checks . . . account book or ledger. A desk drawer, small filing case, or even a sturdy box will serve to keep necessary information together.

6. Find a safe place for valuable papers and records such as insurance policies, savings bonds, receipts for stock purchases, personal records, automobile receipts and title, tax records. A safety deposit box in your bank is

the safest place for valuable papers. A fireproof container should be used if these things are kept in the home.[2]

Where to Get Additional Help

Practically everyone will need expert help on money matters sometime during adult life. Much general information can be obtained by reading various publications, especially those published by the Household Finance Corporation. Government publications are available describing most of the agencies which federal government controls. However, many personal problems require professional help.

An attorney-at-law who specializes in money matters should be consulted when a legal opinion is needed. This is especially true in making contracts, selling real property, and collecting bad debts. Additional information in this area of study is discussed in Chapter 11.

Many banks employ people who will provide free information to customers. Information is available on investments and on bank loans for purchase of homes, equipment, cars, and other property.

Additional help in money matters may be obtained by discussing the problem with your supervisor. A few companies have people employed who will provide legal and financial information for their employees. University extension classes dealing with a number of consumer problems are scheduled in the large cities. Classes are also offered by high school and junior college adult education departments. Individual and group instruction on consumer problems can be furnished by the county agricultural agent and the county home demonstration agent.

High school students should remember that their teachers can help them in this area. Teachers in agriculture, business, homemaking and industrial arts specialize in consumer education.

The wise management of money has a vital bearing on

---

[2]Household Finance Corporation, "Money Management-Your Budget," (Leone Ann Heuer), Chicago, 1950.

the success and happiness of individuals and their families. It is important that young people join the world of work with a high level of skill and knowledge in the wise use of money. With the help which is available today, no one should permit his future to be jeopardized by lack of skill in the use of money.

Ask for Financial Advice If You Have Trouble Living Within Your Budget
(Courtesy of Oklahoma State University Extension)

Study Helps

New Terms

economic problems
financial responsibility
money management
budget
flexibility

competency
estimate
categories
safety deposit box

Study Questions

1. What is a "budget"?
2. List five reasons for planning a budget.
3. What are the two basic steps involved in planning your budget?
4. What must you decide in order to estimate expenses?
5. What four groups of expenses should be listed in your budget?
6. How do you decide the amount to be saved for your future goals?

Discussion Problems

1. Why should you plan a budget while you are attending school? Should you keep the same budget after you are employed?
2. How would you estimate your income? How would you estimate your expenses?
3. Why is it sometimes difficult to follow the budget you have planned? What should be done if you cannot follow your budget?
4. Imagine you and your friend are discussing making a budget. Your friend thinks making a budget is just too much trouble. Try to convince him that the budget will really help and that it is worth the time required to prepare and keep within the estimated budget.
5. Was budgeting as important to the young man in 1870 as it is today? Explain the problems encountered by both groups.
6. What would be a good goal for saving your money earned from summer work?

Chapter 9

Buying Goods and Services

Consumer Problems

Benjamin Franklin is credited with the saying, "A penny saved is a penny earned;" but because inflation has lowered the value of the penny, perhaps we should say today that "a dollar saved is a dollar earned." The basic way to save dollars is to learn how to buy the goods and services needed at the best price. We shall consider how one determines the "best price" when several selections are available.

Good shopping requires careful planning. The first phase of planning requires that you develop a budget by listing an approximate amount under each expense area. Then you should decide exactly what you want before you begin your shopping. If a number of items are to be purchased, an inventory of needs is helpful to determine which items are most needed and which purchases could be postponed. Deciding on the quality required is the second important consideration. The type of article to be purchased and the way in which the article is to be utilized will determine the quality required. A long-lasting article (such as furniture) which will be used every day should be of higher quality construction than an article for occasional use (such as a picnic basket). It is wise to prepare a shopping list from the inventory according to greatest need and quality desired. The third step involves reading advertisements and comparing prices and styles to save time for yourself and the sales people. The value of comparative shopping is that you will learn prices and styles which will help you make better judgments on the best buys. The persuasiveness of a good salesman and your own impulsiveness will not influence you to make poor purchases. Finally, postponing purchase of articles not presently required in order to take advantage of sale prices offers an opportunity to save as much as half of the original cost.

Good buying habits and good money management are closely related. To make our money buy more for us, we need to learn how to shop effectively. Learning to buy effectively is like learning other skills; it takes time and practice. Learning is much easier if one follows a few simple guidelines.

Long Range Planning

Having a well planned budget for the year is helpful in developing a long range buying plan. An approximate dollar amount should be designated for each expense. Few families or individuals can purchase everything needed at one time; the budget allowance is just not enough. Thus, things needed first will be purchased first. Long range planning applies especially to goods that will be used for some time, and must also take into consideration the relationship of what is purchased first and last.

Buying clothing for the school year is a good example. Your entire wardrobe is more important than one individual garment. When your clothing budget is limited, a long range purchase plan for clothing should include the colors you like and what fits your personality. Additional purchases should fit into your particular color and style scheme. It would be very foolish to buy a brown suit when all of your other garments and accessories are gray or black.

Every purchase of clothing needs to fit into your master plan for the year. Two factors are important to your long range plan. First, take inventory of what you have at the present time. Second, plan what you need and hope to buy during the year.

Making an Inventory

Making an inventory of your wardrobe is quite simple. All that is needed is a list of garments and the condition of each one. Probably a mental list is all that is needed. What do you have for work, school, and formal occasions? In which area do you need the most replacement? Should you consider a new color combination? Will the styles change much? The problem here is to think in terms of what you have, what you will need, and then decide what your shopping should include.

Planning for Quality Shopping

After you have completed your inventory, the next step is to make tentative shopping plans. Here compromises will have to be made. Few people have enough money to buy everything desired. Planning for your future shopping is not as easy as making an inventory. Here judgment and knowledge are important. Careful study on how to buy will include:

1. Consideration of which items receive heavy use and therefore need to be durably constructed;
2. Knowledge of what makes one article more durable than another article; and
3. What difference in cost is appropriate for various qualities of merchandise.

Most of us will make mistakes from time to time. However, careful study will prevent many errors and help develop good buying habits.

Understanding the difference in cost of various qualities of merchandise requires further consideration of prices and quality of goods. The price of goods is not always a good guideline for quality. Price is determined in several ways. You may wonder why a pair of shoes priced at $25 at a downtown store may be listed at $18 in a discount store located at the edge of the city. Is quality involved here? The answer, of course, is "no." The difference in pricing is most likely based on the cost of distribution. The cost of distribution is more in the city. Rent costs more; the store is more centrally located; and there are more salesmen to serve you. Therefore, quality of the shoes is not the only factor in pricing. The service and convenience given by the city store make it necessary to charge more for the shoes. Thus, quality is not the entire basis for the difference in price between the downtown shoe store and a discount store.

The difference in pricing may be based on factors other than good service and convenience. Supply and demand enter the picture. A limited supply of needed merchandise in demand will sell for a higher price. When food products are scarce, the prices are higher. A shortage of milk will result in higher prices, for agricultural products are particularly affected by supply and demand.

When one company is the only manufacturer of a needed item, that company may be able to hold a monopoly and charge prices much higher than production costs. Federal and state laws have been passed to prevent groups of firms from holding down production and raising prices. However, some firms still have a monopoly on certain products. The price of these items may not be based on supply and demand.

Determining the quality of merchandise is not easy, and deciding on the level of quality which you will need is more difficult. It has been said that the quality of a product can be assured when buying well-known brands of merchandise. In most cases this is probably true. However, it may be possible to get the same product sold under a retail store brand for less.

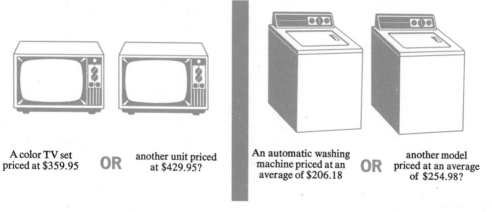

A color TV set priced at $359.95 OR another unit priced at $429.95? An automatic washing machine priced at an average of $206.18 OR another model priced at an average of $254.98?

The Difference in Pricing Is Influenced by Several Factors

For example, Whirlpool manufactures appliances for Sears who sell them under the Kenmore brand name. Montgomery Ward's brand name for appliances is *Signature*, but the appliances are made by a number of well-known manufacturers of appliances. The smart shopper learns that it is possible to get high quality products under different brand names.[1] Much information on the quality of appliances is available through consumer reports.

Consumer Fraud

Fraud may be defined as an intentional untruth or a dishonest scheme to take unfair advantage of a person or group of persons. From the consumer's viewpoint, any scheme by which one's rights or interests are impaired is fraud. The legal definition of fraud is restricted to cases in which deliberate intent can be proved. Actual fraud occurs when something is said, done, or omitted by a person with the plan to continue what he knows to be a deception. Consumer fraud is defined as acts or words that may mislead another person. An example is a man selling his car without informing the buyer that the transmission is failing. Damages in fraud cases may be collected by legal action. However, this process is expensive, time consuming, and embarassing to the plaintiff.

Fraud is as old as the human race. There is hardly an area of human need that has not been subjected to exploitation. Attractive fields for fraud are in products and services sold in large volume, especially in the preparation and sale of food, repair services, beauty aids, hair and health restoratives, advertising, and numerous other fields. In our complex technical society, fraud is much easier to commit than in colonial times when few consumer goods and services were available. Nevertheless, fraud did occur even then.

Fraud will be possible so long as we have greedy producers and gullible consumers. Both groups are guilty. The wise buyer can protect himself to a certain degree. However, in more and

---

[1]"A Hotpoint by any other name would be a": *Everybody's Money*. (Winter 1968-69), Vol. VIII, No. 4, pp. 8-9.

more cases today, the federal and state governments must act to protect the consumer. This is especially true in foods and drugs. The objective of the United States Food and Drug Administration is to insure safety and effectiveness of drugs and therapeutic devices by requiring proof of a safe and useful product.

Federal government activity has increased in protecting the interest of the consumer. New laws have been passed which require truth in packaging, truth in lending and truth in advertising. This has resulted in automotive safety devices and more testing of drugs before sale to the public.

Laws with severe penalty will not entirely prevent fraud. The buyer himself must accept some of the responsibility in protecting himself. Thus, it is necessary for the consumer to keep continuously informed and to carefully study the product and markets.

A Dishonest Scheme That Takes Advantage of Another Person Is Fraud

Evidence of Fraud in Foods

Food frauds have been numerous and include adulteration, misrepresentation, short measuring, deceptive branding, and overpricing. As a result, strict laws have been passed by Congress regarding food packaging. If you take the time to study the label, you may learn a great deal about canned or packaged food because fraudulent claims on the labels carry severe federal penalties. For example, the list of ingredients on the label begins with the item weighing the most and goes down the line to the one weighing the least. The shopper can then select the better buy of a canned stew with the label "potatoes,

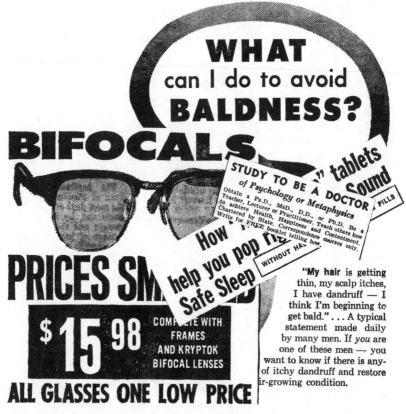

Good Consumers Are Not Mislead by Advertising

beef, carrots, peas, water" than the stew with the label printed "water, carrots, peas, potatoes, beef." The amount of water added to canned food must be considered when determining the quality and quantity.

Fraud, unfortunately, is practiced to a greater extent on persons who know least how to protect themselves. This group includes the poor, especially in minority groups, who frequently have a language difficulty. Education to reduce consumer ignorance is an objective of many government agencies and public schools in various cities and states.

Fraud in Auto Repair

Recent research in the auto repair services clearly shows that the consumer is being victimized by fraudulent practices on the part of some garages. Fraud occurs when a mechanic in a garage replaces many parts which are not defective. The cost of the labor for a job may also be padded by a few unscrupulous garage owners. Not all cases involve fraud, for some of the abuse can be the result of untrained auto mechanics who make incorrect diagnoses of the auto malfunction.

Fraud Occurs When a Mechanic in a Garage Replaces Parts Which Are Not Defective

A number of auto service departments, especially those in large franchise dealerships, practice preventive maintenance on customer's cars. This routine maintenance is required to keep the car warranty in force. However, preventive maintenance involves the replacement of only parts recommended by the factory manual. Fraud occurs when other parts are changed when there is no need.

Today many service stations stock auto accessories, and the service station attendants are urged to sell them. One sales pitch is for the attendant to remove the air filter from the engine and attempt to sell the customer a new one. The same sales pitch is used to sell batteries, radiator hoses, shock absorbers, fan belts, windshield wiper blades, and tires. Fraud occurs when the attendant knows that replacement is not needed. Women tourists traveling alone are probably the most frequently victimized.

Fraud in Health Service

Today the consumer of health services faces many uncertainties in securing needed health care. In the first place, he has little information to judge the ability, dedication or ethics of a physican. In the second place, he may have no time or choice in case of an emergency when he must take what is available at the particular time.

The public attitude toward health is changing rapidly. For many years adequate medical services were considered as a privilege limited to those who could pay. Today health care is considered as a basic right of all people. Yet we still have disagreement on the basic concepts of health service.

Fraud in the medical profession is difficult to spot and prove. The American Medical Association and the American College of Surgeons have continuously urged the ethical practices of those in the medical profession. The Judicial Council of the Medical Association has recommended expulsion of members proved guilty of unethical and illegal practice. Unfortunately, fraudulent practices, such as fee splitting, unnecessary operations, and rebates from clinical laboratories have been reported. Malpractice suits have been won against members of the medical profession. The cost of insurance protection against malpractice lawsuits is at an all-time high.

Protecting yourself from fraudulent practice in the health service is important to you and members of your family.

1. Keep up to date on current medical costs.
2. Learn the reputation, competency and dedication of the medical doctor you select.
3. It is not unethical to discuss fees before service is rendered.
4. Compare fees with others.
5. When your health insurance pays for the service, be sure the charge isn't padded, for this practice will cost you more in insurance premiums eventually.

Unethical action by anyone engaged in medical service should be reported to the State Medical Association.

Medical Fraud Has Occurred in Unnecessary Operations

Fraud in Drugs

The Food and Drug Administration has considerable control over the sale of useless and harmful drugs. Claims made by manufacturers for products must be proved before being advertised.

Manufacturers Have Been Forced to Change Their Advertised Claims of What Patent Medicine Will Do

Many manufacturers have been forced to change their advertised claims of what patent medicine will do. Harmful products must be labeled with ingredients listed on labels.

One problem in the sale of drugs is the price charged. Drugs sold under a brand name are usually many times more expensive than the same drug sold under the generic name.

Fraud in Business and Industry

Fraud in business and industry has become a matter of national concern in the last few years. New authority has recently been given the Federal Food and Drug Administration to protect the consumer from abuses in this area. The Federal Trade Commission has been given additional authority to control deceptive advertising. Both organizations have certain functions which are closely related. In the area of labeling of products, the authority of the Food and Drug Administration often brings its functions close to that of the Federal Trade Commission, which is responsible for enforcement of regulations dealing with misleading advertising of foods and drugs.

The "truth-in-packaging" law and the "truth-in-lending" law provide the government agencies with more authority to protect the consumer.

Government agencies have only recently moved forward to protect consumers. However, private organizations have fought the fraudulent practices of unethical businesses for a number of years. One of the most effective is the Better Business Bureau, an organization which started in 1912. The Bureau has about 126 local offices in the United States which are financed by local businessmen. The work of the Bureau is to build good relationships between the customer and the businessman by advocating fair dealing by both. The Bureau also:

1. Works to prevent deception in advertising;
2. Acts on the complaints of misleading advertisements;
3. Warns the public against fraud; and
4. In some cases reports fraud to law enforcing agencies.

Persons with complaints should visit or write their Bureau.

The "Consumers' Union" is a group of people who buy *Consumers' Report,* a magazine published monthly which reports on the quality of various products. The Consumers Union's main force is its information on manufactured products. The C.U. expects to increase the size of its circulation of *Consumers Reports* to two and one-half million copies in a few years.

Another effort to protect the consumer has been the one-man effort of Ralph Nader, who wrote *Unsafe at Any Speed,* a documented report on safety defects in cars, especially the early Corvairs, manufactured by General Motors. More recently he has investigated the packing industry. The protection of the consumer from fraud is likely to be a public and government issue for the next few years.

Buying Women's Clothes

Clothes are very important, especially to the young woman who is in high school. The clothes one wears seem to tell a story about the wearer that is easily understood by the keen observer. A person's personality is expressed in part by the clothes she selects and wears. There are styles and colors of clothes that cause people to turn and look; other styles and colors seldom get a second glance, even when worn by the same person.

Many styles, models, and colors are available and worn by the young girl today. There are the ultra-modern styles which may change each season, and the more conservative styles which can be worn an extra year without major alterations.

Each girl has her own particular dress problem which requires an analysis for the selection of the most suitable clothing. The correct clothing for a young lady develops her self confidence. Wearing the right clothes, whether at school, on the job, or at a social event is essential to her feeling of adequacy.

Many girls have the figure and size to select and wear clothing from the sales rack. However, many prefer to select a pattern and the material to make their own clothes. For those who have this skill, it is an excellent way to save money and get the best fit. Once the pattern and material have been selected, a careful study of the material type and width is needed in order to decide on the correct amount of material to buy for the pattern chosen.

Since not all girls buy their dresses ready-made, an example of buying clothing is made by giving suggestions on buying a cloth coat. The purchase of a coat is a major investment. Thus, one should give considerable thought to its selection. This is especially important when purchasing a coat with high quality material and workmanship that will be worn for more than one year.

Points to Consider in Buying a Coat

1. Style

The style of a coat is important, especially if it is to be the only coat in your wardrobe. Conservative lines and color will remain in style longer.

2. Material

The material selected should be of good quality. A high percent of wool is recommended. The weave should be small, firm, and uniform. Tweed is acceptable, depending on taste.

3. Workmanship and Design

Each part of the coat should be cut correctly with the grain of the cloth, and the pieces should be matched. The fastenings should be accurately and firmly attached. Buttons should be simple in design and sewn to provide easy buttoning and allow some play. Button holes should be neatly done, and evenly worked with a durable twist thread. Seams should be evenly stitched on the coat. The lining should be attached at the seams with bar tacks.

4. Brands

A manufacturer is known for his quality of goods. Well-known brands generally assure a standard of quality.

Buying a Car

Planning Before Purchase

Just about every young person is anxious to buy his first car. A number of boys and girls start saving money and planning for a car before reaching the eligibility age for a driver's license.

Buying your first car can be an exciting and satisfying experience, or it can be one of confusion and frustration. A car is expensive to buy and to operate, thus one should develop carefully a buying plan before making a purchase. A few suggestions are offered here which will make the purchase of your first car less hazardous. Few young people will have the money to buy a new car; therefore, the suggestions are for buying a used car.

In developing a plan, the first thing to consider is the amount of money you can afford to spend. Remember, the cost of the car is only a part of car expense. Insurance, taxes, and operating expense must be considered if you are to get the benefit you expect.

After you have decided how much money you will have to spend, the next step is to decide what type of car you want. Good buys can be found in sport cars, full size, and luxury cars. Compact cars are generally less expensive than the larger cars. However, they may be less comfortable than the full size cars. When you decide what type and size car you will buy, it is wise to learn the average price one would expect to pay for different models. The Consumer's Digest of Chicago, Illinois publishes a *Price Buying Directory* each year which lists price ranges for used cars. The information provided in this publication is a great help in getting a fair used car deal.

Once you have an expected price range, the next step is to look at the cars on different used car lots. All car dealers use some form of advertising. The most used are newspapers, radio, and television. It is not difficult to learn which of the dealers use such terms as, "best deals in town," "no offer refused," "going out of business," "must sell all the cars on the lot." Such advertising may often be "bait" and should be considered carefully. Prices advertised in newspapers on new cars also may be misleading because they don't include additional cost of transportation and accessories which are on the car. Recently a federal law was passed requiring manufacturers to post suggested retail prices on all new cars. It would not be possible to require posting of suggested prices for used cars, since the condition of the car must be considered.

Advertising Can Be Helpful for the Consumer

In the larger cities it may be possible to find a car you want by examining the classified ads in the local newspaper. However, there are used car salesmen who sometimes use classified advertisements listing home addresses and telephone numbers. The ads are to mislead prospective buyers into thinking they are buying from a private individual at a lower-than-market price. This type of advertisement is also used by car salesmen to spot prospective buyers. Another sales trick is to advertise for buyers to take over the payments of a repossessed car. Such a deal may be false and will cost as much or more than a car purchased from the lot.

When you have located a car that seems to be what you want, the next task is to determine its condition. This is a difficult task for a person who knows cars. For the person who knows little about cars, it would be best to take the car to a reputable mechanic for an evaluation. However, this will probably cost you $10 or more. Before you pay for this service you may be able to make a general check of conditions of the car by using the following check list.

Car Buyer's Check List

Inspection of exterior condition:
1. Has the car been wrecked? Observe the surfaces of the car in the sunlight. Repaired surfaces can be seen by looking at the surface from a view almost parallel with the painted surface.
2. Do the doors fit properly? A door out-of-line may indicate the car has been involved in a wreck.
3. Have rust spots been repaired? Rust spots generally appear in the bottom section of the body. The paint over repaired areas will not be completely matched with the color of the car.
4. Is the paint in good condition? Faded paint with rust spots means the car has not been garaged.
5. Check for dents. Damages to bumper, grill or painted surface reduce the value of the car.
6. What is the condition of the tires? Tires with ⅛″ or less tread will soon need to be replaced. Tires worn irregularly indicate the alignment needs adjustment. A

badly worn ball joint suspension may be the cause, and a repair job will cost up to $200.

7. Are the shock absorbers good? A car that continues to bounce after being pushed up and down probably needs new shocks.
8. Is the windshield and door glass in good condition?
9. Does the car appear to be level when empty? A car which tilts to one side or to front or back probably needs new springs.

Inspection of inside:

1. Are the brake and accelerator pedals badly worn? Worn pedals generally means the car has been driven many miles.
2. Is the steering wheel paint worn off in spots. When paint is worn off the wheel, the car probably has been driven more than 50,000 miles. If the wheel is newly painted, the meaning is the same.
3. What is the condition of the door sills and arm rests? Excessive wear here means excessive use.
4. What is the condition of the carpets and seats? New carpets and seat covers are sometimes installed to make the car sell, but indicate the car has had rough use.
5. Do the door glass mechanisms work smoothly? Wrecked cars many times have windows difficult to raise or lower.
6. What is the indicated mileage? Speedometers can be changed or reset. Does it seem to be correct when compared with inside wear?
7. Do the instruments and accessories all work?

Inspection of engine:

1. Does the radiator indicate leakage or does the coolant appear dark red? Either condition can cause additional repair bills.
2. Is the oil dip stick free from rust or sludge and is the oil clean? A rusty dip stick can be serious. The engine may have an inside gasket leak or cracked block which contaminates the oil. Black oil may indicate additive treatments used to make the engine run quieter.
3. Is the oil on the automatic transmission dip stick clean and free of odor? Dirty oil with an odor can mean excessive transmission wear and costly repair.

4. Does the engine start easily, run smoothly, and have no unusual knocks when accelerated? If the answer is yes, the engine is probably not badly worn.
5. Is there a warranty date on the battery? Batteries over three years old may need replacement.
6. Is the exhaust system in good condition? A leaky muffler or exhaust pipe is dangerous, also expensive to replace.
7. Does the engine or transmission leak? When oil spots appear on the parking area after driving, the engine and transmission should be checked for serious leaks.

Driving inspection:

1. Does the car steer properly? A car that pulls to one side of the road should be carefully checked.
2. Is there an increase of body noise and rattles on rough roads?
3. Is there any vibration or unusual noise on the open road at speeds from 40 to 70 miles per hour? A rear axle hum or transmission noise can mean expensive repairs.
4. Is the automatic transmission operating properly? A transmission which is noisy when the car is shifted from reverse to drive with the brake on may soon fail. A transmission which fails to shift at the proper speed or is rough in shifting needs adjustment and repair.
5. Will the brakes stop the car smoothly? Brakes which pull a car to one side during panic stops are dangerous and should be repaired.
6. Does the car exhaust blue smoke when accelerated rapidly? Generally a car that exhausts blue smoke has badly worn rings, will use oil, and needs expensive engine work.

Any of the conditions which may require additional expense or repair or cause a dangerous operating condition should be considered in the price. A person who is unfamiliar with used car conditions should not sign a contract until the car is inspected by a good mechanic.

After the car has been thoroughly examined, it is time to bargain with the dealer. Defects found on the car should be called to the dealer's attention. He may agree to make repairs or deduct repair cost from the price of the car. When the dealer agrees to make the repairs, they should be made before the contract is signed.

Contracts

A more detailed study of sales contracts will be made in Chapter 11. However, it seems appropriate to cover a few aspects of entering into a contract at this point. Do not sign a contract or purchase order until it is completed in full, and you have examined all the conditions in detail. A copy of the completed contract should be retained by the buyer.

Many cars are sold on the time payment finance plan. The buyer is required to pay a certain amount of the total cost in cash when the car is delivered. The balance is paid over a period of time in monthly payments. The buyer signs a contract which obligates him for all the terms in the contract. Laws vary in different states concerning interest rates and carrying charges, but the general terms are the same. When the buyer signs a contract that is not filled out completely, the dealer can add additional costs and charges.

Don't sign a purchase contract until you study it carefully. If you plan to buy a car using a time payment plan, make arrangements with a reputable bank or finance company. A buyer who is alert, and knows the score both on the quality of the car and its value, and knows how to figure interest costs is less likely to be taken advantage of by unethical dealers. If the buyer fails to see an overcharge before he signs the contract, it will be difficult to get it changed. Fraud is difficult to prove, and it generally costs more to take a case to court than pay the extra amount added to the car cost.

The most important thing for a young car buyer to do is to plan for the purchase. Know what you are doing. It will save you money. Car dealers may have a price marked on their cars, but most of the dealers will bargain. If you accept their list price, you may pay more than necessary. It is a well known fact that one buyer may pay many dollars more than another buyer for the same brand and model of car purchased on the same day from the same car dealer. It pays to bargain. Most car dealers would rather bargain than lose a sale.

Influences on Choice

The buying problems which were discussed under the heading "Consumer Problems," point out the influences of many factors affecting the decision to purchase. In addition to these influences which are under the control of the buyer, there is a second group of influences which may or may not be within the control of the individual buyer. The latter group includes employment, availability of the product desired, the relative strength of the individual's desire to keep up with his peer group, his personal values and habits, and the influence of advertising. Let us see how each of these influences affects buying.

Employment

The kind of job you have ordinarily determines your salary or income, and the kind of job also determines the kind of clothing budget you will need. For example, Mary is employed as a beautician. Her uniform must be purchased from the uniform company designated by her employer in order that all employees will wear identical uniforms. She has no choice in a major part of her clothing expenditure, and her only unrestricted clothing purchases are used for home and recreational activities. On the other hand, Sue is employed as a secretary and is expected to be attractively and neatly dressed. Sue can take full advantage of seasonal clothing sales for new clothing and can wear older clothing at home or for less dressy occasions. Just as these two girls must consider their employment in planning a clothing budget, so must the boys employed as a machinist or as a shoe salesman in a store consider different budget allowances for clothing.

Employment will influence the free time available and money allotted to entertainment cost and sports equipment. If you are trying to "balance the budget," it may help to compare the cost of recreational activities such as tennis and bowling or the cost of sports equipment needed for bicycle riding or hunting. Each person should consider his or her personal preferences in recreational activities, and the cost of entertainment, and then make appropriate allowances in the budget.

Availability of Merchandise

The principle of economics known as the *law of supply and demand* operates in all selling and buying procedures. This "law" states that if the supply of a product is balanced by the demand, the price is a true one directly related to value of the product. But if the supply is less than the demand, the price rises above true value; or if the supply exceeds the demand, the price falls below true value. This balance between supply and demand is a very important consideration in buying food, clothing, and services.

In order to shop most economically, you will need to purchase food or clothing when the supply is most plentiful. Low supply and demand limits production and usually results in increased selling price.

Shopping is usually more economically done in large stores where the supply of merchandise is greater than in small neighborhood stores or from door-to-door salesmen. The large store is able to buy in quantity, thus receiving a lower wholesale price than the neighborhood salesman. Stores in several locations or towns operating under a central management have the opportunity to buy in quantity when the supply is greatest and retail to customers at a lower price. Thus, the discount store or so called "chain" store can be an economical place to purchase known-brand merchandise.

Peer Group Influence on Buying

Everyone wants to be accepted by his peers, and thus a strong influence to "follow the leader" is developed. One girl or boy who is a popular leader can be very influencial in shaping the economic life of a group and of the individuals involved. If the leader's income is on a par with the majority of the peer group members' income, the group members will normally follow the leader's pattern. It is important for each young person to stop to analyze the situation, asking himself, "Am I planning my budget according to my own income and expenditures, or am I overlooking my personal wishes in order to be 'one of the gang'?" Only by adapting your budget to your own income and expenditures can you become an intelligent consumer.

Personal Values and Habits

Because of the pressure to gain peer acceptance, young people have considerable difficulty in recognizing and maintaining personal values and habits. In planning clothing purchases, for example, resist impulse buying. Shop when you and the sales people are not too rushed to consider workmanship, cost of upkeep, and your own tastes. It is possible that a certain outfit will look very smart on tall, slim Marcia but will be unflattering to petite Helen.

Consider the value of buying better quality everyday clothes than dress clothing. Work clothes are worn more often, seen more, and cleaned more frequently, while dress clothing is worn less frequently and thus may be less expensively constructed. Your own needs must be considered before making purchases.

Plan Your Spending According to Your Income, Not the Joneses

Influence of Advertising

Just as the peer group affects your buying, so does the advertising heard and seen daily on radio, television, and in the newspaper. Advertising is helpful in many ways. It informs the buyer where the merchandise is available and provides an index for comparison of prices. Advertising can also be deceptive and harmful to the consumer.

Perhaps the worst abuse of advertising was in the sale of patent medicine before 1915. Government control of advertising has gradually increased during the last 50 years to help protect the consumer. Business and the advertising industry have also helped reduce deceptive advertising. However, it is still not possible to eliminate all deception.

The Federal Trade Commission has moved forward recently in controlling deceptive, false, unclear, and otherwise misleading advertising. The courts have tended to uphold the FTC in protecting the consumer, especially the ones who are least able to protect themselves.

The FTC and the courts will never be able to fully protect all consumers. Therefore, everyone who buys goods and services should learn to protect himself. Two ways to become successful in using advertising are to enroll in consumer education courses

Advertising Can Be Deceptive

and to read the literature published by consumer organizations, such as *Consumers' Digest.*

Watch for bait ads. These are just a way to get you into the store. You can suspect an ad is bait when an item is offered at a very low price and:

1. You are told the item was sold out and are asked to look at something else—usually more expensive.
2. The salesman is unwilling to show the advertised item.
3. The salesman talks down the advertised product, wants you to buy something else.
4. Only the floor sample is left and you are told it can be ordered but will take a long time.[2]

Advertising is both helpful in economical shopping and costly in deceptive practices. Shop for the best buys by comparing quality and price and by being alert to any dishonesty, fraud, or deceptive advertising.

Study Helps

New Terms

inflation	comparative prices	durable
inventory	persuasive influence	monopoly
quality	cost of distribution	bait ads
priority	consumer fraud	compromise
prey		reduction

Study Questions

1. What is the basic way to save dollars?
2. What three steps should be followed for good shopping?
3. What does "long range planning" mean in buying goods and services?
4. What are two steps required for a long range plan?

---

[2]"Be a Good Shopper," Division of Home Economics Federal Extension Service, U.S. Department of Agriculture, June 1965, p. 5.

5. What are the three points to study in order to do "quality" shopping?
6. How does supply and demand affect prices?
7. Can you buy at "wholesale" prices?
8. How can you maintain personal value and habits when shopping?

Discussion Problems

1. Make an inventory of your clothing, writing beside each item the approximate cost. Add to find total value of your clothing. At your present salary, how long would it take you to replace your wardrobe?
2. Why should you decide what you need to purchase before shopping for needed articles?
3. Which is the better buy—a ten ounce bottle of shampoo at $ .50 or a fifteen ounce bottle at $ .69? .... a 24 ounce can of peanuts at $ .60 or a 36 ounce can at $ .90?
4. How does an employee decide on what kind of clothing is needed for a particular job if he is not required to wear a uniform?

Chapter 10

Credit and Installment Buying

Establishing and Maintaining Credit

You may have gone to the local grocery store to make a purchase, and, instead of paying cash, said "Put it on our bill." You were using credit. Each year credit purchases account for over $5,000,000,000 worth of merchandise in the United States. Some predict that we will become a moneyless society with different forms of credit to purchase all goods and services. This may never happen, but more and more credit cards are available for making purchases. The most recent addition is the use of *bank cards*.

Credit is extended to a greater number of people each year because, as responsible citizens, they have earned "the right to receive credit." You and your family have probably gone through a formal process of applying for credit. Generally, the process is repeated each time you apply for credit with a different business.

The person granting credit wants to know a great deal about the person applying for credit. Business organizations have different procedures. However, most retail businesses belong to credit bureaus which provide them with information about people who have been bad credit risks in the past. When a person fails to pay his debts, must be sued, or is continuously slow in paying his bills, he is labeled a *poor credit risk*.

Good credit is a personal asset. *Asset* means sufficient property to pay debts. The credit bureau only records your performance. You must maintain it by using credit wisely and not using credit beyond your ability to pay.

Credit has been defined in a number of ways. An acceptable definition for credit is "a transaction where there is present an exchange of goods, services, or money with a promise to pay at a future time." Most people and business organizations use credit in some form. Consumer credit is an economic tool used by most of us to buy what we need today and pay for it when we are paid at the end of the month.

Some Predict That We Will Become a Moneyless Society

Credit is also important to big and small businesses, as well as local, state, and the federal government. The federal government probably uses more credit than any other organization. When you purchase a government bond you are extending your government credit as well as making an investment.

Purpose of Credit

Credit is an economic tool that serves not only the individual but business, industry, and government. Consumer credit makes it possible for the family to make purchases and pay for them over a period of time. For example, practically every family who enjoys a nice home must pay for it over a long period of time. It is difficult for an individual to buy a car without credit. Credit also provides a convenient way to buy by paying for all purchases with a check at the end of each month.

The use of consumer credit means much more to the manufacturer of consumer goods. By having credit available to the customers, it may be possible to sell them much more. With

These 6 C's Count for Credit

Character—a sincere attitude toward paying your bills.

Capacity—ability to repay loan from money coming in.

Capital—owning property or things worth more than your debt.

Conditions—agreements made in advance between lender and person borrowing.

Collateral—the possessions of any kind, which are set aside or deposited as security for the debt.

Common Sense—ability to use credit wisely.

sales assured, the manufacturer can take advantage of mass production techniques and produce goods at less cost which can be sold to the consumer at a saving. With low cost and good distribution, the average American family can enjoy the products of a productive economy.

The credit that a government offers makes many services and improvements possible. It is almost impossible for a city to install a new water system, or develop new streets, or build a school without credit.

Reasons for and
Against Credit

Reasons "For"	Reasons "Against"
It's convenient.	It's expensive.
You can use things while paying for them.	You may overspend.
You get better service.	You may not shop around as much.
It's handy in emergencies.	It's hard to understand.

Credit is necessary for most businesses to operate. A business uses commercial credit to cover the cost of producing and selling the product. Credit is needed to buy raw materials, enlarge facilities, and make improvements. The farmer uses credit to purchase farm equipment, seed, and perhaps more land. Many people need credit to start in business.

Where to Get Credit

Charging your purchases at the local grocery store is only one form of consumer credit. There are several others. Service credit is a good example of another form of consumer credit.

When Bill Smith picks up his telephone receiver and dials a long distance call to his mother, he is using *service credit*. The cost of the call is automatically recorded, and Bill will receive a bill for services at the end of the month. Even when he turns on an electric light, he is using service credit. *Service credit* is extended to practically everyone who is provided a utility such as gas, water, electricity and telephone service. Utility service is granted on the basis of confidence in the user that he will pay for the service he receives.

Another type of credit mentioned previously is *charge account credit*. This type of credit is offered to millions of persons to purchase gasoline for the car, pay for motel and hotel services, buy clothing, and other articles. Modern data processing techniques make it possible to use credit cards in handling billings and payment. Bank Americard, Master Charge, and Bankmark Card credit services have many additional purchases and services available through charge account credit.

This service demonstrates the confidence placed in the consumer as well as his responsibility in meeting his financial obligations.

Consumer credit is used to a large extent in buying more expensive things such as cars, furniture, and appliances. This type of credit is known as "installment credit." More than three-fourths of all purchases of durable goods are on an installment plan.

Many times it is necessary for a family to meet unforeseen expenses by borrowing money. This type of credit is known as personal loan credit and may be obtained a number of places. Banks provide small personal loan services at a reasonable interest rate. Those with a good credit rating have little difficulty getting small loans from banks. Credit unions lend money only to members. Interest is charged as a monthly rate on the unpaid balance. To join some credit unions, a person may pay as little as 25¢ per month. When he has deposited $5, he has a full share.

Personal finance and small loan companies require little or no collateral. Interest rates are higher since they must take a greater risk. Many states regulate the amount of interest that can be charged.

The truth-in-lending legislation passed by the U.S. Congress in 1967 requires that the lender tell the borrower total cost of the loan. This information will make it easier to compare cost of loan company services.

Pawnshop operators loan money on items of value, such as radios, watches, musical instruments, etc. Most pawnshop operators charge a high rate of interest for their services. If the loan isn't paid at a stated time, the owner of the pawnship may sell the item you leave.

Some lenders operate outside the law. It is illegal to charge more interest than the maximum set by laws of the state.

The Wise Use of Credit

A good money management plan includes guidelines for the wise use of credit. Making good judgments in buying and the wise use of credit are closely related. Too much credit may bankrupt a business or ruin a family's credit rating. Consumers can use credit wisely when they understand and follow three guidelines.

1. Use credit only when necessary or when the cost and risk can be justified.
2. Using your budget as a guide, assume no more debt than you can expect to repay from your present income.
3. Find the least expensive and most advantageous credit available.

Credit is always a risky thing to use. Should the head of a family lose his job, become ill, or be injured in an accident, it would probably not be possible to overcome a large debt.

The average person is not cautious enough in reading contracts and making judgments when using credit or installment buying. We usually think of the down payment price and of the amount of weekly or monthly payments. What we fail to do is to multiply and add quickly enough so we can determine the price of an article both with and without the installment purchase charges.

Stop Careless Spending

All family members old enough should watch their spending. Are dollars buying what the family wants most?

Are you spending more than you planned to? Are you spending too much on—

- daily needs such as food and clothing
- rent
- transportation—car or bus
- recreation

Do you have too many—

- insurance payments
- time payments.

The Federal Government has felt that credit buying was such a common but complicated procedure that it has issued the following information:

BUYING ON CREDIT

DO . . .

1. Read *each page* of contract or agreement. Be sure is says exactly what the salesman says. If it does not, DO NOT SIGN IT!
2. Know what the total cost will be to you when the payments are finished. That is, cost of item, carrying charges, cost of credit, and any other added charges.
3. Know that the price tag on an item is the price of the item *alone*. It does *not include* cost of credit, delivery charges, installation costs or any other added charges.
4. Be sure to compare prices. This means going to different stores comparing brands and prices.
5. Get in touch with legal services immediately when you are told that there was a mistake on the contract and you are asked to sign again. DO NOT SIGN!
6. Know that interest rates are very deceiving and hard to understand.

DON'T . . .

1. Sign your name to any contract or papers until you have talked with legal services.
2. Buy any item until you know the total amount it will cost you including credit and other charges.
3. Borrow money unless you have to. If you must borrow, try to borrow from a credit union or a bank. These two places charge less interest.
4. Allow fast-talking salesmen to talk you into buying anything you don't particularly want or need or cannot afford to pay for.
5. Allow salesman to leave anything at your house to "try out" if you do not want it. If they insist, tell them you

will not be responsible for it and don't sign your name
to anything.
6. Ever tell a salesman you can't afford an item. He will
   show you how you can afford it. Tell the salesman you
   don't want the item.
7. Buy from salesmen who tell you that you don't have
   to read the contract.
8. Buy anything on credit thinking you can pay for it
   by getting new customers for the salesman.
9. Be afraid to say *no* to a salesman.

Estimating Cost of Credit

Credit Financing

When payment on purchases extends over a long period of
time, the purchaser is charged for this time. This is expected,
because the purchaser is actually using the property of others
while making payments. When a salesman needs a car to do
sales work, it may be necessary to use the bank's money to
finance part of the cost. The salesman pays interest on the
loan. Practically any type of credit will cost the user. The cost
may not be noticeable but is added to the cost of the product.
For example, when you buy gasoline using a credit card, the
company must go to extra expense for billing and mailing. This
costs money and the added cost must be passed on to you, the
consumer.

When a merchant extends credit, he may experience costs
other than bookkeeping and billing. A few customers may be
unable to pay their debts. Thus, the merchant will have reduced
profits. A business expects a certain percent of profit. It also expects loss from bad debts but the loss must be recovered by pass-
ing it on to the consumer. Your credit cost in this case may be
slightly higher prices.

Many merchants operate on a cash basis. However, to be
competitive today and to stimulate sales for a larger business
volume, many merchants provide credit for their customers.
An open charge account may not be expensive if the total
charge is paid on a monthly basis. Should the sales items be

appliances, furniture, or automobiles, payment may extend over several months and a different sales plan is used.

When buying large items, such as television sets, radios, refrigerators, and furniture, payments may be made monthly. This type of credit is granted on a time payment basis and is referred to as *installment credit*. In this situation, the merchant may be unable to finance time payments and will seek assistance from a bank or other financial institution. The customer is expected to pay a carrying charge for purchases made on time.

TYPICAL CREDIT CHARGES

The charge for credit may be added to the beginning balance and the total repaid in 12 equal monthly payments.

When They Say	You Pay Annually
$ 6 per $100 or 6% per year	11.1%
$ 8 per $100 or 8% per year	14.8%
$10 per $100 or 10% per year	18.5%
1% per month	22.2%

When contract is paid in installments, the average amount owed is about one-half of the beginning balance. Thus, actual rate is approximately twice the stated rate.

The charge for credit may be based on unpaid balance.

Rate Per Month on Unpaid Balance	Annual Rate
5/6 of 1%	= 10%
1%	= 12%
1-1/2%	= 18%
3%	= 36%

For example, suppose Bill Smith buys a color television set for $400. He pays $100 down and writes a sales contract to pay the remaining $300 over a 12 month period with payments of $29 per month.

Figuring the Cost of Credit

When Bill Smith buys a television set on the installment plan, he will pay more than if he pays cash. The extra expense is a total of three extra costs:

1. Pure interest must be made on the unpaid balance of $300.
2. Losses from bad debts must be added to the cost of credit.
3. Administrative cost of bookkeeping, billing, and mailing must be also added.

Pure interest charged on the unpaid balance is regulated by laws of the various states. However, the charges made by department stores, finance companies, and banks may vary within a city or state.

The $300 unpaid part of the sale will cost Bill interest plus carrying charges. To figure how much it will cost Bill to use time payment instead of cash, use the following formula:

What Credit
Really Costs?

To Figure the Cost of Credit
1. Multiply the amount of each payment by the number of payments to be made on the television set.
2. Add the down payment to the total sum of the monthly payments.
3. Subtract the cash sale price of the television set from the sum of the down payment plus the total monthly payments. The amount will be the carrying charges Bill is paying.

Step I
Multiple the amount of each payment by the number of payments.

$$12 \times \$29 = \$348$$

Step II
Add the down payment.

$$\begin{array}{r} \$348 \\ \underline{100} \\ \$448 \end{array}$$

Step III
Subtract the cash price from the cost of the installment plan.

$$\begin{array}{r} \$448 \\ \underline{400} \\ \$\ 48 \end{array}$$

The cost of installment payments is $48.

When Bill Smith uses this simple formula, he finds the cost of his carrying charges. However, he needs to figure a constant rate of charge to compare cost with other financing plans.

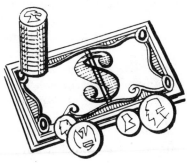

The largest part of the financing charge occurs in the administration of installment sales. Such costs include investigating the credit records of credit applicants, collecting the monthly payments, bookkeeping costs, and mailing. Automobiles sold on time payment must have the cost of insurance added, which increases the administrative cost.

It is easy to compare the cash price of a television set with the cost on the installment plan. However, Bill Smith is still unable to calculate the actual interest rate he is paying. The following formula may be used in finding what cost rate the consumer is actually paying on installment purchases. This formula allows Bill to figure the dollar charge for installment credit costs in terms of the annual percentage rate of credit used.

The formula used is written as follows:

$$CR = \frac{2NT}{B(n+1)}$$

N equals the *number of installment payment periods in one year* on a monthly or weekly basis (12 months or 52 weeks).

T is the *total amount of the financing charge* expressed in dollars and cents.

B represents the *unpaid balance* on which carrying charges will be made.

n equals the *number of payments* to be made in the contract.

When applied to Bill Smith's television purchase the following constant rate is found:

$$\text{Constant Rate (CR)} = \frac{2 \text{ x } 12 \text{ x } \$29}{300 \text{ x } 12 + 1} = \frac{696}{3900} = .178$$

Bill Smith is paying almost 18% carrying charge rate on the installment plan.

The percentage rates charged by different companies may not reflect a true situation. The rates charged by some companies seem quite high. One reason can be attributed to the large number of installment contracts with small sales. The administrative cost is the same for large or small accounts. Since the accounts vary in size, it is difficult to compare rates from company to company unless their credit granting situation is about the same. In Bill Smith's purchase of $400 with an unpaid balance of $300, the cost of administration was probably as expensive if he had purchased a $3000 automobile. Thus, in comparing percentage rates charged, it is necessary to know something of the service provided by the company making the sale. In the next sections we will examine ways in which costs may be compared.

Comparing Credit Charges and Interest Rates

In order to get the best rates on credit, it is necessary to know the sources of credit available. Rates may vary with the risk the company is willing to take in extending credit. Those with good credit ratings generally are able to get the best rates.

The sources of installment credit can be grouped under three classifications:

1. Retailers who finance and operate their own credit plans. This includes department stores, mail order houses, appliance dealers, and others.
2. Retailers who sell their customers' contracts to finance companies. This group includes auto dealers, farm machinery dealers, and appliance dealers.
3. Institutions which make loans directly to customers. These include banks, finance companies, credit unions, and others offering installment credit.

Rates vary among the sources making rates comparable. However, it is necessary to reduce all the rates to a common basis; that is, to compare the rates plus any other charge that is added to the contract. First, determine the complete cost. Some companies advertise low rates and add many other charges which should be added on before the percentage rate is computed for the credit. Second, it is important to learn if a full payment before maturity of the contract will result in reduction of interest and charges. A saving should be made if early payment is made.

After rates have been compared, services provided should also be considered. Some of the services to be considered are:

1. The ease of obtaining credit
2. The ease in making payments
3. Careful bookkeeping

4. The methods used in collecting
5. Whether the company provides low cost insurance on the automobile

After you have compared the rates of all sources of credit and the service provided by each, you are ready to decide if it is wise to use credit for the purpose you desire. You can buy for cash or buy on credit. When you buy on credit, you pay an extra charge. Whether the extra charge is called "service charge," "interest," "carrying charge," or "finance charge," it raises the cost of what you buy. This extra charge can keep you from buying other things you need. For example:

1. An appliance store advertises a refrigerator for $329.95. You can buy it on a 24-month installment contract with a $10 down payment, and you may pay as much as $65 extra for credit—enough to buy 260 quarts of milk.
2. A wool rug, including sales tax, sells for $420.00. Credit charges on a 24-month contract can cost you $180—enough to pay cash for a clothes dryer.

Comparisons on Cost of Credit to Finance Purchase of a $420 Rug for 24 Months

You may want to make similar comparisons before you buy. Costs vary with the institution, business, and State laws.

Item	Bank	Consumer Loan Co.	Dealer	Credit Union	Mail Order Store
Amount financed	$420.00	$420.00	$420.00	$420.00	$420.00
Monthly payments ...	19.95	25.00	19.60	19.75	20.44
Total time price	478.00	600.00	470.40	474.00	490.50
Finance charge	58.80	180.00	50.40	54.00	70.50
Actual annual rate ...	13.4%	36% to $300; 10% above	11.5%	12% on unpaid balance	16.1%

Using Credit

Before signing an installment contract or a note, it is wise to compare the benefits you will get from credit with the extra money it will cost.

Should Bill Smith pay the extra $48 for a television set now, or wait one year and pay cash? Of course no one can answer for Bill. Is a color television set worth an extra $48 cost?

Deciding when to use installment credit is easier when one looks at the following benefits. These benefits can be listed in five general categories.

1. There are benefits from increased earning power. Many businesses started by getting a loan and paying off the loan from monthly earnings from the business. Tom Jones, a high school student, bought a lawnmower on the installment plan after he had contracted with a number of homeowners to keep their lawns cut for the summer. Loans and installment purchases which increase earnings are considered worthwhile. Borrowing for educational purposes is also in this category.

2. Lowering expenses is beneficial and may make a loan worthwhile. If Bill Smith finds that a better car will reduce his car expenses, it may be wise to purchase a better car. He can enjoy driving a safer and more dependable car at the same expense.

3. It may be necessary to use installment credit in emergencies. Suppose the furnace suddenly burns out, or your car breaks down and it must be used to get to work. Many installment purchases are made under emergency conditions. When emergencies occur, such as sickness, accident, or failure of car or equipment, it is worthwhile to use installment credit.

4. Many times it is wise to leave your savings invested and make short-term installment purchases. For example, if Mary Smith had to use her savings in government bonds to replace a dryer in her beauty shop, she would save money by paying installment credit charges rather than lose interest on bonds. Stocks and bonds can be used for security in getting a short-term loan.

5. The final category of benefits to consider is earlier enjoyment of purchases. Generally, earlier enjoyment will be considered in terms of labor saving, time saving, greater convenience, and better family living conditions. Home appliances usually save labor and time. The purchase of

a home for greater convenience and family comfort can generally be justified when compared with the expense of paying rent.

In general, a person receives some benefit from installment credit. The worth of the benefit received must be judged on an individual basis. You will be using installment credit and should be familiar with the costs and problems involved. If you decide

KINDS OF CREDIT

that the benefits are worth the extra cost of an installment purchase, find the best terms available. Ask yourself the following questions before using credit:

1. Is having something now worth the extra cost?
2. Do I need it now?
3. What will I gain from it?
4. Can I meet the payments?
5. Is it worth the risk?
6. Will it help me make more money?
7. What will I give up while paying for it?
8. Am I paying too much in interest and carrying charges?
9. Am I dealing with a fair and honest lender?

If your answers to the questions are "yes" you are most likely prepared to use credit.

Types of Credit

Bank Credit

Most of us, at one time or another need to borrow money in the form of cash. The need for cash may come as a result of an emergency. It is wise to know how to borrow money when you need it.

Institutions who loan money include banks, credit unions, and small-loan companies. Banks have a simple method of making loans with little "red tape" involved. It may be possible to borrow up to $500 on your personal signature. You sign a single-signature promissory note for the amount loaned plus the interest you are requested to pay. The interest is deducted in advance in personal loans.

In obtaining a bank loan, it may be necessary to have a second person, or co-signer, sign your note. This provides the bank additional assurance that the loan will be repaid. In all other ways the co-maker loan and the single signature are the same. Both are promissory notes.

It is also possible to obtain a *collateral loan*. This is a loan in which you furnish stocks, bonds, and/or savings of equal value for security.

Interest rates paid on bank loans are generally lower than percentage rates paid on installment credit purchases or on installment loans.

Installment Loans

Small loan companies operate to provide loans from $20 up to $5000. The money may be repaid on the installment plan. This is the same as installment buying except the borrower receives cash instead of merchandise.

Many small loan companies advertise installment loans to consolidate the debts of the borrower. Should a person be unemployed or have other difficulties, he may borrow enough to pay all his bills and extend payments to the finance company as installments.

Small loan companies are licensed lenders and may charge up to $2\frac{1}{2}\%$ or 3% a month for $300 or less. Rates vary from state to state. Those who need to borrow money on installment should apply the constant rate formula to compare prices charged for the service.

Credit Union Loans

As mentioned earlier in this unit, credit unions provide credit for members only. Members may borrow small amounts without a co-signer or collateral. Rates vary, but generally an interest rate of 1% per month is charged on the actual balance of the debt.

Auto Loans

Loans to purchase automobiles may be secured at a number of places including banks, finance companies, and credit unions. Loans are made under the provisions of the uniform commercial code. Most people purchase their cars on the installment plan. It is important to carefully check the interest rates, insurance costs and other costs involved.

This order is subject to the approval of the Credit Sales Dept. of Sears, Roebuck and Co. There are to be no agreements regarding it, other than those mentioned below or attached hereto in writing.

Retail Installment Contract and Security Agreement

:ARS, ROEBUCK and CO. _____

Address of Store (Street Number, City, State and Zip Code)

_____
(Interviewer)

Date _March 13_ 19 70

I hereby order the following merchandise:

DIVISION	DESCRIPTION	PRICE
46	Kenmore Refrigerator	411 95

OFFICE USE ONLY			
☐ DEFERRED PAYMENT		TERMS CODE	C. LIFE
☐ EMPLOYE SALE	DATE	3	

CASH PRICE	411	95	411	95
CASH DOWN PAYMENT				
AMOUNT FINANCED			411	95
FINANCE CHARGE	124	00	124	00
DEFERRED PAYMENT PRICE	535	95		

TOTAL OF PYMTS.	THIS SALE >	535	95
EXISTING OUTSTANDING BALANCE			
TOTAL OF PYMTS.	NEW BAL. >	535	95

ng _April 8, 1970_, I will pay $ _16.25_ per month for _32_ month(s), and
ng _—_, I will pay $ _—_ per month for _—_ months and a
onthly payment of $ _15.95_ until the amount financed and the finance charge for each purchase is fully paid.

FINANCE CHARGE exceeds $5.00, the ANNUAL PERCENTAGE RATE is 20%, unless a different ANNUAL PERCENTAGE RATE is shown here [X] %

hip of the merchandise remains in Sears until paid for in full. My installment payments shall be applied as follows: In the case of items purchased on different dates, the first purchased shall be deemed first paid the case of items purchased on the same date, the lowest priced shall be deemed first paid for.

greement provides for a series of credit sales by Sears of merchandise and services for my personal, family or household use:

my subsequent purchases, you may charge a finance charge in accordance with your established terms. For **Easy Payment** purchases, I will pay a **FINANCE CHARGE** which will be an amount determined lying an **ANNUAL PERCENTAGE RATE** of 20% to the first $450.00 of the amount financed (or part thereof), 16.50% to the next $550.00 of the amount financed (or part thereof) and 5% to any amount financed in excess of $1,000.00. For **Modernizing Credit Plan** purchases, I will pay a **FINANCE CHARGE** which will be an amount determined by applying an **ANNUAL** :ENTAGE RATE of 14.75% to the amount financed.

accordance with Sears established terms, the finance charge will begin to accrue on my next billing cycle closing date and will be computed only on each new purchase, and the amount financed plus the finance of each new purchase will be added to my existing outstanding balance.

each item is fully paid for, I agree that: I have risk of loss or damage; I will not sell, transfer possession or remove or encumber the property without your written consent; upon default on the terms of this nent, you may declare my existing outstanding balance due and payable and you may repossess the property.

quency charge of 5%, but not more than $2.50 may be assessed once on each installment in default for 16 days or more.

e authorized to investigate my credit record and report to proper persons and bureaus my performance of this agreement.

CE TO BUYER: (1) DO NOT SIGN THIS CONTRACT BEFORE YOU READ IT OR IF IT CONTAINS BLANKS. (2) YOU ARE ENTITLED TO A COPY OF THIS CONTRACT. IT TO PROTECT YOUR LEGAL RIGHTS. (3) UNDER CERTAIN CONDITIONS, YOU MAY REDEEM THE PROPERTY IF REPOSSESSED FOR A DEFAULT OR REQUIRE A LE OF THE REPOSSESSED PROPERTY. (4) SELLER MAY NOT USE UNLAWFUL METHODS TO REPOSSESS THE PROPERTY. (5) IF YOU PAY IN FULL IN ADVANCE, ANY ARNED FINANCE CHARGE WILL BE REBATED UNDER THE RULE OF 78.

IPT OF A COPY OF THIS SECURITY AGREEMENT IS ACKNOWLEDGED:

OMER'S SIGNATURE_____

:ESS _123 Your Street_
Anywhere STATE _USA_ ZIP CODE _90101_

OMER'S _John_ _Q._ _Public_ WIFE'S NAME _Mary_
E (PRINT) FIRST / INITIAL / LAST / FIRST

FIRST PAYMENT DUE_____	
APPROVAL _____	
DATE _____	

683-KS   Rev. 12/69

Study the Kansas Motor Vehicle Installment Contract agreement as an example. Also study the copy of the Security agreement conditions which the purchaser should read before signing the contract.

Revolving Charge Account

The revolving charge account credit plan offered by large department stores, mail order companies, and other retailers

DATE	DIV.	CASH P.	c/c	NEW BAL.	PMT.	CODE

SEARS REVOLVING CHARGE ACCOUNT AND SECURITY AGREEMENT

SEARS, ROEBUCK AND CO.
In consideration of your selling merchandise and services for personal, family or household purposes to me on my Sears Revolving Charge Account I agree to the following regarding all purchases made by me or on my Sears Revolving Charge Account Identification.

1. I have the privilege of a 30-day Charge Account, in which case I will pay the full amount of all purchases within 25 days from the date of each billing statement.

2. If I do not pay the full amount for all purchases within 25 days from the date of each billing statement, the following terms shall be in effect:
(A) I will pay the Deferred Payment Price for each item purchased consisting of:

(1) The cash sale price, and

(2) The **FINANCE CHARGE,** which will be the greater of (a) a minimum charge of 50¢ or (b) an amount determined by applying a periodic rate of 1.5% per month to the first $800.00 of previous balance or part thereof and an amount determined by applying a periodic rate of 1.0% per month to any part of the previous balance in excess of $800.00. If the **FINANCE CHARGE** exceeds 50¢, the **ANNUAL PERCENTAGE RATE** will be 18% on the first $800.00 of previous balance and 12% on that part of the previous balance in excess of $800.00.

(B) I will pay for all purchases in monthly installments which will b[e] puted according to the following schedule:

If the unpaid balance is:	The scheduled monthly payment will be:	If the unpaid balance is:	The sched[uled] monthly pay[ment] will be[:]
$ .01 to $ 10.00	Balance	$300.01 to $350.00	$30.0[0]
10.01 to 150.00	$10.00	350.01 to 400.00	35.0[0]
150.01 to 200.00	15.00	400.01 to 450.00	40.0[0]
200.01 to 250.00	20.00	450.01 to 500.00	45.0[0]
250.01 to 300.00	25.00	Over $500.00	1/10 of accou[nt]

I will pay each monthly installment computed according to the schedule as above upon receipt of each statement. If I fail to pay any installment when due, you may, at your option, take back the merchandise or affirm t[he] and hold me liable for the full balance on my account which shall be imme[diately] due. Ownership of the merchandise purchased on this account shall rem[ain] Sears until I have paid the purchase price in full. My installment payment[s] be applied as follows: in the case of items purchased on different dates, th[e] purchased shall be deemed first paid for; in the case of items purchased [on the] same date, the lowest priced shall be deemed first paid for. I have risk [of loss] or damage to merchandise.

(C) You are to send me a statement each month which will show the balance for purchases, the Finance Charge, and the amount of the n[ext] installment coming due.

(D) I have the right to pay all or any portion of my account in advance.

3. You are authorized to investigate my credit record and report to prop[er per]sons and bureaus my performance of this agreement.

NOTICE TO BUYER: (1) DO NOT SIGN THIS CONTRACT BEFORE [YOU] READ IT OR IF IT CONTAINS BLANKS. (2) YOU ARE ENTITLED [TO A] COPY OF THIS CONTRACT. KEEP IT TO PROTECT YOUR LEGAL RI[GHTS] (3) YOU HAVE THE RIGHT TO PAY IN ADVANCE THE FULL AMOUNT [DUE.] RECEIPT OF A COPY OF THIS SECURITY AGREEMENT IS ACKN[OWL]EDGED:

_____
(CUSTOMER'S SIGNATURE)

F15206-13 (REV. 7-1-69) DATE_____

The Revolving Charge Account Is Used by Department Stores—the Amount and Cost of Credit Is Agreed Upon at the Start of the Account (Courtesy Sears, Roebuck and Company)

is popular with consumers today. Plans used by different companies vary in rates and agreements, but all follow the same general plan.

The customer who buys goods on credit is given the privilege of a 30-day charge account or may extend the payments on a monthly plan. Contracts, conditions, rates charged, amounts which can be purchased, and payment information are printed on the contract.

Interest and charge rates are regulated by state laws. Rates charged may vary from one company to another, but charges are under the maximum set by law. A number of states permit

(PLEASE PRINT)		ACCOUNT NUMBER		LIMIT	DATE OPENED
hn Q. Public	7			60	3-13-70
23 Your Street	INTERVIEWER		AUTHORIZER	RES. 254-1198	PHONE NUMBER
uy where , USA 90101			DATE:	BUS. 235-1700	

AGE ___36___   1. John Q. Public
OWN ☒ MARRIED ☒   DEPENDENTS __w + 3__   2. Mary Public
RENT ☐ SINGLE ☐   WIFE'S NAME __Mary__   3. _____
BOARD ☐ WIDOWED ☐   HOW LONG AT PRESENT ADDRESS ___12 yrs___

R Sheffield Steel Corp   ADDRESS Anywhere , USA   HOW LONG 14 yrs
ION __Engineer__   TIME CARD OR BADGE NUMBER 7501   EARNINGS $ 4200   WK. ☐ MO. ☒
EMPLOYER (IF LESS THAN R WITH PRESENT EMPLOYER)   HOW LONG _____
OF BANK First National Bank, Anywhere, USA   CHECKING ☒
OTHER IF ANY Rental Property $ 100 per month   SAVINGS ☒
ADDRESS (IF LESS THAN RS AT PRESENT ADDRESS)   HOW LONG _____   LOAN ☒

CES BELOW ARE TO BE FILLED IN WHEN THE MERCHANDISE ORDERED IS TO BE ATTACHED TO THE PROPERTY.
S WHERE MATERIAL INSTALLED _____ COST OF PROPERTY $ _____ AMOUNT OF MORTGAGE $ _____
F PERSON LEGAL TITLE _____ NAME AND ADDRESS OF MORTGAGE HOLDER _____

PREVIOUS SEARS ACCOUNTS		CREDIT REFERENCE	DATE OPENED	HIGH CREDIT	BALANCE DATE CLOSED	AMOUNT PAYMENTS	HOW PAID
☐	S.R.C. ☐	1. United Finance Anywhere, USA	9/65	1,500	5/68	46 00	I-1
DATE ___ LIMIT ___		2. Boyer Furniture Your City, USA	2/62	700	1/65	19 50	I-1
ACCT. NO. ___		3. First National Bank Anywhere, USA	1/60	3,000	500	50 00	I-1
E.P.	S.R.C.	4. Wilburs Department Store Anywhere, USA	10/66	195	160	15 00	R-1
IED							
T		5.					
ALANCE ED							
PAYMENTS							
DELINQUENT							

add-on rates of 17% to 20% a year. Study the "Sears Revolving Charge Account and Security Agreement," a sales contract used to familarize customers with conditions, rates, etc. of their revolving charge account.

Those who wish to take advantage of charge account purchases are required to make application and furnish the company with needed information. Study the example of an application form used for this purpose.

Home Loans

Many young men and women look forward to the time when they can own their own home. There has been a definite trend toward individual ownership for the last 20 years. Few families have the money to pay cash for a home; thus, a long term loan is needed.

Housing loans are available from a number of financial institutions including banks, building and loan companies, insurance companies, mortgage companies, and private investors. The rates and contract terms offered by lending agencies differ to some extent, but operate under the laws of the state regulating sales of real estate.

Buying a home is a major financial step for a family and should be undertaken only after careful study and advice from knowledgeable people. Perhaps the most important thing to consider is the family's ability to take on such a financial obligation. Before considering anything else, it is necessary to make this decision. There is no one "pat" answer to this question. However, if a family is able to meet all present expenses and save money out of the present income, chances are good it will be possible to buy a home.

The size of the financial obligation a family should assume in buying a home is not easy to decide. A general guideline is to limit the debt to two times the family's yearly income or the monthly payment should be no larger than 25% of the take home pay of the head of the house. However, this figure may vary depending on the individual family situation.

A down payment is required, and the amount of the down payment will vary with the cost of the home and the institution making the loan.

The Federal Housing Administration, established in 1939, aids prospective home buyers by insuring mortgage loans made by approved private institutions. The financial protection provided to lending agencies makes it possible for them to finance home mortgages at a lower rate of interest and a lower down payment. The monthly payment is generally equal to rent for a comparable house, and maturity of the mortgage is long term. One of the main advantages of an FHA loan is the assistance the buyer gets in an inspection of the house and lot by experts in the field.

Before the contract to buy a home is signed, an attorney should be employed to examine the contract and deed for validity, back taxes, etc.

WHEN YOU USE CONSUMER CREDIT

- Do you ask yourself this: "Is having this item *now* worth the added credit costs?"

- Do you know the sources of consumer credit in your community?

- Do you shop around to find where the credit rate is the lowest and most convenient?

- More important, do you have a credit rating that labels you as an outstanding credit risk?

- Do the items you buy on installment last far beyond the time the last payment is made?

- Do you make as large a down payment as possible without upsetting the family budget?

- Do you pay it off as quickly as possible without making the budget too tight?

- How does your decision fit into your family's budget and plans?

- Are you sure you can meet this payment, plus all other monthly expenses?

Study Helps

New Terms

balance	credit risk	default
borrower	credit rating	repossession
collateral	creditor	principal
contract	charge account	truth-in-lending
credit	installment	per annum
credit charge		

Study Questions

1. How would you define the word "credit"?
2. What is the difference between a bank and a credit union?
3. Suppose that you plan to buy a TV set which costs $300. The dealer has agreed to accept $100 as down payment with the balance paid in $25 per month payments with a carrying charge of 18% per annum on the unpaid balance. What will be the total cost of the television in the eight months payment period? Now suppose that the dealer tells you he gives a 10% discount for cash sales, and you decide to deposit the installment payments each month in a savings account paying 5% per annum interest. When your account totaled $300 and you paid cash for the TV set, how much would you have saved?

Chapter 11

Contracting for Goods and Services

Wherever people live together, it is necessary for them to develop rules of conduct. Without rules, there are no guidelines to follow in dealing with one another. Laws are a set of rules that government enforces through the courts and other agencies. You have heard people say, "It is against the law." This means it is against the rules of the country or community to do certain acts. Laws are made by men to meet conditions of the time. New laws are made each year, others are repealed (revoked). Laws make it possible for people to live together peacefully.

There are two major classifications of laws: public law and civil law. Public law includes constitutional law, international law, administrative law, and criminal law. *Public laws* are passed to regulate the relationships between individuals and the government. *Private law* and *civil law* include the rules that regulate the relationship among people and is concerned with contracts, real estate, and personal injury.

You probably have heard more about criminal law. However, more court action and lawyers' time is spent in civil law cases. Young people know it is against the law to steal, or commit crimes of violence against other people, but they may not know much about the laws concerned with contracts, personal injury or real estate.

The Use of Legal Advice

Laws vary from state to state. However, most states have adopted a uniform commercial code which deals with sales and contracts. The code standarizes laws, making them similar in all states. It is good business to secure the services of an attorney for legal advice on important problems. This is especially true where a complicated contract or will is to be written.

It must be remembered that questions given to a lawyer will be answered in the form of an opinion. It is not wise for a lawyer to give a definite statement since all the circumstances may not be known and a higher court may later reverse the lower court decision.

Contracts

In our modern society, there is an increasing need to depend on others for the necessities of life. When dealing with people we often make promises that are legal obligations enforceable through court action. In fact, many of these promises are legal contracts. Thus, it is important for the young worker to understand the legal aspects of entering into a contract.

A contract is an agreement between two or more competent parties which makes an enforceable obligation. Should one party fail to keep the agreement, the other party may take the case to court for enforcement.

Contracts may result from informal or formal action. *Informal contracts* are made when you make purchases of clothing at the local store, have clothes cleaned at the dry cleaner, or have your shoes repaired at the shoe shop. Other contracts, such as purchasing real estate, are *formal transactions* and may require legal assistance in drawing up the agreement and checking the accuracy of ownership. Some agreements relate to personal matters for practical purposes and are not enforceable by the courts.

Certain elements are necessary in order for a contract to be valid and enforceable by law. These essentials are as follows:

1. Mutual assent. There must be an offer and acceptance.
2. Competent parties. All parties must be legally qualified to make enforceable contracts.

3. Legal agreement. The purpose must be lawful.
4. Consideration. There must be something of value exchanged between the parties to make the contract binding.
5. Legal form. Most contracts must be in writing to be enforceable.

LEGAL QUESTIONS

The answer to each of these questions is "YES":

1. Is a contract binding if it is signed without being read?
2. Is a contract binding if you sign it just to get rid of a persistent salesman?
3. Is a contract binding if you misunderstand part of it?
4. Is an installment sale agreement a contract?
5. Must a contract to purchase real estate be in writing?

The answer to each of these questions is "NO":

1. Is a contract binding if it involves breaking the law?
2. Is a contract binding if it is entered into under pressure or threat?
3. Is an agreement of a boy 14 years of age to buy a bicycle binding?
4. Is it necessary to sign a written order for the purchase of a suit of clothes in order for the contract to be binding?
5. Are you obligated to return or pay for merchandise sent to you that you did not order?

Element One: Mutual Assent

In every contract there is an offer and an acceptance. Mutual assent takes place between the parties when they are in complete agreement on the terms of the contract. At law, this is called "the meeting of the minds," meaning that both parties understand and are willing to enter into the agreement. Under the principles of law, a contract is not valid unless the parties freely and intentionally agree. Thus, to determine the validity of an offer, a three-item test can be used:

1. Is the offer made with the obvious intention of the first party (the offeror) to enter into legal agreement with the party accepting the offer?
2. Is the offer clear and definite?
3. Has the offer been properly communicated by words or actions to the party accepting?

Let's see how this test applies. Advertisements in newspapers have not been legally considered offers since the dealer may not be in a position to sell his product to everyone. It is apparent that the dealer cannot be required or does not intend to enter into a purchase contract with everyone who may want to purchase his product. He may point out this fact in his advertisement with the words, "quantities limited," or "dealer reserves the right to limit sales."

An offer must be clear and definite in order to be considered a legal contract. For example, Mr. Jones, a farmer, had 50 riding horses for sale; and he told Mr. Smith that he would sell him a horse for $150. Mr. Jones had horses priced from $150 to $300. However, Mr. Smith understood he could take any one of the horses. This offer was not properly communicated and so was not a legal contract to sell a specific horse.

Terminating (ending) an offer can be accomplished in several ways. Most frequently, it is terminated in a stated length of time or at a given date. If no time to terminate the offer is stated, it is good for a "reasonable period of time." An offer also is terminated upon the death of the offeror. The offer may be withdrawn at any announced time in cases of rewards. Withdrawal of any offer may be made if the offer has not been accepted in the specified or "reasonable" period of time.

Acceptance of an offer may be by direct communication or by mail. When an acceptance of an offer is made by mail, the contract is not made until the offeror receives the letter of acceptance from the offeree—except in the case where the offer was communicated by mail.[1]

Element Two: Competent Parties

For a contract to be valid, the parties making a contract must be considered competent. This means that the person involved must have the ability to fully understand the extent of his rights and obligations in the matter. Certain individuals are prevented by law from making enforceable contracts. The various state laws define who is competent to make contracts.

Among those considered not competent under the law are minors. A minor is a person who has not reached a specified age which is considered in his state to be the age of full maturity with the ability to make judgments. In most states anyone under the age of 21 years old is not considered competent and may not enter into legal contracts. Usually the contracts made by minors are voidable (may be broken) by the minor. However, when an agreement is made with an adult, the adult is required to fulfill the terms of the agreement if it is a legal contract. The privilege to cancel contracts is given only to the minor, and the adult party to the contract must carry out his part of the contract.

AGE OF MAJORITY (BECOMING OF AGE)

(Minimum legal age to make a contract)

18 years for women and 21 years for men in Arkansas, Idaho, Illinois, Montana, Nevada, North Dakota, Oklahoma, South Dakota, and Utah

18 years for men and women in Kentucky

19 years for men and women in Alaska

20 years for men and women in Hawaii

21 years for men and women in all other states

---

[1] In this case, the U.S. Post Office is the offeror's "agent," and the contract is binding as soon as the acceptance is dropped in the mailbox.

Bill Brown, a 14 year old high school student, ordered a $36 radio kit through the Jones Appliance Store. When the kit finally arrived, the price had gone up to $46; and the dealer requested that Bill pay the $46 or return the kit. Legally, Mr. Jones was required to deliver the kit at the price stated in the contract. However, Bill could have refused to honor his agreement because he was a minor.

Although a minor may cancel many of his contracts, he or his parents will be obligated on contracts for purchases of things the minor actually needs to sustain life. The law generally considers necessities to include food, clothing, shelter, and medical attention. Some exceptions will arise. Johnny, a 14 year old freshman, purchased an expensive leather jacket from the local sports clothing store. Since Johnny's parents had already bought him several jackets, this jacket was not actually needed and it could not be considered a necessity. The store was forced to accept the return of the jacket and refund the full amount of the purchase.

The minor is responsible for medical attention. In an emergency case where a minor requires medical attention, the physician and hospital can collect any money due for services offered.

Contracts for luxuries are voidable by the minor, although the adult may be obligated by the contract. The problems arising from voidable contracts made by the minor have prompted merchants to ask parents of minors to countersign contracts for purchases. Many department stores have established charge accounts for minors countersigned by the parents. This practice reduces the problem of voidable contracts on the part of minors.

Many contract problems have been caused when a minor deliberately misrepresents his age to purchase a car or other articles. In such cases the adult may hold the minor liable for deceit and collect money and damages for the loss. Laws differ from state to state in dealing with this problem. Most merchants prevent these situations and protect themselves by demanding proof of age. Idenification cards, driver's licenses, and draft cards are used for this purpose.

When a person does not have the mental ability to understand the nature of contracts, he may be declared incompetent in a court of law. In addition to those who are mentally deficient, persons intoxicated when the contract was made, and insane persons may be declared incompetent by the court. Contracts made with such people are not enforceable.

Element Three: The Legal Purpose

To be valid, a contract must not be contrary to the law or to the interest of society. The terms of any agreement which are illegal or are harmful to the public health or morals are in fact not a contract because they are not enforceable. Examples of illegal agreements include those involving agreement to steal or to accept stolen goods. Agreements dealing with gambling or wagering are illegal in most states. Should you make a bet with someone and win, it is not possible to take legal action to collect the money won since the agreement is not legal. In a few states where betting on dog and horse racing has been legalized, winnings could be collected if the bets were made according to state law.

It is also illegal to enter into agreement to give false testimony or obstruct justice for a fee. Such agreements do not meet the requirements of being lawful.

In many cities and states certain business, craft, and professional men are licensed to practice or perform work. Contracts with individuals or firms without required licenses are not valid. For example, an unlicensed electrician contracts to install the wiring in a house you are building. You later learn the city will not provide you service until the job is approved by an inspector. The inspector will not approve work done by an unlicensed electrician. Thus, your contract is void.

All states have established maximum interest rates which may be charged the borrower. Charging interest beyond the maximum contract rate is called *usury* and is illegal. Penalties for usury vary, but in some states the penalty may call for the forfeiture of both the principal and the interest of the contract loan.

Recent legislation passed by Congress, known as "truth in lending legislation," clarifies some of the problems concerned with usury laws.

Element Four: Consideration

In order to be enforceable, a contract must be an agreement by which one party agrees to do something; and the other party agrees to do something of value in return. What either party agrees to do in return for the promise received is known as *consideration*. For example, Mr. Smith agreed to permit the electrical company to run a line across a part of his farm. When Mr. Smith signed the agreement (contract) to permit the erection of the power line, he received $1 as consideration. Although Mr. Smith would profit indirectly from having the power line installed, the consideration was necessary to make the contract legal. Consideration is not always in the form of money. It may include services, goods, or a promise to refrain from doing something one has the legal right to do.

Element Five: Legal Form

A contract may be informal or formal. Many contracts are simple and informal, and few of such contracts would involve the exchange of much money. Problems arising in making informal contracts may be resolved without court action. Other contracts, such as the purchase of real estate, must be formal—for they involve the exchange of large amounts of money for buildings and land.

Contracts may be either written or oral. In the sale of goods priced at less than $500, an oral agreement is enforceable. The nature of some transactions require written contracts. A contract for labor and materials is not always in writing, but a written contract helps to avoid misunderstandings.

Certain contracts are required by law to be writing. These contracts include the following:

1. An installment credit or purchase contract.
2. A contract to sell or buy real estate, including buildings, land, mineral rights, and trees.
3. A contract to guarantee the debt of another person in case of default or ligation.
4. An agreement to sell personal property valued at over $500 (amount and conditions may vary in different states).

5. An agreement that is not to be performed within a year from the date it is made.

Contracts are not required to be written in any particular form. However, to be legal, they should include:

1. The date and place of the agreement.
2. The names and addresses of the parties entering into the agreement.
3. A statement of the purpose.
4. A statement of the amount of money, goods, or services given in consideration of the agreement.
5. The signatures of parties or their legal agents.
6. Signatures of witnesses when required by law in certain transactions.

Preparing Contracts

Problems result when people enter into agreements when there is a misunderstanding on the part of one or both parties. Sometimes fraud is involved. In any event, when entering into an important contractual agreement, be extremely cautious in signing contracts. The following suggestions are made for making contracts:

1. When the contract is complex or of sufficient importance, it should be prepared by an attorney-at-law.
2. Read the contract carefully before signing. Be sure the terms and amounts of money listed are accurate.
3. If part of the contract is in small print and you are unable to understand, ask your attorney for help.
4. Always get a copy of what you sign with the signature of the other party, and file it in a safe place, preferably a bank box.
5. Any change made in the terms of the contract should be signed by both parties.

Defective Contracts

When a contract is found to be defective, it cannot be enforced. Such contracts are classified as void or voidable and may be broken by either party. A contract may be void under the following conditions:

1. When a contract is made by compulsion through threats or by violence.
2. When terms of the contracts are fraudulent, misrepresenting the actual situation.
3. When a clearly proven mistake has been made.

When to See a Lawyer

Only a small percent of our population breaks the law and requires an attorney for a court defense. Nevertheless, a family with honest intentions may get into legal difficulties. Most everyone needs the services of a lawyer sometime during his lifetime. Let's look at some of the occasions when you may need legal advice.

Just about every young family looks forward to buying a home. The purchase of real estate may be the first time you need a lawyer.

Many real estate agents encourage the buyer to engage a lawyer to examine the legal papers that are involved in buying real estate. The contract and mortgage papers will need to be examined. Help is needed to determine if the property is free of back taxes and liens. How is the property ownership to be listed. You should ask your lawyer if you and your wife should hold the property you purchase in joint tenancy, or tenants in common, or otherwise. Your lawyer knows the laws in the state in which you live and can explain the advantages and disadvantages of the several ways to hold property.

If you are not married, you may hold property in your own name and have none of the problems of joint holdings. Some may think that joint tenancy will take the place of a will. However, this may not be to the advantage of you or your family. A lawyer is needed to help you select the type of property holding best for your situation.

Suppose you have decided to buy a home and the real estate agent asks you to make a down payment. Be sure you have a written statement from the seller that the down payment will be returned to you if either of you fail to go through with the deal. Otherwise, you will probably have to forfeit your deposit.

Some of the things a buyer of real estate should carefully check are listed below.

1. Is the selling price firmly fixed in the terms of the contract? Contracts for new or remodeled houses may contain a clause that will permit the contractor to add increased cost. If such an escalator clause is acceptable, be sure you can meet the additional costs.
2. Terms describing the down payment and remainder of the cost must be established to your satisfaction.
3. The contract should state the date on which you may have possession without a penalty or returning your money.
4. Be sure you have a clear title and learn what restrictions are placed on the property. Back taxes and any liens for work on the property should be paid by the seller before the contract is signed. A lawyer's fee here may save you much trouble and money.
5. The contract should state who is responsible for the property during the time between contract date and possession date.
6. Be sure the contract states the seller's responsibility for the function of heating, air conditioning, and plumbing, especially if you are buying a new house. Also, included in the contract should be the builder's responsibility for expected function of all parts of the house (roof, doors, walks, etc.) for a given length of time after occupancy.
7. If you are contracting for a new house, be sure you have in writing conditions under which you or the builder can change plans or materials.
8. It is unwise to sign a contract with an escape clause for the builder.
9. Sign your contract after your lawyer has checked the terms and given you his opinion.

Young people need legal protection and assistance in making important contracts.

Take the case of James Young, a recent technical school graduate, who was working for City Electric, a company located about two miles from James' home.

Since there was no bus service to the plant and little chance of James finding a ride with fellow workers, James decided he would need a reliable car. James couldn't afford to spend much money for a car. After looking over his budget for the year, he decided $500 was all he could spend for a car.

James looked at several cars during the evenings and finally found a clean-looking car at "Jack's Quality Cars," a used car lot on Broadway. The price of the car seemed lower than others of the same brand, style, and age. The salesman mentioned that he had just bought the car from a boy who needed the money to start to college, and that he could sell the car to James at a lower price.

James should have been more cautious, but what appeared to be such a good deal was hard to pass up.

James started the car easily and drove it a few blocks. Everything seemed to be functioning properly. However, the transmission did seem to slip slightly. He knew that the car should be checked by his friend, Roger, who was an expert mechanic at Westside Motors. However, it was Saturday afternoon, the service department was closed at Westside Motors, and Roger had gone to visit his brother in another city.

The salesman had the contract ready for James to sign when he returned from the drive. James paid the $100 down and signed the contract which required 12 additional payments of $55 each. The payments included charges for credit, insurance and taxes for the year.

The following Monday, James drove his car to work. The car ran smoothly and functioned perfectly.

James' trouble started on the way home. The car seemed to lose power when accelerated to pass a truck. Something smelled hot. Then there was a ripping sound in the automatic transmission. James' car lost all power, and he was forced to pull off to the side of the road.

He called Roger, who drove out and looked at the car. It didn't take Roger long to see what the trouble was. The transmission was ruined.

The car was towed to the garage and the transmission was further examined. Roger estimated that it would cost $225 to replace the transmission. James called Jack, the used car dealer, and was told that at the low price James paid for the car, he shouldn't expect any guarantee that the transmission wouldn't fail.

James didn't have $225 to replace the transmission. In desperation he called his father for advice. His father suggested that he bring the contract by for his lawyer to examine.

When Mr. Walker, the lawyer, read the contract, he knew that James had failed to read it in detail. The salesman at Jack's Quality Cars had typed in, "This vehicle sold as is." James had signed the contract which released the seller of any responsibility.

Mr. Walker called James' father and explained the mistake made in signing the contract in the first place. James had lost his rights as a buyer by signing a contract containing such a clause. James had given up his right to expect any warranty on the car. He was stuck with a $225 repair job and a $600 debt on the car. Things looked bad for James, who was 21 years old and could not disaffirm the contract on the basis of age.

Roger's discovery when he removed and disassembled the transmission saved James part of the loss. It was discovered that the transmission had been burned out recently and was patched up in order to function for a few more miles. When confronted with this information, Jack offered to give James a serviceable transmission to replace the ruined one. However, James still had to pay the labor cost for the repair job.

Practically everyone is involved in contracts each week. Most of our contracts involve only a small amount of money and are implied. For example, when you buy a can of tuna at the supermarket, the clerk checks your purchase and rings it up on the cash register. The contract is simple; you accept the offer to buy a can of tuna at 49¢ and pay for it. In return for the money you paid, the supermarket promises the tuna to be safe for edible purposes. Should the contents be spoiled, replacement or return of your money is expected.

When large sums of money are used in contracts, and formal procedures are used, you may need a lawyer to protect you. The small cost of legal assistance is a good investment and may save you considerable time and money.

Study Helps

New Terms

law	commercial code	reverse
contract	enforceable obligation	legal opinion
consultation	formal transaction	competent
voidable	mutual assent	valid
countersign	termination of offer	communicated
usury	binding contract	necessity
hazardous	ligation	consideration

Study Questions

1. What are the different classifications of laws?
2. What type of law requires the most legal consultation and court action?
3. When should legal advice be obtained?
4. What are the essential elements of a valid contract?
5. Who is considered incompetent and unable to enter into a contract agreement?
6. Is an advertisement considered to be a legal offer?
7. What items are considered necessities in a contract? What are luxuries?
8. Is a minor responsible for emergency medical attention costs?
9. Is it legal for a minor to make purchases using his father's credit card?
10. What are four types of considerations that may be used in a contract?
11. Can a merchant legally collect a bill made by an intoxicated person?
12. Under what conditions can a gambling debt be legal?
13. What types of contracts are legally required to be in writing?

14. When can an unlicensed craftsman be refused payment for work performed?
15. What are five suggestions that can be made to persons preparing and/or signing a contract?
16. Under what conditions can a contract be declared defective?
17. Under what conditions can a sales contract be oral?

Discussion Problems

1. It is necessary to revise laws occasionally because they are no longer appropriate. Can you think of a law that has been changed since the Constitution was written? Do you know of any law that has been changed in your town? Why were these changes made?
2. Imagine that you are a lawyer, and you have been asked if a certain contract is legal and can be enforced. What points will you study in the contract to help you decide if it is valid?
3. When should you ask a lawyer to examine a contract?
4. What can you do to avoid legal problems?

Chapter 12

Using Bank Services

Two hundred years ago few people needed to know much about banking. In the agricultural society of that day, most of the population lived on farms and paid for goods and services with cash or by the barter system. There was little need for substitutes for money as there is today. In our modern complex society practically everyone who earns or handles money will need the services of banks. Many payments of bills for goods and services cannot be paid over the counter. A check must be used. For example, if you wish to order a clock from a mail order business, you will need to use a substitute for money. In this case, it would probably be a personal check. The check would provide a means of safe transit for the money and also provide a receipt for your records.

Our national system of banks provides us with this service. Without such a system, it would be very difficult to operate our industries and businesses.

Since you will need to have some knowledge and skill in using banking services, this unit is prepared to provide you with useful information needed to develop skill and knowledge.

Banking Institutions

Banks are business firms specializing in the transfer of money and credit. They are authorized by state or federal

governments to perform a certain financial function, such as:
1. To receive deposits of money subject to withdrawal by depositors,
2. Make loans to customers,
3. Pay interest to depositors, and
4. Invest money.

There are several types of banks. However, only one type may be of prime interest since it is the type used by most people in managing their money. It is called a *commercial bank*. The main functions of a commercial bank are:
1. To receive deposits of money,
2. To loan money to individuals and businesses.

Another type of bank is the savings bank, known as a *savings and loan association*. A savings bank accepts deposits of money, and it loans or arranges credit to business, industry, and governments who borrow large amounts of money.

A *trust company* is authorized to administer trust funds and serve as administrators of the estates of deceased persons. Some banks are authorized to serve as trust companies and also

The Modern Bank Is Designed and Located with Parking and a Drive-In Window for the Convenience of the Customer. (Courtesy of The National Bank of Pittsburg, Kansas)

to carry on regular banking functions. Present trends indicate that more banking institutions are being chartered (given authority) to perform commercial, savings, and trust functions.

Bank Classification

Banks are classified on the basis of their authorization either by state or federal goverment.

State Bank

A state bank is organized as a corporation and is chartered by the state in which it operates. A state bank may be a commercial bank, a savings bank, or a trust company. State banks may also be members of the Federal Reserve System.

The Interior of a Modern Bank Is Both Spacious and Pleasant
(Courtesy of The National Bank of Pittsburg, Kansas)

National Bank

A national bank is organized as a corporation and chartered by the federal government. National banks are subject to federal banking laws and regulation of the Federal Reserve System.

The Federal Reserve System

By 1913, the population and economy of the United States had grown so large that the Congress enacted a law to standardize banking practice and improve the banking service. This act was known as the *Federal Reserve Act*. This act established the Federal Reserve system which organized the country into 12 geographical banking districts. In each district there is a Federal Reserve bank. The functions of the 12 Federal Reserve banks are co-ordinated by a seven-member Board of Governors. The members of the Board of Governors are appointed by the President of the United States. Each district Federal Reserve bank is managed by a nine-member Board of Directors. Six members are elected by the member banks in the district, and three members are appointed by the Board of Governors.

The Federal Reserve system has five important functions, which are:

1. Holding of reserves of member banks;
2. Supplying the needs of member banks for cash;
3. Controlling the volume of bank credit extended by banks in the United States;
4. Acting as a clearing house for checks of member banks;
5. Providing fiscal services for the United States Goverment.

Federal Deposit Insurance Corporation

Under the present FDIC plan, all national banks and state banks that are members of the Federal Reserve system are required to insure their deposits with the Federal Deposit Insurance Corporation. The deposits of an individual are insured to a maximum of $15,000, which provides needed protection for the small depositor.

Use of Checking Account

One of the most useful and important functions provided by a bank is the checking service. This service provides you with a substitute for cash. Although it is possible to pay local bills and make local purchases with cash, most people must maintain a checking account to pay out-of-town bills and to keep their money in a safe place. It is not safe to send cash through the mail or to keep large amounts of cash in the home. Thus, maintaining a checking account is an important service to those managing money.

Opening a Checking Account

Opening a checking account is a very simple procedure. First, you visit the bank of your choice and introduce yourself to an officer of the bank. You will probably be interviewed by the cashier or someone assigned to meet new depositors. You will be required to sign a signature card using the signature you will use on all checks written on your account. You may also be assigned a depositor's number which is written on each check you write. You are now ready to deposit your money.

Most banks provide a deposit slip which you prepare in duplicate; one copy is retained by the bank and the other copy by you.

Checking accounts may be opened as individual accounts or joint accounts, depending on the needs of the person or persons starting the checking account.

Making Bank Withdrawals

Great care should be exercised in writing a check. It is important to write clearly and be sure the check is accurate before releasing it. All checks should be written in ink, which

Authorizing Resolution

This certifies that on 20th day of *May,* 19 7 0   a meeting of the directors of

---

adopted a resolution authorizing those officers whose names appear below, to sign checks against funds of the corporation in The National Bank of Pittsburg, Pittsburg, Kansas

---

Secretary	President

Account Information

Occupation or business *Machinist*

Business Address *Pittsburg Machine Tool Co.* Tel. *714-1000*

Resident Address *66 Illinois Drive,* Tel. *714-8211*

Date Opened *May 20, 1970* Account *Pittsburg, Kansas*
Accepted by *J. Boyce* Amount $ *125.00*

Other Information

DEPOSITOR'S CONTRACT AND SIGNATURE CARD

DATED *May 20, 1970* | Account Number *13 - 064 - 2*

The Bank is authorized to recognize any of the signatures subscribed below in payment of funds or the transaction of any business for this account; and I/we further agree to the terms of the Depositor's Contract as printed on the reverse side of this card.

TYPE OF ACCOUNT: ☒ Individual   ☐ Joint   ☐ Partnership   ☐ Corporation
☐ _____

Signature *Bill Smith*

Signature

KBA—Revised 8-68 Pittcraft, Inc.

Signature Card
Checking accounts may be individual accounts or joint checking accounts.
The illustration above indicates the account is an individual checking account.
(Courtesy of The National Bank of Pittsburg, Kansas)

makes them more difficult to change. Each check is dated, and a check number may be inserted in the upper right corner of the check. The name of the person or company to whom the check is written should be carefully written on the second line from the top. You will notice in the illustration that the amount of the check is written twice. First, write the amount in figures,

Deposit Slip

The amounts of currency and silver should be recorded separately. The amount of each check should be recorded individually. Deposit slips should be made in duplicate.

(Courtesy of The National Bank of Pittsburg, Kansas)

giving dollars and cents. Next, on the third line from the top, write the dollar amount spelled out and the cents amount of the check written as a fraction of one dollar. It is customary to draw a line to the end of the space. Many banks today require that you list your account number. Most checks today have the account number and check number preprinted on them. These numbers provide ease in processing as well as a means of protecting the depositor. Then sign your name for identification exactly as written on the signature card.

The Check Stub

The check stub provides the depositor with a space to record information concerning the transaction. It is wise to carefully complete the stub of the check first, otherwise it may be forgotten. The stub provides a place for deposits as well as withdrawals. When the records of all transactions have been recorded accurately, an up-to-date balance of the checking account is available to the writer.

In some cases, it may be wise to write the purpose of the check at the bottom, especially if the check is to be used as a

Check and Stub
The check stub provides a space to keep all information needed in keeping an accurate record of your bank account.
(Courtesy of The National Bank of Pittsburg, Kansas)

receipt of payment. Some businesses assign a number to each charge account. When paying bills for which you have such a charge account number, it may help eliminate errors if you write that account number on the check.

A check may be used to withdraw cash from the bank. In this case, the check is written to "cash." However, a check for cash should be written at the bank and cashed immediately. Such a check, if lost, can be cashed by anyone.

Check Endorsement

Bill Smith, a student enrolled in the high school work experience program, is employed by the Pittsburgh Machine Tool Company. He received a $24 check from the company for his first week of work. Before Bill cashed the check, he signed his name on the back of the check at the left end exactly as it appeared on the front of the check. By using this procedure, the company will know that Bill did cash his check and received cash for his work. This is called a *blank endorsement* of a check, and is necessary to cash it. It is not wise to make a blank endorsement until you are at the bank. If you are not known at the bank, it is best to endorse the check at the teller's window.

In addition to the blank endorsement, there are other endorsements. Should Bill wish to deposit the total amount of the check, he can use a *restrictive* endorsement by writing in "For deposit only" above his signature. No one could cash and receive money from Bill's check; it can only be credited to his account. This is the best way to endorse a check which must be mailed to the bank. If Bill wishes to use the check to pay a debt to his friend John Brown, he can use the special endorsement by writing in "Pay to the order of John Brown" and sign his name. Only John Brown can cash the check, by signing his name below Bill's signature to receive money from the check.

Two considerations which the use of checks involve are care of checks and promptness of depositinig or cashing checks received. Checks from companies or individuals should not be held for an extended length of time. A delayed check makes book-keeping much more difficult.

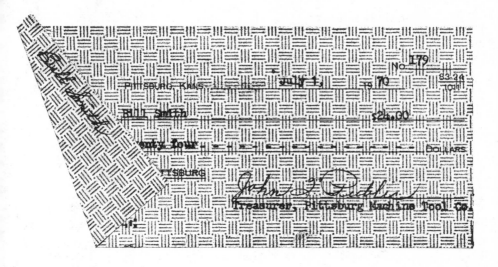

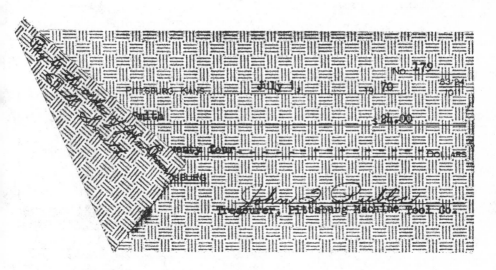

Check Endorsement
The name signed on the back of the check is the endorsement signature
and should match the spelling of the name on the face of the check.
(Courtesy of The National Bank of Pittsburg, Kansas)

Cancelled Checks

Checks which you write will be returned to you after payment. The checks are called "cancelled checks" and are useful to you as a receipt for payment and as a record of your bank

THE NATIONAL BANK
OF PITTSBURG   PITTSBURG, KANSAS 66762

	ACCOUNT NUMBER
	13-064-2

Bill Smith
66 Illinois Drive
Pittsburg, Kansas

DATE OF STATEMENT
11 19 70

CHECKS AND OTHER DEBITS		DEPOSITS	DATE	BALANCE
		BALANCE FORWARD →	08 30	139.69
		200.00	09 09	339.69
121.00			09 11	218.69
19.63			09 12	199.06
24.50			09 23	174.56
25.00			09 30	149.56
77.25			10 24	72.31
		50.00	11 06	122.31
38.00			11 15	84.31

BALANCE PREVIOUS STATEMENT	NUMBER OF ENCLOSURES	CHECKS		DEPOSITS		SERVICE CHARGE	CLOSING BALANCE
		NUMBER	AMOUNT	NUMBER	AMOUNT		
13969	6	6	30538	2	25000	00	8431

SC - SERVICE CHARGE   LS - LIST   RI - RETURNED ITEM   DM - DEBIT MEMO   OD - OVERDRAFT CHARGE   IF - INSUFFICIENT FUNDS

The Bank Statement
The bank statement includes all the deposits made to the checking account and checks paid by the bank during the period.
(Courtesy of The National Bank of Pittsburg, Kansas)

account. Most banks return all cancelled checks to depositors each month. It is good business to file all the cancelled checks with the bank statement after you have made sure all the transactions are correct and the bank balance is accurate.

Your Bank Statement

When you receive the cancelled checks from your bank, a bank statement will be included. The bank statement is an itemized list of checks that have been cancelled during the month. The statement will provide the balance at the start of the period and the balance at the end of the period.

The bank statement provides a record that can be used in checking your banking transactions for the month. Most of the checks will be returned to you with the bank statement.

How to Balance Your Checkbook

Many banks provide a printed form on the back of the statement which makes balancing an account much easier. In the illustration below you will see how to determine whether your balance and the balance on the bank statement agree. Any errors found in the bank statement should be reported at once.

The procedure for balancing your checking account each month is as follows:

1. Sort your checks numerically or by date issued.
2. Check off in your checkbook each of the checks paid by the bank and list the numbers and amounts of those not paid in the space provided at the left. Be sure to include any check still outstanding from a previous statement.
3. Enter and subtract from your checkbook any other charge appearing on the statement.
4. Reconcile your statement in the space provided.

Substitutes for Cash

Personal Checks

The advantages of using a personal checking account are many.

1. Checks are a substitute for money which may be safely sent through the mail. If the check is lost or stolen, it cannot easily be cashed.

You Can Easily

BALANCE YOUR CHECK BOOK

FILL IN BELOW AMOUNTS FROM YOUR CHECK BOOK AND BANK STATEMENT

Balance Shown on
Bank Statement: $ *84.31*

Add Deposits
Not on Statement: $_____

Total . . . $ *84.31*

Subtract Checks Issued but
Not on Statement:

$ *15.00*
5.00
_____
_____
_____
_____
_____
_____

Total . . . $ *20.00*

Balance . . . . $ *64.31*

Balance Shown in
Your Check Book $ *64.31*

Add any Deposits Not
Already Entered in
Check Book: $_____
_____
_____

Total . . . $ *64.31*

Subtract Service Charges
and other Bank Charges
Not in Check Book:

$ *00.00*
_____

Total . . . $ *64.31*

Balance . . . . $ *64.31*

These totals represent the correct amount of money you have in the bank and should agree.
Please examine your statement promptly and report any errors immediately.

Reconciliation of Your Bank Statement

It is necessary to make a reconciliation of the bank statement with your checkstubs. Any errors should be corrected as soon as possible.

(Courtesy of The National Bank of Pittsburg, Kansas)

2. A checking account makes it possible to keep only a small amount of cash in the home or on your person, reducing the chance of robbery.
3. Cancelled checks, endorsed by the person paid, furnish receipts of payment.
4. The record in the checkbook stub is a valuable record of money available for use.

Bank Card Service

The Bank Americard, Master Charge, and Bankmark are new credit services provided by banking institutions. Persons desiring to use this service should understand the rules before making application for a card.

Bank Card Service

A more recent type of banking service is the *Bank Card Service*, a type of credit provided by large organizations in cooperation with banks and business establishments. A special embossed plastic identification card is issued to those who desire the service. Each card has the name and serial number of the cardholder with a place for his signature. Purchases may be made by the holder of a bank card at business

Agreement

Use of this card by, or with the consent of, the holder constitutes agreement by holder to be bound by rules adopted for use of said card and included in this application as follows: Holder agrees (1) to assume responsibility for credit extended by this Issuer or other party to assignee thereof on the basis of this card; (2) to pay, at such place as this Issuer or such other party or assignee thereof designates, obligations evidencing such credit, and service charges in accordance with billings and the current Customer Payment Schedule, including a reasonable attorney's fee in the event of suit; (3) to notify Issuer promptly in writing of loss of this card; (4) this card may be cancelled by the Issuer at any time; (5) to surrender this card upon demand; (6) to waive and release Issuer from all defenses, rights and claims holder may have against any person or entity honoring this card; (7) any claim of Issuer against holder shall at Issuer's option become immediately due and payable if holder fails to perform any terms thereof or make any payments as otherwise agreed; (8) all transactions involving credit extended by Issuer on basis of this card shall be controlled by the laws of Missouri which are hereby expressly adopted to control all transactions hereunder.

Rules for use of card

The following rules together with the agreement set forth on the reverse side of the BankAmericard shall govern all purchases of merchandise, services furnished or cash advanced to holder or anyone authorized to use holder's BankAmericard:

1. Issuer will furnish cardholder a monthly statement showing all purchases and cash advances made. Such statement shall be deemed conclusively correct and accepted by cardholder unless issuer is notified in writing of any errors therein within 10 days from receipt of statement. Cardholder agrees to pay issuer within 25 days from the date of each statement as follows: (a) the full amount of all merchandise purchased, services furnished or cash advanced; or (b) no less than the minimum monthly payment shown thereon which shall be computed by issuer in accordance with the extended payment chart.

2. If holder pays the full amount within 25 days from the date of such statement no time price differential, service charge or interest shall be charged. If holder elects to use the extended payment plan holder agrees to pay time price differential, service charge or interest computed at a rate not in excess of that permitted by law on amounts owing for purchases or cash advances, such charges to commence as of the statement date.

3. Holder shall have the right of paying in advance the full amounts due at any time.

4. Issuer shall not be responsible by reason of refusal of anyone to honor holder's BankAmericard.

5. Holder shall not make or permit use of his BankAmericard for any purchase or cash advance which would exceed the limit issuer has established on the aggregate amount of credit available to cardholder at any one time through use of his BankAmericard.

6. Issuer shall have no responsibility for merchandise or services purchased by holder, and any dispute with respect thereto shall be settled by the holder and the seller involved. Cash refunds will not be made on purchases made through use of BankAmericard but seller in granting any refund or adjustment will initiate a credit to holder's account with issuer.

7. Issuer has the right to revoke the privileges attaching to holder's BankAmericard at any time without notice to holder. Should holder fail to comply with any term or condition in these rules or in the agreement, fail to make payments when due, dies, or becomes subject to bankruptcy or insolvency proceedings, issuer shall have the right to accelerate the full amount owing to issuer.

8. These rules are subject to amendment at any time.

EXTENDED PAYMENT CHART	
If New Balance is	Minimum Payment
$10 to $200....................................	$10
over $200..........................5% of new Balance	
(Balances under $10 are payable in full)	

Fill out the application, tear here and mail for your incredible credit card!

® Service marks owned and licensed by BankAmerica Service Corporation. Licensee in this area is Mid-America Financial Corp., a subsidiary of Commerce Bancshares, Inc.

Persons Who Use Bank Card Service Should Understand All Conditions of the Agreement

establishments honoring the service. The issuer of the card furnishes the cardholder a monthly statement showing all purchases and cash advances made. The cardholder is expected to pay the full amount of purchase within 25 days.

Certified Checks

A few companies today may refuse personal checks, especially if the amounts are large. Those who desire rapid service on orders may use a *certified check.* Your bank can provide this service. Money from your account will be withdrawn to cover the amount and held for payment. The certified check is stamped and signed by a bank official. The signature and the stamped information by the bank official makes payment of the check guaranteed. The company will not have to wait to see if your check is good before delivering the merchandise you ordered.

Cashier's Check

For a small charge, it is possible to use a cashier's check to make payments. The *cashier's check* may be used for the

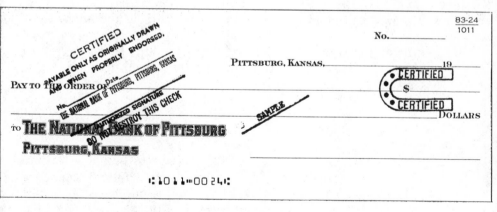

Many Companies Request Payment with a Certified Check for Goods or Services
(Courtesy of The National Bank of Pittsburg, Kansas)

same purpose as a certified check. However, a person need not have a checking account at the bank issuing a cashier's check. You pay the amount of the check, plus the charge, to the bank; and the bank writes the check.

Money Orders

A number of agencies furnish money orders for those making money transactions by mail. These include the American Express Company, the Railway Express Agency, and the United States Post Office. Postal money orders are most commonly used. They are sold at the post office for a small charge. When you need a postal money order, you make the purchase from the money order clerk at the post office who completes the order. The name of the purchaser and person to receive the money order is written in by the purchaser and mailed. The receiver must take the money order to the post office to cash it. The maximum amount of a postal money order is $100, which limits its use in sending large sums.

Telegraphic Money Orders

In emergencies, or when speed in sending money is important, a Western Union Telegraphic Money Order can be used. The cost of sending money by wire depends on the amount but is more expensive than by mail. If desired, a message may be sent at the same time. For safety in sending money, a return reply may be requested to make sure the person intended is getting the money.

Traveler's Checks

One of the most used and safest ways to take a substitute for cash on trips in the United States or to foreign countries is the use of traveler's checks. They can be purchased at banks, railroad offices, or express offices in $10, $20, $50, or $100 denominations. The purchaser signs his name on each check at the time of purchase and signs his name on each check when cashed. Signatures must be identical before the check will be cashed. Traveler's checks can be replaced if lost or stolen, which makes this service a valuable one for the traveler. The cost of the service is low. The purchaser pays one dollar fee for each $100 in traveler's checks.

The Savings Account

Banks provide a savings account for their customers as well as a checking account. Several types of banks provide this service. Commercial banks accept savings of time deposits on which they pay interest. The interest rate paid on deposits may range from 4% to 7½% and are compounded at different periods during the year. Banks have different rules and regulations on withdrawals. Some banks require at least 30 days notice before withdrawal. Special saving certificates may not be withdrawn for six months, while other certificates may not be withdrawn for one year.

Other types of banks accepting deposits for the purpose of saving and investments include savings banks, stock savings banks, and mutual savings banks.

AMERICAN EXPRESS TRAVELERS CHEQUES

The safe money that's spendable everywhere. Your signature is both your identification and your protection.

Sign here when you buy them

Sign here when you spend them

The Traveler's Check Is the Safest Substitute for Money That Can Be Used by the Traveler

It is a good idea to find out by asking your employer and other adults which types of savings banks are located in your community. Then ask at the banks what savings plans are available, what the interest is, how it is paid, and what rules govern savings deposits and withdrawals. You may find the

WITHDRAWAL	DEPOSIT	DATE	INTEREST	BALANCE
	50.00	Jan 2'70		50.00
	75.00	Jan 16'70		125.00
	60.00	Feb 6'70		185.00
	50.00	Feb 20'70		235.00
	25.00	Feb 27'70		260.00
	100.00	Mar 6'70		360.00
	100.00	Apr 3'70		460.00
		Apr 30'70	9.60	469.60
	50.00	May 8'70		519.60
	100.00	Jun 5'70		619.60
	100.00	Jul 3'70		719.60

IN ACCT. WITH Bill Smith   ACCT. NO. 50000

BANK OF PITTSBURG
Pittsburg, Kansas

interest rate varies from one bank to another and according to the type of savings account. After making sure that your account will be insured by the Federal Deposit Insurance Corporation or another reliable plan, you are in a position to look forward to achieving future goals.

The question you may ask is, "How much money should I save?" Some financial experts recommend that, as a reserve, you should have from three to six month's salary in your savings account to meet an emergency. Since each individual has special needs, there is no absolute amount to recommend. However, anything extra you may be able to save can be used for special goals that you have set.

The amount saved each month in relation to salary after taxes is shown in the chart below. The guide may be helpful to you in planning your savings.

If your monthly salary after taxes is...	You should save per month...
$200 to $300	$7 to $30
$300 to $400	$25 to $50
$400 to $500	$50 to $90
$500 to $600	$90 to $100
$600 to $700	$95 to $120
$700 to $800	$115 to $165
$800 to $900	$135 to $185
$900 to $1000	$150 to $220

Study Helps

New Terms

commercial bank	checking account	signature
savings bank	bank statement	depositor
trust funds	bank balance	withdrawal
Federal Reserve	money order	transaction
certified check	traveler's check	endorsement
cashier's check	promissory note	check stub
bank card		reconciliation

Study Questions

1. What are the different kinds of banks?
2. What the the two main functions of commercial banks?
3. What are the functions of the Federal Reserve system?
4. What is a bank deposit? A time deposit?
5. What is the procedure in starting a checking account?
6. How does a check stub help you to keep your checking account accurate?
7. How may a check be endorsed?
8. What procedures should be used in reconciling a bank statement with the check stubs?
9. What advantage is the use of a checking account?
10. Why do some companies request certified or cashier's checks for payment of goods and services?
11. Where can you purchase traveler's checks?
12. What is the FDIC and how does it operate?

Discussion Problems

1. Is your money "safer" in a state bank or a national bank? Why?
2. What advantage is there to you in being a depositor in a bank which is a member of the Federal Deposit Insurance Corporation?
3. List the steps required to open a checking account.
4. Pretend that your friend has just received his first paycheck. What would you tell him to do to get money from the check?
5. Rank the following according to which you think are the best ways of having money while on a vacation trip. Write (1) before the best choice, (2) before the next best way, (3) before the next choice, etc.

   ...... low denomination bills   ...... bank card

   ...... personal checks   ...... money order

   ...... traveler's checks   ...... certified checks

6. Make up an imaginary food order. What should you do before and when paying this bill?

Chapter 13

Buying and Using Government Services

Understanding Taxation

Taxation is a process by which people pay the expenses of their government. Taxation is as old as government itself. Historians indicate that even the earliest forms of government needed a way to finance the cost of government services, and many of them collected taxes in the form of goods and services rather than in cash. This type of tax payment is called "payments in kind."

Taxation has been a problem to most governments. Deciding who shall pay taxes, how much to collect, and how to use the money has never been determined to the satisfaction of all the people.

The preamble of the Constitution of the United States sets forth the general function of our government as follows:

We the People of the United States, in Order to form a more Perfect Union, establish Justice, insure domestic tranquility, provide for the common defense, promote the general welfare, and secure the Blessing of Liberty to ourselves and our posterity, do ordain and establish the Constitution of the United States of America.

Section 8 Article I of the Constitution establishes the responsibility and power of Congress in matters of taxation.

The Congress shall have the power to lay and collect Taxes, Duties, Imposts and Excises, to pay the Debts and provide for the Common Defense and general Welfare of the United States: but all Duties, Imposts, and Excises shall be uniform throughout the United States.

The voters in the United States have a voice in the structure of our tax system. This is the way it should be in a democracy. Our taxes are not imposed for the use of a dictator or a privileged few, but to pay for the goods and services we need and want. When you reach voting age in your state, it will not be possible for you as an individual to decide what taxes you will pay. Tax laws are designed to give equal justice to all citizens. In some cases, small groups may be hurt by laws passed for the general population. However, under our system the individual can vote for people to represent his interest. He can write and speak out against destructive practices. The important thing for a young citizen to learn is that he has a responsibility as a voter to know where each of the candidates for political office stands on tax issues and other financial problems of the country. The voter must be alert and informed on important questions which will affect everyone.

Our tax system is one in which the taxpayer assesses his own tax and in part is dependent upon a positive act of the citizen. At times the responsible taxpayers may lose faith in the tax system and become envious of those who cheat on tax returns. However, there is little reason for the honest taxpayer to feel envious of the tax evader. The chances of getting caught are high, and the penalties are severe for those who are convicted of tax evasion. Honesty in paying one's legally established share is not only an act of good citizenship, but one of pride and clear conscience.

Types of Taxes

Many types of taxes have been used in the United States and other nations. Taxes may be classified in many ways. Important classifications are as follows:

Direct and Indirect Taxes

Direct taxes are paid directly to the government by the taxpayer, hence, the term "direct." The best example of a direct tax is our federal individual income tax which will be discussed later. *Indirect taxes* are taxes on goods and services. Such taxes include excise or sales taxes, cigarette stamp taxes, and duties on imports.

Progressive and Regressive Taxes

Taxes may be classified as progressive or regressive when considered in relation to the ability to pay. A tax is called progressive when the tax is levied proportionately on the ability of the person to pay. The graduated income tax is levied on the amount of income, and the person with a high income is taxed more than a person with a low income. A tax is classified as regressive when the taxation rate remains the same regardless of the so-called ability to pay. Sales tax is considered to be a regressive tax since the tax rate is the same for every purchase of goods without consideration of total purchase which is assumed to reflect ability to pay. Taxes are not planned to be regressive, but in application they many times are. A sales tax is considered regressive since a wealthy family pays less sales tax in proportion to their earnings than a poor family spending one-half of their earnings on items on which sales tax is levied.

State and Local Taxes

To finance the operation of state and local government, several types of taxes are used today.

Property taxes. Property tax is levied on real estate. Each local tax district sets an annual rate which may vary widely with adjoining districts. The rate is based on the assessed valuation of the property. One of the problems is assessing property fairly. Property taxes are still the main source of revenue for operating schools. The following tables compare the state and local tax *sources* in 1963, as well as the *expenditures* for the same year.

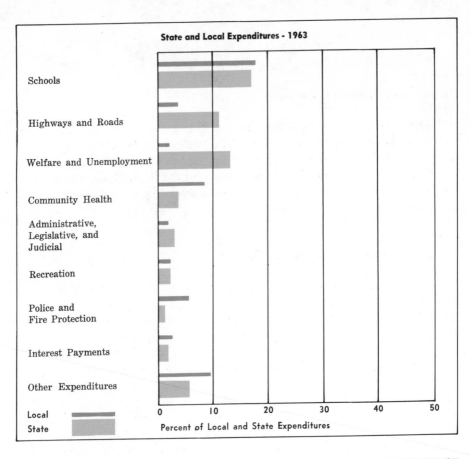

State and Local Expenditures - 1963

Schools

Highways and Roads

Welfare and Unemployment

Community Health

Administrative,
Legislative, and
Judicial

Recreation

Police and
Fire Protection

Interest Payments

Other Expenditures

Local
State

Percent of Local and State Expenditures

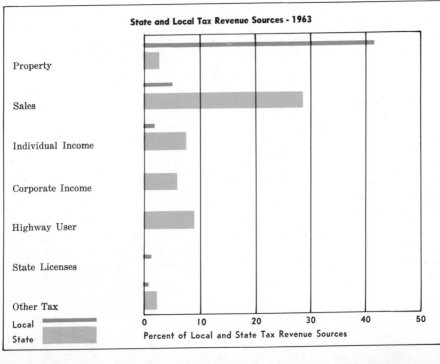

State and Local Tax Revenue Sources - 1963

Property

Sales

Individual Income

Corporate Income

Highway User

State Licenses

Other Tax

Local
State

Percent of Local and State Tax Revenue Sources

Property tax assessed valuation is generally highest on new homes in the suburbs. State income tax is being used to replace property taxes.

Sales taxes. Most states have started using sales tax to raise revenue for state and local government expenses. The rates are as high as 5% on retail sales in a few states.

Highway-user taxes. One of the chief sources of revenue for highway construction and maintenance is the tax on gasoline. Each state sets the rates in cents per gallon of gasoline. Another type of highway-user tax is the license fees for cars, trucks, busses, and trailers. Some cities also levy a tax on gasoline sold in the city. A federal tax is added to finance the interstate highway system.

Payroll and Business taxes. States and cities often require business organizations to buy a license for the privilege of operating a business. States also tax the net earnings of business establishments.

All states charge up to 3% on payrolls in occupations covered by Social Security. The revenue is used to finance unemployment compensation.

State Personal Income taxes. About three-fourths of all the states levy an income tax on individual earnings above certain levels. State income taxes are generally based on information in the federal reporting form.[1]

State Inheritance taxes. Thirty-eight states report some form of inheritance tax.[2] These rates vary widely among the states. The tax rate increases with the value of the estate.

Federal Income Tax

The United States Government's largest single source of revenue is through a graduated individual income tax. The Internal Revenue Service of the United States Treasury Department operates the nationwide collection service.

---

[1]Analysis Staff, Tax Division, U.S. Treasury Department, 1968.
[2]*Ibid.*

Everyone under 65 years of age who resides in the United States and has a gross income of $600 or more during the year must file a Federal Income Tax Return. Persons over 65 who earn $1,200 or more during the year must also file a return. Since the federal income tax affects most people who earn money, we will give it special study.

The history of taxation in our country is closely related to the history of the United States itself. One of the reasons we have the type of tax system we do is in part the result of bitter experiences with taxation during colonial times. Under the rule of the British Empire, taxation grew more oppressive. The cry went out through the land that it was taxation without representation. Finally, after a number of tax schemes were tried by the British, the colonists rebelled in 1776 and declared their independence. One of the chief causes claimed for fighting the Revolutionary War was this taxation without representation. It was not until 1788 that the colonists were able to organize a constitution. Because of the experiences with unfair taxation, our Founding Fathers limited the power of the federal government to tax.

After the war debts were paid, it was possible for President Jefferson and the Congress to abolish the whole system of collecting internal taxes. However, the War of 1812 was expensive and the system of internal taxation was revised. Again, after the war was over, the federal government was able to pay the debts and abolish the excise tax which was the same type of tax used to pay the war debts of the Revolution.

Taxes were raised again during the Civil War, when President Lincoln signed a comprehensive tax law to raise money to fight the war.

The law enacted in 1862 provided for taxation according to income. It also authorized the federal government to levy taxes on real estate, public utilities and many consumer goods such as beer and tobacco. The law authorized a tax-collecting agency which was the forerunner of our present Internal Revenue Service. Agents were employed to collect taxes and special investigators were employed to detect fraud and to enforce the tax laws.

After the war was over and the debts were paid, the tax system was again repealed. By 1877 most of the levies had been removed and the federal government returned to tariff for operation expense rather than taxes.

During the last quarter of the 19th century (1875-1900), more attention was given to the need for a federal income tax system. The country experienced economic panic and depression during this period, causing hardship and suffering. The economic unrest during this period was partly responsible for the rise of a new political party called the "Populist Party." The members of the party included farmers and city labor groups who advocated a federal income tax to collect needed money and serve as a mechanism to regulate the economy, especially during depression and periods of expansion. The same group advocated public ownersip of transportation and comunication systems.

Because of the early experience with oppressive tax laws, most citizens of the United States had a strong feeling against taxes of any kind, especially federal. The Constitution, when adopted, specifically prohibited the levying of direct taxes. On several occasions the courts ruled tax laws unconstitutional because they were considered direct.

During the 1890's income tax laws were challenged in the federal courts. In 1895 the Supreme Court ruled that income tax was a form of direct tax and was therefore unconstitutional. The Income Tax Division in the Office of Internal Revenue was disbanded after that court ruling.

In order to enact an income tax law, is was necessary to change the Constitution. The increased need for money to operate the federal government and the need to reform the tax system of the country led to the proposal for an amendment to the Constitution. This amendment would give Congress the power to tax without apportionment among the States.

The 16th Amendment to the Constitution was passed by Congress in 1909, and was ratified by two-thirds of the states in February, 1913. Provisions of the amendment were as follows:

"The Congress shall have power to lay and collect taxes on incomes, from whatever sources derived, without apportionment among the several states, and without regard to any census or enumeration."

The cost of World War I was the greatest expenditure to the United States Government up to that time. The $35 billion cost of World War I was more than the cost of the federal government from 1791 to 1917. About one-third of the money was raised in taxes under the federal income tax system. The total income tax collection reached about $5½ billion per year in 1920.[3] The per capita cost of government was $178.

After the war, income tax was again reduced and the per capita cost of government fell to $28 under the Coolidge administration. However, when the great depression of 1929 hit the country and millions of people were unemployed, the country started a new economic practice of using federal money to revive the national economy. From 1933 to 1940, much social legislation was passed during the administration of President Franklin D. Roosevelt. The Bureau of Internal Revenue was given the responsibility for the collection of Social Security payroll taxes.

Only a small number of people paid federal income tax before World War II. The number has increased from 8,000,000 to 60,000,000 today.

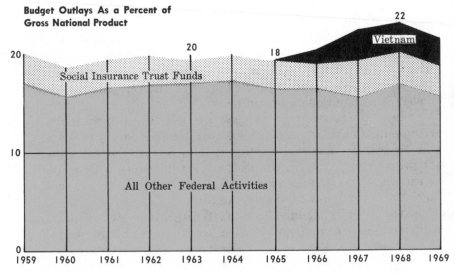

Increased Cost of the Social Security Program and the Vietnam War
Has Required a Higher Percentage of the Gross National Product for Taxes

[3]Department of the Treasury, Internal Revenue Service, "Understanding Taxes, Teaching Taxes Program," 1970 ed., pp 2-4.

Since the end of World War II, the personal income tax rate has remained at a high level. Cost of expensive programs, such as the Marshall Plan after the war, required billions of additional dollars. The Korean War, the Vietnam War, and the Cold War with Russia and China have required additional tax dollars. Today, the single largest expenditure in our national government is for national defense. Also, the cost of federal spending in health, education, and welfare continues to rise. The chart indicates how money is spent in relation to our gross national product.

During President Johnson's administration, Congress passed a new type of income tax law to assess a surcharge on the income tax one pays. The surcharge tax was added to income tax to raise additional revenue to finance the Vietnam War and to reduce inflation. The surcharge rates are shown in the table below. Collection of the surcharge tax started April 1, 1969.

1969 Tax Surcharge Tables

[1] Your tax—Amount shown on line 16, Form 1040 or line 8, Schedule T.
[2] Enter your tax Surcharge on line 17, Form 1040 or line 9, Schedule T.

TABLE 1—Single Taxpayers and Married Persons Filing Separate Returns

If your tax[1] is at least:	But less than	Your tax surcharge[2] is:
0	$148	0
$148	153	$1
153	158	2
158	163	3
163	168	4
168	173	5
173	178	6
178	183	7
183	188	8
188	193	9
193	198	10
198	203	11
203	208	12
208	213	13
213	218	14
218	223	15
223	228	16
228	233	17
233	238	18
238	243	19
243	248	20
248	253	21
253	258	22
258	263	23
263	268	24
268	273	25
273	278	26
278	283	27
283	288	28
288	295	29
295	305	30
305	315	31
315	325	32
325	335	33
335	345	34
345	355	35
355	365	36
365	375	37
375	385	38
385	395	39
$395	$405	$40
405	415	41
415	425	42
425	435	43
435	445	44
445	455	45
455	465	46
465	475	47
475	485	48
485	495	49
495	505	50
505	515	51
515	525	52
525	535	53
535	545	54
545	555	55
555	565	56
565	575	57
575	585	58
585	595	59
595	605	60
605	615	61
615	625	62
625	635	63
635	645	64
645	655	65
655	665	66
665	675	67
675	685	68
685	695	69
695	705	70
705	715	71
715	725	72
725	735	73

If $735 or more multiply your tax[1] by .10

TABLE 2—Married Taxpayers Filing Joint Returns and Certain Widows and Widowers

If your tax[1] is at least:	But less than	Your tax surcharge[2] is:
0	$293	0
$293	298	$1
298	303	2
303	308	3
308	313	4
313	318	5
318	323	6
323	328	7
328	333	8
333	338	9
338	343	10
343	348	11
348	353	12
353	358	13
358	363	14
363	368	15
368	373	16
373	378	17
378	383	18
383	388	19
388	393	20
393	398	21
398	403	22
403	408	23
408	413	24
413	418	25
418	423	26
423	428	27
428	433	28
433	438	29
438	443	30
443	448	31
448	453	32
453	458	33
458	463	34
463	468	35
468	473	36
473	478	37
478	483	38
483	488	39
$488	$493	$40
493	498	41
498	503	42
503	508	43
508	513	44
513	518	45
518	523	46
523	528	47
528	533	48
533	538	49
538	543	50
543	548	51
548	553	52
553	558	53
558	563	54
563	568	55
568	573	56
573	578	57
578	585	58
585	595	59
595	605	60
605	615	61
615	625	62
625	635	63
635	645	64
645	655	65
655	665	66
665	675	67
675	685	68
685	695	69
695	705	70
705	715	71
715	725	72
725	735	73

If $735 or more multiply your tax[1] by .10

TABLE 3—Unmarried (or legally separated) Taxpayers Who Qualify as Heads of Household

If your tax[1] is at least:	But less than	Your tax surcharge[2] is:
0	$223	0
$223	228	$1
228	233	2
233	238	3
238	243	4
243	248	5
248	253	6
253	258	7
258	263	8
263	268	9
268	273	10
273	278	11
278	283	12
283	288	13
288	293	14
293	298	15
298	303	16
303	308	17
308	313	18
313	318	19
318	323	20
323	328	21
328	333	22
333	338	23
338	343	24
343	348	25
348	353	26
353	358	27
358	363	28
363	368	29
368	373	30
373	378	31
378	383	32
383	388	33
388	393	34
393	398	35
398	403	36
403	408	37
408	413	38
413	418	39
$418	$423	$40
423	428	41
428	433	42
433	438	43
438	445	44
445	455	45
455	465	46
465	475	47
475	485	48
485	495	49
495	505	50
505	515	51
515	525	52
525	535	53
535	545	54
545	555	55
555	565	56
565	575	57
575	585	58
585	595	59
595	605	60
605	615	61
615	625	62
625	635	63
635	645	64
645	655	65
655	665	66
665	675	67
675	685	68
685	695	69
695	705	70
705	715	71
715	725	72
725	735	73

If $735 or more multiply your tax[1] by .10

16—80392-1

Taxes and the Federal Budget

The Federal budget serves the same purpose as an individual's budget (to plan expenditures). The federal budget is prepared by the Bureau of the Budget under the direction of the President. It is a financial plan covering programs proposed by the President to meet the needs of the United States. The budget contains an estimate of income and expenses for one *fiscal year*, running from July 1 to June 31.

The budget is completed and sent to Congress in January before the fiscal year starts on July 1. Congress can make additions and deletions in the budget. The House of Representatives is responsible for appropriations to meet the expenses estimated in the budget.

The 1969 federal budget receipts reached $187.8 billion, with expenditures totaling $184.8 billion which netted a surplus of over $3 billion to apply on the national debt. In the bar chart below, the source of income in 1969 is shown by categories and percentages. Receipts come mainly from income taxes: $123.9 billion or 66 percent; social insurance and retirement taxes total $39.9 billion or 21 percent of the total; excise accounts for $15.2 billion or 8 percent of the total.

Where It Comes From

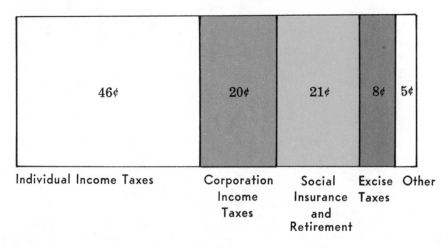

| 46¢ | 20¢ | 21¢ | 8¢ | 5¢ |

Individual Income Taxes   Corporation Income Taxes   Social Insurance and Retirement   Excise Taxes   Other

Source of Federal Income — 1969

The way in which the revenue is spent is shown in the following graph. A breakdown of expenses on a percentage basis is as follows:

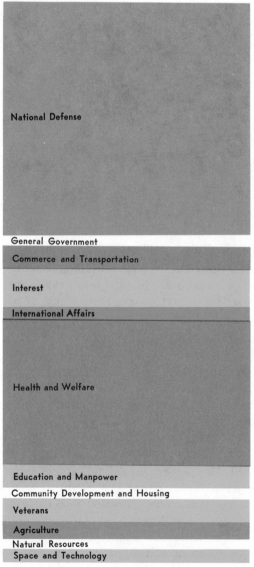

National Defense

General Government

Commerce and Transportation

Interest

International Affairs

Health and Welfare

Education and Manpower

Community Development and Housing

Veterans

Agriculture

Natural Resources

Space and Technology

Notes:
  (1) The figures above add to more than total outlays because they include certain transactions which are entirely within the Government and are thus deducted prior to arriving at the total.
  (2) Detail may not add to totals due to rounding.
  (3) More information on the budget is available in *The Budget in Brief,* which may be obtained for 45 cents from the Superintendent of Documents, U.S. Government Printing Office, Washington, D. C. 20402.

Federal Government Expenditures

National Defense: $81,300,000,000

43¢ of each dollar received by the government in 1969 went for improving our military power, for military assistance abroad, and for atomic energy programs. This includes $29.1 billion for our military operations in Vietnam.

International Affairs: $4,100,000,000

2¢ of each dollar went for international programs, such as economic and technical assistance, Food for Freedom, the operation of embassies and information activities abroad, and the Peace Corps.

Veterans: $7,700,000,000

Pensions and compensation, hospital care and medical treatment, education and training of Vietnam veterans, life insurance benefits, and other veterans programs took about 4¢ of the government dollar.

Interest: $12,800,000,000

Interest payments on the debt held by the public took about 7¢ of each government dollar in 1969.

Space Research and Technology: $4,200,000,000

Manned space flight, space science, and technological and supporting activities required about 2¢ of each government dollar in 1969.

Health and Welfare: $49,000,000,000

This category includes Social Security, Medicare, unemployment and retirement benefits which are financed by taxes specifically levied for these programs. It also includes public assistance grants, medical research, health services, food and nutrition programs, and vocational rehabilitation. These programs accounted for 26¢ of each government dollar in 1969.

Education and Manpower: $7,600,000,000

Programs to improve the quality of education at all levels, to assist science education and basic research, vocational education, and manpower training, took 4¢ of each dollar of the federal budget. Special emphasis is being placed on improving the education of disadvantaged children and enlisting the help of private business in training and hiring the hard-core unemployed.

Community Development and Housing: $1,100,000,000
Through loans and grants, the federal government helps provide public housing, urban renewal, model cities planning, parks, water and sewer facilities, mass transportation, and neighborhood facilities. It also aids private housing through support of the mortgage market and rent supplements. These programs took 1¢ of the government dollar.

Commerce and Transportation: $8,000,000,000
4¢ of the 1969 government dollar went for specially financed highway construction; operation of the federal airways, the Post Office, and the Coast Guard; aids to economically distressed areas and small business; and for related programs.

Agriculture: $6,100,000,000
3¢ of each government dollar were used for the stabilization of farm income, financing rural electrification and housing, soil conservation, research, and food inspection.

Natural Resources: $2,100,000,000
Flood control, navigation, irrigation, power projects, combating water pollution, management and protection of the national parks and forests, and related programs cost 1¢ of each dollar received in 1969.

General Government: $2,900,000,000
2¢ of each dollar went for strengthening efforts to control crime, making and enforcing our laws, managing government finances and property, and other activities.[4]

Preparing Income Tax Returns

Under the provisions of our federal income tax law, every citizen or resident of the United States, whether single or married, who has a gross income of $600 or more per year ($1200 for persons 65 or older) must file a federal income tax return even though the person filing will have deductions and exemptions to release any final tax liability. Also, a person having less

---

[4]*Ibid.* p. 5.

than the required gross income must file an income tax return and pay any tax due if he has uncollected Social Security tax on self-employed income or tips of $400 or more.

The answer to the question, "Do high school students have to file income tax returns?", is yes if he or she earns $600 or more. However, for high school students working during the summer earning less than $600, and whose employers withhold income tax from their wages, it will be necessary to file an income tax return in order to get a refund.

Using Your Social Security Account Number in Tax Reporting

It was the first of April when Carol Wallis decided she would make application with the Employment Security Office for work as a typist. She planned to finish her junior year in high school on May 26, and wanted to use the typing skills learned during the year.

When Carol made application, her Social Security account number was requested. Since she had never worked outside the home, an application for a number had never been made.

APPLICATION FOR SOCIAL SECURITY NUMBER
(Or Replacement of Lost Card)
Information Furnished On This Form Is CONFIDENTIAL
See Instructions on Back.   Print In Black or Dark Blue Ink or Use Typewriter.
DO NOT WRITE IN THE ABOVE SPACE

1 Print FULL NAME YOU WILL USE IN WORK OR BUSINESS — (First Name) **Carol** (Middle Name or Initial—If none, draw line—) **A.** (Last Name) **Wallis**

2 Print FULL NAME GIVEN YOU AT BIRTH **Carol Annette Wallis**

6 YOUR DATE OF BIRTH (Month) (Day) (Year) **May 3, 1951**

3 PLACE OF BIRTH (City) **Plaintown** (County if known) **Jeff** (State) **Kansas**

7 YOUR PRESENT AGE (Age on last birthday) **17**

4 MOTHER'S FULL NAME AT HER BIRTH (Her maiden name) **Annette Mae South**

8 YOUR SEX MALE ☐ FEMALE ☒

5 FATHER'S FULL NAME (Regardless of whether living or dead) **Carl James Wallis**

9 YOUR COLOR OR RACE WHITE ☒ NEGRO ☐ OTHER ☐

10 HAVE YOU EVER BEFORE APPLIED FOR OR HAD A SOCIAL SECURITY, RAILROAD, OR TAX ACCOUNT NUMBER? DON'T KNOW ☐ NO ☒ YES ☐ (If "Yes" Print STATE in which you applied and DATE you applied and SOCIAL SECURITY NUMBER if known)

11 YOUR MAILING ADDRESS (Number and street) **201 East Third,** (City) **Plaintown** (State) **Kansas** (ZIP Code) **66672**

12 TODAY'S DATE **April 30, 1969**

13 Sign YOUR NAME HERE (Do Not Print) **Carol A. Wallis**

TREASURY DEPARTMENT Internal Revenue Service
Form SS-5 (12-64)
Return completed application to nearest SOCIAL SECURITY ADMINISTRATION DISTRICT OFFICE
HAVE YOU COMPLETED ALL 13 ITEMS?

Carol was instructed to go to the Social Security office or the local post office to obtain the Form SS5, which is a form used to apply for a Social Security account number.

The local post office was in a more convenient location than the Social Security office, so Carol went to the post office where she was given Form SS5. The card was easy to complete, and after she had checked everything entered on the card, she entered the date and signed the card. Within a short time, her Social Security card was received. The account number stamped on the card was the one she would use the rest of her life for reporting income taxes and Social Security taxes.

Carol was interviewed at several companies and accepted a job with the Jackson Manufacturing Company as a typist and file clerk.

When Carol started to work on June 5, the Director of Personnel at Jackson's gave her a Form W-4 Employee's Withholding Certificate to fill out for tax purposes. Carol printed her full name and Social Security number on the first line and her full address on the second line. Since Carol had no dependents, she claimed only herself as a dependent. She signed her name and entered the date before returning the form to the personnel office.

The information on Carol's W-4 Form will be used by her employer to determine income tax deduction. Along with income tax deductions, 4.8% additional deductions from her wages must

---

FORM W-4 (Rev. Jan. 1967)
U.S. Treasury Department
Internal Revenue Service

EMPLOYEE'S WITHHOLDING EXEMPTION CERTIFICATE

Type or print full name _Carol A. Wallis_   Social Security Number _499-14-8524_

Home address _____ City _____ State _____ ZIP code _____

EMPLOYEE:	
File this form with your employer. Otherwise, he must withhold U.S. Income tax from your wages without exemption.	**HOW TO CLAIM YOUR WITHHOLDING EXEMPTIONS**
	1. If SINGLE (or if married and wish withholding as single person), write "1." If you claim no exemptions, write "0" . . . _1_
	2. If MARRIED, one exemption each is allowable for husband and wife if not claimed on another certificate.
	(a) If you claim both of these exemptions, write "2"; (b) If you claim one of these exemptions, write "1"; (c) If you claim neither of these exemptions, write "0" . . .
EMPLOYER: Keep this certificate with your records. If the employee is believed to have claimed too many exemptions, the District Director should be so advised.	3. Exemptions for age and blindness (applicable only to you and your wife but not to dependents):
	(a) If you or your wife will be 65 years of age or older at the end of the year, and you claim this exemption, write "1"; if both will be 65 or older, and you claim both of these exemptions, write "2" . . .
	(b) If you or your wife are blind, and you claim this exemption, write "1"; if both are blind, and you claim both of these exemptions, write "2" . . .
	4. If you claim exemptions for one or more dependents, write the number of such exemptions. (Do not claim exemption for a dependent unless you are qualified under Instruction 4 on other side.). . .
	5. If you claim additional withholding allowances for itemized deductions fill out and attach Schedule A (Form W-4), and enter the number of allowances claimed (if claimed file new Form W-4 each year) . . .
	6. Add the exemptions and allowances (if any) which you have claimed above and write total . . . . _1_
	7. Additional withholding per pay period under agreement with employer. (See Instruction 1.) . . . . . $

I CERTIFY that the number of withholding exemptions claimed on this certificate does not exceed the number to which I am entitled.

(Date) ____June 5____, 19_69_   (Signed) _Carol A. Wallis_   c48—16—79001-1

be made for Social Security taxes. In Chapter 14 more attention will be given to Social Security taxes.

Carol worked 13 weeks for Jackson Manufacturing Company before she went on a vacation with her parents in August. When she left her job, the personnel clerk gave Carol two copies of

1

Jackson Manufacturing Company
Plaintown, Kansas   66672

Type or print EMPLOYER'S Federal identification number, name, and address above.

WAGE AND TAX STATEMENT—1969
(For use in States or Cities authorizing combined form)

Employer's State Identification Number

51-0174610

Copy A—
For Internal Revenue Service

FEDERAL INCOME TAX INFORMATION			SOCIAL SECURITY INFORMATION		STATUS	*
Federal income tax withheld	Wages paid subject to withholding in 1969 ¹	Other compensation paid in 1969 ²	F.I.C.A. employee tax withheld ³	Total F.I.C.A. wages paid in 1969 ⁴	1. Single 2. Married	**
$50.70	**$546.00**		**$26.26**		**1**	

EMPLOYEE'S social security number ▶   **499-14-8529**

Name of State	State Form No.	State income tax withheld
Kansas	**K-2**	**.00**
Name of City	City Form No.	City income tax withheld

Carol A. Wallis
203 East Third
Plaintown, Kansas   66672

*See Circ. E for sick pay reporting. **Gross wages for State if different from Federal.
¹ Includes tips reported by employee. Amount is before payroll deductions or sick pay exclusion.
² Report salary or other employee compensation which was not subject to withholding. See Circular E.
³ One-eighth of this amount was withheld to finance the cost of Hospital Insurance Benefits. The remainder is for old-age, survivors, and disability insurance.
⁴ Includes tips reported by employee.

Type or print EMPLOYEE'S name and address (including ZIP code) above.

FORM **W-2** U.S. Treasury Department, Internal Revenue Service   16—80184-1

Uncollected Employee Tax on Tips . . . . $

EMPLOYER: See instructions on back of copy D.

NOTICE TO EMPLOYEE:

1. **Income Tax Wages.**—This statement is important. Copy B must be filed with your U.S. Income Tax Return for 1969 and Copy 2 must be filed with your State or City Income Tax Return for 1969. If your social security number, name, or address is stated incorrectly, correct the information on copies B and 2 and notify your employer.

2. **Social Security Wages.**—If your wages were subject to social security taxes, but are not shown, your social security wages are the same as wages shown under "FEDERAL INCOME TAX INFORMATION," but not more than $7,800.

3. **Credit For F.I.C.A. Tax.**—If more than $374.40 of F.I.C.A. (social security and hospital insurance) employee tax was withheld during 1969 because you received wages from more than one employer, the excess should be claimed as a credit against your Federal income tax. See instructions for your Federal income tax return.

4. A copy of this form has been sent to the Internal Revenue Service.

This is not a tax return but you must file it with your tax return. See instructions on back of copy C.

☆☆☆☆ U.S. GOVERNMENT PRINTING OFFICE : 1969—O-337-016   25-1118272   16—80184-J

Instructions to the Employee Are Given on the Back Side of Copy B
of the Form W-2

Form W-2, "Wage and Tax Statement." Carol's total earnings were $546 with federal income tax withholdings of $50.70 and FICA tax (Federal Insurance Contributions tax) of $26.26. The Social Security taxes (FICA) are payable on wages up to $7,800 a year. The employer must match the 4.8% deducted from the employee's wages.

The W-2 Form (shown) is made with five carbon copies. *Copy A,* the original, is forwarded to the Internal Revenue Service Office. *Copy B* is to be filed with Carol's income tax return Form 1040. *Copy C* is for Carol's individual records. Jackson Manufacturing Company retains *Copy D* for their records, and *Copy 1* is used for filing the state income tax.

The New Form 1040

In 1969, the forms used for filing income tax returns were changed. The old Form 1040A, or short form, was no longer used. Instead, the new Form 1040 was adopted. Form 1040 and Form 1040A, previously used, were combined into a single form. Everyone filing a return was required to use the new form.

Since Carol's total income for 1969 was in the form of wages totaling $546, the Form 1040 without any supporting schedule was used (see the example). As long as Carol's earnings were not more than $5000 and she received no dividends or interest over $200, she may compute her own tax liability or let the Internal Revenue Service do it for her. Since Carol had received instructions in computing tax returns, she decided to complete the Form 1040 herself. The example shown is a copy of the Form 1040 used by Carol. She printed her name, address, Social Security account number, and job title in the first section. Carol entered the reason for not filing a return in 1968 as "None" in the blank space reserved for "Name and address of employer at time of filing." This was her first time to file an income tax return. In the next block toward the bottom of the form she checked box 1, labeled "single." In the exemptions section she listed herself in line 7a as the only dependent claimed. In the section for reporting income she entered the amount of $546 from the Form W-2 on lines 11, 15a and 15c. In sections 19 and 23 she entered the $50.70 withholding from the Form W-2.

Form **1040** Combined with Form 1040A — **US** Department of the Treasury / Internal Revenue Service — **Individual Income Tax Return** 19**69**

For the year January 1–December 31, 1969, or other taxable year beginning ...., 1969, ending .... 19......

First name and initial (If joint return, use first names and middle initials of both)	Last name	Your social security number
Carol A.	Wallis	499 14 8529

Present home address (Number and street or rural route)
201 East Third

Your occupation
Typist

City, town or post office, State and ZIP code
Plaintown, Kansas 66672

Spouse's social security number

Enter below name and address used on your return for 1968 (if same as above write "Same"). If none filed, give reason. If changing from separate to joint or joint to separate returns, enter 1968 names and addresses.
First return

Spouse's occupation

Name and address of employer at time of filing

Your Filing Status— (Check only one)

1 ☒ Single
2 ☐ Married filing joint return (even if only one had income)
3 ☐ Married filing separate return **and** spouse is also filing a return. If this item checked give spouse's social security number in space provided above and enter first name here ▶
4 ☐ Unmarried Head of Household
5 ☐ Surviving widow(er) with dependent child
6 ☐ Married filing separate return and spouse is not filing a return

Your Exemptions

Check boxes for exemptions which apply — Regular — 65 or over — Blind

7a Yourself . . . . ☒ ☐ ☐ } Enter number of boxes checked ▶
7b **Spouse** (applies only if line 2 or line 6 is checked) . . . . ☐ ☐ ☐

8 First names of your dependent children who lived with you

Enter number ▶

9 OTHER DEPENDENTS	(a) NAME—Enter figure 1 in the last column to right for each name listed (if more space is needed, use other side)	(b) Relationship	(c) Months lived in your home. See instructions, B-2.	(d) $600 or more income?	(e) Support you furnished. If 100% write "ALL."	(f) Support furnished by dependent and others
					$	$
						▶
						▶

10 Total exemptions from lines 7, 8, and 9 above . . . . ▶ | 1

Your Income

11 Wages, salaries, tips, etc. (Attach Form W-2 to back. If unavailable, explain on back) . | 11 | 546 00

12a Dividends [Total before exclusion] $ .... [See item 2 on 1040-1] 12b Less Exclusion $ .... Balance ▶ | 12c

13 Interest (Enter total here and if over $100, also list in Schedule B, Part II) . . . . | 13

14 Other income: Total from attached schedules (check schedules used—C ☐, D ☐, E ☐, F ☐) . . | 14

15a Total [Add lines 11, 12c, 13 & 14] $ 546.00, 15b Less Adjustments [See 1040-1] $ .... Adjusted Gross Income ▶ | 15c | 546 00

Your Tax and Surcharge

● If line 15c is $5,000 or more, go to Schedule T, to figure tax and surcharge. (Omit lines 16 and 17.)
● Go to Sch. T to figure tax and surcharge if you itemize deductions; or claim retirement income credit, foreign tax credit, or investment credit; or if you owe self-employment tax or tax from recomputing prior year investment credit. (Omit lines 16 and 17.)
● If neither of above two items applies, go to Tax Tables instead of Sch. T. Complete lines 16, 17, & 18.

16 Tax from Tax Table (see tables on T-2 and T-3) . . . . . | 16 | 0 00
17 Tax surcharge on line 16 (see T-1 for tax surcharge tables) . | 17 | 0 00
18 Enter total of lines 16 and 17 **OR** amount from Schedule T, line 18, if applicable (check if from Tax Table A ☒, B ☐, C ☐; Tax Rate Sch. ☐, Sch. D ☐, or Sch. G ☐) . | 18 | 0 00

See 1040-1 for rules under which the IRS will figure your tax and surcharge.

Your Credits

19 Total Federal income tax withheld (attach Forms W-2 to back) | 19 | 50 70
20 Excess F.I.C.A. tax withheld (two or more employers—see R-2) . . . | 20
21 ☐ Nonhighway Federal gasoline tax, Form 4136; ☐ Reg. Inv., Form 2439 | 21
22 1969 Estimated tax payments (include 1968 overpayment allowed as a credit) | 22
23 Total (add lines 19, 20, 21, and 22) . . . . | 23 | 50 70

Make check or money order payable to Internal Revenue Service.

Balance Due or Refund

24 If line 18 is larger than line 23, enter BALANCE DUE. Pay in full with return ▶ | 24

25 If line 23 is larger than line 18, enter OVERPAYMENT ▶ | 25 | 50 70

26 Line 25 to be: (a) Credited on 1970 estimated tax ▶ $ ....; (b) Refunded ▶ $ 50.70

Under penalties of perjury, I declare that I have examined this return, including accompanying schedules and statements, and to the best of my knowledge and belief it is true, correct, and complete.

Sign here

Your signature Carol A. Wallis Date 1/15/70

Signature of preparer other than taxpayer, based on all information of which he has any knowledge. Date

Spouse's signature (If filing jointly, BOTH must sign even if only one had income)

Address

16-80588—1

(left margin) Please attach Copy B of Form W-2 to back

(left margin) Please attach Check or Money Order here

1969 Tax Rate Schedules

If you do not use one of the Tax Tables, then figure your tax on the amount on line 5, Schedule T, by using the appropriate Tax Rate Schedule on this page. Enter tax on line 6. Also see Tax Surcharge Tables below for tax surcharge.

Schedule I—Single Taxpayers and Married Persons Filing Separate Returns

If the amount on line 5, Schedule T is: Enter on line 6, Schedule T:

Not over $500......14% of the amount on line 5.

Over—	But not over—		of excess over—
$500	$1,000	$70+15%	$500
$1,000	$1,500	$145+16%	$1,000
$1,500	$2,000	$225+17%	$1,500
$2,000	$4,000	$310+19%	$2,000
$4,000	$6,000	$690+22%	$4,000
$6,000	$8,000	$1,130+25%	$6,000
$8,000	$10,000	$1,630+28%	$8,000
$10,000	$12,000	$2,190+32%	$10,000
$12,000	$14,000	$2,830+36%	$12,000
$14,000	$16,000	$3,550+39%	$14,000
$16,000	$18,000	$4,330+42%	$16,000
$18,000	$20,000	$5,170+45%	$18,000
$20,000	$22,000	$6,070+48%	$20,000
$22,000	$26,000	$7,030+50%	$22,000
$26,000	$32,000	$9,030+53%	$26,000
$32,000	$38,000	$12,210+55%	$32,000
$38,000	$44,000	$15,510+58%	$38,000
$44,000	$50,000	$18,990+60%	$44,000
$50,000	$60,000	$22,590+62%	$50,000
$60,000	$70,000	$28,790+64%	$60,000
$70,000	$80,000	$35,190+66%	$70,000
$80,000	$90,000	$41,790+68%	$80,000
$90,000	$100,000	$48,590+69%	$90,000
$100,000	......	$55,490+70%	$100,000

Schedule II—Married Taxpayers Filing Joint Returns and Certain Widows and Widowers (See B-2)

If the amount on line 5, Schedule T is: Enter on line 6, Schedule T:

Not over $1,000......14% of the amount on line 5.

Over—	But not over—		of excess over—
$1,000	$2,000	$140+15%	$1,000
$2,000	$3,000	$290+16%	$2,000
$3,000	$4,000	$450+17%	$3,000
$4,000	$8,000	$620+19%	$4,000
$8,000	$12,000	$1,380+22%	$8,000
$12,000	$16,000	$2,260+25%	$12,000
$16,000	$20,000	$3,260+28%	$16,000
$20,000	$24,000	$4,380+32%	$20,000
$24,000	$28,000	$5,660+36%	$24,000
$28,000	$32,000	$7,100+39%	$28,000
$32,000	$36,000	$8,660+42%	$32,000
$36,000	$40,000	$10,340+45%	$36,000
$40,000	$44,000	$12,140+48%	$40,000
$44,000	$52,000	$14,060+50%	$44,000
$52,000	$64,000	$18,060+53%	$52,000
$64,000	$76,000	$24,420+55%	$64,000
$76,000	$88,000	$31,020+58%	$76,000
$88,000	$100,000	$37,980+60%	$88,000
$100,000	$120,000	$45,180+62%	$100,000
$120,000	$140,000	$57,580+64%	$120,000
$140,000	$160,000	$70,380+66%	$140,000
$160,000	$180,000	$83,580+68%	$160,000
$180,000	$200,000	$97,180+69%	$180,000
$200,000	......	$110,980+70%	$200,000

Schedule III—Unmarried (or legally separated) Taxpayers Who Qualify as Heads of Household (See B-2)

If the amount on line 5, Schedule T is: Enter on line 6, Schedule T:

Not over $1,000......14% of the amount on line 5.

Over—	But not over—		of excess over—
$1,000	$2,000	$140+16%	$1,000
$2,000	$4,000	$300+18%	$2,000
$4,000	$6,000	$660+20%	$4,000
$6,000	$8,000	$1,060+22%	$6,000
$8,000	$10,000	$1,500+25%	$8,000
$10,000	$12,000	$2,000+27%	$10,000
$12,000	$14,000	$2,540+31%	$12,000
$14,000	$16,000	$3,160+32%	$14,000
$16,000	$18,000	$3,200+35%	$16,000
$18,000	$20,000	$4,500+36%	$18,000
$20,000	$22,000	$5,220+40%	$20,000
$22,000	$24,000	$6,020+41%	$22,000
$24,000	$26,000	$6,840+43%	$24,000
$26,000	$28,000	$7,700+45%	$26,000
$28,000	$32,000	$8,600+46%	$28,000
$32,000	$36,000	$10,440+48%	$32,000
$36,000	$38,000	$12,360+50%	$36,000
$38,000	$40,000	$13,360+52%	$38,000
$40,000	$44,000	$14,400+53%	$40,000
$44,000	$50,000	$16,520+55%	$44,000
$50,000	$52,000	$19,820+56%	$50,000
$52,000	$64,000	$20,940+58%	$52,000
$64,000	$70,000	$27,900+59%	$64,000
$70,000	$76,000	$31,440+61%	$70,000
$76,000	$80,000	$35,100+62%	$76,000
$80,000	$88,000	$37,580+63%	$80,000
$88,000	$100,000	$42,620+64%	$88,000
$100,000	$120,000	$50,300+66%	$100,000
$120,000	$140,000	$63,500+67%	$120,000
$140,000	$160,000	$76,900+68%	$140,000
$160,000	$180,000	$90,500+69%	$160,000
$180,000	......	$104,300+70%	$180,000

Carol's earnings are not sufficient to require payment of income tax, thus she enters the $50.70 on line 26b which is for the amount to be refunded. After checking all entries for accuracy, Carol signs and dates the Form 1040, attaches the Copy B of Form W-2 and mails it in the envelope provided to the Internal Revenue Service.

Carol found the instructions easy to follow and learned that filing for an income tax refund is not difficult. However, filing income tax returns becomes more complicated as earnings increase and come from several sources such as wages, interest, and estates.

The information on the federal income tax system and filing of individual returns was taken from the Internal Revenue Service's "Understanding Taxes, Teaching Taxes Program," 1970 edition. The example of Carol's income tax return is only a small part of what is involved in filing returns. Additional information may be obtained by purchasing publications of the Department of the Treasury, Internal Revenue Service.

Legal Requirements for Taxpayers

The law requires that every taxpayer keep records that will enable him to prepare a complete and accurate income tax return. The records should include accurate records on income, deductions, credits, and items required in filing income tax returns. Records for this purpose should include all receipts, cancelled checks, and other evidence to prove the amount claimed for deductions.

The taxpayer must also retain tax records on income and deductions until after the expiration of the statute of limitations, which is ordinarily three years from the date the return was due or filed.

April 15 of each year is the final date for filing income tax returns without penalty. When the last day for filing falls on Saturday, Sunday, or a legal holiday, the next succeeding day (which is not Saturday, Sunday, or a legal holiday) is considered the final day for filing. If the return is mailed, the postmark must show a date no later than the final filing date.

Under certain conditions, a person who is a resident of the United States may be granted an extension of time to file a return. Form 2688 is used for this purpose and may be obtained at the local Internal Revenue Office.

Taxpayers who discover mistakes after having filed tax returns before the final date of April 15, have a chance to rectify their error without penalty. "Form 1040X, Amended U.S. Individual Income Tax Return," is used for this purpose.

As young men and women earn more money and start a family, it is good money management to become familiar with income tax matters. Many certified public accountants specialize in income tax service and can provide income tax filing assistance for a small fee.

Characteristics of a Good Tax System

Few people enjoy paying taxes. Yet few of us would be willing to go without most of the services provided by local, state, and national governments. Since most young workers will be paying taxes for all their working lives, they should be interested in understanding what makes a good tax system.

One of the first questions to be asked is, "How much should I have to pay?" Everyone has not agreed on this question. However, arguments of the past have centered on certain principles which should be considered in order to develop an equitable or just tax system. Adam Smith, a classical economist, presented guidelines for a good tax system before the Constitution of our nation was written. In his book titled, *Wealth of Nations*, he listed four principles of taxation. These principles are concerned with equity, certainty, convenience, and economy.

Equity is the idea that everyone should contribute to the support of his government according to his ability in the proportion to the revenue enjoyed as a citizen.

Certainty was a term used to describe the application of a tax law in respect to each individual. The amount assessed, the time of payment, and the manner of payment should be made clear and not applied arbitrarily.

Convenience means that taxes should be levied and collected at a time and place most convenient for the taxpayer.

Automated Federal Tax System

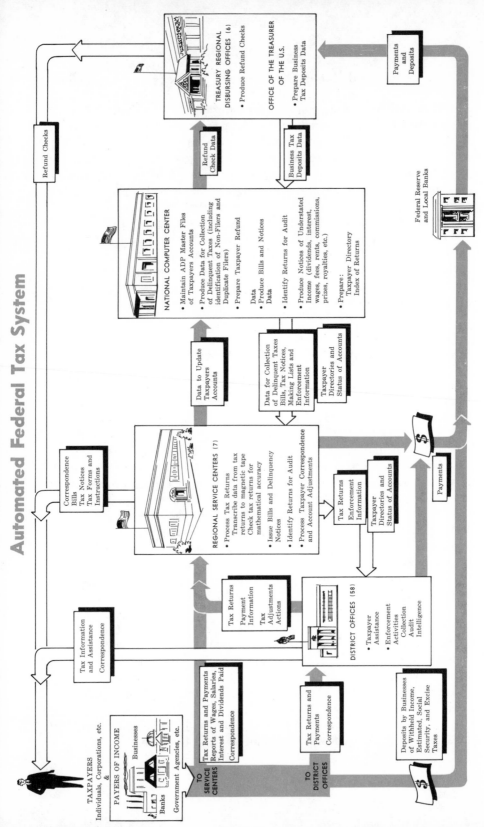

An Automated Tax System Helps to Improve the Efficiency of Taxation

Economy was a term used to indicate that no more tax money should be collected than is necessary, and administrative costs should be kept at a minimum.

The principles of taxation are not discussed as much today as in the past. Most people recognize the merits of such principles as:

1. The ability to pay;
2. Benefits rendered from the taxes;
3. Sacrifice made by individuals; and
4. Cost of service.

Today, economists still do not fully agree on what makes a good tax system. Arguments center on the following principles: cost of service rendered, ability of a person to pay, the sacrifices of individuals, and the benefits one derives from the taxes. All the above principles have merit as well as disadvantages. The ability to pay principle is in evidence when one studies the federal income system. However, we still depend on real estate tax to raise money on the local and state level. State and local governments are hard pressed to provide the services that are needed, especially in support of city services, such as police protection and street maintenance. Many believe the ability to pay principle is the most practical. A proportional tax system which can be made flexible is perhaps the least harmful tax. It does not kill business initiative, but can still supply money for the operations of the government and social and economic progress.

Study Helps

New Terms

direct taxes	wage and tax statements
excise taxes	tax deductions
federal budget	sales tax
inheritance taxes	highway-user tax
property taxes	

Study Questions

1. What is the difference between direct and indirect taxes?
2. What determines the tax rate on property tax?
3. What is the sales tax rate in your state?
4. How does one pay highway-user tax?
5. Does your state have a state income tax?
6. Who is required to file a federal income tax return?
7. When was the federal income tax law enacted?
8. Why has it been necessary to retain a high level of personal income tax since 1940?
9. Who is responsible for the preparation of the federal budget?
10. What government agency is the largest user of tax dollars?
11. What is the purpose of Form W-2 in the tax system?
12. When you buy an auto license what type of taxes are you paying?
13. What is the procedure in getting a Social Security account number?
14. What percentage of your wages does your employer withhold for social security?
15. What is the number of the form used in filing income tax returns?
16. How many copies of the Form W-4 must be completed in your state?
17. Is it possible to correct an error in your income tax returns if you have already mailed them to the Internal Revenue Service office?
18. What are the characteristics of a good tax system?
19. Since tax laws change, where can you go each year to get the latest information on filing your income tax returns?
20. Is it necessary to keep a record of earnings and tax returns?
21. What is the tax surcharge and how is it completed?
22. Why is federal income tax called "graduated income tax"?
23. Can you file an income tax return without a Social Security account number?

Discussion Problems

1. What percent of your personal income should go to finance government activities?
2. What action can the voting citizen take in regard to the tax structure of the United States?
3. What is the argument for a strong federal taxing system?
4. Will an improved automated tax collector and checking system reduce tax evasion?

Chapter 14

Social Security
and Retirement

Most Americans wish to be self-supporting during their lifetimes. The pioneer was taught the value of thrift and saving during his childhood. Saving money started at an early age. Since most of the farmers depended on agriculture for an occupation, money was saved when crops and prices were good. The money they were able to save was invested in more land and livestock. Many were able to save enough to live comfortably during old age. If the farmer became disabled through accident or disease his family or friends took care of him.

With the change in America from a mainly agricultural economy to an urban industrial economy, problems developed for the people employed in business and industry. For many, it was not possible to make enough money during a lifetime to retire. Workers were required to take easier jobs and keep working as long as they were able. Many who were able to save money for retirement lost their savings and investments when economic depressions hit. During the great economic depression of the 1930's, farmers and most businessmen experienced great loss of money and property. The leaders of business, industry, and government started searching for ways in which economic security could be acquired for those reaching retirement age. Thus, in 1935, after the people in the United States had experienced the greatest economic panic in the history of the nation, Congress passed the Social Security Act and established the Social Security Administration.

A number of workers in the United States were protected by private social insurance programs before 1930. These programs were established by labor unions and by the employees of particular industries. Many of the insurance groups were financed by the contributions of the employees and their employers. Through these plans, the employees could have some of their monthly earnings deducted from their checks and invested in the pension fund. At age 65 or older, the workers who had worked for the company long enough were able to receive monthly checks for retirement. Some workers were also able to have health insurance as a part of their retirement. Many of the railroad companies, in cooperation with the workers and the union, were providing hospital care for the workers and retired workers.

Private Retirement Plans Provide Good Benefits for Workers

Many private insurance and retirement plans provided good retirement benefits for their workers. However, the majority of the workers in business and industry were unable to secure jobs with companies providing retirement plans and were forced to live on the money they had saved. Many people felt that the only way to provide insurance coverage for the majority of the people was to establish a national social insurance program operated by a special agency of the federal government.

Social Security Act of 1935

The Social Security Act of 1935 was the first attempt by the federal government to provide a social insurance plan on a nationwide basis. The major purpose of the act was to (1) provide unemployment insurance for persons out of work, and (2) to provide financial benefits for retirement, the needy aged, dependent children, the blind, and for the heirs in case of death. The unemployment insurance phase is handled primarily by the states with federal financial assistance. The second part of the act is directly under the control of the Social Security Administration, which is in the Department of Health, Education, and Welfare.

The young worker will find it to his advantage to fully understand the provisions of the Federal Social Security Act. Parts of the Act are important to the welfare of young families, especially the survivors and disability provisions.

Old Age, Survivors, and Disability Insurance (OASDI)

Part two of the Social Security Act includes the old age, survivors, and disability insurance. Since passage of the Act, several changes have been made. Major changes occured in 1950, 1954, and 1956 when amendments to the Act extended old age and survivor insurance to self-employed people. In 1965, another addition was enacted to provide health insurance for people 65 and older. Many additional changes will probably be made in the future, making published information out of date. However, the basic idea and principles involved in the plan will probably not change.

HOW IT WORKS

More than 9 out of 10 working people are building protection for themselves and their families under the social security program. To pay for this protection, workers make contributions based on their earnings covered by social security and their employers pay an equal contribution. A self-employed person pays contributions at a slightly lower rate than the combined employee-employer rate for retirement, survivors, and disability insurance. However, the hospital insurance contribution rate is the same for the employer, the employee, and the self-employed person.

The earnings covered by social security are reported, and a record of the covered earnings of each worker is kept by the Social Security Administration. The amount of the monthly retirement, survivors, or disability insurance payment is figured from the average monthly earnings in covered employment.

Social security contributions are placed in three special trust funds in the U.S. Treasury—one for retirement and survivors insurance, one for disability insurance, and the third for hospital insurance.

A fourth trust fund holds the assets of the medical insurance program. Into this trust fund go the premiums for medical insurance paid by the people enrolled and the matching amounts from the Federal Government.

Benefit payments and administrative expenses are paid from these funds. By law they can be used for no other purpose.

Basic Ideas of Social Security

The basic idea of the Social Security plan is a simple one. During the working years the employees, their employers, and self-employed persons are enrolled in the program and make Social Security contributions. The contributions are placed in three trust funds. When earnings stop or are reduced due to the worker's retirement, disability or death, the monthly cash benefits are paid to the worker or his family.

Part of the contributions go into the hospital insurance trust fund to provide workers and dependents assistance in paying medical expenses after they reach 65 years of age.

Benefits

The amount of a person's monthly retirement or disability benefit is based on his average earnings and contributions over a period of years. The amount paid to dependents in case of death also depends on the amount of average earnings. The exact amount is not determined until the application for benefits is made. However, an estimate of the worker's benefits can be made using the following steps:

Who Can Get Benefits Because of Disability?

The Social Security program provides disability protection in three different situations. Monthly benefit checks can be paid to:

- Disabled workers under 65 and their families.
- Persons disabled in childhood (before 18) who continue to be disabled. These benefits are payable when a parent receives Social Security retirement or disability benefits, or when an insured parent dies.
- Disabled widows, disabled dependent widowers, and (under certain circumstances) disabled surviving divorced wives of workers who were insured at death. These benefits are payable as early as 50.

Basic Conditions for Payment of Disability Benefits

• How much work is required for disability benefits?

Like other cash Social Security benefits, disability benefits are payable on the basis of credit for work under Social Security. In the case of a disabled worker, his own work is the basis for his benefits. A person disabled in childhood gets benefits based on the earnings of a parent. A widow, widower, or surviving divorced wife gets benefits based on the earnings of the deceased spouse.

To have disability protection, most workers need Social Security credits for at least 5 years out of the 10-year period ending when their disability begins. For the worker who becomes disabled before 31, the requirement ranges down with age to as little as 1½ years.

• When is a person considered "disabled?"

A worker or a person disabled in childhood is considered "disabled" under Social Security if he has a physical or mental impairment which:

Prevents him from doing any substantial gainful work,

and is expected to last (or has lasted) for at least 12 months, or is expected to result in death.

(Payments may be made to a person who meets these requirements even if he is expected to recover from his disability.)

If a worker or childhood disability applicant has an impairment that prevents his doing his usual work, then his age, education, and work experience also may be considered in deciding whether he is able to engage in any other type of work. If he can't do his regular work but can do other substantially gainful work, generally he will not be considered disabled.

A widow or widower may be considered disabled only if he or she has a condition which is so severe that it would ordinarily prevent a person from working and which is expected to last at least 12 months. Age, education, and work experience cannot be considered in deciding whether a widow or widower is disabled.

Special Provisions for the Blind

A person whose vision is no better than 20/200 even with glasses (or who has a limited visual field of 20 degrees or less) is considered "blind" under the Social Security law. If he is not working, he can generally get monthly benefits.

If a person who meets this test of blindness is actually working, he may nevertheless be able to have his future benefit rights protected under other special provisions in the law for blind people. Check with your Social Security office for further details.

Disability Benefit Payments

Disability insurance is very important to the young worker and his family. Since 1954, Social Security has provided this protection at low cost. Many improvements and wider coverage has been extended since that time. Today 67 million workers under 65 and their families are eligible for Social Security. You should know the provisions of Social Security for disabled persons. Perhaps you know of someone who can qualify and has made no application.

The Social Security Administration offers the following information concerning disability insurance benefits.

EXAMPLES OF MONTHLY RETIREMENT AND DISABILITY INSURANCE BENEFITS

Average yearly earnings after 1950	Retirement benefits at 65 or later, or disability benefits	Reduced retirement benefit for worker starting at—			Wife of retired worker, starting at—			
		62	63	64	62	63	64	65 and over
Less than $900	$ 55.00	$ 44.00	$ 47.70	$ 51.40	$20.70	$23.00	$25.30	$ 27.50
$1800	88.40	70.80	76.70	82.60	33.20	36.90	40.60	44.20
$3000	115.00	92.00	99.70	107.40	43.20	48.00	52.80	57.50
$4200	140.40	112.40	121.70	131.10	52.70	58.50	64.40	70.20
$5400	165.00	132.00	143.00	154.00	61.90	68.80	75.70	82.50
$6600	189.90	152.00	164.60	177.30	71.30	79.20	87.10	95.00
$7800*	218.00	174.40	189.00	203.50	78.80	87.50	96.30	105.00

EXAMPLES OF
MONTHLY SURVIVORS INSURANCE BENEFITS

Average yearly earnings after 1950	Widow, widower, or one aged parent—62 or over	Widow under 62 and one child	Widow at 60, no child	Disabled widow at 50, no child
Less than $900	$ 55.00	$ 82.50	$ 47.70	$ 33.40
$1800	73.00	132.60	63.30	44.30
$3000	94.90	172.60	82.30	57.60
$4200	115.90	210.60	100.50	70.30
$5400	136.20	247.60	118.10	82.70
$6600	156.70	285.00	135.90	95.10
$7800*	179.90	327.00	156.00	109.20

● **How much will the benefits be?**

Benefits can amount to as much as $189.90 monthly for a disabled worker and up to $395.60 a month for a family. The amount depends on the worker's average earnings under social security over a period of years.

● **When can benefit payments begin?**

The law provides that payments to a disabled worker and his family or to a disabled widow or widower generally can not begin until the seventh full month of disability. A son or daughter disabled in childhood may be eligible for benefits as soon as one of his parents begins getting retirement or disability benefits, or dies (after having worked long enough under the law to make payments possible).

If a person has been disabled for more than 7 months before he applies, some benefits may be payable for months before the application was made. It is important to apply soon after the disability starts because back payments are limited to the 12 months preceding the date of application.

WHO GETS CASH BENEFITS

YOU

- As a retired worker (at 65, or in a permanently reduced amount beginning between 62 and 65)
- As a disabled worker at any age before 65

When you qualify for benefits at retirement or if you become disabled or at your death, certain of your dependents can receive benefits. Usually these are:

YOUR WIFE

- When 65 (permanently reduced amount as early as 62)
- At any age if caring for a child entitled to benefits, except student benefits

YOUR DEPENDENT HUSBAND

- At 65 (permanently reduced amount as early as 62)

YOUR UNMARRIED CHILDREN

- Under 18
- 18 and over if disabled before 18th birthday
- Between 18 and 22 if full-time students

YOUR WIDOW

- At 62 (permanently reduced amount as early as 60)
- At 50-60 in reduced amount if severely disabled
- At any age if caring for a child entitled to benefits, except student benefits

YOUR DEPENDENT WIDOWER

- At 62
- 50-62 in reduced amount if severely disabled

YOUR DEPENDENT PARENTS (after your death)

- At 62

LUMP-SUM DEATH BENEFIT

- Surviving spouse who was living in the same household
- If there is no spouse, to the person who paid the burial expenses or to the funeral home

● **Where should you go to apply?**

If you are disabled and can't work, you should get in touch with the nearest Social Security office right away. The people there can give you more information about disability benefits and will help you complete an application. If you can't get to the office because you are hospitalized or housebound, a Social Security representative will arrange to call on you.

Health Insurance and Medical Care Under Social Security

Many of our older people living on fixed incomes are unable to meet all the costs of medical care that they need. Private companies have provided some insurance for the older group of citizens. However, insurance for persons over 65 is expensive and many cannot pay the high cost. In 1965, after much debate among different political and professional groups, Congress passed an amendment to the Social Security Act to provide health insurance for persons 65 and over.

Your Social Security Card

Each of you should already have a Social Security card which indicates your Social Security number. If you do not have such a card you should apply immediately to the Social Security Office in your area.

Our concern in this chapter has been with the financial benefits from the Social Security Act. There are a number of other uses for the number on your Social Security card.

Your Social Security number may be required for issuance of a public library card. Your application for employment requires a record of your Social Security number; this number and the wages paid to you are reported each year to the federal Internal Revenue Department as a verification for federal withholding taxes. If you enter military service, your Social Security number becomes your military identification number. As you begin to save a part of your earnings, you will find that the bank requires a record of your Social Security number, for they, like your employer, must report annually to the federal government the amount of interest paid to you on your savings account.

THE KEY TO YOUR SOCIAL SECURITY

SOCIAL **SECURITY**
ACCOUNT NUMBER
000-00-0000
HAS BEEN ESTABLISHED FOR
John Q. Public
SIGNATURE, *John Q. Public*
FOR SOCIAL SECURITY PURPOSES • NOT FOR IDENTIFICATION

Your social security number is your key to the benefits you have earned. You only need one number in your working lifetime, no matter how many jobs you have. And you keep the same number for life.

Your social security record is kept under the name and number on your social security card. You should always show your card to your employer. He needs the information on the card for his report of the amount of your earnings. Be sure his record of your number is correct.

If you are self-employed, copy the number directly from your social security card when you make out the self-employment part of your Federal personal income tax return.

Your social security number is also your tax number. Upon request, show it to anyone who pays you interest, dividends, or other income that must be reported.

You can easily see that your Social Security number is an important link between the government, your employer, and you. This number should be memorized in order that you will be able to write it without checking your Social Security card. To avoid loss of this number before it has been memorized, the Social Security Administration issues duplicate cards, one of which should be placed in your safety deposit box at the bank. The other card should be carried constantly in your billfold. In case one card is lost, the Social Security Office will issue a duplicate if you can show one card; otherwise, a new number must be assigned. Remember—your Social Security card is one of your most vital possessions and you should make every effort not to lose that card.

If you have a

Social Security Card

Be sure to notify the

nearest social security office

when you change your name.

You'll get a social security card

with the same account number,

and the social security records

will be changed to show your

new name.

U.S. DEPARTMENT OF HEALTH, EDUCATION, AND WELFARE
Social Security Administration   SSI–69

STATE OF KANSAS—LABOR DEPARTMENT
EMPLOYMENT SECURITY DIVISION
****
CLAIM SUPPLEMENT

(Do not write in this space)

A _____ C _____

ENTER
YOUR
NAME_____

SOCIAL
SECURITY
NUMBER_____

A. 1. (a) Do you expect to return to your last job?. . . . . ☐ YES   ☐ NO

   (b) Do you have a definite prospect for work with any other employer?. . . . ☐ YES   ☐ NO

   2. How many months have you been employed in the past year? . . . . _____

   3. Do you expect to obtain work through a union?. . . . . ☐ YES   ☐ NO

   If 'Yes', in what union, local and city, are you in good standing?_____

   _____

C. 1. (a) What kind of work are you seeking? _____ At what wage?_____

   (b) List any other kinds of work you can do_____

   2. How many different employers have you worked for during the past year?_____

   3. What means of transportation do you have to get to work?_____

   4. Have you been employed in this area in the past year? . . . . ☐ YES   ☐ NO

   5. (a) Are you or any member of your household engaged in, or planning a
          farming activity?. . . . . ☐ YES   ☐ NO

   (b) Are you self-employed or in business of any kind?. . . . . ☐ YES   ☐ NO

   6. Do you attend, or plan to attend school?. . . . . ☐ YES   ☐ NO

   If 'Yes', when will you enter school?_____, 19_____

   7. Do you receive, or have you applied for a pension or Social Security?. . . . ☐ YES   ☐ NO

   If 'Yes', from what source?_____

   8. Is there any reason why you cannot accept a permanent full time job at once? ☐ YES   ☐ NO

   If 'Yes', check reason: ☐ Home responsibilities   ☐ Care of children   ☐ Aged Persons

        Other (Explain)_____

   9. Are you physically able to accept regular full time employment?. . . . . . . ☐ YES   ☐ NO

   10. To be answered by women only:

   (a) Are you pregnant?. . . . . ☐ YES   ☐ NO

   (b) If you have minor children, give their ages:_____

11. ALL CLAIMANTS ANSWER: During the past 18 months have you worked for any employ-
    er to whom you are related, or for any business in which you have or had a
    financial interest?   ☐ YES   ☐ NO

I certify that the above answers are true and correct to the best of my knowledge.

Date_____   _____
                                              (Claimant's Signature)

L. O. Code_____

K-Ben 15 (2-69) Succeeds KUC 609-5

Unemployment Insurance

Unemployment insurance is not directly related to Social Security insurance, but it is a form of social insurance which we will consider here.

Each state has set up its own law to manage and adminster an unemployment insurance system. The system is managed jointly by the state and the federal government. Most states started paying unemployment benefits to workers in 1938 or 1939.

The Unemployment Act was made a federal law during the Great Depression of the thirties when much of our present social legislation was passed. In a number of states the tax is levied directly upon the employer. A few states finance the system by requiring the employer to make contributions to pay for unemployment or disability.

The laws vary among the states on the amount and length of time an unemployed person may be paid. The table on the following page lists the compensation maximums paid in the states as of July 1, 1969.

Conditions Under Which the Worker Can Collect Compensation

Some unemployment seems to be unavoidable in the work force of our modern industrial world. Many jobs are seasonal and factories are forced to lay off employees during periods of retooling and model changes. The young worker who has little seniority may be the first to experience unemployment and needs to understand the provisions of his state's unemployment compensation laws.

A worker may receive unemployment compensation benefits if he meets certain provisions of the state law. These provisions may include the following:

1. He has become unemployed through no fault of his own.
2. He must register at a public employment office for a job.
3. He must be willing to take a comparable job.
4. He must make a claim for benefits.

5. He had earned a certain amount of money or worked a given length of time.
6. The job in which he is working is covered by state law.

State Unemployment Compensation Maximums, July 1, 1969

State	Maximum weekly benefit amount[1]	Maximum duration, weeks	State	Maximum weekly benefit amount[1]	Maximum duration, weeks
Alabama	$44	26	Montana	$42	26
Alaska	60-85	28	Nebraska	44	26
Arizona	50	26	Nevada	47-67	26
Arkansas	47	26	New Hampshire	54	26
California	65	26	New Jersey	65	26
Colorado	71	26	New Mexico	53	30
Connecticut	70-105	26	New York	65	26
Delaware	55	26	North Carolina	42	26
D. C.	63	34	North Dakota	51	26
Florida	40	26	Ohio	47-66	26
Georgia	47	26	Oklahoma	38	39
Hawaii	72	26	Oregon	49	26
Idaho	53	26	Pennsylvania	60	30
Illinois	42-70	26	Puerto Rico	36	12
Indiana	40-52	26	Rhode Island	56-76	26
Iowa	58	26	South Carolina	50	26
Kansas	53	26	South Dakota	41	26
Kentucky	52	26	Tennessee	47	26
Louisiana	50	28	Texas	45	26
Maine	52	26	Utah	54	36
Maryland	60	26	Vermont	56	26
Massachusetts	57[2]	30	Virginia	48	26
Michigan	46-76	26	Washington	42	30
Minnesota	57	26	West Virginia	49	26
Mississippi	40	26	Wisconsin	66	34
Missouri	53	26	Wyoming	53	26

[1]Maximum amounts. When two amounts are shown, higher includes dependent's allowances. [2]Amount limited only by average weekly wage. Source: U.S. Department of Labor, Manpower Administration, Unemployment Insurance Service.

A worker may not draw unemployment compensation under the following conditions:

1. If unemployed as a result of a labor dispute. (Some
   states have exceptions to this rule.)
2. If he quits his job without cause.
3. When discharged for misconduct. (The waiting period
   is usually longer with fewer payments for persons in
   this category.)
4. When the worker refuses to apply or take a suitable job.
5. When the worker misrepresents facts or makes fradu-
   lent claims.
6. When the worker is discharged after conviction of theft.
7. Other restrictions on payments include leaving the job
   for marriage or pregnancy or to further education.

A Worker May Not Draw Unemployment Insurance If
He Refuses to Take a Suitable Job

The unemployed worker is required to go to his local state employment service office and register for work. He may file for unemployment compensation in some offices. If a job which he can do is available, he must take the job or lose his unemployment benefits. When a worker moves to another state, he can still collect unemployment insurance at the new residence. The new state will act as his agent in most cases.

Benefits under the unemployment insurance program can be paid to unemployed workers who have recent employment or earnings in a job covered by the state law which he resides. The amount of earnings and the period of employment is used to calculate the amount of benefits the worker may receive. The formula used varies from state to state. Generally, the benefits received are equal to one-half the worker's weekly salary. In a number of states the benefits the worker may receive are based on a prior 12-month period of work as well as a stated number of weeks. All workers may not receive the benefits for the number of weeks listed in the table on page 304.

Employer Finance of Unemployment Insurance

The cost of providing unemployment insurance is paid by the employer in all but three states, Alabama, New Jersey, and Alaska. The standard rate of payment for most states is set at 2.7% of the taxable payroll. Employers who have little unemployment in their work force receive lower than average rates. The taxable amounts on which employers pay for unemployment insurance varies in different states. For example, the limit was set in 1964 as the first $3,000 of a worker's wages. However, in Alaska the amount is $7,200.

The employer pays an extra 0.4% unemployment tax to the federal government on the first $3,000 paid to each employee. This money is used to cover the administration cost of the program.

Not all workers are covered by unemployment insurance. Employers who employ four persons for 20 weeks or more per year are required to pay unemployment payroll tax unless they are exempt in the states. Employers that are exempt include

CONTRIBUTION RATE SCHEDULE EMPLOYER-EMPLOYEE, EACH
Percent of Covered Earnings

Years	For Retirement, Survivors, and Disability Insurance	For Hospital Insurance	Total
1968	3.8	0.6	4.4
1969-70	4.2	.6	4.8
1971-72	4.6	.6	5.2
1973-75	5.0	.65	5.65
1976-79	5.0	.7	5.7
1980-86	5.0	.8	5.8
1987 and after	5.0	.9	5.9

SELF-EMPLOYED PEOPLE
Percent of Covered Earnings

Years	For Retirement, Survivors, and Disability Insurance	For Hospital Insurance	Total
1968	5.8	0.6	6.4
1969-70	6.3	.6	6.9
1971-72	6.9	.6	7.5
1973-75	7.0	.65	7.65
1976-79	7.0	.7	7.7
1980-86	7.0	.8	7.8
1987 and after	7.0	.9	7.9

state employer, employer of non-profit organizations, farm and domestic workers, members of the employer's family, and others.

The occupations covered by unemployment insurance have gradually increased during the last 35 years. Perhaps all workers will eventually be covered by some type of unemployment insurance in the future.

Objectives of Unemployment Insurance

Unemployment can cause a family many hardships. This is especially true of a young family which has little financial reserve to fall back on during periods of unemployment. The unemployment system provides some money while a person is temporarily unemployed or has lost his job and is seeking another.

The system has another objective which is equally important to the individual, his family, and the country. The system is a "built in economic stabilizer." When a worker is laid off his job, he starts to receive payments from the unemployment compensation fund. When he returns to work, payments stop and reserves are again collected for the next period of unemployment. When unemployment is low, funds build up. When unemployment is high, the funds go into circulation again. Multiply this process by millions of unemployed men and you find a sizeable amount of money going into the economy.

Several other stabilizers are also in operation in the United States which include the "automatic changes in tax receipts" and the "farm-aid programs."

Workmen's Compensation

The industrial worker of 75 years ago faced many dangers from the crude machinery with which he worked and the unsafe methods used. Accidents killed or injured workers at an alarming rate. Accidents were considered a normal part of a worker's risk and some employers were rather lax in practicing safety in industry. When a worker was injured in an industrial accident, it was difficult to get compensation for injuries. In many cases, only expensive lawsuits allowed the injured worker to get payment for his injuries.

As the number of industrial workers increased and accidents increased, attention to the problem was brought to the general public. Gradually, the philosophy of accident responsibility changed to one placing a larger part on the employer rather than the employee.

Social Security and Retirement 309

CLAIMANT: Do not write
in items 'A' or 'B'

UNEMPLOYMENT INSURANCE APPLICATION

A. Office No.	B. B. Y. E.	**1** PRINT—First Name, Initial, Last Name	**2** SOCIAL SECURITY NUMBER

3 SEX ☐ Male ☐ Female	**5** MAIL ADDRESS Street and Number, P. O. Box or RFD	**6** SHOW OTHER NAMES or Social Security Numbers worked under during past 18 months, if any

4 Year Born

City, State
and ZIP Code:

7 LAST JOB

EMPLOYERS' NAME AND PAYROLL ADDRESS		Details of Job						
LAST EMPLOYER (Regardless of state in which worked or size of firm)	Reason for Leaving Last Job		Began Work			Last Day Worked		
			Mo.	Day	Year	Mo.	Day	Year
Firm Name of Employer___	☐ Quit ☐ Fired ☐ Leave of Absence ☐ Laid off—Lack of Work ☐ Labor Dispute							
Street and Number___					19			19
City, State and Zip Code	KIND OF WORK DONE (Job Title)		Rate of Pay on Last Job					
			$		per			

8 NEXT TO LAST JOB (Omit if "next-to-last-job" ended more than 6 months ago)

NEXT TO LAST EMPLOYER	REASON FOR LEAVING NEXT TO LAST JOB		Began Work			Last Day Worked		
			Mo.	Day	Year	Mo.	Day	Year
Firm Name of Employer___	☐ Quit ☐ Fired ☐ Leave of Absence ☐ Laid off—Lack of Work ☐ Labor Dispute							
Street and Number___					19			19
City, State and Zip Code	KIND OF WORK DONE		RATE OF PAY					
			$		per			

9 HAVE YOU BEEN EMPLOYED by the Federal government in the past 18 months?..................................... ☐ Yes ☐ No

10 HAVE YOU SERVED IN THE ARMED FORCES of the United States in the past 18 months?.......................... ☐ Yes ☐ No

11 HAVE YOU BEEN EMPLOYED OUTSIDE the State of Kansas in the past 18 months?................................. ☐ Yes ☐ No

12 HAVE YOU FILED A PREVIOUS CLAIM for Unemployment Insurance in the past 12 months?.................... ☐ Yes ☐ No

If "YES", Where?
(City & State)___   When?
(Date)___   Against what
State?___

13 REMARKS:

14 CERTIFICATION: I register for work and apply for Unemployment Insurance benefits. All entries on this application are true and correct. I so certify knowing that the law provides penalties if I make false statements or withhold material information to obtain benefits not due me.

CLAIM ACCEPTED BY:___	**15** WRITE YOUR NAME HERE X

CLAIMANT—Do Not Write in Boxes Below

C. Law(s)	D. B. Y. B.	E. Type	F. Claim Date	G. 1 2 3 4 5 6 7 8 9 0	H. BRE Today ☐ Yes	I. Res. Code	J. To Report
K. Occ. Code		L. Industry	M. Suspense Effective		by:	N. K-Ben Atchd.	O.

INSTRUCTIONS TO CLAIMANT

Complete items '1' through '12'. Use item '13', if needed. READ item '14'. WRITE your name in item '15' as it should appear in item '1': first name, initial of middle name and last name.

Entry of your CORRECT Social Security Number is most important. A mistake will delay your claim.

Make NO entries in items lettered 'A' through 'O'.

PRINT all entries except your signature. Press hard enough to make a good carbon imprint on the three forms underneath.

K-Ben 10   (9-67)   Unemployment Insurance Application—Kansas Employment Security Division   ROBERT R. (BOB) SANDERS, STATE PRINTER   1654-1

Laws were passed to protect the worker in case of accidents on the job. The laws are called "Workmen Compensation Laws." There are different responsibilities on the part of employers and employees in reporting accidents and action taken in accidents.

The cost of industrial accidents is very high, not only in money lost, but in suffering by the worker and his family. Claims of injured workers have increased tremendously.

, Compensation claims reached near $1,800,000,000 in 1965 compared with $500,000,000 in 1950. The increase in 15 years represents a larger work force and a higher rate of compensation. However, the average worker of today has many other sources of social insurance to protect him, while the early worker had only workmen's compensation for protection.

One important thing for a young worker is remember if he or she is injured on the job is that it is most important to report the injury to the employer. The requirement that the employee reports an injury is for the protection of both employee and employer. A delay in reporting an injury creates doubt about the accident. A prompt notice protects the employee and also protects the employer against a fraudulent claim.

The time limit in reporting accidents and occupational diseases vary from state to state. All reports are processed, numbered, and coded. A screening process is involved and the accident is analyzed. From reports and analysis, safety experts can study the data and hopefully prevent other such accidents, thereby reducing the cost to the worker and employer.

Persons who are disabled by industrial accidents may become productive citizens again through rehabilitation programs. Here again, state programs are different. It is important for each worker to learn of the rehabilitation program available in the state in which he lives.

Study Helps

New Terms

social legislation   Social Security Administration
economic depression   Social Security Act

Medicare

Old Age and Survivors Insurance

benefits

retirement

contributions

compensation

disability

Medicaid

eligibility

major risks

Study Questions

1. Why do we need state and federal insurance programs?
2. How is the Social Security plan financed?
3. When was the Federal Social Security Act implemented?
4. At what age can a disabled worker qualify for Social Security benefits?
5. How may one check his Social Security contribution?
6. Will a girl receive a new Social Security number when she marries?
7. At what age can a healthy male worker start drawing Social Security retirement benefits?
8. What is the basis for calculating a person's monthly cash benefits for retirement?
9. Will a widow over 65 lose her Social Security benefits if she remarries?
10. Are farmers covered under the provision of the Social Security Act?
11. What is the use of Form SS-5?
12. Under Social Security laws, are cash benefits paid by the federal government?

Discussion Problems

1. List as many reasons as possible why social insurance is needed today.
2. What are the advantages and disadvantages of operating a federally controlled social insurance program?
3. What are the three major risks for which protection is provided in the Social Security Act? Which one is most important to a high school student?

4. What is the maximum amount of cash benefits available to a worker upon retirement? Is the amount adequate?
5. Under what conditions can workers between the ages of 18 and 65 claim Social Security benefits?
6. Is it wise for a young worker to invest in other retirement plans?

REQUEST FOR

STATEMENT

OF EARNINGS

ACCOUNT NUMBER ➡

| 000 | 00 | 0000 |

DATE OF BIRTH ➡

| MONTH | DAY | YEAR |
| January | 1 | 1970 |

Please send me a statement of the amount of earnings recorded in my social security account.

NAME { MISS / MRS. / MR. }   John Q. Public

STREET & NUMBER

CITY & STATE _____ ZIP CODE

} Print Name and Address In Ink Or Use Type- writer

SIGN YOUR NAME AS
YOU USUALLY WRITE IT   *John Q. Public*

Sign your own name only. Under the law, information in your social security record is confidential and anyone who signs someone else's name can be prosecuted.
If your name has been changed from that shown on your social security account number card, please copy your name below exactly as it appears on that card.

Chapter 15

Insurance

Sharing Economic Losses

The Indians who roamed the plains and woodlands many years ago had little need for the types of insurance available to us today. Their way of life was simple compared with ours. However, the Indians did need a form of insurance which they supplied for themselves. The basic idea in insurance is to have many people share the risk of economic loss. The Indians pooled their labor and time to insure the health and safety of all members of the tribe. They lived off the land and had little interest in individual ownership of real estate. The braves hunted wild game to provide meat while the squaws and children raised corn and other grains to insure the food supply for the winter. In case of injury or death of the father, other members of the tribe cared for the family. This was a simple form of insurance.

Ever since the dawn of history, people have banded together to share economic loss and other hazards. As early as 900 B.C., sea-going people who lived on the islands of Rhodes in the Mediterranean Sea organized a plan to share the loss or damages to their ships and cargos. Like the Indians banding together for mutual protection, this illustrates the insurance principle of sharing economic loss. The Romans organized a type of life insurance for their soldiers during the 7th century. They also organized burial societies to share the cost of funerals. Members of guilds banded together and organized insurance plans for the protection of each member and his family.

Marine insurance to protect ship owners and shippers developed rapidly in England during the 17th Century when a new method of insuring ships and cargos evolved. Those who had the money and were willing to share the risk of a shipment would sign a contract to underwrite, or guarantee, a percent of loss in case the ship and cargo were lost. Should the ship reach port and sell the cargo, the underwriter would profit. However, in case of shipwreck the underwriter would lose.

Life insurance started over 300 years ago. The first policies probably grew out of marine insurance where protection was made available to the ship's passengers during a voyage.

There are early records of an Englishman who wrote a life insurance policy in 1583, and the first successful life insurance company was founded in England in 1705. The first life insurance company in America was founded in Philadelphia and was called "A Corporation for the Relief of Poor and Distressed Presbyterian Ministers and of the Poor and Distressed Widows and Children of Presbyterian Ministers".[1] A mutual fire insurance company was founded in Philadelphia by Benjamin Franklin.

Insurance Needs of Young Workers

The insurance needs of young workers are quite different from the needs of those with a family. John Smith is working on his first job since graduating from high school. He lives in a furnished apartment and has little personal property other than his wardrobe and an old car. His insurance needs are different from his sister Mary's who operates a beauty shop with an inventory of $10,000 and a mortgage of $5,000 on the equipment. The risks are different in these two situations, but both need insurance for protection against economic loss.

As a worker, you face risks every day. You may become ill and need hospitalization, or you may be injured on the high-

---

[1]R. Wilfred Kelsey and Arthur C. Daniels. *Handbook of Life Insurance,* Institute of Life Insurance, New York. pp. 8-9.

way or on the job. The young worker faces other risks, too. Should Mary's beauty shop be destroyed by fire or by a wind storm, a property insurance policy would protect her from a disastrous loss. Mary could be sued if a patron was injured in her shop. Liability insurance would protect her and the patron in case of an accident of this kind.

Many kinds of insurance are needed. As a single young man or woman with few responsibilities and little property, a life insurance policy plus a health and disability policy may be all the insurance you need. If you own a car, it will be necessary for you to buy car insurance. Many states require liability insurance before licensing a driver. For those owning business or real estate, property insurance will protect them from loss.

When a young man marries and starts a family, a larger percentage of his insurance budget may be needed for life insurance. Mary will need to continue liability insurance for herself and her employees in the beauty shop. Retirement is probably not a big worry for young workers. However, it is wise to start saving through an insurance policy or a savings plan at an early age for retirement.

A large percent of your insurance budget should go for life insurance. People who buy insurance protect themselves by sharing economic loss with their fellow workers and friends. Insurance helps to reduce some of the uncertainties of life and gives peace of mind not otherwise possible.

Planning for Personal Insurance

In planning your insurance program, it is necessary to first determine the risk you face at home, on the highway, and on the job. List all the risks which you may encounter in groups under headings of (1) property, (2) liability, (3) life, and (4) health insurance. Secondly, you must determine which risk you cannot afford to take without the protection of insurance. It will not be economically possible to protect yourself from all risks. Also, in planning you must consider the insurance you have in the form of social insurance and insurance protection furnished by your employer. A few people actually buy more

INSURANCE P OR?

Now have all you need with one easy monthly payment—through State Farm

insurance than they can afford and are pressed to meet all the other expenses. Such a person may be called "insurance poor."

Many large insurance companies furnish guidelines to assist persons in deciding how much to budget for insurance. The services of a good insurance agent from a recognized company are important. The young worker should select the agent and company carefully. One important check to make is to learn if the agent and his company has a state license to operate. The reputation of an agent may be determined by how long he has been with his company and recommendations from his policyholders. The premium (payments) on insurance policies may vary with the company. It is wise to compare the cost of insurance in different companies before buying.

Few young workers will have the experience or knowledge to buy insurance without cautious consideration and help from their parents, employers, and friends. Thus, in the remainder of this unit we will consider the different types of insurance available and suggest pointers for buying insurance.

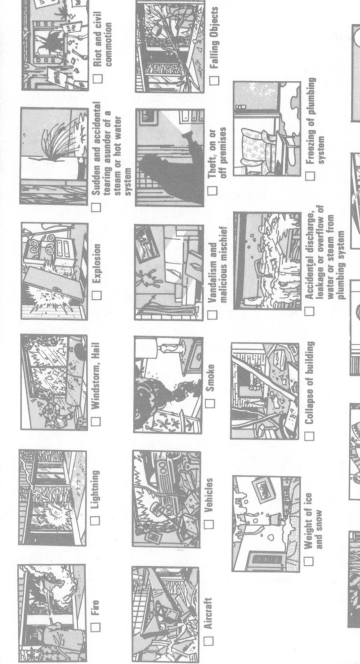

☐ Fire
☐ Lightning
☐ Windstorm, Hail
☐ Explosion
☐ Sudden and accidental tearing asunder of a steam or hot water system
☐ Riot and civil commotion

☐ Aircraft
☐ Vehicles
☐ Smoke
☐ Vandalism and malicious mischief
☐ Theft, on or off premises
☐ Falling Objects

☐ Artificially generated electrical currents
☐ Weight of ice and snow
☐ Collapse of building
☐ Accidental discharge, leakage or overflow of water or steam from plumbing system
☐ Freezing of plumbing system

☐ Personal liability
☐ Medical payments (other than to insureds)
☐ Physical damage to property of others
☐ All costs of defending suits (whether you are liable or not)

Insurance Covers Loss from All These Perils
(Courtesy State Farm Fire and Casualty Company, Bloomington, Illinois)

Types of Insurance

Property Insurance

Many large insurance companies in the United States are licensed to sell property insurance. For a small premium payment each year, a policyholder can protect his investment in a home or other property. A family investment in a home built with savings over a 20-year period may be lost in minutes in a fire or tornado. Insurance makes it possible to rebuild.

The home owner policy provides insurance coverage for owner and occupants of one- and two-family private residences. Many homeowners buy a comprehensive insurance policy which includes protection against many perils. The chart shows the basic coverage included in a comparative homeowner policy.

An inventory of personal property should be made and a copy placed in your bank safety deposit box. If a claim is made, it is easier to settle when a complete inventory is available.

Liability insurance may also be included under the homeowners policy. The liability insurance part of the homeowner's policy protects against claims in areas of personal liability, medical payments, and damage to the property of others. This coverage will protect persons injured on the homeowner's property or cover property damage.

Automobile Insurance

The owners and operators of automobiles must assume a great deal of responsibility. The National Safety Council estimated that more than 50,000 persons were killed in accidents in 1969, and billions in property loss result from accidents each year. The rise in accidents is a great problem both to the insured and to the insurer. Cost of auto insurance accident claims are increasing each year at an alarming rate. No driver can afford to drive without adequate protection.

Those who own or operate a motor vehicle should have a complete understanding of automobile insurance and should consider the following types of coverage.

First, bodily injury liability coverage is very important since those riding in the car or injured by the car can be protected. The driver can also be protected against suits of persons

INSURANCE INVENTORY	HOMEOWNERS*

DWELLING (Including Garage)   VALUES

Replacement Cost (Estimate) $_____

Actual Value
(Replacement cost
Less Depreciation) (Estimate) $_____

Present Insurance (Amount) $_____

Premium (Present Insurance) $_____

PRESENT COVERAGE

• Fire and Extended Coverage   ☐

• Broad Form   ☐

• Dwelling & Special Form   ☐

Other Forms   ☐

EXPIRATION DATE_____

PERSONAL PROPERTY

(Replacement Cost, Less Depreciation)   Actual Value

Furniture (Living Room,
Dining and Bedrooms) $_____

Appliances $_____

Clothing $_____

Linens, Rugs, Etc. $_____

China, Silverware $_____

Other Articles (Books, Sports
Equipment, Etc.) $_____

TOTAL $_____

Present Insurance (Amount) $_____

Premium (Present Insurance) $_____

EXPIRATION DATE_____

HOMEOWNERS*

FORM NO(s)._____

Expiration Date

COVERAGE: AMOUNTS

A DWELLING . . . . .   _____

B PRIVATE STRUCTURES . .   _____
Detached Garage, Etc.

C UNSCHEDULED
PERSONAL PROPERTY
On Premises . . . . . .   _____

Off Premises . . . . . .   _____

D ADDITIONAL LIVING
EXPENSE . . . . . .   _____

E COMPREHENSIVE
PERSONAL LIABILITY . .   _____

F MEDICAL PAYMENTS . .   _____
(Per Person)

G PROPERTY DAMAGE . .   _____

ADDED COVERAGES:

End. No. _____   _____

End. No. _____   _____

End. No. _____   _____

Premium: 1st Year $_____

2nd Year $_____

3rd Year $_____

TOTAL $_____

If Paid In Advance . . TOTAL $_____

*COVERAGE SUBJECT TO POLICY TERMS.

Insurance Inventory
It is important to have an inventory of all property insured. The inventory should be current and a copy filed for safe keeping.
(Courtesy of State Farm Insurance, Bloomington, Illinois)

injured or killed by the insured's vehicle. Different amounts of coverage may be purchased. It is possible to carry as much as $100,000 for one person or a total of $300,000 should more than one person be injured in an accident.

Second, medical payment coverage is also available. This coverage is similar to the protection offered in a homeowner's policy. It will pay medical expenses for a person who may be injured while a passenger in your car. You should consider this type of insurance if you transport persons to work or children to school.

Third, collision insurance is available. If you have a large investment in your car, collision insurance is recommended. Complete coverage is very expensive. A $50 or $100 deductible policy is less expensive. The owner pays the first $50 or $100 of the damage.

Fourth, property damage liability insurance protects you and the owner of another car or property from loss when your

Bodily Injury Liability Insurance Is a Must

vehicle causes the damage. Property damage liability insurance is available in amounts of $5000 to $100,000. This coverage is generally purchased with bodily injury liability insurance and is equally important. In many states the law requires all drivers to carry these two types of insurance.

Fifth, comprehensive insurance protects you against loss due to damage to your automobile from fire, lightning, flood, and windstorm. Glass breakage is also covered under this section of a policy. You also have protection against theft of your car or parts of the car under comprehensive coverage.

Sixth is protection against uninsured drivers who may involve you in an accident. This type of coverage is limited to the amount of liability required under the laws of the various states.

Automobile insurance is expensive and we should buy only the insurance necessary for protecting ourselves and others. No one should drive a car without liability insurance. Both bodily injury and property damage coverage is needed unless a person has the wealth to pay damages resulting from accidents which may be his fault. Most young people should also buy insurance for medical payments to protect others riding in their cars. Collision insurance is rather expensive. Individual circumstances must be considered in deciding if this type of insurance is necessary. For example, if your car is old and has little value you should probably not carry collision insurance. On the other hand, if you use your car in sales work, and have most of your money invested in the car, it would be wise to purchase collision insurance. If your car is essential for your job, you may carry insurance to provide transportation while your auto is being repaired.

There are many factors affecting the rates of the insurance charged by different companies.

1. The rates set by an insurance company reflect the cost of claims over a three-year period of time, and companies who are selective in choosing drivers they insure will probably have lower rates. Therefore, drivers who have good records should buy from selective companies.

2. The area where you live is a second factor. Congested urban areas have a higher rate of accidents than rural

DAMAGE by your automobile

  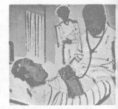

☐ Bodily Injury and Property Damage Liability —including bailbond expense, attorney fees and court costs.

Medical Payments— reimbursement for medical expenses arising out of an auto accident.
☐ Major Medical
☐ Standard Form

DAMAGE to your automobile

Comprehensive . . . accidental loss or damage* including theft rental.

☐ 100% Coverage
☐ $50 Deductible

Collision or Upset
☐ 80% Collision
☐ Deductible

☐ Emergency Road Service service expense for mechanical first aid.

* luggage and wearing apparel for certain listed perils

PLUS these special coverages

☐ Uninsured Automobiles—bodily injuries caused by a legally liable but uninsured or unknown driver.

☐ Rental Reimbursement— Car rental (up to a specified amount) while insured auto is being repaired.

☐ Automobile Death Indemnity, a scheduled amount payable if caused by an automobile accident

☐ Total Disability— Weekly payments for total disability caused by an automobile.

☐ Personal and residence liability, including medical payments

NOTE: These are brief explanations of coverages, but not a contract. Your legal contract is contained only in your policy. If you have any questions, please contact your State Farm agent. Some coverages (or certain features of some coverages) may not be available in your state.

Automobile Insurance Brochure
Automobile insurance is needed to protect your investment and persons who may be injured by your automobile.
(Courtesy State Farm Insurance, Bloomington, Illinois)

areas, thus a higher rate must be charged the policy holder.

3. The cost of car repair affects insurance rates. Charges are higher in some areas and some cars are more expensive to repair.

4. A fourth factor in determining rates is the classification of the driver himself. The young male driver under 25

Explanation of

Private
Passenger
Automobile
Classifications

See Your
State Farm Agent
for further details

Private passenger automobiles are classified and rated for liability, comprehensive, and collision insurance in accordance with 3 broad classification categories:

I   Age, sex, and marital status of the operator (s) of the automobile.

II   Use of the automobile, estimated annual mileage driven, and age of the operators under 25.

III   Discounts — 2 or more cars insured, driver training, good student, and student over 150 miles away from home.

The 3 digit code beside the word CLASS on your policy or premium notice indicates how your automobile is classified on the Company's records. *For example: CLASS 2AO.*

I.   The first digit from the left (the *2* in the example *2AO*) indicates the DRIVER CLASSIFICATION:

No Male Owner or Operator Under 25 and No Unmarried Female Owner or Operator Under 25
- 1 — Principal Operator 30 thru 64
- 2 — Principal Operator 65 or over
- 3 — Principal Operator Unmarried Male 25 thru 29

No Male Owner or Operator Under 25
- 4 — Unmarried Female Under 25, Occasional Operator
- 5 — Unmarried Female Under 25, Owner or Principal Operator

No Unmarried Male Owner or Operator Under 25
7 — Married Male Under 25, Owner or Operator

No Unmarried Male Owner or Principal Operator Under 25
- 8 — Unmarried Male Under 25, Occasional Operator
- 9 — Unmarried Male Under 25, Owner or Principal Operator

Continued on Reverse

II. The following use classifications, such as *A* in the example *2AO*, are applicable to driver classifications 1, 2, or 3:

*A — Pleasure use/7500 miles or less annually.
*B — Pleasure use/Over 7500 miles annually.
**C — Driven to or from work 10 miles or less one way/7500 miles or less annually.
**D — Driven to or from work 10 miles or less one way/Over 7500 miles annually.
**E — Driven to or from work over 10 miles one way/7500 miles or less annually.
**F — Driven to or from work over 10 miles one way/Over 7500 miles annually.
G — Business use/12,000 miles or less annually.
H — Business use/Over 12,000 miles annually.
J — Farmer—not used in any other occupation/7500 miles or less annually.
K — Farmer—not used in any other occupation/Over 7500 miles annually.
L — Non-farm utility vehicle used for business purposes.
M — Farm utility vehicle.
S — Antique auto—limited use.

The following use classifications are applicable to driver classifications 4, 5, 7, 8, or 9:

*A — Pleasure use/Operator is 21 thru 24.
*B — Pleasure use/Operator is under 21.
**C — Business use or driven to or from work/Operator is 21 thru 24.

**D — Business use or driven to or from work/Operator is under 21.
J — Farmer—not used in any other occupation/Operator is 21 thru 24.
K — Farmer—not used in any other occupation/Operator is under 21.
L — Non-farm utility vehicle used for business purposes.
M — Farm utility vehicle.
S — Antique auto—limited use.

III. The 3rd digit from the left (the *O* in the example *2AO*) indicates the applicable discount:

0 — Single, car—no discount.
1 — Good student.
2 — Good student and two or more cars.
3 — Two or more cars insured by State Farm.
4 — Driver training.
5 — Driver training and two or more cars.
6 — Good student and driver training.
7 — Good student, driver training, and 2 or more cars.
8 — Student over 150 miles from home.
9 — Student over 150 miles from home and two or more cars.
C — Student over 150 miles from home and driver training.
D — Student over 150 miles from home, driver training, and two or more cars.

* Pleasure use includes driving to or from work 30 miles or less weekly.   ** This means driving to or from work over 30 miles weekly.

STATE FARM MUTUAL AUTOMOBILE INSURANCE COMPANY / STATE FARM FIRE AND CASUALTY COMPANY
G 5361 e   MISSOURI / KANSAS • 2000 HIGHWAY 70 WEST / COLUMBIA, MISSOURI 65201

Private Passenger Automobile Classifications

Automobile insurance classifications are important to the person buying insurance. The above lists automobile classifications for insurance purposes. (Courtesy State Farm Insurance Company, Bloomington, Illinois)

years of age has a greater accident claim rate than any other group. Since persons in this classification have more accidents, a much higher rate is charged.

Some companies give special discounts for students who have high grades in high school or college. Drivers must remember that insurance rates are based on accidents and claims over the last three years of the company's experience. The more money a company must spend for accident claims, the higher insurance rates will go.

The table on page 323 is used to compare various liability rates by driver classifications in large cities.

Automobile owners and drivers should familiarize themselves with the rules and regulations of their respective insurance companies and state laws. Generally, the following procedures should be observed in reporting accidents when there is bodily injury and/or damages of $50 or more.

IN CASE OF ACCIDENT

1. Call the city police or highway patrol.
2. Obtain the names and addresses of driver, persons injured, passengers, and witnesses of the accident.
3. Write a brief description of injuries and property damage.
4. Write a description of the accident, time of day, visibility, road conditions, and other observed information.
5. Check the accident area for skid marks and tire marks.
6. Notify your insurance company representatives.
7. Your insurance company prefers that you not discuss the accident with other persons, but remember remarks and discussion by those at the scene of the accident.

25% OFF
Good Student Discount

car insurance-wise

Life Insurance

When starting your first full-time job, you may have little interest in buying life insurance. However, in a few years you will probably be married and have young children. Life insurance will then be of real interest. First, life insurance will give economic protection to the family should the father die as a result of accident or disease. Second, life insurance will provide a way to save money for some future use such as education for the children or income for retirement years and to meet financial emergencies, should they arise. Third, life insurance is a good method to save during working years.

Life insurance is especially important to the young man who has dependents. If he should die or become disabled, they could be left without any income. The risk is greatest when the family is young and expenses are largest. Little or no money has been saved; but with life insurance, the dependents can be protected. First, insurance can provide cash for immediate expenses such as payments on furniture, an automobile, a home, or funeral debts. Large, long-term debts, such as home mortgages, may be covered by a mortgage-cancellation clause in the policy. Second, insurance can provide money for the family to live on while adjustments are being made. Many times a young widow will need money to train for a job outside the home. If enough life insurance money is available, the young mother will be able to stay at home and provide good care for the children when they are young. Life insurance combined with federal Social Security benefits will generally provide enough money to keep the family together until the children are through school and able to provide for themselves.

Thus, life insurance provides economic protection for a young man's family in case of his death. It also provides certain benefits for the insured himself. Several types of policies have cash or loan values which may be used by the policyholder in case of a financial emergency. A policy with adequate value can be used in securing a loan in case of an immediate need for cash.

A number of life insurance contracts are available. The contracts, referred to as policies, are listed under five major types. These are straight life, limited payment, endowment, annuity, and term policies. Some policies are quite simple, others combine a number of elements to provide special coverage.

Kinds of Life Insurance

The **straight life insurance policy** provides protection over a long period of time. Premiums are payable as long as the insured person lives or as long as he wishes to keep the policy in force. This type of insurance policy is one of the better ones for the man or woman who desires protection for dependents and at the same time wants to accumulate a cash value over a number of years. The straight life policy has one of the lowest rates, and when combined with certain other plans, such as a term policy, provides adequate protection for most families. Many policyholders do not continue paying straight life premiums after retirement, but take a reduced *paid-up policy* which has a face value of 60 to 70% when the policyholder reaches the age of 65 years.

The **limited payment life insurance** contract is the same as the straight life, except that the premiums are paid for a limited number of years instead of for life. The contract can be written for the premiums to be paid-up in 10, 20, or 30 years.

Many young people prefer a limited payment policy instead of the straight life payments. In most situations the straight life gives more protection at lower cost because the premiums are lower at a time when a young family needs more protection. For example, if John Smith at age 20 years old decides to buy a $10,000 straight life policy, his yearly premiums will be $121.50, while for a 25-year limited policy his premium will be $161.10 per year. The cash value of the life policy will be $2350 while the 25-year policy will be $3380 after 20 years.

Under an **endowment insurance plan** the policyholder pays a stated premium for a given length of time. If the insured is living when the policy reaches maturity, he receives the full amount of the policy. However, if he should die, the amount will go to his beneficiary at the time of his death. The amount paid to the beneficiary may be paid in a lump sum or in monthly payment for a number of years.

AGE **20** — 𝕄𝕄 FACTOR PER POLICY A-$10.00 S-$6.00 Q-$4.00 BSP-$1.00

$1,000		EXEC†	SWL	20 PL	20 E	LP 65	LP 60
MALE	A	$10.06	$10.64	$19.02	$41.55	$11.57	$12.15
	S	5.13	5.43	9.70	21.19	5.90	6.20
	Q	2.62	2.77	4.95	10.80	3.01	3.16
	BSP	.86	.90	1.62	3.53	.98	1.03
FEMALE	A	$9.53	$10.11	$18.53	$41.19	$11.04	$11.63
	S	4.86	5.16	9.45	21.01	5.63	5.93
	Q	2.48	2.63	4.82	10.71	2.87	3.02
	BSP	.81	.86	1.58	3.50	.94	.99
CASH VALUE							
5th YR		$13	$18	$58	$164	$25	$25
10th YR		60	70	159	401	80	86
20th YR		176	195	412	1000	219	235
AT 60		480	504	638		586	638
AT 62		512	536	662		629	662
AT 65		560	583	696		696	696
PAID UP							
5th YR		$56	$64	$206	$254	$82	$89
10th YR		223	219	497	538	250	269
20th YR		489	474	1000	MATURES	533	571
AT 60		806	791			919	1000
AT 62		825	811			952	
AT 65		852	839			1000	

$1,000		10 E	15 E	10 PL	15 PL	25 PL	30 PL
MALE	A	$98.53	$59.90	$34.28	$24.01	$16.11	$14.27
	S	50.25	30.55	17.48	12.25	8.22	7.28
	Q	25.62	15.57	8.91	6.24	4.19	3.71
	BSP	8.38	5.09	2.91	2.04	1.37	1.21
FEMALE	A	$98.32	$59.58	$33.82	$23.54	$15.61	$13.75
	S	50.14	30.39	17.25	12.01	7.96	7.01
	Q	25.56	15.49	8.79	6.12	4.06	3.58
	BSP	8.36	5.06	2.87	2.00	1.33	1.17
CASH VALUE							
5th YR		$441	$256	$129	$81	$44	$35
10th YR		1000	599	321	212	128	109
20th YR				412	412	338	290
AT 60				638	638	638	638
AT 62				662	662	662	662
AT 65				696	696	696	696
PAID UP							
5th YR		$511	$344	$457	$287	$156	$124
10th YR		MATURES	694	1000	663	400	341
20th YR						822	705
AT 60							
AT 62							
AT 65							

$1,000		E 65	E 60	E 55	20 PE 65	20 PE 60	T 65
MALE	A	$13.95	$16.18	$19.40	$22.88	$25.22	$6.54
	S	7.11	8.25	9.89	11.67	12.86	3.34
	Q	3.63	4.21	5.04	5.95	6.56	1.70
	BSP	1.19	1.38	1.65	1.94	2.14	.56
FEMALE	A	$13.45	$15.69	$18.92	$22.43	$24.77	$6.31
	S	6.86	8.00	9.65	11.44	12.63	3.22
	Q	3.50	4.08	4.92	5.83	6.44	1.64
	BSP	1.14	1.33	1.61	1.91	2.11	.54
CASH VALUE							
5th YR		$35	$45	$60	$77	$88	$.0
10th YR		107	131	165	202	227	.19
20th YR		285	344	427	518	578	69
AT 60		806	1000		869	1000	84
AT 62		878			918		60
AT 65		1000			1000		0
PAID UP							
5th YR		$101	$117	$139	$222	$229	
10th YR		270	298	333	510	516	
20th YR		551	596	653	1000	1000	
AT 60		928	MATURES	MATURES		MATURES	
AT 62		958					
AT 65		MATURES					

834 † $25,000 MINIMUM

𝕄𝕄 FACTOR PER POLICY A-$10.00 S-$6.00 Q-$4.00 BSP-$1.00 — AGE **20**

$1,000		RI 70	RI 65	RI 62F	RI 60	RI 55
MALE	A	$15.05	$19.49	$25.41	$26.23	$35.99
	S	7.68	9.94	12.96	13.38	18.35
	Q	3.91	5.07	6.61	6.82	9.36
	BSP	1.28	1.66	2.16	2.23	3.06
FEMALE	A	$14.55	$19.01	$24.96	$25.79	$35.60
	S	7.42	9.70	12.73	13.15	18.16
	Q	3.78	4.94	6.49	6.71	9.26
	BSP	1.24	1.62	2.12	2.19	3.03
CASH VALUE						
5th YR		$39	$58	$84	$89	$133
10th YR		118	164	226	235	338
20th YR		314	430	584	605	858
AT 60		906	1279	1740	1796	
AT 62		992	1397	1898		
AT 65		1132	1588			
PAID UP						
5th YR		$122	$167	$228	$232	$308
10th YR		324	414	537	534	682
20th YR		664	832			
AT 60					MATURES	MATURES
AT 62				MATURES		
AT 65			MATURES			

PLAN	PREMIUM RATES — MALE				PREMIUM RATES — FEMALE			
	A	S	Q	BSP	A	S	Q	BSP
5 YR	LEVEL TERM INSURANCE — $1,000 FACE AMOUNT							
10								
15								
10 YR	INCOME EXTENSION BENEFIT — $10.00 MONTHLY INCOME							
10 YR	$2.16	$1.10	$0.56	$0.18	$2.08	$1.06	$0.54	$0.18
11	2.28	1.16	.59	.19	2.19	1.12	.57	.19
12	2.42	1.23	.63	.21	2.32	1.18	.60	.20
13	2.56	1.31	.67	.22	2.45	1.25	.64	.21
14	2.67	1.36	.69	.23	2.55	1.30	.66	.22
15	2.81	1.43	.73	.24	2.68	1.37	.70	.23
16	FAMILY INCOME BENEFIT — $1,000 FACE AMOUNT							
16	2.93	1.49	.76	.25	2.78	1.42	.72	.24
17	3.04	1.55	.79	.26	2.88	1.47	.75	.24
18	3.14	1.60	.82	.27	2.96	1.51	.77	.25
19	3.27	1.67	.85	.28	3.08	1.57	.80	.26
20	3.41	1.74	.89	.29	3.19	1.63	.83	.27
21	3.51	1.79	.91	.30	3.27	1.67	.85	.28
22	3.61	1.84	.94	.31	3.34	1.70	.87	.28
23	3.72	1.90	.97	.32	3.42	1.74	.89	.29
24	3.83	1.95	1.00	.33	3.50	1.79	.91	.30
25	3.95	2.01	1.03	.34	3.59	1.83	.93	.30
30	4.54	2.32	1.18	.39	3.96	2.02	1.03	.34
35	5.26	2.68	1.37	.45	4.38	2.23	1.14	.37
	FAMILY INCOME BENEFIT — $1,000 FACE AMOUNT							
10 YR	MORTGAGE PROTECTION BENEFIT — $1,000 INITIAL AMOUNT							
10 YR	$2.21	$1.13	$0.57	$0.19	$2.12	$1.08	$0.55	$0.18
15	2.28	1.16	.59	.19	2.18	1.11	.57	.19
20	2.36	1.20	.61	.20	2.22	1.13	.58	.19
25	2.48	1.26	.64	.21	2.28	1.16	.59	.19
30	2.61	1.33	.68	.22	2.32	1.18	.60	.20
10 PL	GUARANTEED ISSUE BENEFIT — $1,000 FACE AMOUNT							
10 PL	$1.47	$0.75	$0.38	$0.12	$1.35	$0.69	$0.35	$0.11
15 PL	1.27	.65	.33	.11	1.15	.59	.30	.10
20 PL	1.18	.60	.31	.10	1.06	.54	.28	.09
OTHER	1.18	.60	.31	.10	1.06	.54	.28	.09

	A	S	Q	BSP
FAMILY SUPPLEMENT	$30.00	$15.30	$7.80	$2.55
CHILDREN'S SUPPLEMENT	10.00	5.10	2.60	.85
ACCIDENTAL DEATH BENEFIT	1.00	.51	.26	.09
RPB Factor 15%		Interim Term $0.36 Per Month per $1,000		

Life Insurance Premium Rates Factor

Selecting the type of life insurance policy needed to protect your family is difficult. This rate factor table is to help you better understand the types of policies available. It is recommended that one consult his insurance agent for additional information.

(Courtesy of the United Benefit Life Insurance Company, Omaha, Nebraska)

UNITED FAMILY PLAN

Any and all of the family needs can now be taken care of in one package with the Family Plan. In addition to providing coverage for every member of the family, the right amount can be provided on the father to take care of one or all of the basic needs—Last Expense, Dependency Income, Widow's Income, and Retirement—by a choice of Family Plan 1, 2 or 3. The mother and children are covered under the Family Supplement (see page A16 for description). The table at the bottom of page C5 gives the income period and the amount of insurance on the wife.

The production credit on No. 1 is $8,000 ($5,000 SWL+$3,000 FS) and No. 2 is $19,000 ($5,000 SWL+$3,000 FS+$11,000 IEB). For No. 3, the production credit is $14,000 ($3,000 FS+$11,000 IEB) plus the coverage on the father's life.

United Family Plan No. 1

$5,000 Select Whole Life with 1 Unit Family Supplement

WP and ADB Included

Age of Husband	Premium* Annual	Premium* B.S.P.	Cash Value 10th Year	Cash Value 20th Year	Cash Value Age 65
18	$ 94.95	$ 8.25	$315	$ 905	$2960
19	96.55	8.40	330	940	2935
20	98.20	8.50	350	975	2915
21	99.90	8.65	365	1010	2900
22	101.70	8.80	380	1045	2880
23	103.60	9.00	400	1085	2860
24	105.55	9.15	420	1125	2840
25	107.60	9.30	440	1165	2820
26	109.75	9.50	460	1205	2795
27	111.95	9.70	480	1245	2770
28	114.30	9.90	500	1285	2750
29	116.80	10.10	525	1330	2720
30	119.45	10.35	545	1370	2695
31	122.90	10.55	570	1415	2665
32	125.10	10.80	590	1460	2635
33	128.10	11.05	615	1500	2605
34	131.40	11.35	640	1545	2570
35	134.75	11.65	665	1590	2535
36	138.35	11.95	685	1635	2495
37	142.15	12.25	710	1680	2455
38	146.10	12.60	735	1725	2415
39	150.30	12.95	760	1770	2370
40	154.60	13.30	790	1820	2325
41	159.20	13.70	815	1865	2275
42	164.15	14.15	840	1910	2225
43	169.20	14.55	870	1960	2170
44	174.50	15.00	895	2005	2110
45	180.05	15.50	925	2060	2060

United Family Plan No. 2

$5,000 Select Whole Life with 1 Unit Family Supplement and $100 Monthly Income—20 Year I.E.B.

WP and ADB Included

(Medical examination required for ages 26 and over)

Age of Husband	Premium* Annual	Premium* B.S.P.	Cash Value 10th Year	Cash Value 20th Year	Cash Value Age 65
18	$128.25	$11.05	$315	$ 905	$2960
19	130.25	11.30	330	940	2935
20	132.30	11.40	350	975	2915
21	134.40	11.55	365	1010	2900
22	136.60	11.80	380	1045	2880
23	139.00	12.00	400	1085	2860
24	141.45	12.25	420	1125	2840
25	144.00	12.40	440	1165	2820
26	146.85	12.70	460	1205	2795
27	149.85	12.90	480	1245	2770
28	153.00	13.20	500	1285	2760
29	156.60	13.50	525	1330	2720
30	160.45	13.85	545	1370	2695
31	165.10	14.15	570	1415	2665
32	170.00	14.60	590	1460	2635
33	175.70	15.05	615	1500	2605
34	182.00	15.65	640	1545	2570
35	188.85	16.25	665	1590	2535
36	196.95	16.95	685	1635	2495
37	205.65	17.65	710	1680	2455
38	215.10	18.60	735	1725	2415
39	225.20	19.35	760	1770	2370
40	236.10	20.20	790	1820	2325
41	248.40	21.30	815	1865	2275
42	261.75	22.45	840	1910	2225
43	275.90	23.65	870	1960	2170
44	291.30	24.90	895	2005	2110
45	307.85	26.40	925	2060	2060

*MM Factor Included

United Family Plan No. 3

$15.00 Monthly B.S.P.*

Select Whole Life with 1 Unit Family Supplement and $100 Monthly Income—20 Year I.E.B.

WP and ADB Included

(Medical examination required for all ages)

Age of Husband	Amount of Select Whole Life	Cash Value 10th Year	Cash Value 20th Year	Cash Value Age 65
18	$9202	$579.73	$1665.56	$5429.18
19	8814	581.72	1657.03	6173.82
20	8836	604.52	1684.02	5034.79
21	8382	611.89	1683.16	4861.58
22	8048	611.65	1682.03	4635.65
23	7792	620.16	1682.18	4434.14
24	7455	626.22	1677.38	4234.44
25	7261	638.97	1691.81	4095.20
26	6933	637.84	1670.85	3975.55
27	6707	643.87	1670.04	3715.68
28	6417	641.70	1649.17	3529.35
29	6145	645.23	1634.57	3342.88
30	5845	637.21	1601.80	3150.99
31	5607	639.20	1586.78	2988.53
32	5276	622.57	1540.59	2780.45
33	4967	610.94	1490.10	2587.81
34	4583	586.82	1416.15	2355.66
35	4228	562.32	1344.50	2143.60
36	3839	525.94	1255.35	1915.66
37	3477	493.73	1168.27	1707.21
38	3066	450.70	1057.77	1480.88
39	2686	408.27	950.84	1273.16
40	2333	368.61	849.21	1084.85

*MM Factor Included

Insurance Benefits on Wife

$1,000 Plus $50 Monthly Income

Age of Wife	Income Period in Years	Initial Amount of Insurance	Income Period in Years	Age of Wife	Initial Amount of Insurance
16	25	$11,691	14	31	$ 7,870
17	24	11,300	14	32	7,870
18	23	11,001	13	33	7,468
19	22	10,693	12	34	7,054
20	21	10,376	12	35	7,054
21	20	10,049	11	36	6,628
22	19	9,712	11	37	6,188
23	19	9,712	10	38	6,188
24	18	9,365	9	39	5,736
25	18	9,365	8	40	5,269
26	17	9,008	8	41	5,269
27	16	8,640	7	42	4,289
28	16	8,640	6	43	4,295
29	15	8,261	6	44	4,295
30	15	8,261	5	45	3,785

Short term endowment policies provide good investment, but less protection. The young man or woman who is able to invest in an endowment policy maturing at age 65 is more likely to cover the real needs. A 20-year endowment policy purchased at age 20 will probably be too expensive for most people and mature at a time when a man is reaching his highest rate of earning. Thus, a long-term endowment policy would probably be better.

Life annuity contracts are available from insurance companies in various amounts. The main purpose is to assure a regular income for the policyholder and/or his wife from a given time, usually retirement, until their death. Annuities can be purchased as a lump sum, or can be paid for over a number of years. There are a number of annuity plans, but in all, the chief purpose is to provide income for retirement.

Term life insurance is available for a specific time at a given rate. This insurance provides protection only in case of death of the insured and no cash accumulation is provided. Many people purchase a term policy in combination with other types of insurance. For example, a young man may wish to have additional protection for his family during the years when the children are young and his savings and income low. A term policy will give the financial protection when it is most needed by the family. Many companies require physical examinations for policyholders and may refuse them insurance or deny them the privilege of renewal. Term insurance rates are low but get higher as the policyholder gets older.

Life insurance is also offered as:
1. Industrial
2. Group
3. Savings bank

Industrial insurance is a special type of insurance offered to industrial workers. Premiums are collected by the worker's employer usually as payroll deductions. For a few cents each week, the worker can purchase a small policy of $1000 or less through payroll deduction. Industrial insurance is the only insurance some workers can afford. Medical examinations are usually not required. The policies generally include death and disability features.

Group insurance is available at special rates to workers of some employers. In most instances, the insurance company will accept the company's health records and no individual examinations are required of the workers. Rates are usually low and are based on the group's age, environmental conditions, hazards, etc. Many companies pay part of the premiums.

Group insurance may be purchased as group term insurance or group permanent life insurance which does accumulate a cash value. Group term insurance rates increase as the age of the employee increases and are expensive for the older worker.

Savings bank insurance has been authorized by a few states. The savings banks accept the premium payments for insurance just as they accept savings deposits. Insurance policies sold by savings banks are limited in amount by state regulations.

Savings bank insurance was intended for wage earners as a convenient method of paying for insurance and to take the place of industrial life insurance which is being discontinued in many places.

What Life Insurance Should You Buy?

The type of insurance appropriate for each individual depends on a number of things. Perhaps the best way to answer the question is to decide what you want your life insurance to do for you and your dependents.

First: How much money do you want to leave your dependents if you should die this year? Will you require more insurance to provide for them?

Second: What are your retirement plans? Will insurance be needed or will other investments and pension plans provide the money you will need?

Third: How much can you afford for insurance premiums? Will your income increase during the coming years in relation to increased expenses?

When you have arrived at answers to these three questions you are ready to consult with insurance agents, study their literature, and select an insurance company and agent.

Health Insurance

Medical knowledge and skill has developed rapidly in the last 25 years. People today enjoy better health and have better medical care than ever before. However, more and more people need medical care, and the problem of financing the cost of sickness and accidents is a major one for many people. A lengthy period in the hospital would bankrupt most families. To avoid financial disaster, most families carry health and accident insurance.

Three types of organizations provide health and accident insurance on a voluntary basis. These include insurance companies which pay cash benefits to policyholders and their families in case of sickness or accident. Benefits are paid for loss of income and for hospital, surgical, and medical costs. Nonprofit organizations provide service benefits to members of the plan. For example, Blue Cross is a non-profit company paying for hospital costs and Blue Shield covers doctors' fees and other medical costs. Another plan is the consumer-sponsored plan which provides full hospital and medical costs. Under this plan, an industry may own its own hospitals and employ a medical staff to serve those covered.

Accident and health contracts may also be purchased by an individual for himself and his family. Health insurance policies may provide coverage under any one or all five of the following types of health and accident services:

1. **Hospital expense.** Hospitalization insurance provides for a part or all the cost of a hospital room for a given number of days. Additional benefits usually provide for the cost of X-rays, use of the operating room, anesthesia, and laboratory services.

2. **Surgical expense.** This type of insurance pays the cost of a surgeon and is based on a schedule of fees set for different operations. Surgical expense insurance ranks second in use among other forms of health insurance.

3. **General medical expense.** This type of insurance pays part or all expenses of calls made by doctors at the hospital. Some policies will also cover the cost of home calls by the doctor, or at the doctor's office.

4. **Major medical expense.** This type of insurance covers the cost of longer periods of hospitalization and nursing care. It

takes up where the other forms of health insurance stop. Serious accidents or major illness which may cost several thousands of dollars are covered by major medical expense insurance.

5. Loss of income. Many times accidents or illness causes loss of income for a number of months, or in some cases, the person is disabled for life. Loss of income insurance provides protection for the worker and his family. Premium rates are based on the time covered and the amount of monthly loss.

The following six suggestions are planned to help you save money on health care. These suggestions, plus an adequate health insurance policy, offer excellent protection to the young workers.

---

6 WAYS YOU CAN STRETCH YOUR HEALTH CARE DOLLARS

1. HAVE A REGULAR FAMILY DOCTOR
The doctor who sees you regularly knows you best. Generally, he is able to diagnose your illness quicker with more certainty than a physician who is seeing you for the first time without the benefit of your past medical history. And because a regular family doctor does have your complete medical record, he may be able to avoid duplication of many expensive, time-consuming tests.

2. IF POSSIBLE, VISIT THE DOCTOR IN HIS OFFICE
Office calls are far less expensive since they don't involve the travel time required to make a house call. The doctor is better able to treat you at the office, too, where he has a vast array of medical equipment and trained personnel to assist him.

3. BE SURE TO HAVE REGULAR CHECKUPS
Oftentimes a routine physical checkup will reveal an unsuspected illness that might otherwise go undetected until it has reached a serious or incurable state. The small fee charged for a physical examination may save you an expensive bill later on. It could even save your life!

4. CHOOSE A SEMIPRIVATE HOSPITAL ROOM
Unless your doctor feels a private room is absolutely necessary, consider the semiprivate room when you are hospitalized. It can cut your hospital bill considerably and, unless you're seriously ill, it's nice to have someone to talk to during the long hours you'll spend in bed.

5. MAKE CERTAIN YOU TAKE ALL YOUR TAX DEDUCTIONS
You're allowed to deduct all medical expenses that exceed 3% of your income as well as drugs and medicines that exceed 1% of your income. Keep accurate records of all your medical expenses to make sure you don't overlook any deduction to which you are rightfully entitled.

6. MOST IMPORTANT, KEEP YOUR PRESENT HEALTH INSURANCE IN FORCE
Over the past few years, medical care costs have increased at a faster pace than any other kind of personal expense. Since the 1957-1959 base period, the Consumer Price Index for medical care has risen more than 31%. The chart below graphically portrays the spiraling cost of medical care in relation to other items in your family budget.

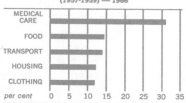

Percentage Increase in Consumer Prices
(1957-1959) — 1966

MEDICAL CARE							
FOOD							
TRANSPORT							
HOUSING							
CLOTHING							
per cent	0	5	10	15	20	25	30	35

Even greater increases have occurred in the area of hospitalization. Since 1960, hospital expense each patient-day has risen from $32.00 to $46.00—a 44% increase!

Because of this steadily increasing cost of medical care, it is more important than ever before that you retain the fine protection you now carry with Mutual of Omaha. There's no substitute for the feeling of financial security this coverage can offer you when you're sick or hurt . . . security that can play an important role in your ability to get well.

Suggestions for Buying Insurance

Buying life insurance is more important than buying auto-mobile insurance because life insurance continues year after year.

The following suggestions are made for life insurance specifically. However, they may apply to most types of insurance.

1. Select a good company and a reliable agent. Both can be recognized by a little investigation of past service to their customers and rates charged.

2. Analyze your needs. Too many buyers don't study their needs enough to make a wise decision. The buyer should be careful not to buy more insurance than he can afford. A few make real sacrifices to pay insurance premiums.

3. Program your insurance purchases. Your insurance needs will change and your income will most likely increase. Purchase a policy that can be adjusted to fit your needs.

4. Don't drop one policy to buy another. In most situations it is not wise to change policies or companies. You will lose a part of the cash loan value and rates go higher as the policyholder gets older.

5. Arrange the best terms for payment of premiums. The least expensive plan to pay premiums is on an annual basis. Semiannual or monthly premium payments cost the company more bookkeeping time and therefore must cost more.

6. Keep your policy in a safe place. Your insurance policy and other valuable papers should be placed in a safe place. It is good planning to have your wife and members of your family or close relatives know where the policy is located.

Life insurance is complicated, and all the information you need to select an insurance policy cannot be discussed here. It is, therefore, very important for the young worker to study carefully all the facets of a policy before entering into a contract.

Study Helps

New Terms

property insurance
liability insurance
comprehensive insurance
personal property
bodily injury
term policy
group insurance

coverage
protection
deductible
endowment
annuity
premium
benefits

collision insurance
home-owner's policy
insurance claim
savings bank insurance
straight life
limited payment
industrial insurance

Study Questions

1. What nationality groups had a form of insurance during historically ancient times?
2. What type of insurance was the forerunner of life insurance?
3. What is meant by the term, "liability insurance"?
4. Why should every homeowner maintain a homeowner's insurance policy?
5. What six types of insurance should be carried by everyone who operates a motor vehicle?
6. What are the factors which determine insurance rates?
7. What kinds of life insurance could you buy?
8. What types of organizations provide health and accident insurance?
9. What coverage provisions should be included in a health insurance policy?
10. Why should a young, healthy wage-earner pay for health insurance?

Discussion Problems

1. Study each of the accident photos on the following pages.
   a. Make an imaginary report of the personal injury resulting from each accident. What would you estimate each injured person will pay for medical care? What kind of insurance protection should the person have to pay the doctor and hospital charges?

b. Make an imaginary report of the property damage in each accident. What kinds of insurance protection are needed?

c. In which of the seven photos of accidents is there an obvious need for liability insurance?

d. Which of the following insurance plans could be needed by the accident victims in the photo?

life	liability	accident-income
property	hospital-surgical	major medical
collision	accidental death	accident-income
theft	legal defense cost	mortgage-pay

2. Why is there greater need for insurance protection in 1970 than there was in 1670?

3. What is the difference between property and liability insurance? Should you have both types of insurance?

4. Give some imaginary examples of use of property and liability insurance. Do you think the premium payment required was "worth it" in these cases?

5. Take the role of the person who has just had an auto accident while driving his friend's car and tell what you would do.

Accident Photographs
Courtesy of Mutual of Omaha

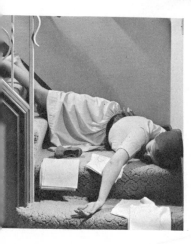

PART III

Meeting Future
Responsibilities

Introduction

From about the time we begin kindergarten until the time we retire from an active working life at age 65 or 70, society expects us to take on certain responsibilities. These change throughout life. If we are to meet these responsibilities in such a way as to make the greatest contribution to the good of society and to our own happiness, we must go through certain stages of vocational development. If we miss a stage, we cannot successfully go on to the next stage.

As we move toward the year 2000, our lives will surely be affected by these expected changes:[1]

The 1970's and 1980's will bring—
1. A great era of invention, discovery, and social change.
2. A great increase in technological advances.

---

[1]*America's Next 30 Years—Business and The Future.* Council on Trends and Perspective Economic Analysis and Study Group, Chamber of Commerce of the United States, Washington, D.C., 1970.

3. More money to spend by most—although there will be a growing gap between the wealthy and the poor. More will be spent for education, recreation, and travel.
4. A learning society. Education will not stop for most people when they graduate from high school—or even college. They will continue their education throughout their lifetime.

The way in which you can move through the stages of vocational development in order to successfully fulfill your responsibilities is discussed in Part III. Much of this development depends upon a plan of continuous education. The means of getting this education is brought into focus for you too, perhaps for the first time.

Chapter 16

Vocational Development and Changing Responsibility

In the first chapter of this book, we said that you can expect to live for *about* another 50 years and that if you are a boy you will work for about 40 of these years. If you are a girl, you will work for about 25 years. These, of course, are averages. Some people do not work so many years, others work longer. Neither do we know how long *you* will live. However, mortality tables used by insurance companies to determine rates show that the *average* 18-year old boy can expect to live until he is 70. The average 18-year old girl can expect to live about three years longer. Of course, many people die younger, and if you are still alive on your 70th birthday, you can expect to live *about* another ten years.

Average Person's Vocational and Responsibility Growth

Even though none of us knows how long we will live or exactly how many years we will work, we make plans based on what we know about the *average* person.

We have discussed the importance of satisfying work to a satisfying life—that the work a person does largely determines his *way of life*. Because of this, psychologists have recognized certain stages through which each person passes in his vocational development. With each stage there are certain responsi-

bilities; and as we move from one stage of vocational development to the next, our responsibilities change. The stages of
vocational development and responsibility may be identified
according to the following chart.

Stages of Vocational Development and Life Responsibility

Stage	Age	Vocational Development	Life Responsibilities
2	10-25	Learns to identify workers by parents' work, TV.	Personal cleanliness, closely supervised household chores school responsibilities.
1	5-10	Develops work habits.	Organize school assignments, added household chores not so closely supervised.
3	15-25	Learns about self and how to fit into the world, selects and prepares for career, begins work.	To succeed on job, manage money; if married, responsibility to family.
4	25-55	Growth and productivity.	Family and home responsibilities, education for children; may need larger home, two cars.
5	55-65	Preparing for retirement.	Children grown and establishing own homes, need for smaller home, saving for retirement.
6	65-	Relaxing and contemplating.	Little or no responsibility to job, free to travel.

Stage I — 5 to 10 Years Old

The things we do and learn before **stage 1** in the chart are of
great importance but are not directly related to our vocational
development. The child who receives a great deal of attention
and direction of learning activities during the first four or five

years of his life finds learning easier and more fun than the child who is neglected. This is probably the reason that the oldest child in the family usually performs better in school than his younger brothers and sisters. During his early years, the oldest child received all of the attention. The oldest child usually completes more years of education and has greater drive to succeed than younger members of the family. Most of our great presidents have been the oldest member of their families. The more interest people take in us, and the more active we (and they) keep our mind, the easier it will be for us to succeed in the next stages of our lives.

The Child Who Receives Attention and Direction of Learning at Home Finds Learning Easier and More Fun Than the Neglected Child

Stage 1 in our vocational development takes place between the ages of 5 and 10. It is at this time that we begin to notice that people are identified by the kind of work they do. We learn this mainly from seeing how closely our parents are identified with their work, and from watching television. The responsibilities which we should assume during stage 1 are limited to our school assignments, some supervised household chores, and taking care of our own cleanliness.

Stage 2 — 10 to 15 Years Old

In stage 2, we develop work habits which will be with us for a long time. Those who have not developed good work habits by the time they are about 15 years old will find it very difficult to succeed in stage 3. If, at age 16 or 17, they realize this, they *can* improve their work habits. Unfortunately, those who have not developed them by this time usually never do. Responsibilities in stage 3 include school assignments and added household chores which are not so closely supervised.

Stage 3 — 15 to 25 Years Old

Stage 3 takes place mainly between the ages of 15 and 25. This book deals mainly with what happens to you during these years. We have discussed selecting appropriate career goals, how to locate job vacancies, how to apply for a job, and how to improve your chances of being successful on the job. These responsibilities, along with getting the appropriate educational preparation necessary to reach your long range career goal are critical. They are critical because you cannot successfully move on to stages 4, 5, and 6 unless you have been at least fairly successful in stage 3. Success in each stage depends upon how successful you were in the previous stage. Our main life responsibilities during stage 3 are job success, learning to manage money, and—if married—responsibility to family.

Stage 4 — 25 to 55 Years Old

Someone has said that the success a man achieves by age 25 is of no great credit to him, but is due mainly to the education provided by his parents and society. That is, if we have equal education and ability, we are all at about the same level of success at age 25. What happens after we are 25 is due mainly to our own efforts. Vocational development in **stage 4** is growth and increased productivity. It occurs between the ages of 25 and 55, and it is a chance to continue to improve ourselves through our efforts on the job and a continuing educational program. This continuing education may take many forms. You may take courses in adult evening school or through university extension —or you may continue your study through selective reading. Thus, our responsibilities to ourselves and to our work has changed from what it was in stage 3. Our responsibilities to others have changed too. By the time we enter stage 4, most of us are married—or will soon be married. It is during these years, age 25 to 55, that we raise our children and provide encouragement for their success in each of the first three stages of vocational development and life responsibilities. The more successful we have been in each stage, the more guidance we can give our children as they pass through these same stages.

Stage 5 — 55 to 65 Years Old

When we reach **stage 5**, our children are probably grown and have established their own homes. Thus, our responsibilities change again. We may no longer need such a large home. Perhaps one car will do instead of two. Our living expenses may be less during stage 5 than they were while our children were home and in school, but we will need to save some money for retirement, travel, and possible medical expenses.

Stage 6 — Over 65 Years Old

Stage 6 is retirement. It is a time to relax and contemplate —to look back over one's life. If we have been successful in each of the stages up to retirement, we will look back over life with satisfaction. We will feel that we have made a contribution to society and feel that life is worthwhile after all.

As we said, success in each stage depends upon success in the previous stage. Because of this, many people are frustrated by a feeling that they are not as successful in their work, or in life, as they should be. Most often, it is because they did not get all they should have out of their experiences in stages 2 and 3. If you feel that your own vocational development is not keeping pace with your life responsibilities, talk it over with your school counselor. The person who is successful in one stage moves on to the next stage knowing he will succeed in the experiences appropriate for the new stage.

Case Studies

The four cases which follow were based upon studies conducted by Dr. Robert J. Havighurst of the University of Chicago. They were previously reported in *Man In A World At Work*, Houghton Mifflin Company, Boston, 1964. These are presented here to illustrate the significance of success in the various stages of vocational development.

JOSEPH

Joseph's father is a high school teacher. The boy went through elementary school and high school with a good record. In high school he got credit for four years of mathematics and four years of science, partly through studying by himself with the assistance and encouragement of a science teacher in high school. When he entered the state university, he was given advanced standing and encouraged to begin sophomore work in science and math. Upon graduation with honors in physics, Joseph had his choice of several scholarships for graduate study; he decided to apply for one of the NASA awards, which he won.

Joseph is one of many people for whom a career is the axis of life. His thoughts and aspirations have centered on his occupation since he was 12 years old, when he began to study algebra by himself, having finished his seventh-grade arithmetic textbook by Christmas of that school year. Indeed, some of his teachers feel that he is too narrowly devoted to a career, and that such concentration and single-mindedness have cost him something. He has had very little interest in girls, and his male frinds think of him as one who fails to enjoy social events, music, or a good conversation . . . .

Joseph identified with his father when he was a young boy, and in this way the concept of himself as a worker became a part of his ideal self. From the age of 10 he could not see himself in the future except as a man who worked and supported a family. Then, from about the age of 10 to 15, he formed a set of basic work habits which he has maintained all his life. He learned to do a job which was clearly his responsibility, whether this meant doing chores at home or getting his school lessons done as soon as they were assigned, and not putting them off in favor of seeing a movie or watching television.

His next step was to decide to become a scientist and to prepare for this career by his choice of studies in high school and college. As he progressed through college, he decided to pursue graduate work in the field of physics. During his senior year in college he examined the possibilities. When he heard of the NASA fellowship program, he applied for it.

For what will follow in Joseph's life, we can predict some such course as the following: He will work on a government assignment in space science for a few years, then find himself in a responsible position in this area, with younger men working on his team. By the time he is 40, he will be one of the outstanding men in space science. He will choose between research and administration in a university or a government science agency. For the next twenty years he will be at the peak of his productivity and influence.

During this period, Joseph will be helping his own children get started in their careers, and he will probably take a leading position on committees of scientists for the recruiting and training of young scientists. He will also become active as a citizen, serving on advisory boards to the President or to Congress. Eventually, in his 60's, Joseph will slowly reduce his work load. He will lecture frequently, advise frequently, and publish less than he did in earlier years. At about the age of 70, he will retire from his formal position but remain active as a kind of elder statesman of science. Perhaps he will write and publish his memoirs as a pioneer in space science.

Thirty years ago, Anderson and Davidson said, "The work a man does to earn his livelihood stamps him with mental and physical traits characteristic of the form and level of his labor, defines his circle of friends and acquaintances, affects his use of leisure, influences his political affiliations, limits his interests and the attainment of his aspirations, and tends to set the boundaries of his culture."[1] This is true of Joseph. It is also true of two other boys who grew up in the same town and attended the same schools as Joseph—but their vocational development was different from Joseph's, and different from that of each other.

PHIL

Phil was a very bright boy with an I.Q. of 140. He learned rapidly in school. At home he had a variety of interests, mainly pet animals and games which he played with neighborhool children. His father was in charge of canned goods and packaged food at a supermarket. Neither of his parents read much beyond looking at the

---

[1]H. D. Anderson and P. E. Davidson, *Occupational Trends in the United States* (Stanford, California: Stanford University Press, 1940), p. 1.

daily papers. They were active in their church and were constantly working on committees in preparation for a church dinner or some similar activity.

Phil identified with his father as a worker and a man who did things with and for other people. Phil's own energy was largely used in active play in the neighborhood. At home he early developed the habit of reading comic books, of which he always had a stack of twenty or thirty on hand. When he had finished reading them, he traded them with other boys for books he had not read. In school, Phil got his assigned lessons quickly and usually had everything finished in class so that he had little or no homework to do. However, he did not develop the kind of intellectual curiosity that Joseph had. Thus, when Phil finished his arithmetic lesson for the day, he used the rest of his time "fooling around" and bothering other children until the teacher had a talk with him about it; they agreed that Phil could read comic books whenever he had finished his school work for the day. Joseph, on the other hand, worked ahead in his arithmetic and soon finished the book. He then went on to study an algebra book while Phil read his comic books.

In spite of this apparent waste of time, Phil learned the basic habits of industry in two ways. First, he went to work selling newspapers . . . . His ability to put work ahead of other things is illustrated by an incident which occurred when he was in the sixth grade. Phil sprained his ankle. The doctor put a plaster cast around it, telling Phil's mother that he could go around normally except when it rained, for he was not to get the cast wet. Phil went to school and to his newspaper business on dry days. On rainy days, he stayed home from school; but he always went to his job, rain or shine.

By the time Phil was 15 years old, he was working on Saturdays in a shoe store. The summer he was 16 he practically ran the store while his employer played golf. His employer came to rely more and more on Phil, and he began to talk of the time when Phil would be through high school and would work full time. Meanwhile, Phil attracted customers with his effective sales personality; and he committed himself more and more to the business. His school grades dropped from A's to B's, and one or two of his teachers spoke to him about his apparent loss of interest in school. Phil remarked that he was getting what he needed from school. He was the senior class president and a popular boy, well regarded in the school as well as the community.

In spite of urging by some of his teachers, Phil did not go to college. Instead, he entered the shoe business where, by the time he was 25, he was a minor partner. We can see Phil growing into the mastery of his business, becoming sole owner before he is 40, and becoming a leader in the chamber of commerce and in his service club. He may serve on the school board and take an active interest in the vocational education program of schools. His own children will be given the best education he can get for them in local schools, and he will encourage them to go to college "to take advantage of things I didn't have time for," as he will perhaps put it.

From the age of 40 to perhaps 70, Phil will be one of the leading local merchants, generally pleased with himself though occasionally wondering whether he made the right choice when he decided to go into business locally rather than to college. This choice, he will see, both made possible his rapid rise to local business success and also denied him the opportunity of getting into a broader sphere of work, possibly a position in a large business where he might have gained statewide or national fame.

RAY

Ray had a very different career from that of Joseph and Phil, though work was for him also a central axis. His father, an unskilled worker on a construction gang, managed to keep fairly steady work, although there

were slack times when he supplemented his unemployment compensation with a part-time commercial fishing on the big river that ran by the city. Ray's mother
also worked at times, in a laundry, when money was
needed and she could get away from home without ne-
glecting her four children. Ray's identification was with
a hardworking man who kept busy at one thing or
another.

In school, Ray did not do at all well. He had a reading disability that began to handicap him seriously by
the time he reached the fifth grade. His mother took
him out of a parochial school and put him in a public
school where she was told by neighbors that Ray might
get special help. But there was very little improvement
and Ray made less and less effort to master his school
work. A "tough" lad, he took the leadership among a
small group of boys who were failing in school. They
became quite unruly, sometimes openly defiant of the
assistant principal of the school. They also began to
miss school regularly. Ray's parents tried punishing
him when poor report cards and complaints about his
behavior came home. But Ray became stubborn at such
times, and his mother and father said privately that
perhaps there was not much to be done. Neither of them
had gone beyond the eighth grade in school.

Ray learned something about work through delivering papers after school in the afternoons, and
through chores at home which his father insisted on his
doing. By the time he was 14, he was actively looking
for odd jobs and for such seasonal work as berry
picking.

School was less and less attractive to Ray, and
when he dropped out a month before his sixteenth
birthday, the principal made no effort to call him back.
Ray immediately went to work in the laundry where
his mother was employed, and in a few months he had
a job on a construction crew. He worked steadily, got
along well with foremen and his fellow workers, and
learned the essentials of his job quickly.

When he was about 17 years of age, Ray married a girl a year younger, and by the time he was 20 they had two children. They lived in a very small house with low rent, but they had not gone into debt and were slowly accumulating furniture that would last them a long time. Ray's wages increased slowly, and when he was 21 he became assistant foreman of a road-working crew. At 25, he was regarded by the road contractor who employed him as one of his most responsible men and was told that the next vacancy in a foreman's job would go to him.

This is probably as good a job as Ray will ever have. He may be able to keep this type of job until he is 60. He will raise his children and send them through high school, urging them to get more education than he was able to get. He is likely to buy a house on the edge of the city and to do a good deal of work on it, adding a room when his growing family needs it, and keep a vegetable garden. Perhaps he will buy a motor boat to use on the river for fishing.

As he gets on into his 60's, he may have to give way to a younger man as foreman, a man who knows the newer road-building methods and can read technical journals. Ray probably will take a less responsible job and then retire willingly on his Social Security pension at 65. He may do what work he can find in the neighborhood for a few years, helping younger men who are repairing their homes. In any case, he will regard himself as a man who did his share of work in life who enjoyed his family and friends.

"All three of these boys reached manhood in 1960, but their stories could have been matched many times in any year during the preceding 60 years of the 20th century. However, before the advent of space science, it is likely that Joseph would have become a chemist or an engineer. There would be a growing number of boys like Joseph as the century wore on, while life stories like those of Phil and Ray would grow less frequent."[2] Meanwhile, the story of Kenny will likely become more frequent.

KENNY

Kenny grew up in the poorest part of the same city where the other three boys lived. He never knew his father. His mother had two later husbands. The one with whom she lived when Kenny was 5 to 10 years old was a truck driver who spent much time away from home, except when he was not working, when he loafed around home, drinking a good deal and beating Kenny for little or no reason. Kenny probably never identified with this man, or with any man who set an example of regular work and a regular life. When Kenny was about 10, his stepfather deserted his mother, leaving her with two younger children. She then received Aid for Dependent Children for about four years, when she married again. This husband was a fairly steady worker but paid very little attention to his stepchildren. He was a silent, gloomy man who worked in a factory.

Kenny was at least average in intelligence and got average grades in the first few years of school. But as school work grew harder and more demanding, Kenny lost interest. There was no one at home to show an interest in the lessons, and he soon quit doing homework. He and several boys in the neighborhood spent their free time playing exciting games together. Their first contact with the police came when Kenny was 10 years old and the gang walked barefoot one night along a strip of freshly laid cement sidewalk. From this time on, Kenny and his gang were always dodging the

[2]Robert J. Havighurst, "Youth in Exploration and Man Emergent," *Man In A World At Work*. Edited by Henry Borow, National Vocational Guidance Association, c1964 (printed by Houghton Mifflin Co., Boston), p. 220.

police as a result of one escapade or another. By the time Kenny was 16, he had been arrested several times and brought to court twice, both times for stealing.

At school Kenny made little or no effort to do his work. He was known to teachers as a bright, mischievous boy who had to be watched constantly. By the time he was 14, his behavior was so bad that he was expelled from one class after another. At 15, he had only two regular classes, being consigned to study hall the rest of the time. To the relief of everybody, he left school the day he was 16.

During the next year, Kenny worked at eight or ten jobs briefly. They were not good jobs by his standards, and his work was seldom satisfactory by the standards of his employers. He was arrested twice . . . . and placed on probation both times. When he reached 17, he volunteered for the Navy. In six months he was discharged because he did not work satisfactorily at anything.

Back at home, Kenny loafed a while, then was arrested and sent to prison briefly for burglary. At the age of 19, he married a 17-year-old girl and began to hold jobs for longer periods of time. By the time he was 25, he was working as long as a year at a time at one or another factory job, but he was still a marginal worker, likely to be laid off when work was slack or to quit a job when he did not like the foreman or his fellow workers. He was learning to live on a combination of unemployment compensation, as long as it lasted, and wages for unsteady work.

It is a question whether Kenny will ever become a steady, responsible worker. Automation may push him out of work, and he does not seem to care much about what happens as long as there is income from one or another government source. He is in danger of becoming permanently unemployed. One cannot see him at 30, or 40, or 50 as maintaining a responsible role as a worker and citizen and provider for his family.

Study Helps

Study Questions

1. How do you expect your responsibilities to change between now and a year from now? Two years from now? Five years from now?
2. What kind of planning do you think might help you to assume your new responsibilities?

Chapter 17

Post High School
Education and Training

The Nature of Work Today

We live in an age characterized by the high rate of change. Persons who retire during this decade have witnessed the greatest technological advances ever known to man. Perhaps one of the best illustrations of change is in the area of air travel. Through the ages, people have been interested in flight, but it was necessary to wait until this century for progress. In 1903 the Wright brothers flew the first "heavier-than-air" plane at Kitty Hawk, North Carolina. Charles A. Lindberg made his famous solo flight from New York to Paris in 1927. Commercial airlines started flying across the oceans in the next decade. Interplanetary travel started in 1969 when Neil Armstrong and his crew made the first moon landing. Man has traveled at speeds of 25,000 miles per hour, a speed undreamed of when the Wright brothers flew 120 feet in 12 seconds. In practically all technical areas we see evidence of amazing changes. Radio, the telephone, and television have all been developed for practical use in this century. Color television has been developed in the last few years. The use of nuclear energy has increased considerably since 1950. Computers have revolutionized the business world.

Technology has advanced so far that most of the unskilled jobs are no longer available. Automation is rapidly replacing

355

machine operators in manufacturing. Production has increased greatly with less manpower needed. Business and industry have become so complex today that workers must be educated if they expect to be employed and must continue learning to advance in their jobs.

Education and training are greatly needed by the workforce of today. Young people should take advantage of every possible opportunity to learn the skills and knowledge for their future work.

Increasing Your Earnings

The education you have and the skills you learn are closely related to the money you will earn during a lifetime. In 1966 it was estimated by the United States Department of Labor

The Education You Have and the Skills You Learn Are Closely Related to the Money You Will Earn During Your Life

that persons who quit school at the eighth grade could expect a lifetime earnings of $154,000. The high school graduate of 1966 could expect total earnings of $282,000 during his lifetime, and the expected average earning for college graduates would be $451,000.

Practically all surveys made on lifetime earnings of workers indicate that there is a close relationship between education and earnings. Some say that an individual's lifetime earnings depends more on his willingness to work hard and save money for investment. This may be partly true, but education and training will give the individual an advantage over the person who has equal initiative and abilty.

Education and Job Security

The importance of education and job security cannot be overlooked. The Labor Department Survey, made in 1968, clearly reveals a relationship between the unemployment rate of 18 and 19 year-old men and women and the level of their educational attainments. The survey report indicated that of all the unemployed in the United States in March 1968, 22% were from the 18-19 year old group who had only 5 to 7 years of elementary education. 14% of the unemployed in this age range had attended high school. Persons who had completed high school had the lowest unemployment and accounted for 8.6% of the unemployed.

It was also noted that 40% of the male workers were employed in the lowest paid occupations. Workers who failed to finish high school represented a total of 76.8%, and the occupations offered little opportunity for advancement.

The jobs for which those without training can qualify are decreasing each year. For example, farm employment has continued to drop since World War II. Three million jobs were lost in agriculture between 1947 and 1962. It appears that job loss will continue among farm workers for several years. Those with little training who have worked in this occupational area are forced to prepare for other employment or be among the unemployed.

The best job security is found in the jobs that require the most education and training. Employment in the professional, technical, and related occupational group has increased rapidly since 1950. Employment in these areas will continue to increase for some time, especially in the technical areas. Thus, young people who desire employment in these areas must prepare through additional education and training.

Preparation for Work

Most jobs available to young men and women require additional specialized training. In deciding which occupation you wish to make a life work, it is necessary to evaluate yourself.

Many Jobs Are Available in the Technical Occupations, But One Must Have Training to Enter the Field

After you have all the data available, the final decision must be yours. Preparation for the professions requires considerable ability, effort, and time. The rewards for those successful may be great. However, many rewarding jobs are available in areas of business, industry, and government which do not require years of training.

There are many ways to prepare for work. Of course, it is wise to remain in high school and graduate if possible. Your efforts and application in high school studies will provide a good background for further preparation.

For the 610,000 boys and girls who dropped out of school below the 12th grade in 1967-1968, jobs in a number of occupations are available. Many may be learned on the job, others require apprenticeship training. The following occupations may be learned through "on the job" training or in an apprenticeship program. The list is from the *Occupational Outlook Handbook* and includes only general categories of various occupations.

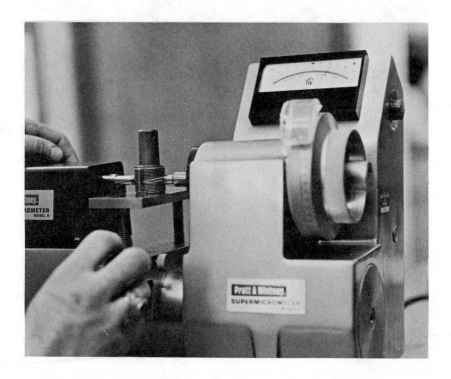

Jobs for Which a High School Education Is Preferred

Occupation   Employment Opportunities

Health Occupations

- Dental Laboratory   Very favorable opportunities.
  Technician   Rapid employment increase.

**Other Professional and
Related Occupations**

- Photographer   Portrait and commercial fields
                             crowded, but demand will con-
                             tinue strong for industrial pho-
                             tographers. A small increase in
                             employment expected.

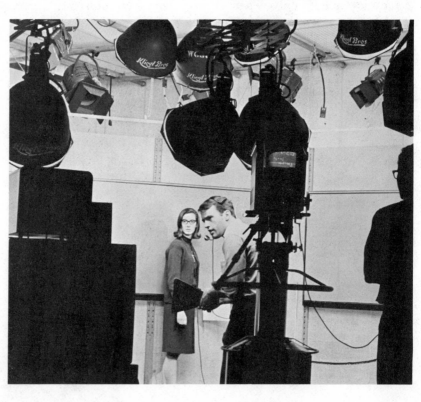

Occupation	Employment Opportunities
Clerical and Related Occupations	Tens of thousands of openings yearly, but competition keen. Many opportunities for part-time work. Very rapid employment increase.
• Shipping or Receiving Clerk	Thousands of openings annually. Many applicants, so keen competition.

Sales Occupations

• Automobile Parts Counterman	A few thousand openings yearly. Continued employment growth.
• Salesman or Saleswoman (Retail Trade)	Many opportunities for full- or part-time work. Moderate increase in employment.

Service Occupations

• Barber	Several thousand openings annually. Moderate rise in employment.
• Cook and Chef	Excellent employment opportunities. Thousands of openings annually.
• Cosmetologist	Job opportunities expected to be very good. Very rapid employment expansion.
• Hospital Attendant	Very rapid rise in employment.
• Private Household Worker	Excellent employment opportunities. Many thousands needed annually. Moderate employment rise.

Occupation	Employment Opportunities
• Waiter and Waitress	Good opportunities. Majority of jobs for women; however, men preferred for jobs in formal dining establishments.

Building Trades

• Asbestos and Insulating Worker	Several hundred openings annually. Moderate employment increase.
• Bricklayer	Several thousand openings each year. Moderate rise in employment.

• Carpenter	Slow increase in employment, but many openings each year in this very large occupation.
• Cement Mason and Terrazzo Worker	A few thousand openings each year. Moderate increase in emment.

Occupation	Employment Opportunities
• Construction Laborer or Hod Carrier	Many thousands of openings each year. Slow increase in employment.

• Floor Covering Installer	Several hundred openings yearly. Moderate increase in employment.
• Lather	About 1,000 opening annually. Moderate increase in employment.
• Painter or Paperhanger	Many thousands of opening each year. Slow increase in employment.
• Plasterer	A few thousand openings each year. Moderate increase in employment.
• Plumber or Pipefitter	Several thousand openings each year. Moderate increase in employment.
• Roofer	A few thousand openings annually. Moderate increase in employment.

Occupation	Employment Opportunities
• Stonemason, Marble Setter, and Tile Setter	Small number of openings yearly. Slow growth in employment.
• Structural, Ornamental, and Reinforcing Iron Worker	A few thousand openings annually. Rapid increase in employment.

Driving Occupations

• Bus Driver	Small number of opportunities for new workers yearly, but overall employment expected to decline.
• Routeman	Several thousand openings each year. Slight rise in employment.
• Taxi Driver	Many opportunities for new workers, though number of cabs is declining. Instability of income causes high turnover.
• Truck Driver	Rapid increase in employment.
• Truck Driver, Over-the-Road	Thousands of new drivers needed each year. Rapid increase in employment.

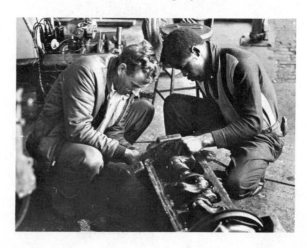

Occupation   Employment Opportunities

Machining Occupations

- Machine Tool Operator   Little or no overall employment growth, but thousands of replacement openings yearly.

Mechanics and Repairmen

- Appliance Serviceman   Thousands of openings yearly. Rapid increase in employment.

- Automobile Body   A few thousand openings annually. Moderate employment growth.
  Repairman

- Automobile Mechanic   More than 20,000 job openings yearly. Moderate employment growth.

- Bowling-Pin Machine   A few hundred replacement openings each year. Little or no change in employment.
  Mechanic

- Diesel Mechanic   Very rapid employment increase.

- Electric Sign   Several hundred openings annually. Rapid increase in employment.
  Serviceman

Occupation	Employment Opportunities
● Electrician (Maintenance)	An increase of a few thousand annually.
● Farm Equipment Mechanic	About 2,300 openings yearly. Moderate rise in employment.
● Industrial Machinery Repairman	Several thousand openings annually. Moderate increase in employment.
● Millwright	Several thousand openings yearly. Slow increase in employment.
● Truck or Bus Mechanic	A few thousand truck mechanics and a few hundred bus mechanics will be needed annually.

Manual Occupations

● Automobile Upholsterer	A few thousand openings annually.
● Boilermaking Worker	About 600 replacement openings annually. Slow employment growth.
● Electroplater	A few hundred jobs open annually. Limited employment growth.
● Furniture Upholsterer	Continuing shortage of workers.
● Gasoline Service Station Attendant	Several thousand full-time and part-time openings annually. Moderate employment increase.
● Jeweler or Jewelry Repairman	Continuing shortage of workers.
● Manufacturing Inspector	Slow increase in employment.
● Motion Picture Projectionist	Slight increase in employment, but openings will be scarce in this relatively small occupation.

Occupation	Employment Opportunities
● Photographic Laboratory Worker Semi-skilled	A few hundred openings annually. Many of the semi-skilled jobs will be filled by women. Moderate employment increase.
● Power Truck Operator	Moderate increase in employment.
● Production Painter	Several thousand replacement opportunities annually.
● Shoe Repairman	Continuing shortage of workers.
● Stationary Fireman	Few employment opportunities. Decline in employment.
● Welder, or Oxygen and Arc Cutter	Several thousand new workers needed yearly. Rapid increase in employment.

Occupation   Employment Opportunities

Foundries

- Foundry Coremaker   Several hundred openings annually, chiefly for replacements. Slow growth in employment.

Jobs for Which a College Education Is Usually Required

Business Administration and Related Professions

- Accountant   Very good employment prospects. Rapid expansion in employment.

- Advertising Worker   Rapid employment increase; but stiff competition.

- Marketing Research Worker   Very good employment opportunities.

Occupation

Employment Opportunities

- Personnel Worker

Favorable employment outlook. Opportunities best for college graduate with major in the field.

- Public Relations Worker

Rapid expansion in employment.

Clergy

- Protestant Clergyman

The supply of well-qualified Protestant ministers probably will continue to be less than demand.

- Rabbi

The number of rabbis expected to be inadequate to meet the expanding demands for their services.

- Roman Catholic Priest

Growing number of priests needed.

Occupation	Employment Opportunities
Conservation Occupations	
• Forester	Good employment opportunities.
• Range Manager	Favorable employment opportunities in this small field. Probably best opportunities in federal agencies.
Counseling	
• Counselor, Rehabilitation	Excellent employment opportunities.
• Counselor, School	Excellent employment opportunities. Rapid employment increase.
• Counselor, Vocational	Excellent employment opportunities in this small field.
Health Occupations	
• Chiropractor	Employment outlook favorable; uncrowded field.
• Dentist	Very good opportunities for employment. Employment will increase.
• Dietitian	Excellent and increasing employment opportunities.
• Hospital Administrator	Excellent employment prospects for those with master's degree in hospital administration.
• Medical Record Librarian	Excellent employment prospects.
• Medical Technologist	Excellent prospects for jobs. Many opportunities for part-time employment.
• Occupational Therapist	Excellent employment opportunities; shortage of workers.

Occupation	Employment Opportunities
● Optometrist	Favorable employment prospects.
● Osteopathic Physician	Excellent job prospects.
● Pharmicist	Very favorable employment opportunities. Gradual increases in new positions is anticipated.
● Physical Therapist	Excellent employment prospects. Demand expected to exceed supply.
● Physician	Excellent employment opportunities.
● Podiatrist	Employment opportunities good. Though the field is small, the number graduating each year is also small.
● Sanitarian	Very favorable employment prospects as state and local health agencies expand activities in field of environmental health.
● Speech Pathologist: Audiologist	Good employment opportunities, best for those with a graduate degree.
● Veterinarian	Very good employment prospects. The demand will probably exceed the supply.

Mathematics and Related Fields

● Actuary	Excellent employment opportunities for professional actuaries in this small occupation. Good demand for well-qualified actuarial trainees.

Occupation	Employment Opportunities
● Mathematician	Excellent opportunities for those with graduate degree and well-qualified bachelor's degree holders; increasing competition for entry positions in this very rapidly growing field.
● Statistician	Good employment opportunities.

Natural Sciences

● Biological Scientist	Very good employment opportunities for graduate degree holders. Those with only bachelor's degree may be limited to semiprofessional jobs. Very rapid employment growth.
● Earth Scientist: Geologist	Favorable employment prospect for those with only bachelor's degree will face some competition for entry positions. Relatively slow employment increase expected.
● Geophysicist	Favorable employment prospects, though field is small. Best opportunities for those with graduate degree. Employment expected to grow slowly.
● Meteorologist	Good job opportunities in this small field. Space-age activities contribute to demand.
● Oceanographer	Good employment opportunities, particularly for advanced degree holders. Rapid growth in this small field.

Occupation   Employment Opportunities

Physical Sciences

- Astronomer   Favorable employment outlook
                              in this small field. Excellent
                              prospects for those with Ph.D.
                              degree.

- Biochemist   Very good employment prospects,
                              especially for those with Ph.D.
                              degree. Very rapid employment
                              growth.

- Chemist   Very good employment prospects.
                              Growing demand expected to ex-
                              ceed the number of new chemist-
                              ry graduates.

- Physicist   Excellent employment opportu-
                              nities, particulary for advanced
                              degree holders and well-qualified
                              bachelor's degree holders. Very
                              rapid employment growth.

Occupation

Employment Opportunities

Art Related Occupations

● Industrial Designer

Employment will expand moderately in this small field. Prospects are best for those with a college degree and outstanding talent.

Social Sciences

● Anthropologist

Very rapid increase expected in this very small field. Largest increase will be in teaching jobs.

● Economist

Excellent employment opportunities for those with graduate degrees. Applicants with B.A. degree will find many opportunities in government agencies. Very rapid employment increase.

● Geographer

Favorable employment outlook, but field is relatively small.

Occupation	Employment Opportunities
• Historian	Excellent employment opportunities in teaching for those with graduate degrees, but openings scarce for those without advanced degree.
• Policitial Scientist	Excellent employment prospects for Ph D's., especially in college teaching. Good employment prospects for those with master's degree, but limited for those with only B.A.
• Sociologist	Rapid increase in employment. Best opportunities for those with Ph. D. degree.

Teaching

• Teacher; College or University	Excellent job opportunities, especially for those with doctoral degree; many opportunities for those with master's degree, particularly in junior colleges.

Occupation	Employment Opportunities
• Teacher; Kindergarten, Elementary, and Secondary School	Large number of openings. Greater emphasis expected to be placed on quality of applicant's training and academic achievement.

Writing Occupations

• Newspaper Reporter	Good employment opportunities for the well qualified and talented. Others face keen competition. Small town papers offer most openings.
• Technical Writer	Many opportunities for beginners with good writing ability and appropriate education. Moderate employment increase.

Other Professional and Related Occupations

• Architect	Good employment prospects in this rapidly growing field.

Occupation	Employment Opportunities
• College Placement Officer	Very rapid employment increase expected, but a very small field.
• Home Economist	Very good employment opportunities especially for teachers in secondary schools and colleges. Employment will expand.
• Landscape Architect	Favorable employment opportunities. Continued expansion in employment.
• Lawyer	Very good prospects for graduates from widely recognized law schools and those who rank high in class. Others may encounter difficulty finding salaried jobs.
• Librarian	Excellent employment prospects. Shortage expected to continue, particularly in school libraries.
• Psychologist	Excellent employment opportunities. Large employment increase expected in state and local agencies.
• Recreation Worker	Excellent job chances for well-qualified workers. Very rapid increase in employment.
• Social Worker	Excellent employment opportunities for those with a master's degree in social work; good opportunities for those with a bachelor's degree.
• Systems Analyst	Excellent employment opportunities in this rapidly expanding occupation.

Occupation	Employment Opportunities
● Urban Planner	Very good employment prospects. Shortage of qualified planners in this relatively small but rapidly growing field.

Managerial Occupations

● Purchasing Agent	Good employment opportunities for the well qualified. Rapid growth of employment.

Sales Occupations

● Manufacturer's Salesman	Good opportunities for the well-trained; but employers will be selective. Rapid increase in employment.
● Securities Salesman	Good employment opportunities. Turnover high among beginners. Rapid employment rise.

Occupation	Employment Opportunities
Service Occupations	
• F.B.I.	Personnel turnover low.
Agriculture	
• Cooperative Extension Service Worker	Favorable employment opportunities, especially for work in depressed rural areas.
Civil Aviation	
• Airline Dispatcher	Little change expected in this very small field.
Banking	
• Bank Officer	Entry opportunities are very good. Thousands of openings each year. Very rapid employment increase.

Many companies offer "on-the-job" training programs for beginners. The length of training varies from a few weeks to two years. The pay for these jobs is generally low, but many provide an opportunity to continue learning and make progress on the job.

To find "on-the-job" training, one may apply to the State Employment Service, to companies advertising openings, and to private employment agencies.

Vocational Schools

Since 1963 local, state, and federal educational agencies have cooperated in developing vocational schools and programs. Under the provisions of the Vocational Educational Act of 1963, millions of dollars have been spent in buildings and equipment for vocational education. These schools offer both high school and post-high school work of less than college grade. Opportunities for interested students include preparation in agriculture and business occupations, trade training, health occupations, and technical work.

The cost of attending public vocational schools is very low. In many cases, fees for supplies and books are the only cost. In some of the larger cities, students may have an opportunity to work part time to help cut expenses. Loans for students are also available to those who can qualify. Most high school courses require two years and 1080 hours for completion. Post-high school courses may require as much as 2100 hours of instruction.

Graduates are assisted by the school in locating jobs in the area. A larger number of young people are taking advantage of vocational education.

Community Junior Colleges

In the last 20 years the enrollment in community junior colleges has increased, and the curriculum has been expanded. Traditionally, the junior college offered transfer college credit. However, the objectives have been broadened to include tech-

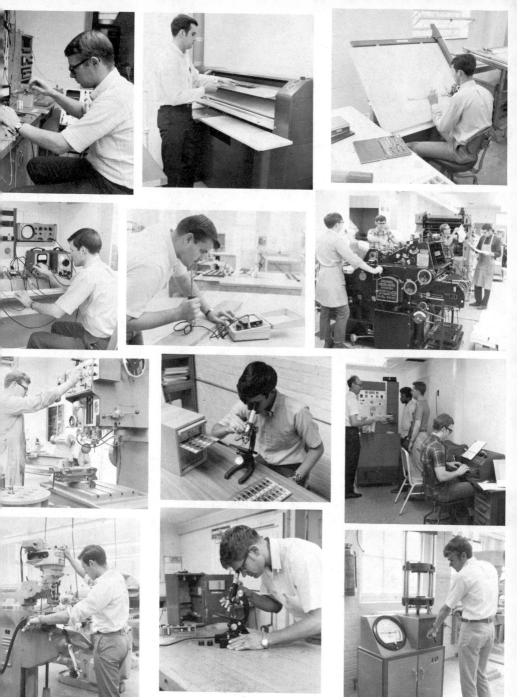

Work in the Skilled Trades Is Open to Those Who Have Completed an
Apprenticeship Program or a Vocational Education Course in
High School or Junior College

nical courses and provide adult education and community services.

Those who desire the first two years of college transfer credit may attend a junior college near their homes. Generally, public junior colleges are less expensive to attend than a four-year college or university. Many academic fields of study are offered in the junior college as well as the two-year technical program.

Technical areas of study include automotive technology, business, data processing, chemical technology, drafting, and design, electronic technology, tool and manufacturing technology, and many other areas of study. It has been estimated that about 50% of our manpower will be given instruction on the post-high school level in area vocational schools and community junior colleges.

In many areas, a community junior college or an area vocational-technical school is within commuting distance of persons who desire the additional instruction.

Four-Year Colleges and Universities

Young men and women who plan to enter professional work are generally expected to prepare in a college or university. Over 2,000 colleges and universities offer professional and highly technical training for those qualified after high school. Only 20% of the young people graduating from high school earned a Bachelor Degree from a college in 1969. This percent is about equal to the percent of the labor force working in professional and technical occupations.

Many professional occupations require at least four years of college. A few require six to eight years of college preparation for entry. A number of professions may be entered without a college degree, but related experience and education are required to enter work.

Planning a college education should be started while in high school, and all aspects of planning should be completed before actually enrolling in college. Public institutions of higher learning have been organized in each state. However, each state follows an individual plan with individual requirements. Generally, the more expensive programs, such as medicine and law are offered in the state university, while the less expensive and less lengthy programs are offered in state colleges.

In selecting a college or university, it is wise to make a study of those offering the program you desire. A comparison of the costs, convenience, reputation, and entry requirements would be useful. In many of the areas of study, the institution can accept a limited number of students each year; thus, it is wise to make application at several institutions.

Colleges and universities publish catalogs which give most of the information you need. Additional information may be obtained by writing to the college or university.

Estimating the cost of college training is important— especially if you are on a close budget. Costs vary from school to school. Private colleges are usually more expensive. Public universities charge higher fees than state colleges. In 1969, estimated cost of attending college varied from $1500 to several thousand dollars a year. If you live at home while attending college, you will save several hundred dollars each year.

Persons Who Wish to Prepare for the Professions Should Start Planning to Attend College Before High School Graduation

Financial aid is available to deserving students. Both private and public schools offer scholarships and fellowships to a number of students each year. Students who hope to qualify for financial awards should apply early. Students may borrow money for their educational expenses. National Defense Student Loans have been available for several years. Students may borrow up to $5,000 in a four-year period and repay the money after finishing college. Most students work to pay part of their educational expenses. Some students work enough to pay all of their expenses. However, it may take an additional year or two to finish a four-year program. Recent research indicates grades are not drastically affected when a student works part time while attending college.

Many students who start to college do not finish. Latest statistics indicate only one-half of those attending earn a degree. It is therefore important to carefully plan for college before enrollment. Students, parents, and guidance counselors should work together in answering the question "should I go to college?" A few questions you should answer:

1. Do I really want to make the sacrifice of time, effort, and money to complete a college degree?
2. Do I have the ability to master the knowledge and skill involved to perform effectively after graduation?
3. Am I really interested in the work for which I am preparing?
4. Can my parents afford to pay for my college education?

Perhaps many other questions concerning a college educations should be asked. College study is rigorous and success requires interest, maturity, and self-discipline.

Adult Education

College education is not the only road to a successful career. There are still opportunities for the self-made man. One avenue for success is through adult or continuing education. This route takes longer, but the satisfaction may be greater. More attention is being given to informal adult education today. Most city high schools offer evening courses in business and industrial subjects. Private schools offer evening programs for those who work during the day. Correspondence courses are offered in many subjects. Those interested in learning have numerous opportunities.

Many have developed into successful professionals through adult education. The adult who has been self-reliant for a number of years approaches educational opportunities realistically and with a determination to succeed.

Study Helps

New Terms

interest test   automation   lifetime earnings
ability test   aptitudes   occupational aspirations

Study Questions

1. What are the technological changes which have caused occupational changes? How have these changes affected your preparation for a job?
2. Based on the life-time earnings estimate of the United States Department of Labor, how much more money will a college graduate earn than a high school graduate?
3. What occupation has lost a great many job opportunities in the past twenty years? Why do you think this has occurred?

Discussion Problems

1. Suppose your best friend wants to quit school at the end of the 10th grade. Think of as many reasons as you can to persuade your friend that staying in school is the better thing to do.
2. At the present time, what occupation do you plan to enter? What influenced you to select this occupation? Why do you think you will be successful in this job? Is it the only occupation which interests you?

3. Study the employment opportunities for each occupation listed on pp. 360-79. For which occupations are the employment opportunities discouraging? For which occupations is the demand for workers greatest? Which occupations should have an increase in employment opportunities?

Understanding
Mathematics

Our System of numbering is made up of ten basic symbols:

O, 1, 2, 3, 4, 5, 6, 7, 8, 9,

These numbers are called "digits," and they can be combined to make larger numbers, for example:

36,   456,   3,914,   14,672

Each digit in the above numbers tell how many of something. Let's look at the number 36. It is the same as 30 + 6. It is not the same as 63. The *placement* of each digit makes a difference. The digit on the *right* tells us the number of "1's." The next digit tells us the number of "10's." Thus, in the number 36, we know that there are 6 "1's" and 3 "10's." The chart below shows the meaning of digit placement.

hundred millions	ten millions	millions	hundred thousands	ten thousands	thousands	hundreds	tens	ones
6	3	2,	2	8	9 ,	1	4	6

The number in the chart would be read, "Six hundred thirty-two million, two-hundred eighty-nine thousand, one hundred forty-six." Notice that each group of three digits in the chart is separated by commas for easier reading.

What is meant by each digit in the number 456? Is this the same as 400 + 50 + 6? They are both the same. In the number 456, we know that there are 4 "100's," 5 "10's," and 6 "1's." A clear understanding of this makes all mathematics easier.

What is meant by each digit in the following numbers?

3,914   14,672   127,684

Addition Review

This is the way we add:

(1) count the number of "1's" (in the right column)

(2) if the column total is one digit, write it down and on to the next column left

(3) if the column total is more than one digit, write down only the "one's" digit and add the rest to the next column on the left

(4) continue this procedure until all columns have been added.

Add these numbers:

DO NOT WRITE ANSWERS IN YOUR BOOK. . . . For all the following mathematical problems. Use a separate sheet of paper to record your answers.

36	16	46	53	75
+45	+38	+29	+69	+49

417	864	219	765	436
+266	+916	+784	+544	+988

Check your answers on page 403. If you missed more than two, ask your teacher to watch you add a few numbers so that he can see where you are having difficulty. Usually, it is either (1) you don't understand how to "carry," or (2) you haven't memorized the combinations of basic numbers. Check yourself by working these as fast as you can, and see how long it takes you.

2	4	4	5	6	8	7	9
+3	+3	+5	+3	+4	+6	+5	+7

3	5	9	7	9	8
+6	+7	+6	+6	+9	+4

If you really know these combinations, you should be able to answer them all in 15 seconds. Check your answers on page 403. If you missed more than one, or if it took more than 25 seconds, you will improve your math skills by practicing these combinations for a few minutes every day for a week.

If the combinations above were easy for you, add these numbers as fast as you can, checking your time:

41	16	71	67	34	19
26	29	62	91	17	82
39	71	38	43	28	76
62	46	14	22	63	48

87	79	58	89	78	85
66	68	95	74	99	97
47	84	89	98	87	73
91	76	63	85	92	98

Check your answers on page 404. If your answers are all correct and you finished in less than 2 minutes, you probably have little or no difficulty with addition. If you missed more than one and required more than two minutes to finish, you can improve by practicing the addition problems on the next three pages for a few minutes each day for a week.

Addition Practice

I

9	6	4	7	8	7
4	5	8	7	6	3
6	8	4	2	4	8
4	5	8	6	3	6

II

7	5	8	6	9	5
8	6	7	8	6	8
4	8	6	7	8	7
5	7	4	9	7	9

III

2	4	6	9	7	5
6	8	9	4	6	8
5	7	4	8	6	7
9	7	5	3	8	6

IV

8	7	4	3	6	8
9	6	3	8	5	1
8	6	9	3	7	8
7	5	8	9	6	4

Check Your Answers on Page 404

V

16	21	18	13	17	19
14	18	19	11	13	18
17	12	13	12	14	15
11	13	14	10	19	18

VI

14	17	19	16	10	17
17	19	15	14	18	19
10	12	11	13	17	18
12	14	18	17	16	13

VII

17	18	16	15	14	12
20	23	25	28	26	23
19	17	15	21	19	26
13	18	22	27	27	29

VIII

27	29	15	28	30	31
19	31	40	16	41	53
32	41	19	64	35	48
31	48	52	49	62	59

Addition Practice

I	64	48	87	62	52	86
	27	95	35	13	75	64
	31	15	19	73	59	38
	97	34	23	48	42	49

II	54	31	45	75	66	48
	36	27	65	77	53	86
	27	17	43	12	25	53
	19	39	71	43	97	36

III	13	38	54	39	26	78
	58	27	39	46	49	11
	39	58	47	68	88	47
	44	32	19	28	64	47

IV	95	38	41	76	85	89
	22	45	58	74	89	40
	51	17	46	97	20	18
	31	67	49	50	32	25

Check Your Answers on Page 404

V	32	45	19	21	31	40
	16	31	28	40	33	19
	21	32	17	24	18	40
	25	16	43	18	47	21

VI	48	75	18	92	35	64
	58	87	69	57	44	74
	68	98	56	76	59	68
	84	75	96	84	77	85

VII	68	64	75	79	72	94
	68	74	73	62	58	68
	84	83	96	52	74	69
	71	53	68	82	91	58

VIII	99	75	82	51	79	52
	51	42	73	94	68	67
	57	63	58	97	24	61
	47	96	48	58	73	96

Addition Practice

I	33	41	27	53	31	42
	52	34	18	31	46	28
	48	38	53	57	37	61
	38	19	27	41	37	38
	53	53	79	51	62	85
	41	29	53	59	63	25

II	49	37	28	32	64	85
	59	42	19	71	58	62
	43	58	49	64	41	38
	75	63	29	59	55	31
	88	46	29	43	82	19
	64	18	29	43	18	86

III	38	51	37	66	49	82
	39	64	48	13	27	48
	44	18	21	63	91	65
	19	55	42	78	61	74
	63	40	75	24	38	55
	28	43	12	33	72	20

Check Your Answers on Page 404

IV	116	314	110	112	120	135
	101	95	125	100	110	114
	150	123	52	19	16	14
	132	46	118	163	150	18
	16	131	45	84	19	65
	156	119	125	141	19	185

V	31	29	116	118	145	76
	135	211	21	9	161	136
	46	197	186	415	208	6
	316	143	263	190	154	117
	149	16	213	16	43	218
	119	63	117	321	116	110

VI	158	211	184	301	195	265
	185	461	139	410	210	312
	148	213	186	297	315	115
	75	142	63	18	119	219
	8	85	4	138	42	18
	105	118	19	128	200	16

Subtraction Review

This is the way to subtract:

(1) Begin with the "1's" (right column). If the bottom number is less than the top number, subtract and go to the next column left.

(2) If, in any column, the bottom number is larger than the top number, we must "borrow." To borrow, the top number of the next column left becomes one less and the number above the number being subtracted becomes 10 more.

(3) Continue until all columns have been subtracted.

Examples:

$$
\begin{array}{r}
\overset{4}{7}\overset{}{5}2 \\
-\ 38 \\
\hline
714
\end{array}
\qquad
\begin{array}{r}
\overset{41}{5}23 \\
-167 \\
\hline
356
\end{array}
\qquad
\begin{array}{r}
\overset{29}{3}00 \\
-\ 54 \\
\hline
246
\end{array}
$$

Subtract the bottom numbers from the top numbers:

$$
\begin{array}{r} 29 \\ -15 \\ \hline \end{array}
\qquad
\begin{array}{r} 38 \\ -21 \\ \hline \end{array}
\qquad
\begin{array}{r} 46 \\ -36 \\ \hline \end{array}
\qquad
\begin{array}{r} 52 \\ -23 \\ \hline \end{array}
\qquad
\begin{array}{r} 47 \\ -29 \\ \hline \end{array}
$$

$$
\begin{array}{r} 114 \\ -\ 90 \\ \hline \end{array}
\qquad
\begin{array}{r} 165 \\ -146 \\ \hline \end{array}
\qquad
\begin{array}{r} 258 \\ -199 \\ \hline \end{array}
\qquad
\begin{array}{r} 753 \\ -545 \\ \hline \end{array}
\qquad
\begin{array}{r} 641 \\ -155 \\ \hline \end{array}
$$

Check your answers on page 405. If you missed more than two, ask your teacher to watch you subtract so that he can see where you are having difficulty. Usually, it is either (1) you don't understand how to "borrow," or (2) you haven't memorized the subtraction of basic numbers. Check yourself by working these as fast as you can, and see how long it takes you.

8	7	9	16	13	18	14
− 2	− 5	− 5	− 7	− 9	− 9	− 8

12	15	17	13	11	16	17
− 8	− 9	− 8	− 6	− 4	− 8	− 9

If you really know these, you should be able to answer them all in 20 seconds. Check your answers on page 405. If you missed more than one, or if it took you more than 30 seconds, you will improve your math skills by practicing the subtraction of these basic numbers for a few minutes every day for a week.

If the subtraction of the basic numbers above was easy for you, subtract these numbers as fast as you can, checking your time:

86	75	95	115	250	160	500	75
− 50	− 66	− 54	− 85	−165	−145	−155	− 48

47	85	66	758	315	130	404	80
− 39	− 36	− 27	−169	−255	− 95	−135	− 18

Check your answers on page 405. If your answers are all correct and you finished in less than 1 minute, you will have no difficulty with subtraction. If you missed more than one and required more than one minute to finish, you can improve by practicing the subtraction problems on the next two pages for a few minutes each day for a week.

Subtraction Practice

I	26 − 16	31 − 10	53 − 12	28 − 15	32 − 11	41 − 9
II	33 − 11	19 − 12	53 − 13	60 − 15	35 − 15	46 − 17
III	44 − 12	75 − 61	62 − 51	83 − 72	56 − 45	48 − 17
IV	39 − 23	66 − 17	37 − 22	46 − 35	28 − 17	77 − 18
V	62 − 25	84 − 33	59 − 51	84 − 45	97 − 58	49 − 17
VI	31 − 21	60 − 17	55 − 13	78 − 27	47 − 39	32 − 27

Check Your Answers on Page 405

VII	75 − 14	48 − 19	66 − 59	95 − 73	88 − 28	54 − 33
VIII	87 − 31	92 − 41	76 − 27	69 − 19	84 − 21	72 − 48
IX	84 − 21	66 − 39	59 − 18	93 − 49	55 − 21	75 − 48
X	46 − 33	76 − 17	98 − 47	75 − 66	58 − 19	47 − 26
XI	85 − 42	68 − 51	77 − 38	42 − 31	71 − 45	39 − 26
XII	97 − 64	81 − 35	76 − 29	95 − 64	88 − 47	42 − 19

Subtraction Practice

I	115 − 95	128 − 62	142 − 31	181 − 75	143 − 48	111 − 17
II	185 − 83	164 − 116	197 − 38	172 − 41	131 − 39	195 − 48
III	121 − 114	165 − 39	188 − 36	154 − 82	133 − 111	129 − 113
IV	216 − 120	139 − 37	215 − 150	312 − 125	425 − 240	130 − 108
V	118 − 95	415 − 63	365 − 175	391 − 158	418 − 265	333 − 157
VI	405 − 58	315 − 119	125 − 108	740 − 516	515 − 143	811 − 558

Check Your Answers on Pages 405 and 406

VII	586 − 342	419 − 119	638 − 511	532 − 411	896 − 716	518 − 144
VIII	775 − 519	511 − 430	588 − 217	915 − 689	824 − 641	732 − 489
IX	950 − 758	870 − 532	584 − 189	916 − 684	488 − 217	748 − 539
X	689 − 481	761 − 187	860 − 255	995 − 158	178 − 126	815 − 748
XI	964 − 483	818 − 649	764 − 164	998 − 596	789 − 318	778 − 682
XII	887 − 188	795 − 713	658 − 511	418 − 365	666 − 319	785 − 347

Multiplication Review

This is the way to multiply:

(1) Begin by multiplying the "1's" digit of the top number by the "1's" digit in bottom number.

(2) If the product (answer) is a one-digit number, write it down and next multiply the "10's" digit of the top number by the "1's" digit of the bottom number.

(3) If the product (answer) is a two-digit number, write down only the "1's" digit and after the next multiplication add the "10's" digit of this number to the product.

(4) Continue this procedure until each digit in the top number has been multiplied by the "1's" digit of the bottom number.

(5) If multiplying by a two-digit or larger number, multiply each digit of the top number by the "10's" digit of the bottom number following the procedure above, but indent your answer one digit to the left—so that the "1's" digit of this product is placed under the "10's" digit of the first product.

(6) Continue multiplying until all top digits have been multiplied by each digit in the bottom number, indenting the new product one place to the left each time.

(7) All products are added together to get the final answer.

Examples:

```
   4              14
 361            526
× 7            × 72
2,527          1052
              3682
             37,872
```

Multiply the top numbers by the bottom numbers:

```
  35      42      55      73      96      68     125
× 8     × 6     × 7     × 5     × 4     × 9     × 3
```

85	37	75	174	213	389	768
×12	×16	×25	× 38	× 47	× 96	× 35

Check your answers on page 406. If you missed more than three, ask your teacher to watch you multiply some numbers so that he can see where you are having difficulty. It may be that you do not fully understand the procedure, but for many the problem is simply that the "multiplication tables" haven't been completely memorized. Check yourself by multiplying these combinations as fast as you can, and see how long it takes you.

5	7	6	4	9	8	3	9	7
×4	×3	×8	×7	×5	×7	×5	×4	×5

6	7	4	9	6	9	3	9	8
×7	×7	×6	×7	×9	×8	×9	×9	×8

If you really know these combinations, you should be able to answer them all in 20 seconds. Check your answers on page 406. If you missed more than two, or if it took you more than 30 seconds, you will improve your math skills by practicing the combinations on page 399.

If the combinations above were easy for you, multiply these numbers as fast as you can, checking your time:

654	395	506	419	725	386	853
× 37	× 24	× 34	× 25	× 36	× 21	× 74

742	905	186	614	372	125	498
× 16	× 37	× 79	× 83	×145	×346	×125

Check your answers on page 406. If your answers are all correct and you finished in less than six minutes, you will have no difficulty with multiplication. If you missed more than two, or if it took you more than ten minutes, you will improve your math skills by practicing multiplication problems on the next three pages for a few minutes each day for a week.

Multiplication Practice

I	45 × 7	75 × 6	62 × 5	38 × 4	47 × 6	36 × 3
II	65 × 4	57 × 6	78 × 7	81 × 3	45 × 4	31 × 5
III	53 × 3	44 × 5	68 × 4	34 × 5	38 × 6	52 × 7
IV	68 × 6	91 × 7	45 × 6	86 × 5	95 × 6	51 × 5
V	59 × 5	48 × 3	61 × 5	78 × 4	46 × 7	39 × 5
VI	82 × 3	43 × 6	35 × 7	77 × 4	95 × 4	76 × 6

Check Your Answers on Page 406

VII	115 × 4	108 × 6	116 × 5	111 × 7	109 × 3	114 × 4
VIII	125 × 5	136 × 6	118 × 3	141 × 7	155 × 6	163 × 4
IX	158 × 4	215 × 6	185 × 7	201 × 6	135 × 5	211 × 7
X	257 × 6	313 × 6	351 × 5	148 × 4	318 × 7	255 × 3
XI	275 × 5	190 × 4	512 × 6	374 × 7	408 × 3	522 × 6
XII	601 × 5	755 × 3	484 × 5	950 × 7	382 × 6	615 × 4

Multiplication Practice

I	41 ×12	73 ×11	61 ×13	37 ×14	47 ×15	35 ×17
II	62 ×21	55 ×17	76 ×23	82 ×45	44 ×25	57 ×32
III	52 ×25	48 ×56	66 ×47	85 ×61	37 ×35	72 ×44
IV	68 ×66	23 ×52	49 ×34	86 ×46	53 ×32	78 ×55
V	59 ×27	36 ×19	77 ×36	42 ×73	75 ×56	53 ×43
VI	82 ×26	49 ×35	95 ×53	74 ×67	67 ×43	88 ×35

Check Your Answers on Page 407

VII	54 × 8	57 × 9	62 × 9	38 × 8	46 × 9	35 × 8
VIII	39 ×18	55 ×19	74 ×28	83 ×39	72 ×82	58 ×91
IX	75 ×83	84 ×92	77 ×85	49 ×96	33 ×48	47 ×83
X	88 ×29	29 ×38	41 ×49	36 ×95	95 ×58	48 ×87
XI	79 ×74	38 ×83	68 ×91	93 ×82	31 ×48	78 ×98
XII	99 ×28	47 ×95	85 ×86	68 ×74	37 ×46	89 ×98

Multiplication Practice

I	645 × 21	358 × 42	605 × 34	491 × 53	368 × 36
II	385 × 61	724 × 32	510 × 25	273 × 54	931 × 61
III	675 × 44	950 × 26	145 × 37	357 × 17	229 × 37
IV	752 × 31	684 × 55	591 × 32	523 × 15	687 × 22
V	522 × 16	435 × 33	789 × 12	618 × 56	531 × 66
VI	168 × 55	632 × 46	731 × 71	719 × 28	737 × 37

Check Your Answers on Page 407

VII	134 × 18	318 × 29	218 × 81	375 × 93	415 × 84
VIII	385 × 85	538 × 92	423 × 86	487 × 95	518 × 88
IX	864 × 81	532 × 87	486 × 96	799 × 99	534 × 97
X	775 ×121	534 ×114	898 ×211	661 ×412	458 ×312
XI	853 ×412	666 ×513	874 ×423	397 ×561	521 ×234
XII	753 ×354	518 ×687	628 ×674	555 ×789	425 ×698

Division Review

This is the way we divide:

(1) In the following problem, we are to divide 273 by 21. The number to be divided, 273, is placed inside the division sign and is called the *dividend*. The number 21 is placed outside the division sign and is called the *divisor*. The answer to the problem is called the *quotient*.

(2) In division we try to find a number, the *quotient*, which when multiplied by the *divisor*, the answer (product) is equal to or less than the *dividend*.

(3) If the product is equal to the dividend, you have completed the division problem. If the product is less than the dividend, subtract—placing the difference over the divisor as a fraction and make it part of the quotient.

(4) The techniques of division will be illustrated by example:

$$
\begin{array}{r}
13 \\
21\overline{)273} \\
21 \\
\hline
63 \\
63 \\
\hline
0
\end{array}
\qquad
\begin{array}{r}
307 \\
15\overline{)4605} \\
45 \\
\hline
10 \\
0 \\
\hline
105 \\
105 \\
\hline
0
\end{array}
\qquad
\begin{array}{r}
2014 \quad ^{9}/_{36} = \\
36\overline{)72513} \\
72 \\
\hline
05 \\
0 \\
\hline
51 \\
36 \\
\hline
153 \\
144 \\
\hline
9
\end{array}
\qquad 2014\,\tfrac{1}{4}
$$

Divide the numbers inside the division sign by the outside numbers:

6$\overline{)54}$ 7$\overline{)42}$ 9$\overline{)108}$ 8$\overline{)56}$ 12$\overline{)96}$ 13$\overline{)273}$ 15$\overline{)180}$ 14$\overline{)154}$

16$\overline{)128}$ 19$\overline{)475}$ 24$\overline{)264}$ 35$\overline{)630}$ 46$\overline{)1,430}$ 18$\overline{)220}$

Check your answers on page 407. If you missed more than two, ask your teacher to watch you divide some numbers so that he can see where you are having difficulty. If you missed more than two of these problems, you can improve your skill at division by practicing these problems for a few minutes each day for a week.

Division Practice

I	24)126	14)155	15)810	31)1,395	55)2,915
II	68)3,536	17)765	58)2,494	25)705	85)1,275
III	38)2,166	32)2,448	12)4,260	85)37,740	26)16,744
IV	44)3,740	36)1,050	42)9,429	54)13,716	68)3,604
V	39)14,313	76)4,256	34)11,730	63)2,709	43)7,439
VI	55)19,470	33)12,375	57)13,338	48)30,912	86)46,784
VII	49)3,339	74)18,944	64)16,392	66)24,690	99)4,653
VIII	72)97,632	84)11,928	65)980	83)19,588	54)13,932
IX	95)14,825	76)42,864	84)38,976	51)14,025	23)33,741
X	121)4,114	215)7,525	125)30,625	545)12,535	764)25,976

Check Your Answers on Pages 407 and 408

Answers to Math Problems

Pages 388 and 389

	81		54		75		122	124
	683		1,780		1,003		1,309	1,424
5	7	9	8	10	14	12	16
9	12	15	13	18	12		

Page 389

168	162	185	223	142	225
291	307	305	346	356	353

Page 390

I	23	24	24	22	21	24
II	24	26	25	30	30	29
III	22	26	24	24	27	26
IV	32	24	24	23	24	21
V	58	64	64	46	63	70
VI	53	62	63	60	61	67
VII	69	76	78	91	86	90
VIII	109	149	126	157	168	191

Page 391

I	219	192	164	196	228	237
II	136	114	224	207	241	223
III	154	155	159	181	227	183
IV	199	167	194	297	226	172
V	94	124	107	103	129	120
VI	258	335	239	309	215	291
VII	291	274	312	275	295	289
VIII	254	276	261	300	244	276

Page 392

I	265	214	257	292	276	279
II	378	264	183	312	318	321
III	231	271	235	277	338	344
IV	671	828	575	619	434	531
V	796	659	916	1,069	827	663
VI	679	1,230	595	1,292	1,081	945

Page 393

14	17	10	29	18
24	19	59	208	486

Page 394

6	2	4	9	4	9	6	
4	6	9	7	7	8	8	
36	9	41	30	85	15	345	27
8	49	39	589	60	35	269	62

Page 395

I	10	21	41	13	21	32
II	22	7	40	45	20	29
III	32	14	11	11	11	31
IV	16	49	15	11	11	59
V	37	51	8	39	39	32
VI	10	43	42	51	8	5
VII	61	29	7	22	60	21
VIII	56	51	49	50	63	24
IX	63	27	41	44	34	27
X	13	59	51	9	39	21
XI	43	17	39	11	26	13
XII	33	46	47	31	41	23

Page 396

I	20	66	111	106	95	94
II	102	48	159	131	92	147
III	7	126	152	72	22	16
IV	96	102	65	187	185	22
V	23	352	190	233	153	176
VI	347	196	17	224	372	253

VII	244	300	127	121	180	374
VIII	256	81	371	226	183	243
IX	192	338	395	232	271	209
X	208	574	605	837	52	67
XI	481	169	600	402	471	96
XII	699	82	147	53	347	438

Pages 397 and 398

280	252	385	365	384	612	375
1,020	592	1,875	6,612	10,011	37,344	26,880

Page 398

20	21	48	28	45	56	15	36	35
42	49	24	63	54	72	27	81	64
24,198		9,480	17,204	10,475	26,100		8,106	63,122
11,872		33,485	14,694	50,962	53,940		43,250	62,250

Page 399

I	315	450	310	152	282	108
II	260	342	546	243	180	155
III	159	220	272	170	228	364
IV	408	637	270	430	570	255
V	295	144	305	312	322	195
VI	246	258	245	308	380	456
VII	460	648	580	777	327	456
VIII	625	816	354	987	930	652
IX	632	1,290	1,295	1,206	675	1,477
X	1,542	1,878	1,755	592	2,226	765
XI	1,375	760	3,072	2,618	1,224	3,132
XII	3,005	2,265	2,420	6,650	2,292	2,460

Page 400

I	492	803	793	518	705	595
II	1,302	935	1,748	3,690	1,100	1,824
III	1,300	2,688	3,102	5,185	1,295	3,168
IV	4,488	1,196	1,666	3,956	1,696	4,290
V	1,593	684	2,772	3,066	4,200	2,279
VI	2,132	1,715	5,035	4,958	2,881	3,080
VII	432	513	558	304	414	280
VIII	702	1,045	2,072	3,237	5,904	5,278
IX	6,225	7,728	6,545	4,704	1,584	3,901
X	2,552	1,102	2,009	3,420	5,510	4,176
XI	5,846	3,154	6,188	7,626	1,488	7,644
XII	2,772	4,465	7,310	5,032	1,702	8,722

Page 401

I	13,545	15,036	20,570	26,023	13,248
II	23,485	23,168	12,750	14,742	56,791
III	29,700	24,700	5,365	6,069	8,473
IV	23,312	37,620	18,912	7,845	15,114
V	8,352	14,355	9,468	34,608	35,046
VI	9,240	29,072	51,901	20,132	27,269
VII	2,412	9,222	17,658	34,875	34,860
VIII	32,725	49,496	36,378	46,265	45,584
IX	69,984	46,284	46,656	79,101	51,798
X	93,775	60,876	189,478	272,332	142,896
XI	351,436	341,685	369,702	222,717	121,914
XII	266,562	355,866	423,272	437,895	296,650

Pages 402 and 403

9	6	12	7	8	21	12	11
8	25	11	18	31	2/23	12 2/9	

I	5 1/4	11 1/14	54	45	53
II	52	45	43	28 1/5	15
III	57	76 1/2	355	444	644
IV	85	29 1/6	224 1/2 254		53

V	367		56	345		43	173
VI	354		375	234		644	544
VII	68	1/7	256	256	1/8	374	1/11	47
VIII	1,356		142	15	1/15	236	258
IX	156	1/19	564	464		275	1,467
X	34		35	245		23	34

Parliamentary Procedure

I. The Need for Parliamentary Procedure

Members of a democratic society need a set of rules to obtain group consensus in solving problems and making decisions. In arriving at decisions, a group of people must have a leader skilled in rules of discussion and debate. The pariliamentary procedure is a logical method of working with groups and has been used for this purpose for many years. The English Parliament used the procedure to conduct its business. This became known as parliamentary law. Many modifications have been made to fit the needs of different groups. However, the purpose is still the same—to carry on orderly group meetings conducted on the basis of democratic principles.

A. Democratic Principles:

Parliamentary procedure is based upon a number of democratic principles which are as follows:

1. Debate of the group members must be fair to all present.
2. All entitled members of the group are free to debate under the rules established.
3. The majority has the right to decide the issues.
4. The minority is also guaranteed the right to express

their opinion with protection from the majority provided through parliamentary law.

5. The minority members are expected to abide with the decision when made by the majority.

B. Parliamentary Terms

In order to participate in groups using parliamentary procedure, members need to learn the terms used. When persons participating know the terms and the rules, the organization can move ahead with efficiency.

1. *The chair*: Means the office or dignity of one who presides. A President, Chairman, Speaker, Moderator, etc.
2. *The House*: The members, group or body assembled.
3. *The Meetings:* A gathering of members.
4. *A Quorum*: The number of entitled members who must be present to legally transact business and make decisions.
5. *Minutes*: The official record of the proceedings of an organization.
6. *Proxy:* A signed statement by a member authorizing another member to vote in his absence.
7. *Pro tem*: Acting during the absence of another officer.
8. *Pro and Con:* Means for or against a motion or rule.

C. Other Terms Used in Parliamentary Procedure:

1. *The Motion:* Is a proposal by a member of the house that certain action be taken by the organization.
2. *Second the Motion:* Is stated when a second member of the house approved the motion.
3. *Amending a Motion:* To change the first motion.
4. *The Question*: Means for the presiding officer to call for a vote by the members.
5. *New Business:* Business brought before the house for the first time.

6. *Unfinished Business:* Old business brought before the house for the second or more times.
7. *Table the Question:* To delay decision on a motion.
8. *To Adjourn:* To offcially close the meeting by a majority vote of those present.

II. Conducting a Business Meeting

It is not the purpose of this guide to give the rules of parliamentary procedure in detail. Persons who are elected to office, or who serve as the group's parliamentarian, should study Rules of Order by H. M. Robert, published by Scott, Foresman and Company, Glenview, Illinois.

A. Steps in Holding a Meeting:

No business can legally be transacted at a meeting of any organization unless a quorum is present. Usually a quorum is a majority of members. However, it may be a number fixed by the rules of the organization.

When a quorum is present the usual conduct of the meeting is as follows:

1. The presiding officer takes the chair and calls the meeting to order.
2. He presents the order of business as prescribed by the rules of the organization. If the organization has not adopted an order of business, it may follow a play similar to the one described in B, conducting a meeting.

B. Conducting a Typical Club Meeting:

Many high school organizations have adopted national order of business with ceremonies for meeting. The Future Farmers, Future Homemakers, Distributive Education Clubs, and the Vocational Industrial Clubs of America have adopted general procedures for their meetings.

The meeting described here will be typical of many organizations.

1. President: takes the chair, rises, raps the gavel on wood block and calls, "Meeting will come to order."
2. President: "Bill Smith will lead us in the pledge of allegience to the Flag."
3. President: "Carol Wallis will lead us in singing America."
4. President: "Marie Smith, the secretary, will read the minutes of the previous meeting."
5. President: "Are there corrections to the minutes?" If no corrections are made from the house, the president says, "The minutes are approved as read." If corrections are necessary, the president will ask the secretary to correct the report and say, "Are there any other corrections?" "The minutes stand approved as corrected."
6. President: "The next order of business are the reports of other officers." (May include corresponding secretary, treasurer's report, and other officer reports).
7. President: "The next order of business is the reports of standing committees."
   a. Report of the membership committee
   b. Report of the finance committee
   c. Report of the program committee
   d. Report of other committees
8. President: "The next order of business are reports from the special committees."
   a. Report of the picnic committee
   b. Report of other committees
9. President: "Is there any unfinished business to act upon today? (If no unfinished business, the next order of business is new business.)
10. President: "Is the any new business to be considered today?" (Under new business a number of actions are considered, such as communications, presenting of bills for payment, future plans, setting dates for other activities, etc.)
11. President: "The program committee will now present the program." (The president presents the program

chairman who introduces the speaker or whoever presents the program. When the program is concluded, the program chairman returns the meeting to the chair after thanking the participants.)

12. President: "Is there future business or announcements to come before the meeting?" (After announcements, etc., the president may ask for a motion to adjourn. After a motion, a second to the motion, and a majority voting in favor of adjournment.)

   President: The meeting is adjourned."

III. Classification of Motions

Motions are classified as to their importance. The rank of importance is called the order of precedence. For the purpose of this guide in parliamentary procedure, main motions and secondary motions will be considered.

A main motion is used to introduce a proposal for action by the organization while a secondary motion may be made while the main motion is pending. Only one main motion may be before the organization at one time. Secondary motions made while the main motion is pending must be disposed of before voting on the main motion.

A. Steps in Making a Motion:

1. Any member who desires to make a motion to introduce an item of business should rise and request recognition from the chair (presiding officer). The proper address is to call out, "Mr. President," "Madam President," "Mr. Chairman," etc. When the chair has recognized the member by name, he may present his motion to the organization. A main motion must have a second. After the second is made the motion may be debated. The final vote is taken after the discussion is ended. A

majority rules. A simple majority is one more than one half of the members present.

a. Example in Using a Main Motion.
John Smith: (Rising) "Mr. President."
President: "Mr. Smith."
John Smith: "I move that the club purchase a new ceremonial emblem before the state contest in April."
Carol Wallis: "I second the motion."
President: "It is moved by John Smith and seconded that the club purchase a new ceremonial emblem before the state contest."
Members: Discussion.
President: "Is there further discussion? (a pause) Are you ready for the question?" Unless there is a response the president continues. "All in favor of the motion say Aye." "Those opposed say No." "The ayes have it." The motion to purchase a new ceremonial emblem before the state contest has passed.

b. Amending a Motion
Many times it is desirable to amend a main motion to make improvements or to make passage of the main motion possible. Suppose for example that Joan Adams thinks new ceremonial flags should also be purchased. To amend the pending motion she followed the following procedure:
Joan Adams: "Mr. President."
President: "Miss Adams."
Joan Adams: "I move to substitute for the pending motion that we purchase ceremonial flags and ceremonial emblem before the state contest in April."
Mike Taylor: "I second it."
Members: Discussion.
President: "It has been moved by Miss Adams and seconded to amend the pending motion by adding ceremonial flags to the motion to purchase a ceremonial emblem." "Are you ready for the question?" "All who are in favor of amending the main motion say Aye." " All opposed to amending the main motion

say No." "The ayes have it, the amendment to the
motion carried." "Are there other amendments?"
(pause) "If there are no other amendments the
question on the main motion is before the assembly."
"All in favor of the motion say Aye." "All opposed
say No." "The ayes have it." "Motion carried."

c. Table a Motion
When the main motion is pending it may be necessary to make a secondary motion to delay or post-
pone action on the pending motion until a more
favorable time.

An example of using the secondary motion is
to lay a question on the table. This can be illustrated
by going back to the main motion after it was
amended again. Suppose the treasurer of the club
was concerned about the purchase of a ceremonial
flag and ceremonial emblem since adequate money
was not available at the time of the meeting but
would probably be before the next meeting a month
later.
Bill Brown: "Mr. President."
President: "Mr. Brown."
Bill Brown: "I move that the pending motion to
purchase a ceremonial emblem be tabled until next
meeting in order to better know our financial
situation."
Roy Hays: "I second it."
President: "It has been moved and seconded to table
the motion to purchase a ceremonial emblem before
the state contest next April." "The motion is unde-
batable, unamendable, and requires a majority vote
of members present." "Those in favor of the motion
say Aye." "Those opposed say No." The ayes have
it, and the motion for the club to purchase a new
ceremonial emblem before the state contest in April
is tabled."

To lay a question on the table is one of seven
motions called subsidiary motions, which should all
be learned and practiced by club members.

IV. Election of Officers

The democratic process requires that person in leadership positions be nominated and elected to the position by their fellow club members.

Nominations are made by a committee, from the floor, and through a nominating ballot.

In many clubs new officers are nominated by a committee who is appointed by the president. The committee should be named with adequate time to make selections and contact persons selected to be nominated. Some clubs instruct the nominating committee to select two persons for each office. Other clubs require the nominating committee to select only one officer for each office.

On the date set for election of officers, the president requests a report from the chairmen of the nominating committee.

Chairman: "Mr. President, the nominating committee submits the following nominations:

For president — Mr. James Thompson

For Vice-President — Miss Jane Green

For Secretary — Miss Katherine Mills

For Treasurer — Mr. Jon Teel

President: "Are there other nominations from the floor?"

If no additional nominations are made from the floor, the following is correct practice.

Bill Smith: "Mr. President, I move that nominations close."

Carol Wallis: "Mr. President, I second the motion."

President: "It has been moved and seconded that nominations for officers be closed." "Are you ready for the question." (pause) "Those opposed please stand." (A two-thirds majority is needed to close nominations.) "There being a two-third majority, the motion is carried and nominations are closed."

After nominations have been closed with one person nominated for each office, a motion for election of officers by acclamation is in order.

Member: "Mr. President, I move that we accept the nominations of the nomination committee and elect the new officers by acclamation."

Oppressive Child Labor Is Defined As Employment of Children Under the Legal Minimum Ages[1]

Age Standards

16—BASIC MINIMUM AGE FOR EMPLOYMENT

At 16 years of age young people *may be employed in any occupation* other than a nonagricultural occupation declared hazardous by the Secretary of Labor. There are no other restrictions. If not contrary to State or local law, young people of this age may be employed during school hours, for any number of hours, and during any periods of time.

18—MINIMUM AGE FOR EMPLOYMENT IN NONAGRICULTURAL OCCUPATIONS DECLARED HAZARDOUS BY THE SECRETARY OF LABOR

16—MINIMUM AGE FOR EMPLYOMENT IN AN AGRICULTURAL OCCUPATION DECLARED HAZARDOUS BY THE SECRETARY OF LABOR AT ANY TIME AND FOR EMPLOYMENT IN AGRICULTURE DURING THE HOURS SCHOOLS ARE IN SESSION IN THE DISTRICT WHERE THE MINOR LIVES WHILE WORKING. (See Child Labor Bulletin No. 102.)

---

[1]*Child Labor Provisions of the Fair Labor Standards Act* (United States Department of Labor WHPC Publication 1258), Jan. 1969, pp. 5-30.

417

*14—MINIMUM AGE FOR SPECIFIED OCCUPATIONS OUT-
SIDE SCHOOL HOURS*

Employment of 14- and 15-year-old youths is limited to certain occupations outside school hours only and under specified conditions of work as set forth in Child Labor Regulation No. 3 (see p. 26).

Coverage of the Child Labor Provision

Employment . . .

IN COMMERCE

Employees engaged in interstate or foreign commerce are covered. This includes, among others, workers in the telephone, telegraph, radio, television, importing, exporting, and transportation industries; employees in distributing industries, such as wholesaling, who handle goods moving in interstate or foreign commerce, as well as workers who order, receive, or keep records of such goods; and clerical and other workers who regularly use the mails, telephone, and telegraph for interstate or foreign communication.

IN THE PRODUCTION OF GOODS FOR COMMERCE

Employees who work in places that produce goods for interstate or foreign commerce, such as manufacturing establishments, oil fields, mines; or in occupations that are closely related or directly essential to the production of such goods are covered.

IN AN ENTERPRISE ENGAGED IN COMMERCE

Employees employed in certain enterprises, as that term is defined in the act, which are engaged in interstate or foreign commerce or in the production of goods for such commerce are covered. Included in this category are such establishments as hotels, motels, restaurants, hospitals, laundries and dry cleaning establishments, institutions for the resident care of the sick or aged, other retail and service establishments, and schools.

The child labor provisions apply to an enterprise even though a business unit of such establishment is exempt under section 13 from the monetary provisions of the act.

IN OR ABOUT AN ESTABLISHMENT PRODUCING GOODS FOR COMMERCE

Producers, manufacturers, or dealers are prohibited from shipping or delivering for shipment in interstate or foreign commerce any goods produced in an establishment in or about which oppressive child labor has been employed within 30 days prior to the removal of the goods. It is not necessary for the employee to be working on the goods that are removed for shipment in order to be covered.

Exemptions from the Child Labor Provisions of the Act

THE CHILD LABOR PROVISIONS DO NOT APPLY TO:

Children under 16 years of age employed by their parents in *agriculture* or in nonagricultural occupations *other than* manufacturing or mining occupations or occupations declared hazardous for minors under 18.

Children under 16 years of age employed by other than their parents in *agriculture*, if the occupation has *not* been declared hazardous and the employment is *outside the hours schools are in session* in the district where the minor lives while working. Children employed as *actors* or *performers* in motion picture, theatrical, radio, or television productions.

Children engaged in the *delivery of newspapers* to the consumer. *Homeworkers* engaged in the *making of wreaths* composed principally of natural holly, pine, cedar, or other evergreens (including the harvesting of the evergreens).

Hazardous Occupations

The Fair Labor Standards Act provides a minimum age of 18 years for any *nonagricultural* occupation which the Secretary of Labor "shall find and by order declare" to be particularly hazardous for 16- and 17-year-old persons, or detrimental to their health and well-being.

A 16-year minimum age applies to any agricultural occupation that the Secretary of Labor "finds and declares" to be particularly hazardous for the employment of children under 16.

Determination of hazardous occupations is made after careful investigation by the U.S. Department of Labor's Bureau of Labor Standards of the occupations to be included within the scope of the investigation. During such an investigation, trained personnel gather statistical data on industrial injuries, visit typical plants to observe the occupations and their hazards under actual operating conditions, and seek the opinion and advice of safety engineers, plant supervisors, trade association officials, union leaders, and State factory inspectors, as well as experts from industrial accident commissions and agencies of the Federal Government. A preliminary report is prepared on the basis of the investigation and is submitted for comment and suggestion to a technical advisory committee appointed from the ranks of employers, associations, trade unions, and experts in the particular field under consideration. After comments and suggestions have been received from the advisory committee, the report is revised and a proposed finding and order, if justified, is prepared.

Upon issuance and publication of the proposed finding and order, opportunity is given for any interested party to make objection to or to suggest revisions in the order at a public hearing. Objections and suggested revisions are carefully considered and, if they are found to be justified, the proposed order is revised. Thereafter, if warranted, the order is adopted and issued by the Secretary of Labor. Once issued, the orders have the force of law, and a violation of their provisions constitutes a violation of the child labor provisions of the Fair Labor Standards Act.

The 17 hazardous occupations orders now in effect apply either on an industry basis, specifying the occupations in the industry that are not covered, or on an occupational basis irrespective of the industry in which found. Investigations and procedures followed in determining hazardous occupations in agricultural employment are similar to those described in connection with industry.

EXEMPTIONS:

Nonagricultural Hazardous Occupations Orders Nos. 5, 8, 10, 12, 14, 16 and 17 contain exemptions for apprentices and student-learners provided they are employed under the following conditions:

I. *Apprentices:* (1) The apprentice is employed in a craft recognized as an apprenticeable trade; (2) the work of the apprentice in the occupations declared particularly hazardous is incidental to his training; (3) such work is intermittent and for short periods of time and is under the direct and close supervision of a journeyman as a necessary part of such apprentice training; and (4) the apprentice is registered by the Bureau of Apprenticeship and Training of the U.S. Department of Labor as employed in accordance with the standards established by that Bureau, or is registered by a State agency as employed in accordance with the standards of the State apprenticeship agency recognized by the Bureau of Apprenticeship and Training, or is employed under a written apprenticeship agreement and conditions which are found by the Secretary of Labor to conform substantially with such Federal or State standards.

II. *Student-Learners:* (1) The student-learner is enrolled in a course of study and training in a cooperative vocational training program under a recognized State or local educational authority or in a course of study in a substantially similar program conducted by a private school; and (2) such student-learner is employed under a written agreement which provides: (i) That the work of the student-learner in the occupations declared particularly hazardous shall be incidental to his training; (ii) that such work shall be intermittent and for short periods of time, and under the direct

and close supervision of a qualified and experienced person;
(iii) that safety instructions shall be given by the school and
correlated by the employer with on-the-job training; and
(iv) that a schedule of organized and progressive work pro-
cesses to be performed on the job shall have been prepared.
Each such written agreement shall contain the name of the
student-learner, and shall be signed by the employer and the
school coordinator or principal. Copies of each agreement
shall be kept on file by both the school and the employer. This
exemption for the employment of student-learners may be
revoked in any individual situation where it is found that
reasonable precautions have not been observed for the safety
of minors employed thereunder.

A high school graduate may be employed in an occupation in
which he has completed training as provided in this paragraph
as a student-learner, even though he is not 18 years of age.

Hazardous Occupations Orders in Nonagricultural Occupations

Those occupations declared to be particularly hazardous for
minors between 16 and 18 years of age (also for minors 14 and
15) are included in the seventeen Hazardous Occupations Orders
listed on following pages:

(1) Occupations in or about plants or establishments manufacturing or storing explosives or articles containing
explosive components.

(2) Occupations of motor-vehicle driver and outside helper.

(3) Coal-mine occupations.

(4) Logging occupations and occupations in the operation
of any sawmill, lath mill, shingle mill, or cooperage-
stock mill.

(5) Occupations involved in the operation of power-driven
woodworking machines.

(6) Occupations involving exposure to radioactive substances and to ionizing radiations.

(7) Occupations involved in the operation of elevators and
other power-driven hoisting apparatus.

(8) Occupations involved in the operation of power-driven
metal forming, punching, and shearing machines.

(9) Occupations in connection with mining, other than coal.

(10) Occupations involving slaughtering, meat-packing or processing, or rendering.

(11) Occupations involved in the operation of certain power-driven bakery machines.

(12) Occupations involved in the operation of certain power-driven paper-products machines.

(13) Occupations involved in the manufacture of brick, tile, and kindred products.

(14) Occupations involved in the operation of circular saws, band saws, and guillotine shears.

(15) Occupations involved in wrecking, demolition, and shipbreaking operations.

(16) Occupations involved in roofing operations.

(17) Occupations in excavation operations.

Text of the Hazardous Occupations Orders in Nonagricultural Occupations

MANUFACTURING OR STORAGE OCCUPATIONS INVOLVING EXPLOSIVES (ORDER NO. 1)

The following occupations in or about plants or establishments manufacturing or storing explosives or articles containing explosive components:

(1) All occupations in or about any plant or establishment (other than retail establishments or plants or establishments of the type described in subparagraph (2) of this paragraph) manufacturing components except where the occupation is performed in a "non-explosives area" as defined in subparagraph (3) of this section.

(2) The following occupations in or about any plant or establishment manufacturing or storing small arms ammunition not exceeding .60 caliber in size, shotgun shells, or blasting caps when manufactured or stored in conjunction with the manufacture of small-arms ammunition:

(a) All occupations involved in the manufacturing, mixing, transporting, or handling of explosive compounds in the manufacture of small-arms ammunition and all other occupations requiring the performance of any duities in the explosives area in which explosive compounds are manufactured or mixed.

(b) All occupations involved in the manufacturing, transporting, or handling of primers and all other occupations requiring the performance of any duties in the same building in which primers are manufactured.

(c) All occupations involved in the priming of cartridges and all other occupations requiring the performance of any duties in the same workroom in which rim-fire cartridges are primed.

(d) All occupations involved in the plate loading of cartridges and in the operation of automatic loading machines.

(e) All occupations involved in the loading, inspecting, packing, shipping and storage of blasting caps.

Definitions

(1) The term "plant or establishment manufacturing or storing explosives or articles containing explosive components" means the land with all the buildings and other structures thereon used in connection with the manufacturing or processing or storing of explosives or articles containing explosive components.

(2) The terms "explosives" and "articles containing explosive components" mean and include ammunition, black powder, blasting caps, fireworks, high explosives, primers, smokeless powder, and all goods classified and defined as explosives by the Interstate Commerce Commission in regulations for the transportation of explosives and other dangerous substances by common carriers (49 CFR Parts 71-78) issued pursuant to the Act of June 25, 1948 (62 Stat. 739; 18 U.S.C. 835).

(3) An area meeting all of the following criteria shall be deemed a "nonexplosives area":

    (a) None of the work performed in the area involves the handling or use of explosives;

    (b) The area is separated from the explosives area by a distance not less that that prescribed in the Amercian Table of Distances for the protection of inhabited buildings;

    (c) The area is separated from the explosives area by a fence or is otherwise located so that it constitutes a definite designated area; and

    (d) Satisfactory controls have been established to prevent employees under 18 years of age within the area from entering any area in or about the plant which does not meet criteria (a) through (c).

(Effective July 1, 1939. Amended February 13, 1943, and June 12, 1952.)

MOTOR VEHICLE OCCUPATIONS (ORDER NO. 2)

    (a) *Except as provided in paragraph* (b). The occupations of motor vehicle driver and outside helper on any public road, highway, in or about any mine (including open pit mine or quarry), place where logging or sawmill operations are in progress, or in any excavation of the type identified in § 1500.68 (a) are particularly hazardous for the employment of minors between 16 and 18 years of age.

    (b) *Exemptions*

        (1) *Incidental and occasional driving.* The finding and declaration in paragraph (a) shall not apply to the operation of automobiles or trucks not exceeding 6,000 pounds gross vehicle weight if such driving is restricted to daylight hours; *provided,* such operation is only occasional and incidental to the child's employment; that the child holds a State license valid for the type of driving involved in the job which he performs and has completed a State approved driver education course; and *pro-*

vided further, that the vehicle is equipped with a seat belt or similar device for the driver and for each helper, and the employer has instructed each child that such belts or other devices must be used. This subparagraph shall not be applicable to any occupation of motor-vehicle driver which involves the towing of vehicles.

(2) *School bus driving.* The finding and declaration in paragraph (a) shall not apply to driving a school bus during the period of any exemption which has been granted in the discretion of the Secretary of Labor on the basis of an application filed and approved by the Governor of the State in which the vehicle is registered. The Secretary will notify any State which inquires of the information to be furnished in the application. Neither shall the finding and declaration in paragraph (a) apply in a particular State during a period not to exceed the first 40 days after this amendment is effective while application for such exemption is being formulated by such State seeking merely to continue in effect unchanged its current program using such drivers, nor while such application is pending action by the Secretary.

(c) *Definitions.*

(1) The term "motor vehicle" shall mean any automobile, truck, truck-tractor, trailer, semitrailer, motorcycle, or similar vehicle propelled or drawn by mechanical power and designed for use as a means of transportation but shall not include any vehicle operated exclusively on rails.

(2) The term "driver" shall mean any individual who, in the course of his employment, drives a motor vehicle at any time.

(3) The term "outside helper" shall mean any individual, other than a driver, whose work includes riding on a motor vehicle outside the cab for the purpose of assisting in transporting or delivering goods.

(4) The term "gross weight" includes the truck chassis with lubricants, water and full tank or tanks of fuel, plus the weight of the cab or driver's compartment, body and special chassis and body equipment, and payload. (Eff. Jan. 1, 1940, amended May 6, 1955; Nov. 1, 1967; and Sept. 5, 1968.)

COAL MINE OCCUPATIONS (ORDER NO 3)

All occupations in or about any coal mine, except the occupation of slate or other refuse picking at a picking table or picking chute in a tipple or breaker and occupations requiring the performance of duties solely in offices or in repair or maintenance shops located in the surface part of any coal-mining plant.

Definitions

The term "coal" shall mean any rank of coal, including lignite, bituminous, and anthracite coals.

The term "all occupations in or about any coal mine" shall mean all types of work performed in any underground working, open pit, or surface part of any coal-mining plant that contributes to the extraction, grading, cleaning, or other handling of coal. (Effective September 1, 1940.)

LOGGING AND SAWMILLING OCCUPATIONS (ORDER NO. 4)

All occupations in logging and all occupations in the operation of any sawmill, lath mill, shingle mill, or cooperage-stock mill except the following:

(1) Exceptions applying to logging:

    (a) Work in offices or in repair or maintenance shops.

    (b) Work in the construction, operation, repair, or maintenance of living and administrative quarters of logging camps.

    (c) Work in timber cruising, surveying, or logging-engineering parties; work in the repair or maintenance of roads, railroads, or flumes; work in forest protection, such as clearing fire trails or roads, piling and burning slash, maintaining fire-fighting equipment, constructing and maintaining telephone lines, or acting as fire lookout or fire patrolman away from the actual logging operations: *Provided,* that the provisions of this paragraph shall not apply to the felling or bucking of timber, the collecting or transporting of logs, the operation of power-driven machinery, the handling or use of explosives and work on trestles.

(d) Peeling of fence posts, pulpwood, chemical wood, excelsior wood, cordwood, or similar products, when not done in conjuntion with and at the same time and place as other logging occupations declared hazardous by this section.

(e) Work in the feeding or care of animals.

(2) Exceptions applying to the operation of any permanent sawmill or the operation of any lath mill, shingle mill, or cooperage-stock mill: *Provided,* that these exceptions do not apply to a portable sawmill the lumber yard of which is used only for the temporary storage of green lumber and in connection with which no office or repair or maintenance shop is ordinarily maintained: and *Further provided,* that these exceptions do not apply to work which entails entering the sawmill building:

(a) Work in offices or in repair or maintenance shops.

(b) Straightening, marking, or tallying lumber on the dry chain or the dry drop sorter.

(c) Pulling lumber from the dry chain.

(d) Clean-up in the lumberyard.

(e) Piling, handling, or shipping of cooperage stock in yards or storage sheds, other than operating or assisting in the operation of power-driven equipment.

(f) Clerical work in yards or shipping sheds, such as done by ordermen, tallymen, and shipping clerks.

(g) Clean-up work outside shake and shingle mills, except when the mill is in operation.

(h) Splitting shakes manually from pre-cut and split blocks with a froe and mallet, except inside the mill building or cover.

(i) Packing shakes into bundles when done in conjunction with splitting shakes manually with a froe and mallet, except inside the mill building or cover.

(j) Manual loading of bundles of shingles or shakes into trucks or railroad cars, provided that the employer has on file a statement from a licensed doctor of medicine or osteopathy certifying the minor capable of performing this work without injury to himself.

Definitions

The term "all occupations in logging" shall mean all work performed in connection with the felling of timber; the bucking or converting of timber into logs, poles, ties, bolts, pulpwood, chemical wood, exclesior wood, cordwood, fence posts, or similar products; the collecting, skidding, yarding, loading, transporting, and unloading of such products in connection with logging; the constructing, repairing, and maintenance of roads, railroads, flumes, or camps used in connection with logging; the moving, installing, rigging, and maintenance of machinery or equipment used in logging; and other work performed in connection with logging. The term shall not apply to work performed in timber culture, timber-stand improvement, or in emergency firefighting.

The term "all occupations in the operation of any sawmill, lath mill, shingle mill, or cooperage-stock mill" shall mean all work performed in or about any such mill in connection with storing of logs and bolts; converting logs or bolts into sawn lumber, laths, shingles, or cooperage stock; storing, drying, and shipping lumber, laths, shingles, cooperage stock, or other products of such mills; and other work performed in connection with the operation of any sawmill, lath mill, shingle mill, or cooperage-stock mill. The term shall not include work performed in the planing-mill department or other remanufacturing departments of any sawmill, or in any planing mill or remanufacturing plant not a part of a sawmill.

(Effective August 1, 1941. Amended September 12, 1942; June 25, 1943; October 18, 1944; September 11, 1946; February 2, 1948; and April 15, 1967.)

*POWER-DRIVEN WOODWORKING MACHINE OCCUPA-
TIONS (ORDER NO. 5)*

The following occupations involved in the operation of
power-driven woodworking machines:

(1) The occupation of operating power-driven woodworking machines including supervising or controlling the
operation of such machines, feeding material into such
machines, and helping the operator to feed material
into such machines, but not including the placing of
material on a moving chain or in a hopper or slide for
automatic feeding.

(2) The occupations of setting up, adjusting, repairing,
oiling, or cleaning power-driven woodworking machines.

(3) The operations of off-bearing from circular saws and
from guillotine-action veneer clippers.

Definitions

(1) The term "power-driven woodworking machines" shall
mean all fixed or portable machines or tools driven by
power and used or designed for cutting, shaping, forming, surfacing, nailing, stapling, wire stitching, fasten-
ing, or otherwise assembling, pressing, or printing wood
or veneer.

(2) The term "off-bearing" shall mean the removal of material or refuse directly from a saw table or from the
point of operation. Operations not considered as off-
bearing within the intent of this section include: (a)
The removal of material or refuse from a circular saw
or guillotine-action veneer clipper where the material
or refuse has been conveyed away from the saw table
or point of operation by a gravity chute or by some
mechanical means such as a moving belt or expulsion
roller, and (b) the following operations when they do
not involve the removal of material or refuse directly
from a saw table or from the point of operation: the
carrying, moving, or transporting of materials from
one machine to another or from one part of a plant to

another; the piling, stacking, or arranging of materials for feeding into a machine by another person; and the sorting, tying, bundling, or loading of materials.

Exemptions

The exemptions for apprentices and student-learners discussed on page 421 apply to this Order.

(Effective August 1, 1941. Amended November 13, 1942; February 18, 1944; July 12, 1944; October 31, 1945; September 27, 1946; November 24, 1951; and September 23, 1958.)

OCCUPATIONS INVOLVING EXPOSURE TO RADIOAC-TIVE SUBSTANCES AND TO IONIZING RADIATIONS (ORDER NO. 6)

Any work in any workroom in which (a) radium is stored or used in the manufacture of self-luminous compound; (b) self-luminous compound is made, processed, or packaged; (c) self-luminous compound is stored, used, or worked upon; (d) incandescent mantles are made from fabric and solutions containing thorium salts, or are processed or packaged; (e) other radioactive substances are present in the air in average concentrations exceeding 10 percent of the maximum permissible concentrations in the air recommended for occupational exposure by the National Committee on Radiation Protection, as set forth in the 40-hour week column of Table One of the National Bureau of Standards Handbook No. 69 entitled "Maximum Permissible Body Burdens and Maximum Permissible Concentrations of Radionuclides in Air and in Water for Occupational Exposure," issued June 5, 1959.

Any other work which involves exposure to ionizing radiations in excess of 0.5 rem per year.

Definitions

As used in this section: the term "self-luminous compound" shall mean any mixture of phosphorescent material and radium, mesothorium, or other radioactive element; the term "work-room" shall include the entire area bounded by walls of solid material and extending from floor to ceiling; the term "ionizing radiations" shall mean alpha and beta particles, electrons, protons, neutrons, gamma, and X-ray and all other radiations which produce ionizations directly or indirectly, but does not include electromagnetic radiations other than gamma and X-ray.

(Effective May 1, 1942. Amended July 9, 1949; June 23, 1957; August 14, 1958; and October 21, 1961.)

POWER-DRIVEN HOISTING APPARATUS OCCUPATIONS (ORDER NO. 7)

The following occupations involved in the operation of power-driven hoisting apparatus:

(1) Work of operating an elevator, crane, derrick, hoist, or high-lift truck, except operating an unattended automatic operation passenger elevator* or an electric or air-operated hoist not exceeding 1 ton capacity.

(2) Work which involves riding on a manlift or on a freight elevator, except a freight elevator operated by an assigned operator.

(3) Work of assisting in the operation of a crane, derrick, or hoist performed by crane hookers, crane chasers, hookers-on, riggers, rigger helpers, and like occupations.

Definitions

The term "elevator" shall mean any power-driven hoisting or lowering mechanism equipped with a car or platform which moves in guides in a substantially vertical direction. The term shall include both passenger and freight elevators, (including portable elevators or tiering machines) but shall not include dumbwaiters.

---

*Note: See "Exception" (p. 434)

The term "crane" shall mean a power-driven machine for lifting and lowering a load and moving it horizontally, in which the hoisting mechanism is an integral part of the machine. The term shall include all types of cranes, such as cantilever gantry, crawler, gantry, hammer-head, ingot-pouring, jib, locomotive, motor truck, overhead traveling, pillar jib, pintle, portal, semi-gantry, semiportal, storage bridge, tower, walking jib, and wall cranes.

The term "derrick" shall mean a power-driven apparatus consisting of a mast or equivalent members held at the top by guys or braces, with or without a boom, for use with a hoisting mechanism and operating ropes. The term shall include all types of derricks, such as A-frame, breast, Chicago boom, gin-pole, guy, and stiff-leg derricks.

The term "hoist" shall mean a power-driven apparatus for raising or lowering a load by the application of a pulling force that does not include a car or platform running in guides. The term shall include all types of hoists, such as base-mounted electric, clevis suspension, hook suspension, monorail, overhead electric, simple drum, and trolley suspension hoists.

The term "high-lift truck" shall mean a power-driven industrial type of truck used for lateral transportation that is equipped with a power-operated lifting device usually in the form of a fork or platform capable of tiering loaded pallets or skids one above the other. Instead of a fork, or platform, the lifting device may consist of a ram, scoop, shovel, crane, revolving fork, or other attachments for handling specific loads. The term shall mean and include high-lift trucks known under such names as forklifts, fork trucks, forklift trucks, tiering trucks, or stacking trucks, but shall not mean low-lift trucks or low-lift platform trucks that are designed for the transportation of, but not the tiering of, material.

The term, "manlift" shall mean a device intended for the conveyance of persons which consists of platforms or brackets mounted on, or attached to, an endless belt, cable, chain or similar method of suspension; such belt, cable, or chain operating in a substantially vertical direction and being supported by and driven through pulleys, sheaves or sprockets at the top or bottom.

Exception

This section shall not prohibit the operation of an automatic elevator and an automatic signal elevator provided that the exposed portion of the car interior (exclusive of vents and other necessary small openings), the car door, and the hoistway doors are constructed of solid surfaces without any opening through which a part of the body may extend; all hoistway openings at floor level have doors which are interlocked with the car door so as to prevent the car from starting until all such doors are closed and locked; the elevator (other than hydraulic elevators) is equipped with a device which will stop and hold the car in case of overspeed or if the cable slackens or breaks; and the elevator is equipped with upper and lower travel limit devices which will normally bring the car to rest at either terminal and a final limit switch which will prevent the movement in either direction and will open in case of excessive over travel by the car.

Definitions

As used in this exception:

For the purpose of this exception the term "automatic elevator" shall mean a passenger elevator, a freight elevator, or a combination passenger-freight elevator, the operation of which is controlled by pushbuttons in such a manner that the starting, going to the landing selected, leveling and holding, and the opening and closing of the car and hoistway doors are entirely automatic.

For the pupose of this exception, the term "automatic signal operation elevator" shall mean an elevator which is started in response to the operation of a switch (such as a lever or pushbutton) in the car which when operated by the operator actuates a starting device that automatically closes the car and hoistway doors—from this point on, the movement of the car to the landing selected, leveling and holding when it gets there, and the opening of the car and hoistway doors are entirely automatic.

(Eff. Sept. 1, 1946, Amended Sept. 30, 1950; Sept. 1, 1955; and Nov. 7, 1967.)

POWER-DRIVEN METAL FORMING, PUNCHING, AND SHEARING MACHINE OCCUPATIONS (ORDER NO. 8)

The occupations of operator of or helper on the following power-driven metal forming, punching, and shearing machines:

(1) All rolling machines, such as beading, straightening, corrugating, flanging, or bending rolls; and hot or cold rolling mills.

(2) All pressing or punching machines, such as punch presses, except those provided with full automatic feed and ejection and with a fixed barrier guard to prevent the hands or fingers of the operator from entering the area between the dies; power presses; and plate punches.

(3) All bending machines, such as apron brakes and press brakes.

(4) All hammering machines, such as drop hammers and power hammers.

(5) All shearing machines, such as guillotine or squaring shears; alligator shears; and rotary shears.

The occupations of setting up, adjusting, repairing, oiling, or cleaning these machines including those with automatic feed and ejection.

Definitions

The term "operator" shall mean a person who operates a machine covered by this Order by performing such functions as starting or stopping the machine, placing materials into or removing them from the machine, or any other function directly involved in operation of the machine.

The term "helper" shall mean a person who assists in the operation of a machine covered by this Order by helping place materials into or remove them from the machine.

The term "forming, punching, and shearing machines" shall mean power-driven metal-working machines, other than machine tools, which change the shape of or cut metal by means of tools, such as dies, rolls, or knives which are mounted on rams, plungers, or other moving parts. Types of forming, punching, and shearing machines, enumerated in this section are the machines to which the designation is by custom applied.

Exemptions

The exemptions for apprentices and student-learners discussed on page 421 apply to this Order.

(Effective October 30, 1950. Amended September 23, 1958, and November 15, 1960.)

Note: This order does *not* apply to a very large group of metal-working machines known as machine tools. Machine tools are defined as "power-driven complete metalworking machines having one or more tool- or work-holding devices, and used for progressively removing metal in the form of chips." Since the Order does not apply to machine tools, the 18-year age minimum does not apply. They are classified below so that they can be readily identified.

Milling function machines	Planning function machines	Grinding function machines
Horizontal Milling Machines	Planers	Grinders
Vertical Milling Machines	Shapers	Abrasive Wheels
Universal Milling Machines	Slotters	Abrasive Belts
Planer-type Milling Machines	Broaches	Abrasive Disks
Gear Hobbing Machines	Keycasters	Abrasive Points
Profilers	Hack Saws	Buffing Wheels
Routers	**Band Saws	Polishing Wheels
**Circular Saws		Stroppers
		Lapping Machines

**See HO 14

Boring function machines	Turning function machines
Vertical Boring Mills	Engine Lathes
Horizontal Boring Mills	Turret Lathes
Jig Borers	Hollow Spindle
Pedestal Drills	Lathes
Radial Drills	Automatic Lathes
Gang Drills	Automatic Screw
Upright Drills	Machines
Centering Machines	
Reamers	
Honers	

OCCUPATIONS IN CONNECTION WITH MINING, OTHER THAN COAL (ORDER NO. 9)

All occupations in connection with mining, other than coal, except the following:

(1) Work in offices, in the warehouse or supply house, in the change house, in the laboratory, and in repair or maintenance shops not located underground.

(2) Work in the operation and maintenance of living quarters.

(3) Work outside the mine in surveying, in the repair and maintenance of roads, and in general clean-up about the mine property such as clearing brush and digging drainage ditches.

(4) Work of track crews in the building and maintaining of sections of railroad track located in those areas of open-cut metal mines where mining and haulage activities are not being conducted at the time and place that such building and maintaining work is being done.

(5) Work in or about surface placer mining operations other than placer dredging operations and hydraulic placer mining operations.

438 Meeting Future Responsibilities

(6) The following work in metal mills other than in mercury-recovery mills or mills using the cyanide process:

    (a) Work involving the operations of jigs, sludge tables, flotation cells, or drier-filters.

    (b) Work of hand sorting at picking table or picking belt.

    (c) General cleanup work.

Provided, however, that nothing in this section shall be construed as permitting employment of minors in any occupation prohibited by any other hazardous occupations order issued by the Secretary of Labor.

Definitions

As used in this section: The term "all occupations in connection with mining, other than coal" shall mean all work performed underground in mines and quarries; on the surface at underground mines and underground quarries; in or about open-cut mines, open quarries, clay pits, and sand and gravel operations; at or about placer mining operations; at or about dredging operations for clay, sand or gravel; at or about bore-hole mining operations; in or about all metal mills, washer plants, or grinding mills reducing the bulk of the extracted minerals; and at or about any other crushing, grinding, screening, sizing, washing or cleaning operations performed upon the extracted minerals except where such operations are performed as a part of a manufacturing process. The term shall not include work performed in subsequent manufacturing or processing operations, such as work performed in smelters, electro-metallurgical plants, refineries, reduction plants, cement mills, plants where quarried stone is cut, sanded and further processed, or plants manufacturing clay, glass, or ceramic products. Neither shall the term include work performed in connection with coal mining, in petroleum production, in natural-gas production, nor in dredging operations which are not a part of mining operations, such as dredging for construction or navigation purposes.

(Effective January 6, 1951.)

OCCUPATIONS INVOLVING SLAUGHTERING, MEAT-PACKING OR PROCESSING, OR RENDERING (ORDER NO. 10)

The following occupations in or about slaughtering and meat-packing establishments, rendering plants, or wholesale, retail or service establishments:

(1) All occupations on the killing floor, in curing cellars, and in hide cellars, except the work of messengers, runners, handtruckers, and similar occupations which require entering such workrooms or workplaces infrequently and for short periods of time.

(2) All occupations involved in the recovery of lard and oils, except packaging and shipping of such products and the operation of lard-roll machines.

(3) All occupations involved in tankage or rendering of dead animals, animal offal, animal fats, scrap meats, blood, and bones into stock feeds, tallow, inedible greases, fertilizer ingredients, and similar products.

(4) All occupations involved in the operation or feeding of the following power-driven meat-processing machines, including the occupation of setting up, adjusting, repairing, oiling, or cleaning such machines: meat patty forming machines, meat and bone cutting saws, knives (*except bacon-slicing machines), head splitters, and guillotine cutters; snout pullers and jaw pullers; skinning machines; horizontal rotary washing machines; casing-cleaning machines such as crushing, stripping, and finishing machines; grinding, mixing, chopping, and hashing machines; and presses (except belly-rolling machines).

(5) All boning occupations.

(6) All occupations that involve the pushing or dropping of any suspended carcass, half carcass, or quarter carcass.

---

*Note: The term "bacon-slicing machine" as used in this Order refers to those machines which are designed solely for the purpose of slicing bacon and are equipped with enclosure or barrier guards that prevent the operator from coming in contact with the blade or blades, and with devices for automatic feeding, slicing, shingling, stacking, and conveying the sliced bacon away from the point of operation.

(7) All occupations involving hand-lifting or hand-carrying any carcass or half carcass of beef, pork, or horse, or any quarter carcass of beef or horse.

Definitions

The term "slaughtering and meat-packing establishments" shall mean places in or about which cattle, calves, hogs, sheep, lambs, goats, or horses are killed, butchered, or processed. The term shall also include establishments which manufacture or process meat products or sausage casings from such animals.

The term "rendering plants" shall mean establishments engaged in the conversion of dead animals, animal offal, animal fats, scrap meats, blood, and bones into stock feeds, tallow, inedible greases, fertilizer ingredients, and similar products.

The term "killing floor" shall include that workroom or workplace where cattle, calves, hogs, sheep, lambs, goats, or horses are immobilized, shackled, or killed, and the carcasses are dressed prior to chilling.

The term "curing cellar" shall include that workroom or workplace which is primarily devoted to the preservation and flavoring of meat by curing materials. It does not include that workroom or workplace where meats are smoked.

The term "hide cellar" shall include that workroom or workplace where hides are graded, trimmed, salted, and otherwise cured.

The term "boning occupations" shall mean the removal of bones from meat cuts. It shall not include work that involves cutting, scraping, or trimming meat from cuts containing bones.

Exemptions

This Order shall not apply to the killing and processing of poultry, rabbits, or small game in areas physically separated from the killing floor.

The exemptions for apprentices and student-learners discussed on page 421 apply to this Order.

(Eff. May 8, 1952; Amended Nov. 15, 1960; Dec. 22, 1962, and Dec. 30, 1963.)

POWER-DRIVEN BAKERY MACHINE OCCUPATIONS (ORDER NO. 11)

The following occupations involved in the operation of power-driven bakery machines:

(1) The occupations of operating, assisting to operate, or setting up, adjusting, repairing, oiling, or cleaning any horizontal or vertical dough mixer; batter mixer; bread dividing, rounding, or molding machine; dough brake; dough sheeter; combination bread slicing and wrapping machine; or cake cutting band saw.

(Effective July 21, 1952. Amended November 15, 1960.)

POWER-DRIVEN PAPER-PRODUCTS MACHINE OCCUPATIONS (ORDER NO. 12)

The occupations of operating or assisting to operate any of the following power-driven paper-products machines:

(1) Arm-type wire stitcher or stapler, circular or band saw, corner cutter or mitering machine, corrugating and single- or double-facing machine, envelope die-cutting press, guillotine paper cutter or shear, horizontal bar scorer, laminating or combining machine, sheeting machine, scrap-paper baler, or vertical slotter.

(2) Platen die-cutting press, platen printing press, or punch press which involves hand feeding of the machine.

The occupations of setting up, adjusting, repairing, oiling, or cleaning these machines including those which do not involve hand feeding.

Definitions

The term "operating or assisting to operate" shall mean all work which involves starting or stopping a machine covered by this Order, placing materials into or removing them from the machine, or any other work directly involved in operating the machine.

The term "paper-products machine" shall mean power-driven machines used in the remanufacture or conversion of paper or pulp into a finished product. The term is understood to apply to such machines whether they are used in establishments that manufacture converted paper or pulp products, or in any other type of manufacturing or nonmanufacturing establishment.

Exemptions

The exemptions for apprentices and student-learners discussed on page 421 apply to this Order.

(Effective September 11, 1954. Amended September 23, 1958, and November 15, 1960.)

OCCUPATIONS INVOLVED IN THE MANUFACTURE OF BRICK, TILE, AND KINDRED PRODUCTS (ORDER NO. 13)

The following occupations involved in the manufacture of clay construction products and of silica refractory products:

(1) All work in or about establishments in which clay construction products are manufactured, except (a) work in storage and shipping; (b) work in offices, laboratories, and storerooms; and (c) work in the drying departments of plants manufacturing sewer pipe.

(2) All work in or about establishments in which silica brick or other silica refractories are manufactured, except work in offices.

(3) Nothing in this section shall be construed as permitting employment of minors in any occupation prohibited by any other hazardous occupations order issued by the Secretary of Labor.

Definitions

The term "clay construction products" shall mean the following clay products: Brick, hollow structural tile, sewer pipe and kindred products, refractories, and other clay products such as architectural terra cotta, glazed structural tile, roofing tile, stove lining, chimney pipes and tops, wall coping, and drain tile. The term shall not include the following non-structural-bearing clay products: Ceramic floor and wall tile, mosiac tile, glazed and enameled tile, faience, and similar tile, nor shall the term include nonclay construction products such as sand-lime brick, glass brick, or nonclay refractories.

The term "silica brick or other silica refractories" shall mean refractory products from raw materials containing free silica as their main constituent.

(Effective September 1, 1956.)

OCCUPATIONS INVOLVED IN THE OPERATION OF POWER-DRIVEN CIRCULAR SAWS, BAND SAWS, AND GUILLOTINE SHEARS (ORDER NO. 14)

The occupations of operator of or helper on the following power-driven fixed or portable machines equipped with full automatic feed and ejection:

(1) Circular saws.

(2) Band saws.

(3) Guillotine shears.

The occupations of setting up, adjusting, repairing, oiling, or cleaning circular saws, band saws, and guillotine shears.

Definitions

The term "operator" shall mean a person who operates a machine covered by this Order by performing such functions as starting or stopping the machine, placing materials into or removing them from the machine, or any other function directly involved in operation of the machine.

The term "helper" shall mean a person who assists in the operation of a machine covered by this Order by helping place materials into or remove them from the machine.

The term "machines equipped with full automatic feed and ejection" shall mean machines covered by this Order which are equipped with devices for full automatic feeding and ejection and with a fixed barrier guard to prevent completely the operator or helper from placing any part of his body in the point-of-operation area.

The term "circular saw" shall mean a machine equipped with a thin steel disc having a continuous series of notches or teeth on the periphery, mounted on shafting, and used for sawing materials.

The term "bandsaw" shall mean a machine equipped with an endless steel band having a continuous series of notches or teeth, running over wheels or pulleys, and for sawing materials.

The term "guillotine shear" shall mean a machine equipped with a moveable blade operated vertically and used to shear materials. The term shall not include other types of shearing machines, using a different form of shearing action, such as alligator shears or circular shears.

Exemptions

The exemptions for apprentices and student-learners discussed on page 421 apply to this Order.

(Effective November 15, 1960.)

OCCUPATIONS INVOLVED IN WRECKING, DEMOLITION, AND SHIPBREAKING OPERATIONS (ORDER NO. 15)

All occupations in wrecking, demolition, and shipbreaking operations.

Definitions

The term "wrecking, demolition, and shipbreaking operations" shall mean all work, including cleanup and salvage work, performed at the site of the total or partial razing, demolishing, or dismantling of a building, bridge, steeple, tower, chimney, other structure, ship or other vessel.

(Effective November 15, 1960.)

OCCUPATIONS IN ROOFING OPERATIONS (ORDER NO. 16)

All occupations in roofing operations.

Definitions

The term "roofing operations" shall mean all work performed in connection with the application of weatherproofing materials and substances (such as tar or pitch, asphalt prepared paper, tile, slate, metal, translucent materials, and shingles of asbestos, asphalt or wood) to roofs of buildings or other structures. The term shall also include all work performed in connection with: (1) The installation of roofs, including related metal work such as flashing and (2) alterations, additions, maintenance, and repair, including painting and coating, of existing roofs. The term shall not include gutter and downspout work; the construction of the sheathing or base of roofs; or the installation of television antennas, air conditioners, exhaust and ventilating equipment, or similar appliances attached to roofs.

Exemptions

The exemptions for apprentices and student-learners discussed on page 421 apply to this Order.

(Effective February 5, 1962.)

OCCUPATIONS IN EXCAVATION OPERATIONS (ORDER NO. 17)

The following occupations in excavation operations:

(1) Excavating, working in, or backfilling (refilling) trenches, except (a) manually excavating or manually backfilling trenches that do not exceed four feet in depth at any point, or (b) working in trenches that do not exceed four feet in depth at any point.

(2) Excavating for buildings or other structures or working in such excavations, except (a) manually excavating to a depth not exceeding four feet below any ground surface adjoining the excavation, or (b) working in an excavation not exceeding such depth, or (c) working in an excavation where the side walls are shored or sloped to the angle of repose.

(3) Working within tunnels prior to the completion of all driving and shoring operations.

(4) Working within shafts prior to the completion of all sinking and shoring operations.

Exemptions

The exemptions for apprentices and student-learners discussed on page 421 apply to this Order.
(Effective May 9, 1963.)

CHILD LABOR REGULATION NO. 3

EMPLOYMENT OF 14- AND 15-YEAR-OLD MINORS IS LIMITED

to certain occupations under conditions which do not interfere with their schooling, health, or well-being.

(a) *14- AND 15-YEAR-OLD MINORS MAY NOT BE EMPLOYED*:

(1) DURING SCHOOL HOURS, except as provided in paragraph (b).
(2) BEFORE 7 a.m. or AFTER 7 p.m. except 9 p.m. from June 1 through Labor Day (time depends on local standards).
(3) MORE THAN 3 HOURS A DAY—on school days.
(4) MORE THAN 18 HOURS A WEEK—in school weeks.
(5) MORE THAN 8 HOURS A DAY—on nonschool days.
(6) MORE THAN 40 HOURS A WEEK—in nonschool weeks.

(b) In the case of enrollees in work training programs conducted under Part B of Title I of the Economic Opportunity Act of 1964, there is an exception to the requirement of paragraph (a) (1) of this section if the employer has on file with his records kept pursuant to Part 516 of this title an unrevoked written statement of the Administrator of the Bureau of Work Programs or his representative setting out the periods which the minor will work and certifying that his health and well-being, countersigned by the principal of the school which the minor is attending with his certificate that such employment will not interfere with the minor's schooling.

Permitted Occupations for 14- and 15-Year-Old Minors in Retail, Food Service, and Gasoline Service Establishments

14- AND 15-YEAR-OLD MINORS MAY BE EMPLOYED IN—

(1) OFFICE and CLERICAL WORK (including operation of office machines).

(2) CASHIERING, SELLING, MODELING, ART WORK, WORK IN ADVERTISING DEPARTMENTS, WINDOW TRIMMING and COMPARATIVE SHOPPING.

(3) PRICE MARKING and TAGGING by hand or by machine, ASSEMBLING ORDERS, PACKING and SHELVING.

(4) BAGGING and CARRYING OUT CUSTOMERS' ORDERS.

(5) ERRAND and DELIVERY WORK by foot, bicycle, and public transportation.

(6) CLEAN UP WORK, including the use of vacuum cleaners and floor waxers, and MAINTENANCE of GROUNDS, but not including the use of power-driven mowers or cutters.

(7) KITCHEN WORK and other work involved in preparing and serving food and beverages, including the operation of machines and devices used in the performance of such work, such as, but not limited to, dishwashers, toasters, dumbwaiters, popcorn poppers, milk shake blenders, and coffee grinders.

(8) WORK IN CONNECTION WITH CARS and TRUCKS if confined to the following:
> Dispensing gasoline and oil.
> Courtesy service.
> Car cleaning, washing and polishing.
> Other occupations permitted by this section.

BUT NOT INCLUDING WORK:
> Involving the use of pits, racks or lifting apparatus or involving the inflation of any tire mounted on a rim equipped with a removable retaining ring.

(9) CLEANING VEGETABLES and FRUITS, and WRAP-

PING, SEALING, LABELING, WEIGHING, PRICING
and STOCKING GOODS when performed in areas physically separate from areas where meat is prepared for
sale and outside freezers or meat coolers.

In Any Other Place of Employment

14- AND 15-YEAR-OLD MINORS MAY BE EMPLOYED IN—
any occupation EXCEPT the excluded occupations listed below:

14- AND 15-YEAR-OLD MINORS MAY NOT *BE EMPLOYED
IN—*

(1) Any MANUFACTURING occupation.

(2) Any MINING occupation.

(3) PROCESSING occupations (except in a retail, food service, or gasoline service establishment in those specific
occupations expressly permitted there in accordance
with the foregoing list).

(4) Occupations requiring the performance of any duties
IN WORKROOMS OR WORKPLACES WHERE
GOODS ARE MANUFACTURED, MINED, OR
OTHERWISE PROCESSED (except to the extent expressly permitted in retail, food service, or gasoline
service establishments in accordance with the foregoing list).

(5) PUBLIC MESSENGER SERVICE.

(6) OPERATION OR TENDING of HOISTING APPA-
RATUS or of ANY POWER-DRIVEN MACHINERY
(other than office machines and machines in retail, food
service, and gasoline service establishments which are
specified in the foregoing list as machines which such
minors may operate in such establishments).

(7) ANY OCCUPATIONS FOUND AND DECLARED TO
BE HAZARDOUS.

(8) OCCUPATIONS IN CONNECTION WITH:

(a) TRANSPORTATION of persons or property by rail, highway, air, on water, pipeline or other means.

(b) WAREHOUSING and STORAGE

(c) COMMUNICATIONS and PUBLIC UTILITIES

(d) CONSTRUCTION (including repair)

Except Office or Sales Work in connection with these Occupations (not performed on transportation media or at the actual construction site).

(9) ANY OF THE FOLLOWING OCCUPATIONS IN A RETAIL, FOOD SERVICE, OR GASOLINE SERVICE ESTABLISHMENT:

(a) WORK performed IN or ABOUT BOILER or ENGINE ROOMS.

(b) Work in connection with MAINTENANCE or REPAIR OF THE ESTABLISHMENT, MACHINES or EQUIPMENT.

(c) OUTSIDE WINDOW WASHING that involves working from window sills, and all work requiring the use of LADDERS, SCAFFOLDS or their substitutes.

(d) COOKING (except at soda fountains, lunch counters, snack bars, or cafeteria serving counters) and BAKING.

(e) Occupations which involve OPERATING, SETTING UP, ADJUSTING, CLEANING, OILING, or REPAIRING power-driven FOOD SLICERS and GRINDERS, FOOD CHOPPERS and CUTTERS, and BAKERY-TYPE MIXERS.

(f) Work in FREEZERS and MEAT COOLERS and all work in PREPARATION OF MEATS for sale (except wrapping, sealing, labeling, weighing, pricing and stocking when performed in other areas).

(g) LOADING and UNLOADING GOODS to and from trucks, railroad cars or conveyors.

(h) All occupations in WAREHOUSES except office and clerical work.

Age Certificates

An employer can protect himself from unintentional violation of the minimum age provisions by obtaining and keeping on file an AGE OR EMPLOYMENT CERTIFICATE for each minor employed, showing the minor to be of the age established for the occupation in which he is employed. Employers should obtain such a certificate and have it on file before the minor starts work.

Age or employment certificates, sometimes called work permits or working papers, issued under State child labor laws are accepted as proof of age in 45 States, the District of Columbia, and Puerto Rico. Special arrangements for proof of age have been made in Alaska. In 4 States—Idaho, Mississippi, South Carolina, and Texas—Federal certificates of age are issued by the Wage and Hour and Public Contracts Divisions.

Age certificates have the twofold purpose of (1) protecting minors from harmful employment as defined by the child labor provisions of the act; and (2) protecting employers from unintentional violation of the minimum age provisions of the act by furnishing them with reliable proof of age for minors employed in their establishment. This protection is specifically authorized by the act.

To make sure that the minors in their employ are of legal age under the act, employers are urged to obtain an age certificate for every minor claiming to be under 18 years of age before employing him in any occupation, and for every minor claiming to be 18 or 19 years of age before employing him in any of the nonagricultural occupations declared hazardous.

The age certificate protects the employer only if it shows the minor to be of the legal age for the occupation in which he is employed.

If an employer has any difficulty in obtaining age certificates for minors he wishes to employ, he should notify the nearest office of the Wage and Hour and Public Contracts Divisions (see pp. 31 and 32) or the Bureau of Labor Standards, U.S. Department of Labor, Washington, D.C. 20210.

Penalties for Violation

The act provides, in the case of willful violation, for a fine up to $10,000; or, for a second offense committed after the conviction of such person for a similar offense, for a fine of not more than $10,000; or imprisonment for not more than 6 months, or both. The Secretary of Labor may also ask a Federal district court to restrain future violations of the child labor provisions of the act by injunction.

State Child Labor Laws

Every State has a child labor law and all but one has a compulsory school attendance law. Whenever a State standard differs from a Federal standard, the higher standard must be observed.

Additional Information

Inquiries about the Fair Labor Standards Act will be answered by mail, telephone, or personal interview at any office of the Wage and Hour and Public Contracts Divisions of the U.S. Department of Labor. Offices are listed in the telephone directory under the U.S. Department of Labor in the U.S. Government listing. These offices also supply publications free of charge.

Offices listed in *italics* are staffed by investigation personnel whose duties frequently require them to be away from the office. Telephone messages and requests for information may be left at these offices when regular personnel are not on duty. Personnel appointments may be arranged by either telephone or mail.

Alabama: *Anniston*, Birmingham, *Dothan*, *Florence*, *Huntsville*, Mobile, Montgomery, *Opelika*, *Selma*, *Tuscaloosa*
Alaska: *Anchorage*
Arizona: Phoenix, *Tucson*

Arkansas: *El Dorado, Fayetteville, Fort Smith, Hope,* Little Rock, *Pine Bluff*

•California: *Bakersfield, Fresno,* Hollywood, Long Beach, Los Angeles, *Modesto, Monterey,* Oakland, *Redding, Riverside,* Sacramento, *San Diego,* San Francisco, *San Jose, San Mateo, Santa Ana, Santa Rosa, Stockton, West Covina,* Whittier

Colorado: Denver, *Pueblo*

Connecticut: *Bridgeport,* Hartford, *New Haven, New London*

Delaware: *Wilmington*

District of Columbia: College Park

Florida: *Clearwater, Cocoa, Fort Lauderdale, Fort Myers,* Jacksonville, *Lakeland, Leesburg,* Miami, North Miami, *Orlando, Ormond Beach, Panama City, Pensacola, St. Petersburg,* Tampa, *West Palm Beach*

Georgia: *Albany, Athens,* Atlanta, *Augusta, Brunswick,* Columbus, *Gainesville,* Hapeville, *Macon, Rome,* Savannah, *Thomasville, Valdosta*

Hawaii: Honolulu

Idaho: *Boise*

Illinois: Chicago, Springfield

Indiana: *Evansville,* Indianapolis, South Bend

Iowa: *Burlington, Cedar Rapids, Davenport,* Des Moines, *Fort Dodge, Mason City, Sioux City, Waterloo*

Kansas: *Great Bend, Pittsburg, Salina, Topeka,* Wichita

Kentucky: *Ashland,* Lexington, Louisville, *Middlesboro, Pikeville*

Louisiana: *Alexandria,* Baton Rouge, *Hammond, Houma, Lafayette, Lake Charles, Monroe,* New Orleans, Shreveport

Maine: Portland

Maryland: Baltimore, College Park, *Hagerstown, Salisbury*

Massachusetts: Boston, *Lowell,* Springfied, *Worcester*

Michigan: Detroit, Grand Rapids, *Lansing*

Minnesota: Minneapolis

Mississippi: *Columbus, Clarksdale, Greenville, Greenwood, Hattiesburg,* Jackson, *Meridian, Tupelo*

Missouri: *Cape Girardeau, Columbia, Joplin,* Kansas City, *St. Joseph,* St. Louis, *Springfield*

Montana: *Great Falls*

Nebraska: *Grand Island, Lincoln,* Omaha

Nevada: *Reno*
New Hampshire: Manchester, *Laconia*
New Jersey: *Camden*, Newark, Paterson, Trenton
New Mexico: Albuquerque, *Las Cruces, Roswell*
New York: *Albany*, Bronx, Brooklyn, Buffalo, Hempstead, New York, *Rochester*, Syracuse
North Carolina: *Asheville*, Charlotte, *Durham, Fayetteville, Goldsboro*, Greensboro, *Hickory, High Point*, Raleigh, *Wilmington, Winston-Salem*
North Dakota: *Bismarck*
Ohio: Cincinnati, Cleveland, Columbus
Oklahoma: *Ardmore, Enid, Lawton, Muskogee*, Oklahoma City, Tulsa
Oregon: *Eugene, Medford*, Portland, *Salem*
Pennsylvania: *Allentown, Altoona, Chester, DuBois, Erie, Greensburg*, Harrisburg, *Hazleton, Indiana, Johnstown, Lancaster, Lewistown*, McKeesport, *New Castle*, Philadelphia, Pittsburgh, *Reading, Scranton, Uniontown, Washington*, Wilkes-Barre
Rhode Island: Providence
South Carolina: *Charleston*, Columbia, *Florence, Greenville, Spartanburg*
South Dakota: *Aberdeen, Rapid City*, Sioux Falls
Tennessee: *Bristol, Chattanooga, Columbia, Jackson, Johnson City*, Knoxville, Memphis, Nashville
Texas: *Abilene, Amarillo, Austin, Beaumont*, Corpus Christi, Dallas, El Paso, Fort Worth, *Galveston*, Harlingen, Houston, *Laredo, Longview, Lubbock, Lufkin, Midland, Odessa, Paris*, San Antonio, *Texarkana, Tyler, Victoria*, Waco, *Wichita Falls*
Utah: *Ogden*, Salt Lake City
Vermont: *Burlington, Montpelier*
Virginia: *Alexandria, Norfolk*, Richmond, Roanoke, *Waynesboro*
Washington: Seattle, *Spokane, Tacoma*
West Virginia: *Bluefield*, Charleston, Clarksburg, *Huntington, Logan*
Wisconsin: Madison, Milwaukee, *Oshkosh*
Wyoming: *Casper, Cheyenne*

Puerto Rico: *Arecibo, Caguas,* Hato Rey, Mayaguez, *Ponce,* Santurce

Canal Zone, Virgin Islands: Santurce, Puerto Rico

American Samoa, Eniwetok Atoll, Guam, Johnston Island, Kwajalein Atoll, Wake Island: Honolulu, Hawaii

Bibliography of Vocational Guidance Materials

Business Administration and Related Professions

Accountants

American Institute of Certified
Public Accountants
666 Fifth Avenue
New York, N.Y. 10019

National Association of
Accountants
505 Park Avenue
New York, N.Y. 10022

Financial Executives Institute
50 West 44th Street
New York, N.Y. 10036

The Institute of Internal
Auditors, Inc.
60 Wall Street
New York, N.Y. 10005

Accounting Careers Council
National Distribution Center
P.O. Box 650
Radio City Station
New York N.Y. 10010

Advertising Workers

American Advertising Federation
655 Madison Avenue
New York, N.Y. 10021

American Association of
Advertising Agencies
200 Park Avenue
New York, N.Y. 10017

Marketing Research Workers

Small Business Administration
Washington, D.C. 20416

American Marketing Association
230 North Michigan Avenue
Chicago, Ill. 60601

Personnel Workers

American Society for Personnel
Administration
52 East Bridge Street
Berea, Ohio 44017

Public Personnel Association
1313 East 60th Street
Chicago, Ill. 60637

Public Relations Workers

The Information Center
Public Relations Society of
   America, Inc.
845 Third Avenue
New York, N.Y. 10022

Conservation Occupations

Foresters

Society of American Foresters
1010 16th Street NW
Washington, D.C. 20036

Forest Service,
U.S. Department of Agriculture
Washington, D.C. 20250

American Forest Products
   Industries, Inc.
1835 K Street NW
Washington, D.C. 20006

American Forestry Association
919 17th Street NW
Washington, D.C. 20006

Forestry Aids

Forest Service
U.S. Department of Agriculture
Washington, D.C. 20250

Range Managers

American Society of Range
   Management
Box 13302
Portland, Oreg. 97213

Bureau of Land Management
U.S. Department of Interior
Washington, D.C. 20240

Forest Service
U.S. Department of Agriculture
Washington D.C. 20250

Soil Conservation Service
U.S. Department of Agriculture
Washington D.C. 20250

Counseling

School Counselors

American School Counselor
   Association
1605 New Hampshire Avenue NW
Washington D.C. 20009

Rehabilitation Counselors

American Psychological
   Association Inc.
1200 17th Street NW
Washington, D.C. 20036

American Rehabilitation
   Counseling Association
1605 New Hampshire Avenue NW
Washington, D.C. 20009

National Rehabilitation
   Counseling Association
1522 K Street NW
Washington, D.C. 20005

U.S. Department of Health,
   Education and Welfare
Vocational Rehabilitation
   Administration
Washington, D.C. 20201

Vocational Counselors

National Vocational Guidance
   Association, Inc.
1605 New Hampshire Avenue NW
Washington, D.C. 20009

National Employment Counselors
   Association
1605 New Hampshire Avenue NW
Washington, D.C. 20009

U.S. Department of Labor,
Bureau of Employment Security,
   U.S. Employment Service
Branch of Counseling and Testing
   Services
Washington, D.C. 20210

Engineering

Engineers' Council for
   Professional Development
345 East 47th Street
New York, N.Y. 10017

Engineering Manpower
  Commission
Engineers Joint Council
345 East 47th Street
New York, N.Y. 10017

National Society of Professional
  Engineers
2029 K Street NW
Washington, D.C. 20006

The American Federation of
  Technical Engineers (AFL-CIO)
900 F Street NW
Washington, D.C. 20004

Aerospace Engineers

American Institute of Aeronautics
  and Astronautics, Inc.
1290 Avenue of the Americas
New York, N.Y. 10019

Agricultural Engineers

American Society of Agricultural
  Engineers
420 Main Street
St. Joseph, Mich. 49085

Ceramic Engineers

National Institute of Ceramic
  Engineers
4055 North High Street
Columbus, Ohio 43214

Chemical Engineers

American Institute of Chemical
  Engineers
345 East 47th Street
New York, N.Y. 10017

Civil Engineers

American Society of Civil
  Engineers
345 East 47th Street
New York, N.Y. 10017

Electrical Engineers

Institute of Electrical and
  Electronic Engineers
345 East 47th Street
New York, N.Y. 10017

Industrial Engineers

American Institute of Industrial
  Engineers
345 East 47th Street
New York, N.Y. 10017

Mechanical Engineers

The American Society of
  Mechanical Engineers
345 East 47th Street
New York, N.Y. 10017

Metallurgical Engineers

American Institute of Mining,
  Metalurgical, and Petroleum
  Engineers
345 East 47th Street
New York, N.Y. 10017

Mining Engineers

American Institute of Mining,
  Metalurgical, and Petroleum
  Engineers
345 East 47th Street
New York, N.Y. 10017

Health Service
Occupations

Chiropractors

American Chiropractic Association
American Building
2200 Grand Avenue
P.O. Box 1535
Des Moines, Iowa 50306

International Chiropractors
  Association
741 Brady Street
Davenport, Iowa 52805

Dental Hygienists

American Dental Hygienists'
  Association
211 East Chicago Avenue
Chicago, Ill. 60611

Dental Laboratory Technicians

American Dental Association
Council on Dental Education
211 East Chicago Avenue
Chicago, Ill. 60611

National Association of Certified
Dental Laboratories, Inc.
1330 Massachusetts Avenue NW
Washington, D.C. 20005

Dentists

American Dental Association
Council on Dental Education
211 East Chicago Avenue
Chicago, Ill. 60611

American Association of Dental
Schools
211 East Chicago Avenue
Chicago, Ill. 60611

Dietitians

The American Dietetic Association
620 North Michigan Avenue
Chicago, Ill. 60611

Hospital Administrators

American College of Hospital
Administrators
840 North Lake Shore Drive
Chicago, Ill. 60611

Association of University
Programs in Hospital
Administration
1642 East 56th Street
Chicago, Ill. 60637

Licensed Practical Nurses

ANA-NLN Nursing Careers
Programs
American Nurses' Association
10 Columbus Circle
New York, N.Y. 10019

National Association for Practical
Nurse Education and Service,
Inc.
535 Fifth Avenue
New York, N.Y. 10017

National Federation of Licensed
Practical Nurses, Inc.
250 West 57th Street
New York, N.Y. 10019

Department of Medicine and
Surgery
Veterans Administration
Washington, D.C. 20420

Medical Laboratory Assistants

Board of Certified Laboratory
Assistants
445 North Lake Shore Drive
Chicago, Ill. 60611

Medical Record Librarians

The American Association of
Medical Record Librarians
211 East Chicago Avenue
Chicago, Ill. 60611

Medical Technologists

American Soceity of Medical
Technologists
Suite 1600
Hermann Professional Building
Houston, Tex. 77025

Registry of Medical Technologists
of the American Society of
Clinical Pathologists
P.O. Box 2544
Muncie, Ind. 47302

Medical X-Ray Technicians

The American Society of
Radiologic Technologists
537 South Main Street
Fond du Lac, Wis. 54935

The American Registry of
Radiologic Technologists
2600 Wayzata Blvd.
Minneapolis, Minn. 55405

Occupational Therapists

American Occupational Therapy
  Association
251 Park Avenue South
New York, N.Y. 10010

Optometrists

American Optometric Association
700 Chippewa Street
St. Louis, Mo. 63119

Osteopathic Physicians

American Osteopathic Associaion
212 East Ohio Street
Chicago, Ill. 60611

Pharmacists

American Pharmaceutical
  Association
2215 Constitution Avenue NW
Washington, D.C. 20037

American Council on
  Pharmaceutical Education
77 West Washington Street
Chicago, Ill. 60602

Physical Therapists

American Physical Therapy
  Associaion
New York, N.Y. 10019

Physicians

Council on Medical Education
American Medical Association
535 North Dearborn Street
Chicago, Ill. 60610

Association of American Medical
  Colleges
2530 Ridge Avenue
Evanston, Ill. 60201

Podiatrists

American Podiatry Association
3301 16th Street NW
Washington, D.C. 20010

Registered Professional Nurses

ANA-NLN Nursing Careers
  Program
American Nurses' Association
10 Columbus Circle
New York, N.Y. 10019

Department of Medicine and
  Surgery
Veterans Administration
Washington, D.C. 20420

Sanitarians

American Public Health
  Association
1790 Broadway
New York, N.Y. 10019

International Association of Milk,
  Food, and Environmental
  Sanitarians
Blue Ridge Road
P.O. Box 437
Shelbyville, Ind. 46176

National Association of
  Sanitarians
1550 Lincoln Street
Denver, Colo. 80203

Speech Pathologists and Audiologists

American Speech and Hearing
Association
9030 Old Georgetown Road
Washington, D.C. 20014

Veterinarians

American Veterinary Medical
  Association
600 South Michigan Avenue
Chicago, Ill. 60605

Agricultural Research Service
U.S. Department of Agriculture
Washington, D.C. 20250

Mathematics and Related Fields

Mathematicians

American Mathematical Society
P. O. Box 6248
Providence, R.I. 02904

Mathematical Association of
America
SUNY at Buffalo
Buffalo, N.Y. 14214

Association for Computing
Machinery
211 East 43rd Street
New York, N.Y. 10017

Society for Industrial and Applied
Mathematics
33 South 17th Street
Philadelphia, Pa. 19103

Statisticians

American Statistical Association
810 18th Street NW
Washington, D.C. 20006

Association for Computing
Machinery
211 East 43rd Street
New York, N.Y. 10017

Institute of Mathematical
Statistics
Department of Statistics
California State College at
Hayward
Hayward, Calif. 94542

Interagency Board of U.S. Civil
Service
Examiners for Washington, D.C.
1900 E Street NW
Washington, D.C. 20415

Society for Industrial and Applied
Mathematics
33 South 17th Street
Philadelphia, Pa. 19103

Actuaries

Casualty Actuarial Society
200 East 42nd Street
New York, N.Y. 10017

Society of Actuaries
208 South LaSalle Street
Chicago, Ill. 60604

Natural Sciences

Biological Scientists

American Institute of Biological
Sciences
3900 Wisconsin Avenue NW
Washington, D.C. 20016

Interagency Board of U.S. Civil
Service Examiners for
Washington, D.C.
1900 E Street NW
Washington, D.C. 20415

Geologists

American Geological Institute
1444 N Street NW
Washington, D.C. 20005

Geophysicists

American Geophysical Union
1145 19th Street NW
Washington, D.C. 20036

Society of Exploration
Geophysicists
Shell Building
Tulsa, Okla. 74119

Meteorologists

American Meteorological Society
45 Beacon Street
Boston, Mass. 02108

American Geophysical Union
1145 19th Street NW
Washington, D.C. 20036

Environmental Science Services
Administration
Washington Science Center
Rockville, Md. 20852

Oceanographers

American Society of Oceanography
906 C. & I. Building
Houston, Tex. 77002

American Society of Limology
and Oceanography
Institute of Ecology
University of California
Davis, Calif. 95616

Interagency Committee on
Oceanography
Building 159 E
Washington Navy Yard
Washington, D.C. 20390

International Oceanographic
Foundation
1 Rickenbacker Causeway
Virginia Key
Miami, Fla. 33149

National Oceanographic
Association
1900 L Street NW
Washington, D.C. 20036

Chemists

American Chemical Society
1155 16th Street NW
Washington, D.C. 20036

Manufacturing Chemists'
Association, Inc.
1825 Connecticut Avenuue NW
Washington, D.C. 20009

Biochemists

American Society of Biological
Chemists
9650 Rockville Pike
Bethesda, Md. 20014

Physicists

American Institute of Physics
335 East 45th Street
New York, N.Y. 10017

Astronomers

The American Astronomical
Society
211 FitzRandolph Road
Princeton, N.J. 08540

Interagency Board of U.S. Civil
Service Examiners for
Washington, D.C.
1900 E Street NW
Washington, D.C. 20415

The Performing Arts

American Guild of Musical Artists
1841 Broadway
New York, N.Y. 10023

Musicians and Music Teachers

American Federation of
Musicians (AFL-CIO)
641 Lexington Avenue
New York, N.Y. 10022

American Guild of Musical Artists
1841 Broadway
New York, N.Y. 10023

American Guild of Organists
630 Fifth Avenue
New York, N.Y. 10020

National Assoiation of Schools of
Music
1501 New Hampshire Avenue NW
Washington, D.C. 20036

Music Educators National
Conference
The National Education
Association of the United States
1201 16th Street NW
Washington, D.C. 20036

Singers and Singing Teachers

National Association of Schools of
Music
1501 New Hampshire Avenue NW
Washington, D.C. 20036

Music Educators National
Conference
The National Education
Association of the United States
1201 16th Street NW
Washington, D.C. 20036

American Guild of Musical Artists
1841 Broadway
New York, N.Y. 10023

Other Related Occupations

Industrial Designers

Industrial Designers Society of
America
60 West 55th Street
New York, N.Y. 10019

National Association of Schools
of Art
50 Astor Place
New York, N.Y. 10003

Interior Designers and Decorators

National Society of Interior
Designers, Inc.
Suite 700
157 West 57th Street
New York, N.Y. 10019

Social Sciences

Anthropologists

The American Anthropological
Association
3700 Massachusetts Avenue NW
Washington, D.C. 20016

Economists

American Economic Association
Northwestern University
629 Noyes Street
Evanston, Ill. 60201

Geographers

Association of American
Geographers
1146 16th Street NW
Washington, D.C. 20036

Historians

American Historical Association
400 A Street SE
Washington, D.C. 20003

Political Scientists

American Political Science
Association
1527 New Hampshire Avenue NW
Washington, D.C. 20036

American Society for Public
Administration
1329 18th Street NW
Washington, D.C. 20036

Teaching

Kindergarten and Elementary School Teacher

U.S. Department of Health,
Education, and Welfare
Office of Education
Washington, D.C. 20202

American Federation of Teachers
716 North Rush Street
Chicago, Ill. 60611

National Commission on Teacher
Education and Professional
Standards
National Education Association
1201 16th Street NW
Washington, D.C. 20036

Secondary School Teachers

U.S. Department of Health,
Education, and Welfare
Office of Education
Washington, D.C. 20202

American Federation of Teachers
716 North Rush Street
Chicago, Ill. 60611

National Commission on Teacher
  Education and Professional
  Standards
National Education Association
1201 16th Street NW
Washington, D.C. 20036

College and University Teachers

U.S. Department of Health,
  Education, and Welfare
Office of Education
Washington, D.C. 20202

American Association of
  University Professors
1785 Massachusetts Avenue NW
Washington, D.C. 20036

American Council on Education
1785 Massachusetts Avenue NW
Washington, D.C. 20036

American Federation of Teachers
716 North Rush Street
Chicago, Ill. 60611

National Education Association
1201 16th Street NW
Washington, D.C. 20036

Technician Occupations

Engineering and Science Technicians

American Society for Engineering
  Education
Technical Institute Council
Dupont Circle Building
1346 Connecticut Avenue NW
Washington, D.C. 20036

Engineers' Council for Professional
  Development
345 East 47th Street
New York, N.Y. 10017

National Council of Technical
  Schools
1507 M Street NW
Washington, D.C. 20005

Draftsmen

American Institute for Design
  and Drafting
770 South Adams Road
Suite 110
Birmingham, Mich. 48011

American Federation of Technical
  Engineers
900 F Street NW
Washington, D.C. 20004

Writing Occupations

Newspaper Reporters

American Newspaper Publishers
  Association
750 Third Avenue
New York, N.Y. 10017

The Newspaper Fund, Inc.
Box 300
Princeton, N.J. 08540

Sigma Delta Chi
35 East Wacker Drive
Chicago, Ill. 60601

American Newspaper Guild,
  Research Department
1126 16th Street NW
Washington, D.C. 20036

American Council on Education
  for Journalism
Ernie Pyle Hall
Bloomington, Ind. 47405

Technical Writers

Executive Secretary
Society of Technical Writers and
  Publishers, Inc.
Suite 421
1010 Vermont Avenue
Washington, D.C. 20005

Other Professional and Related Occupations

Architects

The American Institute of
Architects
1735 New York Avenue NW
Washington, D.C. 20006

Society of American Registered
Architects
1821 Jefferson Place NW
Washington, D.C. 20036

College Placement Officers

The College Placement Council,
Inc.
35 East Elizabeth Avenue
Bethlehem, Pa. 18018

Home Economists

American Home Economics
Association
1600 20th Street NW
Washington, D.C. 20009

Landscape Architects

American Society of Landscape
Architects, Inc.
2000 K Street NW
Washington, D.C. 20006

Lawyers

The American Bar Association
1155 East 60th Street
Chicago, Ill. 60637

Association of American Law
Schools
1521 New Hampshire Avenue NW
Washington, D.C. 20036

Librarians

American Library Association
50 East Huron Street
Chicago, Ill. 60611

Special Libraries Association
31 East 10th Street
New York, N.Y. 10003

Library Services Branch
Office of Education
U.S. Department of Health,
Education, and Welfare
Washington, D.C. 20202

Photographers

Professional Photographers of
America, Inc.
1090 Executive Way
Oak Leaf Commons
Des Plaines, Ill. 60018

Programmers

Data Processing Management
Association
524 Busse Highway
Park Ridge, Ill. 60068

Association for Computing
Machinery
211 East 43rd Street
New York, N.Y. 10017

Psychologists

American Psychological
Association
1200 17th Street NW
Washington, D.C. 20036

Recreation Workers

National Recreation and Park
Association
1700 Pennsylvania Avenue NW
Washington, D.C. 20006

Social Workers

National Commission for Social
Work Careers
2 Park Avenue
New York, N.Y. 10016

Surveyors

American Congress on Surveying
and Mapping
Woodward Building
Washington, D.C. 20005

American Society of
Photogrammetry
105 North Virginia Avenue
Falls Church, Va. 22044

Systems Analysts

American Federation of
Information Processing Societies
211 East 43rd Street
New York, N.Y. 10017

Data Processing Management
Association
505 Busse Highway
Park Ridge, Ill. 60068

Association for Computing
Machinery
211 East 43rd Street
New York, N.Y. 10017

Urban Planners

American Institute of Planners
917 15th Street NW
Washington, D.C. 20005

American Society of Planning
Officials
1313 East 60th Street
Chicago, Ill. 60637

Managerial Occupations

The American Management
Association
135 West 50th Street
New York, N.Y. 10015

The Society for the Advancement
of Management
16 West 40th Street
New York, N.Y. 10015

Industrial Traffic Managers

American Society of Traffic and
Transportation, Inc.
22 West Madison Street
Chicago, Ill. 60602

Purchasing Agents

National Association of
Purchasing Agents
11 Park Place
New York, N.Y. 10007

Clerical and Related Occupations

Office Occupation Unit
Division of Vocational and
Technical Education
Bureau of Adult Vocational and
Library Programs
U.S. Office of Education
Washington, D.C. 20202

Stenographers and Secretaries

United Business Schools
Association
1101 17th Street NW
Washington, D.C. 20036

National Shorthand Reporters
Association
25 West Main Street
Madison, Wis. 53703

Electronic Computer Operating Personnel

Data Processing Management
Association
524 Busse Highway
Park Ridge, Ill. 60068

Association for Computing
Machinery
211 East 43rd Street
New York, N.Y. 10017

Sales Occupations

Automobile Salesmen

National Automobile Dealers
Association
2000 K Street NW
Washington, D.C. 20006

Automobile Parts Counterman

Automotive Service Industry
Association
168 North Michigan Avenue
Chicago, Ill. 60601

National Automotive Parts
Association
29 East Madison Street
Chicago, Ill. 60602

Salesmen in Wholesale Trade

National Association of
Wholesalers
1725 K Street NW
Washington, D.C. 20006

Manufacturer's Salesmen

Sales and Marketing Executives—
International
Youth Education Department
630 Third Avenue
New York, N.Y. 10017

The Council on Opportunities in
Selling, Inc.
630 Third Avenue
New York, N.Y. 10017

Insurance Agents and Brokers

Institute of Life Insurance
277 Park Avenue
New York, N.Y. 10017

Life Insurance Agency
Management Association
170 Sigourney Street
Hartford, Conn. 06105

The National Association of Life
Underwriters
1922 F Street NW
Washington, D.C. 20006

Insurance Information Institute
110 William Street
New York, N.Y. 10038

National Association of Insurance
Agents, Inc.
96 Fulton Street
New York, N.Y. 10038

Insurance Institute of America,
Inc.
270 Bryn Mawr Avenue
Bryn Mawr, Pa. 19010

Real Estate Salesmen and Brokers

Department of Education
National Association of Real
Estate Boards
155 East Superior Street
Chicago, Ill. 60611

Securities Salesmen

New York Stock Exchange
11 Wall Street
New York, N.Y. 10005

Investment Bankers Association of
America
425 13th Street NW
Washington, D.C. 20004

National Association of Securities
Dealers, Inc.
1707 H Street NW
Washington, D.C. 20006

Service Occupations

Private Household Workers

National Committee on Household
Employment
1346 Connecticut Avenue NW
Washington, D.C. 20036

FBI Special Agents

The Federal Bureau of
Investigation
U.S. Department of Justice
Washington, D.C. 20535

Firefighters

International Association of Fire
Fighters
905 16th Street NW
Washington, D.C. 20006

International Association of Fire
Chiefs
232 Madison Avenue
New York, N.Y. 10016

Policemen and Policewomen

International Association of Chiefs
of Police
1319 18th Street NW
Washington, D.C. 20036

International Association of
Women Police
100 North LaSalle Street
Chicago, Ill. 60602

State Police Officers

International Association of Chiefs
of Police
1319 18th Street NW
Washington, D.C. 20036

Cooks and Chefs

Educational Director
National Restaurant Association
153 North Lake Shore Drive
Chicago, Ill. 60610

Council on Hotel, Restaurant, and
Institutional Education
Statler Hall
Cornell University
Ithaca, N.Y. 14850

Waiters and Waitresses

Educational Director
National Restaurant Association
1530 North Lake Shore Drive
Chicago, Ill. 60610

Hospital Attendants

ANA-NLN Nursing Careers
Program
American Nurses' Association
10 Columbus Circle
New York, N.Y. 10019

Division of Health Careers
American Hospital Association
840 North Lake Shore Drive
Chicago, Ill. 60611

Barbers

National Association of Barber
Schools, Inc.
750 Third Avenue
Huntington, W. Va. 25701

Associated Master Barbers and
Beauticians of America
219 Greenwich Road
P.O. Box 17782
Charlotte, N.C. 28211

Journeymen Barbers, Hairdressers,
Cosmetologists, and Proprietors'
International Union of America
1141 North Deleware Street
Indianapolis, Ind. 46207

Cosmetologists

National Association of
Cosmetology Schools, Inc.
3839 White Plains Road
Bronx, N. Y. 10467

National Hairdressers and
Cosmetologists Association
175 5th Avenue
New York, N.Y. 10010

Journeymen Barbers, Hairdressers,
Cosmetologists, and Proprietors'
International Union of America
1141 North Delaware Street
Indianapolis, Ind. 46207

Building Trades

American Federation of Labor and
Congress of Industrial
Organizations
Building and Construction Trades
Department
815 16th Street NW
Washington, D.C. 20006

Associated General Contractors of
America, Inc.
1957 E Street NW
Washington, D.C. 20006

National Association of Home
Builders
1625 L Street NW
Washington, D.C. 20036

Asbestos and Insulating Workers

Insulation Distributor-Contractors
National Association, Inc.
1425 Chestnut Street
Philadelphia, Pa. 19102

International Association of Heat
and Frost Insulators and
Asbestos Workers
1300 Connecticut Avenue NW
Washington, D.C. 20036

Bricklayers

Associated General Contractors of
America, Inc.
1957 E Street NW
Washington, D.C. 20006

Bricklayers, Masons and
Plasterers' International Union
of America
815 15th Street NW
Washington, D.C. 20005

Structural Clay Products Institute
1520 18th Street NW
Washington, D.C. 20036

Carpenters

Associated General Contractors of
America, Inc.
1957 E Street NW
Washington, D.C. 20006

United Brotherhood of Carpenters
and Joiners of America
101 Constitution Avenue NW
Washington, D.C. 20001

Cement Masons

Associated General Contractors of
America, Inc.
1957 E Street NW
Washington, D.C. 20006

Bricklayers, Masons and
Plasterers' International Union
of America
815 15th Street NW
Washington, D.C. 20005

Operative Plasters' and Cement
Masons' International
Association of the United States
and Canada
1125 17th Street NW
Washington, D.C. 20036

Construction Laborers and Hod Carriers

Laborers' International Union of
North America
904 16th Street NW
Washington, D.C. 20006

Electricians (Construction)

International Brotherhood of
Electrical Workers
1200 15th Street NW
Washington, D.C. 20005

National Electrical Contractors
Association
1730 Rhode Island Avenue NW
Washington, D.C. 20036

National Joint Apprenticeship and
Training Committee for the
Electrical Industry
1730 Rhode Island Avenue NW
Washington, D.C. 20036

Floor Covering Installers

American Carpet Institute
Empire State Building
New York, N.Y. 10001

Armstrong Cork Co.
Lancaster, Pa. 17604

Congoleum-Nairn, Inc.
195 Belgrove Drive
Kearny, N.J. 07032

Lathers

Contracting Plasterers' and
Laborers' International
Association
304 Landmark Building
1343 H Street NW
Washington, D.C. 20005

National Bureau for Lathing and
Plastering
938 K Street NW
Washington, D.C. 20001

The Wood, Wire and Metal
Laborers International Union
6530 New Hampshire Avenue
Takoma Park, Md. 20012

Marble Setters, Tile Setters and Terrazzo Workers

National Terrazzo and Mosiac
Association, Inc.
1901 Fort Myer Drive
Arlington, Va. 22209

Tile Contractors' Association of
America, Inc.
1901 Fort Myer Drive
Arlington, Va. 22209

Operating Engineers (Construction Machinery Operators)

Associated General Contractors of
America, Inc.
1957 E Street NW
Washington, D.C. 20006

International Union of Operating
Engineers
1125 17th Street NW
Washington, D.C. 20036

Painters and Paperhangers

Brotherhood of Painters,
Decorators and Paperhangers of
America
1925 K Street NW
Washington, D.C. 20006

Painting and Decorating
Contractors Association of
America
2625 West Peterson Avenue
Chicago, Ill. 60605

Plasterers

Bricklayers, Masons and
Plasterers' International Union
of America
815 15th Street NW
Washington, D.C. 20005

Contracting Plasterers' and
Lathers' International
Association
304 Landmark Building
1343 H Street NW
Washington, D.C. 20005

National Bureau for Lathing and
Plastering
938 K Street NW
Washington, D.C. 20001

Operative Plasterers' and Cement
Masons' International
Association of the United States
and Canada
1125 17th Street NW
Washington, D.C. 20036

Plumbers and Pipefitters

National Association of Plumbing-
Heating-Cooling Contractors
1016 20th Street NW
Washington, D.C. 20036

United Association of Journeymen
and Apprentices of the Plumbing
and Pipe Fitting Industry of the
United States and Canada
901 Massachusetts Avenue NW
Washington, D.C. 20001

Roofers

National Roofing Contractors
   Association
300 West Washington Street
Chicago, Ill. 60606

United Slate, Tile and Composition
   Roofers, Damp and Waterproof
   Workers Association
1125 7th Street NW
Washington, D.C. 20036

Sheet-Metal Workers

Sheet Metal and Air Conditioning
   Contractors' National
   Association, Inc.
107 Center Street
Elgin, Ill. 60120

Sheet Metal Workers'
   International Association
1000 Connecticut Avenue NW
Washington, D.C. 20036

Stonemasons

Bricklayers, Masons and
   Plasterers' International Union
   of America
815 15th Street NW
Washington, D.C. 20005

Structural, Ornamental and Reinforcing-Iron Workers, Riggers, and Machine Movers

Associated General Contractors of
   America, Inc.
1957 E Street NW
Washington, D.C. 20006

Driving Occupations

American Trucking Association
1616 P Street NW
Washington, D.C. 20036

Forge Shop Occupations

The Forging Industry Association
55 Public Square
Cleveland, Ohio 44113

International Brotherhood of
   Boilermakers, Iron Shipbuilders,
   Blacksmiths, Forgers and
   Helpers
Eighth at State Avenue
Kansas City, Kans. 66101

Open Die Forging Institute
440 Sherwood Road
La Grange Park, Ill. 60625

Mechanics and Repairmen

Air-Conditioning, Refrigeration, and Heating Mechanics

Refrigeration Service Engineers
   Society
433 North Waller Avenue
Chicago, Ill. 60644

Appliance Servicemen

Association of Home Appliance
   Manufacturers
20 North Wacker Drive
Chicago, Ill. 60606

National Appliance and Radio-TV
   Dealers Association
364 Merchandise Mart
Chicago, Ill. 60654

Automobile Body Repairmen

Automotive Service Industry
   Association
168 North Michigan Avenue
Chicago, Ill. 60601

Independent Garage Owners of
   America, Inc.
624 South Michigan Avenuue
Chicago, Ill. 60605

Automobile Mechanics

Automotive Service Industry
Association
168 North Michigan Avenue
Chicago, Ill. 60601

Independent Garage Owners of
America, Inc.
624 South Michigan Avenue
Chicago, Ill. 60605

National Automobile Dealers
Association
2000 K Street NW
Washington, D.C. 20006

Diesel Mechanics

International Association of
Machinists and Aerospace
Workers
1300 Connecticut Avenue NW
Washington, D.C. 20036

Amalgamated Transit Union
5025 Wisconsin Avenue NW
Washington, D.C. 20016

Sheet Metal Workers'
International Association
1000 Connecticut Avenue NW
Washington, D.C. 20036

International Union, United
Automobile, Aerospace and
Agricultural Implement Workers
of America
8000 East Jefferson Avenue
Detroit, Mich. 48214

Electric Sign Servicemen

National Electric Sign Association
10912 South Western Avenue
Chicago, Ill. 60643

Farm Equipment Mechanics

Farm Equipment Institute
850 Wrigley Building North
410 North Michigan Avenue
Chicago, Ill. 60611

National Farm and Power
Equipment Dealers Association
2340 Hampton Avenue
St. Louis, Mo. 63139

Industrial Machinery Repairmen

Instrument Society of America
530 William Penn Place
Pittsburgh, Pa. 15200

Scientific Apparatus Makers
Association
Recorder-Controller Section
370 Lexington Avenue
New York, N.Y. 10017

Millwrights

United Brotherhood of Carpenters
and Joiners of America
101 Constitution Avenue NW
Washington, D.C. 20001

Truck Mechanics and Bus Mechanics

American Trucking Associations,
Inc.
1616 P Street NW
Washington, D.C. 20036

Vending Machine Mechanics

National Automatic Merchandising
Association
7 South Dearborn Street
Chicago, Ill. 60603

Watch Repairmen

American Watchmakers Institute
P.O. Box 1101
Cincinnati, Ohio 45211

Retail Jewelers of America, Inc.
1025 Vermont Avenue NW
Washington, D.C. 20005

Machining Occupations

International Association of
Machinists and Aerospace
Workers
1300 Connecticut Avenue NW
Washingtin, D.C. 20036

International Union
United Automobile, Aerospace and
Agricultural Implement Workers
of America
8000 East Jefferson Avenue
Detroit, Mich. 48214

International Union of Electrical
Workers
1200 15th Street NW
Washington, D.C. 20005

Printing (Graphic Arts) Occupations

American Newspaper Publishers
Association
750 Third Avenue
New York, N.Y. 10017

Education Council of The Graphic
Arts Industry, Inc.
4615 Forbes Avenue
Pittsburgh, Pa. 15213

Graphic Arts Technical
Foundation
4615 Forbes Avenue
Pittsburgh, Pa. 15213

Gravure Technical Institute
60 East 42nd Street
New York, N.Y. 10020

Printing Industries of America,
Inc.
20 Chevy Chase Circle NW
Washington, D.C. 20015

Composing Room Occupations

International Typographical Union
P.O. Box 157
Colorado Springs, Colo. 80901

International Typographic
Composition Association, Inc.
2233 Wisconsin Avenue NW
Washington, D.C. 20007

Printing Industries of America,
Inc.
20 Chevy Chase Circle NW
Washington, D.C. 20015

Photoengravers

American Photoengravers
Association
166 West Van Buren Street
Chicago, Ill. 60604

Lithographers and Photoengravers
International Union
233 West 49th Street
New York, N.Y. 10019

Lithographic Occupations

Lithographers and Photoengravers
International Union
233 West 49th Street
New York, N.Y. 10019

International Printing Pressman
and Assistants' Union of North
America
Pressmen's Home, Tenn. 37850

Graphic Arts Technical Foundation
4615 Forbes Avenue
Pittsburgh, Pa. 15213

National Association of Photo-
Lithographers
230 West 41st Street
New York, N.Y. 10036

Printing Industries of America,
Inc.
20 Chevy Chase Circle NW
Washington, D.C. 20015

Electrotypers and Stereotypers

International Stereotypers' and
Electrotypers' Union of North
America
10 South La Salle Street
Chicago, Ill. 60603

International Association of
Electrotypers and Stereotypers,
Inc.
758 Leader Building
Cleveland, Ohio 44114

Printing Industries of America,
Inc.
20 Chevy Chase Circle NW
Washington, D.C. 20015

Printing Pressmen and Assistants

International Printing Pressmen and Assistants' Union of North America
Pressman's Home, Tenn.   37850

Printing Industries of America, Inc.
20 Chevy Chase Circle NW
Washington, D.C.   20015

Bookbinding and Related Workers

International Brotherhood of Bookbinders
1612 K Street NW
Washington, D.C. 20016

Printing Industries of America, Inc.
20 Chevy Chase Circle NW
Washington, D.C.   20015

Other Manual Occupations

Automobile Painters

Automotive Service Industry Association
168 South Michigan Avenue
Chicago, Ill.   60601

Independent Garage Owners of America, Inc.
624 South Michigan Avenue
Chicago, Ill.   60605

Blacksmiths

International Brotherhood of Boilermakers, Iron Shipbuilders, Blacksmiths, Forgers and Helpers
Eighth at State Avenue
Kansas City, Kans.   66101

Boilermaker Occupations

International Brotherhood of Boilermakers, Iron Shipbuilders, Blacksmiths, Forgers and Helpers
Eighth at State Avenue
Kansas City, Kans.   66101

Dispensing Opticians and Optical Mechanics

American Optical Company
Box 1
Southbridge, Mass.   01551

Bausch and Lomb, Inc.
635 St. Paul Street
Rochester, N.Y.   14602

Optical Wholesalers Association
222 West Adams Street
Chicago, Ill.   60606

International Union of Electrical, Radio and Machine Workers
1126 16th Street NW
Washington, D.C.   20036

Guild of Prescription Opticians of America
250 Connecticut Avenue NW
Washington, D.C. 20036

American Board of Opticianry
821 Eggert Road
Buffalo, N.Y.   14226

Electroplaters

American Electroplaters Society, Inc.
56 Melmore Gardens
East Orange, N.J.   07017

National Association of Metal Finishers
248 Lorraine Avenue
Upper Montclair, N.J.   07043

Furniture Upholsterers

Upholsterers International Union of North America
1500 North Broad Street
Philadelphia, Pa.   19121

Gasoline Service Station Attendants

American Petroleum Institute
Marketing Division
1271 Avenue of the Americas
New York, N.Y.   10020

Jewelers and Jewelry Repairmen

Retail Jewelers of America, Inc.
1025 Vermont Avenue NW
Washington, D.C. 20005

Manufacturing Jewelers and Silver-
  smiths of America, Inc.
Sheraton-Biltmore Hotel
Room S-75
Providence, R.I. 02902

International Jewelry Workers'
  Union
Local No. 1
133 West 44th Street
New York, N.Y. 10036

Photographic Laboratory Occupations

Master Photo Dealers' and
  Finishers' Association
603 Lansing Avenue
Jackson, Mich. 49202

Shoe Repairmen

Shoe Service Institute of America
222 West Adams Street
Chicago, Ill. 60606

Stationary Engineers

International Union of Operating
  Engineers
1125 17th Street NW
Washington, D.C. 20036

National Association of Power
  Engineers, Inc.
176 West Adam Street
Chicago, Ill. 60603

Welders and Oxygen and Arc Cutters

The American Welding Society
345 East 47th Street
New York, N.Y. 10017

International Association of
  Machinist and Aerospace
  Workers
1300 Connecticut Avenue NW
Washington, D.C. 20036

International Brotherhood of
  Boilermakers, Iron Shipbuilders,
  Blacksmiths, Forgers and
  Helpers
Eighth at State Avenue
Kansas City, Kans. 66101

United Association of Journeymen
  and Apprentices of the Plumbing
  and Pipe Fitting Industry of the
  United States and Canada
901 Massachusetts Avenue NW
Washington, D.C. 20001

Occupations in Aircraft, Missile, and Spacecraft Manufacturing

National Aeronautics and Space
  Administration
Washington, D.C. 20546

Aerospace Industries Association of
  America, Inc.
1725 DeSales Street NW
Washington, D.C. 20036

International Association of
  Machinists and Aerospace
  Workers
1300 Connecticut Avenue NW
Washington, D.C. 20036

International Union, United
  Automobile, Aerospace and
  Agricultural Implement Workers
  of America
8000 East Jefferson Avenue
Detroit, Mich. 48214

International Union of Electrical
  Radio and Machine Workers
1126 16th Street NW
Washington, D.C. 20036

Electronics Industries Association
1721 DeSales Street NW
Washington, D.C. 20036

Aluminum Industry

The Aluminum Association
420 Lexington Avenue
New York, N.Y. 10017

Apparel Industry Occupations

Amalgamated Clothing Workers of
America
15 Union Square
New York, N.Y. 10003
American Apparel Manufacturers
Association, Inc.
200 K Street NW
Washington, D.C. 20006

Associated Fur Manufacturers, Inc.
101 West 30th Street
New York, N.Y. 10001

Clothing Manufacturers
Association of U.S.A.
135 West 50th Street
New York, N.Y. 10001

National Outerwear and Sportwear
Association, Inc.
347 Fifth Avenue
New York, N.Y. 10016

International Ladies' Garments
Workers' Union
1710 Broadway
New York, N.Y. 10019

United Garment Workers of
America
31 Union Square
New York, N.Y. 10003

Occupations in the Atomic Energy Field

U.S. Atomic Energy Commission
Washington, D.C. 20545

Occupations in the Baking Industry

American Bakers Association
1700 Pennsylvania Avenue NW
Washington, D.C. 20006

Electronics Manufacturing

Electronic Industries Association
20001 Eye Street NW
Washington, D.C. 20006

Occupations in Foundries

Foundry Educational Foundation
1138 Terminal Tower
Cleveland, Ohio 44113

International Molders' and Allied
Workers Union of North America
1225 East McMillan Street
Cincinnati, Ohio 45206

National Foundry Association
9838 Roosevelt Road
P.O. Box 76
Westchester, Ill. 60156

Non-Ferrous Founders' Society
14600 Detroit Avenue
Cleveland, Ohio 44107

Gray and Ductile Iron Founders'
Society, Inc.
National City
East 6th Building
Cleveland, Ohio 44114

American Foundrymen's Society
Golf and Wolf Roads
Des Plaines, Ill. 60016

Malleable Founders' Society
781 Union Commerce Building
Cleveland, Ohio, 44114

Steel Founders' Society of America
Westview Towers
21010 Center Ridge Road
Rocky River, Ohio 44116

Occupations in the Industrial Chemical Industry

American Chemical Society
1155 16th Street NW
Washington, D.C. 20036

Manufacturing Chemists'
Association, Inc.
1825 Connecticut Avenue NW
Washington, D.C. 20009

Occupations in the Iron and Steel Industry

American Iron and Steel Industry
150 East 42nd Street
New York, N.Y. 10017

United Steelworkers of America
1500 Comonwealth Building
Pittsburgh, Pa. 15222

Petroleum and Natural Gas Production and Processing

American Gas Association
605 Third Avenue
New York, N.Y. 10016

American Petroleum Institute
1271 Avenue of the Americas
New York, N.Y. 10020

National Petroleum Refiners Assoc.
1725 DeSales Street NW
Washington, D.C. 20036

Occupations in the Pulp, Paper, and Allied Products Industry

American Forest Products
Industries
1835 K Street NW
Washington, D.C. 20036

American Paper Institute
260 Madison Avenue
New York, N.Y. 10016

Fibre Box Association
224 South Madison Avenue
Chicago, Ill. 60604

National Paper Box Manufacturers
Association, Inc.
12 North Broad Street
Philadephia, Pa. 19107

National Paper Trade Association,
Inc.
220 East 42nd Street
New York, N.Y. 10017

United Papermakers and Paper-
workers
Papermakers Building
Albany, N.Y. 12201

Restaurant Industry

Educational Director
National Restaurant Association
1530 North Lake Shore Drive
Chicago, Ill. 60610

Council on Hotel, Restaurant and
Institutional Education
Statler Hall, Cornell University
Ithica, N.Y. 14850

Occupations in Government

American Society for Public
Administration
1329 18th Street NW
Washington, D.C. 20036

Service and Miscellaneous

Hotel Occupations

American Hotel and Motel
Association
221 West 57th Street
New York, N.Y. 10019

Council on Hotel, Restaurant, and
Institutional Education
Statler Hall, Cornell University
Ithica, N.Y. 14850

National Executive Housekeepers
Association, Inc.
Business and Professional Building
Gallipolis, Ohio 45631

Agricultural Finance

Farm Credit Administration
Washington, D.C. 20578

Farm Credit District—
Springfield, Mass.; Baltimore, Md.;
Columbia, S.C.; Louisville, Ky.;
New Orleans, La.; St. Louis, Mo.;
St. Paul, Minn.; Omaha, Nebr.;
Wichita, Kans.; Houston, Tex.;
Berkeley, Calif.; Spokane, Wash.

Farmers Home Administration
U.S. Department of Agriculture
Washington, D.C.   20250

Agricultural Director
American Bankers Association
90 Park Avenue
New York, N.Y.   10016

Transportation, Communication and Public Utilities

Pilots and Copilots

International Air Line Pilots
Association
55th Street and Cicero Avenue
Chicago, Ill.   60638

Flight Engineers

Flight Engineers' International
Association
100 Indiana Avenue NW
Washington, D.C.   20001

Occupations in the Electric Power Industry

International Brotherhood of
Electrical Workers
1200 15th Street NW
Washington, D.C.   20005

Utility Workers' Union of America
1875 Connecticut Avenue NW
Washington, D.C.   20006

Railroad Occupations

Association of American Railroads
Transportation Building
Washington, D.C.   20006

Telephone Industry Occupations

Alliance of Independent Telephone
Unions
Room 302
1422 Chestnut Street
Philadelphia, Pa.   19102

Communications Workers of
America
1925 K Street NW
Washington, D.C.   20006

International Brotherhod of
Electrical Workers
1200 15th Street NW
Washington, D.C.   20005

Occupations in Finance and Insurance

Banking

American Bankers Association
Personnel Administration and
Management Development
Committee
90 Park Avenue
New York, N.Y.   10016

National Association of Bank
Women, Inc.
National Office
60 East 42nd Street
New York, N.Y.   10017

The National Consumer Finance
Association
1000 16th Street NW
Washington, D.C.   20036

Insurance

Institute of Life Insurance
277 Parke Avenue
New York, N.Y. 10017

Insurance Information Institute
110 William Street
New York, N.Y.   10038

Index

Abilities, 119
Acceptance, 231
Accidents, 308, 324
Accountant, 17, 455
Adaptability, 92
Addition review, 388
Adult, responsibilities of, 151
Adult education, 93, 384
Advertising, 192
  career information, 455
  laws, 183
  practices, 201
Aerospace, career data, 474
Age, 233, 417, 450
Agreement, signing, 211
Agricultural occupations, 379
Air travel, 355
Amendment to motion, 414
Annuities, 330
Apparel industry, career data, 475
Appearance, 52, 129
Application, for job, 38-66
Application forms, 39-42
Appointment, for interview, 53
Apprenticeable trades, 359, 381, 421
Aptitudes, 119
  and jobs, 11
Architect, 24, 464
Arithmetic ability, 120
Art related occupations, 373
Asset, 205
Astronomy, career data, 461
Attitudes —
  inventory of, 135
  on job, 67-86
  and job finding, 63
  toward people, 123
Attorney, *see* Lawyer
Atomic energy, career data, 475
Auto —
  loans, 222
  purchasing, 192
  repair, 185
  reporting accidents, 324
  safety, 183

Automation, 286, 355
Automobile insurance, 318, 323

Bait ads, 202
Bank credit, 209-221, 257
Bank services, 244-264
Bank statement, 255
Banks, 244
  for money counsel, 175
Banking, career data, 379, 477
Bargaining, 197
  collective, 83
Beginner, behavior as, 80
  importance of, 67, 138
Benefits —
  Social Security, 294
  unemployment, 304
Better Business Bureau, 189
Biological science, career data, 460
Blank endorsement, 252
Blind, disability benefits for, 296
Bodily injury liability insurance, 319
Body odor, 143
Borrowing, 211
Boss, being a, 93
Brand names, 181, 191
Breath, 143
Budgeting, 153-177
  basic procedure, 166
  and employment, 198
  federal, 274
  using, 173
Building trades, 18-362, 468
Business administration, 17-368
Business taxes, 269
Buying practices, 178-203

Cancelled checks, 254
Car —
  budgeting for, 167
  buying a, 192, 194, 240
  insurance, 315

Career —
advancments in, 87-110
choosing, 2, 11, 37, 343
long-range goal, 88
planning, 34
Carrying charges, 214
Cash, substitutes for, 256
Casualty insurance, 318
Chair, in parliamentary law, 410
Charge accounts, 208, 225
Checks, 248-255
advantages of, 256
cashier's, 259
certified, 259
as receipt, 252
writing a, 248, 251
Cheerfulness, 139
Chemistry, career data, 461
Child development, 341
Child labor laws, 417-454
exemptions, 419
14- and 15-year-old minors, 446
offices for enforcement, 451
state, 451
Citizens, good, 151
Civil aviation occupations, 379
Civil law, 229
Clothes —
budgeting for, 167, 169
buying, 191, 200
buying women's, 190
at interview, 54
planning buying, 179
Coal mining, 427
Collateral, for loan, 221
Collective bargaining, 83
Commercial bank, 245
Commercial credit, 208
Community colleges, 380
Company courses, 93
Computers, 355
Conservation occupations, 19, 370
Consideration, contract element, 236
Consumer —
protection of, 182
wise, 151
Consumer credit, 206-208
Consumer education, 182, 185, 189, 192
Contracts, 229-230, 243
for car sale, 241

defective, 236
elements of, 230
legal forms, 236
legal purpose, 235
preparing and signing, 211, 237
for real estate purchase, 239
sales, 197
Contribution —
budgeting for, 169
to Social Security, 294
Convenience, of taxation, 285
Cooperation, 71-92
Correspondence courses, 93
Co-signer, 221
Counseling, on money management, 175
Counselor, school, 26, 370
career data, 456
Courtesy, 124-139-141
Co-workers, relations with, 79
Credit, 204, 221
cost of, 211-212, 217
using, 204, 218, 227, 228
wise use, 209
Credit bureau, 204
Credit cards, 208
Credit union, 209
loans, 222
Criminal law, 229
Criticism —
in evaluation interview, 103
taking, 73

Daily living costs, budgeting for, 171
Debate —
on motion, 413
rules of, 409
Deceit, in contracts, 234
Decisiveness, 92
Delegation, 191
Democracy, 266
procedure in, 409
Dental occupations, career data, 458
Dependability, 73-125, 140-142
Deposits, insured by banks, 247
Deposit slip, 258
Depression, 290
Design careers, data on, 462
Desire, 127-139
Dietitians, career data, 458
Direct taxes, 267

Disability benefits, Social Security, 294
Disability insurance, 292
Discipline, on job, 78
Discount store, 199
Disposition, 142
Division, review of, 402
Draftsmen, career data, 463
Dress, appropriate, 139-142
Driving habits, 148
Driving occupations, 364, 470
Dropout's career, 350
Drugs, buying, 188
Drug safety, 183

Earnings, and education, 356
Eating habits, 147
Economy, of taxation, 287
Education —
  and earnings, 357
  continues through life, 339
  and job security, 357
  post-high-school, 355-386
Emergencies, budgeting for, 169
Emotions, controlling, 130
Employee —
  deserves evaluations, 77
  expectations of, 75
  withholding certificate, 279
Employer —
  covered by child labor laws, 418
  evaluates job applicants, 63
  expects of employee, 69
  finances unemployment
    insurance, 306
  for money counsel, 175
Employment, and purchasing plans, 198
Employment agencies, 30
Endowment life insurance, 327
Enthusiasm, 73-125
Equity, of taxation, 285
Evaluations, job, 77
Example, setting an, 96
Excise tax, 274
Expenses —
  budgeting flexible, 169
  of federal government, 276
Eyes, as windows, 146

Family responsibilities, 344
Favoritism, 98

Federal Deposit Insurance
  Corporation, 247
Federal income tax, 269
Federal Reserve System, 247
Finance company, 209
Finances, managing, 152-177
Finger dexterity, 121
Fingernails, 143
First names, use of, 81
Fiscal year, 274
Fixed expenses, 164
Food labels, 184
Foresight, 126
Forging, career data, 470
Formal contract, 230
Formality, at work, 81
Foundry occupations,
  career data, 368, 475
Fraud, 182
Friendliness, 126-141
Friends, at work, 79
Fringe benefits, 84
Funeral society, 313

Gallantry, 140
Gambling contracts, 235
Gasoline tax, 269
General aptitude test battery, 121
Gifts, budgeting for, 169
Goals —
  in budgeting, 167
  long-range, 88, 112
Golden rule, 128
Goods, buying, 4, 178-203
Good will, 8
Government, as employer, 30
Government services, 265-289, 476
Grades, school, 120
Grooming, 130, 139-141
  for interview, 54
Group insurance, 330, 331

Habits, and buying, 200
Hardware salesman, 157
Hazardous occupations, 420-422
Health, 126, 141-142
Health insurance, 292, 315-332
  Social Security, 299
Health occupations, 20, 360-370, 458
Health services, buying, 186
Hoisting apparatus, hazards, 432

Home, buying, 227-238
Home economics, career data, 464
Home loans, 162, 226
Homeowner insurance, 318
Honesty, 8, 71, 78, 127, 139-141
Hospital insurance, 332
Hospital occupations, career data, 459
Household, budgeting for, 171, 226
Humor, sense of, 82, 131, 141-142

Ideas, interest in, 116
Identity, work as, 2, 5, 6
Income, estimating, 163
Income insurance, 332
Income tax returns, 269, 277, 281, 284
Indirect taxes, 267
Industrial insurance, 330
Inflation, 84
Informal contract, 230
Inheritance taxes, 269
Initiative, 71, 91, 127
Injury, reporting, 310
IQ score, 120
Installment credit, 204-228
    sources and costs, 217
    using, 219
Insurance, 313-337
    budgeting for, 164
    career data, 477
    and credit costs, 218
    need for, 314
    of savings, 263
    selecting agent, 316
    social, 291
    suggestions for buying, 334
Intelligence, 120-141
Interest, figuring, 216
Interest rates, 211, 213, 217
    legal, 225
Interests, 113-116, 145
Internal Revenue Service, 269
Interviews, 17, 38, 52, 61, 103
Introductions, 56
    to co-workers, 77
Inventory —
    of attitudes, 135
    and buying, 180
    interest, 113
    personality, 134
    for property insurance, 318
    self, 111-137

Jobs, 11-37
    applying for, 28, 38-66
    apprenticeable, 360
    attitude on, 67-69
    choosing, 26, 290
    education for specific, 360-379
    in complex society, 1
    leaving, 108
    part-time, 13, 25
    progress on, 87-110
    why people don't get, 61
    see also Work
Job security, and education, 357
Joint tenancy, 238
Junior colleges, 380

Labor, 83
Laws —
    and contracts, 229-243
    to protect consumer, 183
Lawyer —
    career data, 464
    for money counsel, 175
    use before signing, 237
    use of, 238, 241
Leader, following, 199
Learning, job attitude toward, 72
Legal advice, 230
Legal form, of contract, 236
Legality, of contract purpose, 235
Lending laws, 183, 189
Letter of application, 43-47
Liability insurance, 315, 318
License taxes, 269
Life, stages, of 343
Life expectancy, 3, 340
Life insurance, 314, 326, 330
    early Rome, 313
    rate factors, 328
Loans, personal, 209
    budgeting repayment, 165
    for education, 384
Local taxes, 267
Logging occupations, hazardous, 427
Loyalty, 8, 74, 128
Luxuries, 4

Main motion, 413
Maintenance, auto, 186
Management occupations,
    career data, 378, 465

Manual dexterity, 121
Manual occupations, career data,
    366, 473
Majority, age of, 233, 409
Major medical insurance, 332
Material, in clothing, 191
Mathematics, 387-408
    data on careers, 460
    interest in, 345
    occupations, 22, 371
Means, living within, 154
Medical care —
    budgeting for, 169
    of minor, 234
    purchasing, 187
    Social Security, 299
Medical insurance, 320, 332
Meeting, holding a, 11
Men, traits women admire, 139
Mental abilities, 120
Mining occupations, hazardous,
    437
Minor, 233
    responsibility of, 410
    right of, 409
Minutes, 410
Money, reason to work, 4
Money management, 153-177
Money orders, 260
Monopoly, 181
Morals, 128, 139, 142
Mortgages, 164, 226
Motion —
    amending, 415
    making, 413
    classes of, 413
Motor vehicle occupations,
    hazardous, 425
Multiplication review, 397
Music, career data, 461
Mutual assent, 231

Natural science occupations, 374
Neatness, 129
Negative attitudes, 69
Negotiations, labor, 83
Neutrality, among employees, 82
Newspaper ads, for jobs, 31
Night school, 93, 384
Nominating committee, 416
Nursing occupations, career data,
    459

Occupations —
    choosing, 9
    covered by child labor laws, 418
    sources of information on,
        455-477
    studying, 15
    trends in specific, 360-379
    see also Work, Job
Occupational diseases, 310
Oceanography, career data, 461
Offer, 231
    nature of legal, 232
Officers, electing, 416
Old age insurance, 292
On-the-job training, 380
Open-mindedness, 129

Packaging laws, 183, 189
Parliamentary procedure, 409-416
Part-time work, 13, 25
Pawnshop, 209
Pay, 7
    and education, 357
    raise in, 87
Payroll taxes, 269
Pension funds, 291
People —
    getting along with, 67
    interest in, 116
Performance, review of job, 102
Perseverance, 91
Personal data sheet, 47-51
Personal effectiveness, 138-150
Personal loans, 209
Personal service careers,
    data sources, 467
Personality, 122
    changing, 144
    and job, 12
    and voice, 132
    rating scale, 134
Personnel work, career data, 455
Pessimists, 124
Physical abilities, 121
Placement office, 26
Positive attitudes, 69
Postal money order, 260
Premiums, scheduling insurance,
    334
Price —
    comparing, 178
    and quality, 180
Professional occupations, 376

Professions, 84
Profits, 84
Programmers, career data, 464
Progress, job, 87-110
Progressive taxes, 267
Promiscuity, 142
Promissory notes, 221
Promotions, 87
Property insurance, 315, 318
Property taxes, 267
Pro tem, 410
Provider, good, 140
Proxy, 410
Public relations, career data, 456
Public service occupations,
    career data, 466
Punctuality, 130
Purchase order, signing, 197

Quality, comparing, 180
Question, call for, 410
Quitting a job, 108
Quorum, 410, 411

Radiation hazards, 431
Railroad retirement, 291
Range management, career data,
    456
Rates, auto insurance, 321
Real estate, buying, 238, 239
    tax, 267
Reasoning ability, 121
Reconciliation, of bank statement,
    256
Records, keeping budget, 174
Recreation, budgeting for, 169
Regressive taxes, 267
Rehabilitation programs, 310
Respect, 139, 142
Responsibility —
    accepting, 94
    delegating, 101
    future, 338, 340-354
    for money management, 156
Restrictive endorsement, 252
Resume', personal, 47-51
Retirement, 290-312, 345
    budgeting for, 165, 326
    preparation for, 344
Revolving charge account, 224
Rudeness, 143
Rules and regulations, employers,
    77

Safety, 183
    job, 76, 84
    of records, 174
Safety deposit box, 174
Salary —
    discussing at job interview, 59
    increases, 101
    level of, 75
Sales occupations, 23, 360, 378, 465
Sales tax, 269
Savings —
    amount of, 263
    budgeting for, 173
Savings accounts, 245, 261, 331
Sawmill occupations, hazardous,
    427
School, classes and work, 15
Schools, as employers, 31
Scientist, as life goal, 346
Scientific occupations, 22
Second, for motion, 414
Secondary motions, 413
Secretary, 19, 160
Self —
    knowing, 111-137
    understanding, 9
Self-control, 130, 141
Self respect, 7, 140, 142, 143
Selfishness, 139, 142
Seniority, 90
Service charges, 218
Service credit, 208
Service occupations, 360, 361, 379
Service station attendant, 25
Services, 4
    buying, 178-203
Severance pay, 109
Shopping practices, 178
Signature, on check, 249
Skills —
    and education, 357
    for work, 15
Small loan companies, 209, 222
Smoking, 143
Social science occupations, 24, 373,
    462
Social Security, 78, 290-312
    costs of, 307
    number, 278-279
Social work, career data, 464
Speech occupations, career data,
    459

Spending, planning, 165
State banks, 246
State taxes, 267
Statisticians, career data, 460
Stolen goods, controls for, 235
Strike benefits, 84
Style, in clothing, 191
Subsidiary motions, 415
Subtraction, review, 393
Success, 7, 87-110
    and attitude, 67-86
    desire for, 125, 139
Summer job, 25
Supervisor, 96, 99
Supply and demand, 181, 199
Surcharge, on income tax, 273
Survivor's insurance, 292
Systems analysts, career data, 464

Table, motion to, 411, 415
Tact, 132
Take home pay, 163
Talents, 119
Tariff, as tax, 270
Taxes, 265, 285
    budgeting for, 164
    history of, 270
    types of, 266
Taxpayers, requirements of, 284
Technology, advance of, 355
Teenage unemployment, 63
Teeth, 141, 142
Telegraphic money order, 260
Telephone, career data, 477
Telephone directory, as job source,
    33
Temperament, 142
Tenants, in common, 238
Tests, 113
Therapists, career data, 459
Time payment plans, 197
Title, to real estate, 239
Training —
    by employer, 77
    planning, 96
    post-high-school, 355-386
    for promotion, 92
Transportation, budgeting for, 171
Transportation careers, data,
    20, 477
Traveler's checks, 260
Tribe, as form of insurance, 313

Truth in lending, 209, 235
Trust company, 245

Underwriter, 314
Unemployment, 308
    personal reasons for, 61
Unemployment compensation, 110,
    269, 292, 303
Uninsured motorist insurance, 321
Unions, 83
Usury, 235
Utilities, budgeting for, 164

Values, 111
    and buying, 200
    comparing, 178
    and personality, 123
Verbal ability, 120
Vocational development, 340-354
Vocational guidance, sources of
    material, 455-477
Vocational schools, 380
Voice, 132, 146
Vote, on motion, 414

Wage, 101
Wage and tax statement, 280
Wardrobe, planning, 129
Welder, career data, 21, 474
Wildcat strike, 84
Willingness to learn, 72
Woodworking occupations,
    hazardous, 430
Work —
    change in nature, 111
    and continuous education, 339
    meaning of, 1
    molds the man, 347
    nature of today's, 355
    preparation for, 358
    quality and quantity, 90
    reasons for, 4
    and way of life, 340
    see also Job
Work-experience education, 2, 13
Work habits, developing, 343
Work permit, 450
Workmen's compensation, 78, 308
Workmanship, in clothing, 191
Writing, career data, 376, 463
Written contracts, 236

Yourself, knowing, 111-137